Forbidden Science 4

Also by Jacques Vallee

In English:

Anatomy of a Phenomenon
Challenge to Science
Passport to Magonia
The Invisible College
Messengers of Deception
The Edge of Reality (with Dr. J. A. Hynek)
Dimensions
Confrontations
Revelations
The Network Revolution
Electronic Meetings (co-author)
Computer Message Systems
A Cosmic Samizdat
Forbidden Science, Vol.1
Forbidden Science, Vol.2
Forbidden Science, Vol.3
The Four Elements of Financial Alchemy
FastWalker (novel)
The Heart of the Internet
Stratagem (novel)
Wonders in the Sky (with Chris Aubeck)

In French:

Le Sub-Espace (novel, Jules Verne Prize winner)
Le Satellite Sombre (novel)
Alintel (novel)
La Mémoire de Markov (novel)
Les Enjeux du Millénaire (essay)
Au Coeur d'Internet
Stratagème (novel)

Forbidden Science 4
The Spring Hill Chronicles

The Journals of Jacques Vallee 1990-1999

ANOMALIST BOOKS
San Antonio * Charlottesville

Forbidden Science 4: The Spring Hill Chronicles

ISBN: 978-1-949501-05-6

This book was originally published in hardback as *Forbidden Science Volume Four* by Documatica Research, LLC, in 2019.

Third Edition

Front cover image: Godruma/iStock
Cover design by Seale Studios

The author can be contacted at:
P.O. Box 641650
San Francisco, CA. 94164

The author's website: www.jacquesvallee.com

For information about Anomalist Books, go to AnomalistBooks.com or write to:
Anomalist Books, 5150 Broadway #108, San Antonio, Texas 78209

Contents

Figures

Introduction

I ran to the treetops, I ran to the sky
Out to the lake, into the rain that matted my hair
And soaked my shoes and skin
Hid my tears, hid my fears
I ran to the forest, I ran to the trees
I ran and I ran, I was looking for me

Mer Girl, by Madonna and William Orbit, 1998

The *Spring Hill Chronicles* are a record of reflections into the natural history of paranormal phenomena, against the background of active researches on human consciousness. These entries were written between 1990 and the end of the millennium. I was able to conduct these activities, including the building and operation of a private observatory, alongside my professional work as a high-technology investor in Silicon Valley that allowed me the freedom of independent thinking about long-term futures.

Paranormal research moved into new directions during this period, while science and business thrived: I was privileged to work alongside some of the experts who built the structures of the World Wide Web and studied the genome. I was also involved in the investigation of close encounters in the USSR in 1990 and of the Haravilliers mystery in France at the end of the decade. These two major episodes--still unexplained today--can be seen as the "bookends" between which a few trusted associates and I studied dozens of remarkable UFO cases yielding veridical data, including material analyzed in the laboratory, a treasure for sciences to come.

The media paid little attention to these events, in part because serious witnesses had learned to demand confidentiality and stayed away from journalists. Besides, there was plenty of cheaper, juicier controversy for television tabloids to exploit: another day, another sexy abduction tale, another leak from a fake intelligence source. In a perfectly illegal caper exploiting professional journalists, government agencies were caught spreading fake data designed to discredit physicist Paul Bennewitz, a contractor who knew too much, while CIA puppets on a

Mission from God tried to make the world believe the U.S. had colonized Mars using Alien technology. Some researchers took the bait and wasted time following false trails.

This fourth volume of *Forbidden Science* pursues the real enigma, taking the reader behind the scenes: to the board room of a private research institute; to meetings with Congressmen and intelligence officials; and to closed sessions where the subject was debated.

Most importantly, this was the first period when scientists were able to study UFOs with adequate resources. Handpicked by knowledgeable men like Colonel John Alexander and space entrepreneur Robert Bigelow, these researchers produced results that will challenge and puzzle the reader. Like my colleagues I was torn between the sincerity of the witnesses and the extraordinary nature of the stories. I kept my own counsel, in privacy.

As Dr. Carl Jung wrote, "It is important to have a secret, a premonition of things unknown. It fills life with something impersonal, a *numinosum*. A man who has never experienced that has missed something important."

Staying away from ideology, much of my research was in the field, meeting with witnesses. I did "run to the forest, run to the trees," and "soaked my shoes and skin." Details of the research were shared among a small circle of trusted colleagues. As always my wife Janine questioned my hypotheses, lovingly tolerated my frustrations and encouraged me to continue keeping these Journals—not because my own life was particularly interesting, but as an instance of the mystery and drama that life itself bestows on all of us. My own contribution is to memorialize unique events that have not been documented anywhere else, and to tell the truth about them.

As Albert Camus advised us, "If a man wants to be recognized, he must simply tell who he is. If he remains silent or lies, he dies alone and everything around him is destined to unhappiness. On the contrary, if he tells the truth, he will no doubt still die, but he will have helped others and himself in life."

San Francisco, December 2014.
Paris, December 2017.

Part Thirteen

ALIEN RUMORS

1

Moscow. Sunday 7 January 1990.

The bells of the Kremlin ringing through the icy night woke me up. At a time when the Soviet regime is collapsing, the thrill of a new decade is palpable even in the stillness of this spartan room. Back in Germany, the once formidable Berlin Wall is being broken up into thousands of chips sold off as souvenirs. Dictators tumble everywhere; socialist "satellites" fall from the rigid orbits they maintained for 40 years. Against this tumultuous backdrop, over the next five days, I will meet researchers of paranormal phenomena in Russia, some of them speaking to a Westerner for the first time.

The press is filled with breathless reports of spacecraft and humanoids. The notoriously conservative Tass news agency shocked its colleagues by printing that scientists in Moscow and Voronezh had authenticated the sightings (**1**). A few weeks ago, over dinner in San Francisco, I suggested to Martine Castello, a journalist with *Le Figaro*, to travel to Moscow to look into the stories (**2**). Her manager agreed but the Russians said *nyet,* until my name was mentioned and there was pressure on the Novosti press agency to authorize our trip.

A young man named Genya was waiting for us at Sheremetievo airport. He drove us to this ugly hotel, the Rossiya, a Stalinian block of a thousand rooms arranged over a central courtyard. As soon as we were able to empty our suitcases and to get rid of our guide, Martine and I went over to Red Square for an evening stroll. Crude white lights on the façade of the Gum department store illuminated the crenellated walls and the Lenin mausoleum, before which a long line was patiently snaking. Hundreds were waiting for the changing of the guard, executed with that beautiful mechanical precision that characterizes mindless military operations but another feeling, a spiritual one, was also palpable. Among this crowd assembled from the four corners of the faltering Soviet empire arose a fervor that bordered on the mystical. It was a delight to watch the people in the glare of the floodlights, the women in gorgeous fur coats, tall white chapkas on proud heads.

The temperature is minus 3 centigrade, and dropping.

A team of researchers from the Urals tell us about a wave of sightings near Perm. Glowing balls of light drifted eerily through the woods, they say, pointing to the photographs they give us. When the officials are away they share details never reported.

Moscow. Monday 8 January 1990.

Over dinner we discussed destiny, cosmology and time symmetry with Russian physicists. The conversation reminded me of Michael Murphy's novel, *An End to Ordinary History* (**3**): His Esalen group inspired their generation. Back in our rooms, however, a different impression: We can only watch unstable pictures on black and white television sets. I was stupefied to see a boring art program in French about Pope Urbain VIII... We imagined 200 million Russians watching this on prime time in their little izbas while the snow fell around them. One needs a solid sense of humor to survive here.

Now, an unexpected honor: The vice-chairman of Novosti welcomed us in person. Our interpreters were stunned to be greeted at this high level. I responded just as formally while secretaries brought some excellent tea. We were introduced to researcher Vladimir Azhazha and we plunged into our beloved subject. Azhazha stressed that the most important characteristic of UFOs was their ability to change shape, their "polymorphism." I gave him my article highlighting that same aspect: "It is as if you and I had been working together for ten years," he said warmly, putting down his papers with a smile.

We spent the next three hours with investigators from the Voronezh Collective. They had brought their films, their notes, and their reconstruction of the landings. The Russians have craftily misled the foreign media about their real findings, keeping the most important facts private, as we discovered once they saw they could trust us.

Moscow. Tuesday 9 January 1990.

The little place at the end of the hall where we have our modest breakfast has run out of coffee powder, so we survive on tea and dry bread. Well-known geology expert Alexis Zolotov has come over to Novosti, where the vice-chairman's office has been put at our disposal. He gave us a demonstration of biolocation, and we spent a great deal of time discussing the Tungunska explosion of 1908.

In the afternoon I was invited to visit Progress, the largest publisher in the Soviet Union, who proposed to translate *Dimensions* into Russian. Later I had the pleasure of meeting my long-time correspondent Alexander Kazantsev in his cosy apartment filled with books and ancient Japanese artefacts. Alexis Zolotov joined us again for a reunion of kindred spirits. We were finally able to discuss sightings and topics we couldn't broach in letters.

Watching the white beards and twinkling eyes around us, I almost felt transported into a meeting of hermetic adepts. In Russia as elsewhere, the most important facets of a paranormal observation are so private, and sometimes so shocking to the rational mind, that they are only shared in confidence.

There is a strange man in the hallway of our hotel. Last night he suggested that we change some money. Tonight he approached me, saying in bad English: "Tomorrow I give woman..." There is a cluster of such characters in front of the hotel lobby: informers, undercover cops and lowly KGB men, pimps, and small-time crooks.

Moscow. Wednesday 10 January 1990.

Again I was awakened by the bells of the Kremlin, and felt hungry. It had started to snow. Not only was there no coffee available in the hotel today, there wasn't even any tea. The little counter at the end of our corridor had its iron curtain drawn shut. In vain, we started exploring the huge building in search of food. When we finally met Sergei, our second guide, he rushed us to a waiting car: We were late for our visit to the City of the Stars. In the deep mush of the miserable roads it took an hour to reach the facility where Soviet cosmonauts are trained.

Along the way, brightly painted blue and green, the little dachas adorned with woodcarvings like Victorian houses provided the only relief from a dreary landscape.

We visited the huge facility where the twin of the Mir space station is housed; we saw the training process for extra-vehicular activities, and its enormous water tank; but I was most impressed by the space capsules recovered after their fiery re-entry. They look like mere specks of burnt metal next to the big and bright space station, a Jules Verne vision of man's first heroic efforts in space.

Coming out of our first meeting at the cosmonaut training center we found out that our car had a flat tire. Sergei explained that we had come along a road that is often strewn with large nails. People throw the nails to puncture the tires of the buses that bring businessmen from the airport. Then they drive up and offer their services. They make 15 rubles each time they take stranded passengers to the city.

As we expressed surprise at such trickery, Sergei told us another anecdote that throws some interesting light on *Perestroika*: A friend of his tried to make some extra money by taking a job in a government program, unloading boxcars at night at the railroad station for 20 rubles an hour. As he reported for work, he found three bullies waiting for him. Once he'd explained his purpose they gave him 50 rubles and told him to go home and shut up. While ordinary citizens starve the Russian mafia takes control of the produce and sells it on the black market. No wonder we'd missed breakfast!

Obviously, many people don't want the system to change. Yet unavoidable transformations are coming, so sweeping they take everyone by surprise. Before my trip an SRI security officer had sternly briefed me about Russia: the KGB tries to compromise visitors, I was told. Don't carry "adult" magazines: Innocent businessmen with a copy of *Playboy* have been threatened with jail for trying to undermine the moral fiber of the socialist paradise. I was thinking of that warning while watching an ad for *Playboy* on Moscow TV, a blatant appeal for socialist girls to be photographed in the nude for a special issue about the novel joys of *Glasnost*.

The high point of the day was the opportunity to spend some quiet, reflective time in the office of Yuri Gagarin, where Soviet cosmonauts come for spiritual retreat on the eve of a launch. Gagarin was flying his jet half-drunk when he crashed. That lesson, too, will not be forgotten: No matter how high a man goes, he is still human, and can still fail.

Moscow. Thursday 11 January 1990.

Now the temperature is 20 below zero, still dropping. The Moskova is frozen. We spent the morning at the Permanent Exposition of the Achievements of the Soviet Union, a sprawling facility where many exhibits are crumbling. It was already a depressing sight when Janine and I visited it in the summer of 1966.

As we boarded the little train that takes visitors from building to building I sat in the front row, next to the ticket dispenser. We put a few kopeks into the machine and pulled out enough tickets for the three of us. At the next stop an old lady got in, handed me some kopeks, and mumbled something in Russian: I was supposed to pay the machine and pull out the corresponding tickets. Over the next ten minutes Sergei and Martine mocked me as I kept pulling out more and more tickets and filling the device with little coins: "Don't laugh," I told them, "I already got myself a job in Russia!"

We finally reached the Space pavilion. It houses a permanent show on UFOs where the organizers proudly display a copy of *Challenge to Science*. They showed me Janine's signature and mine, and our dedication to Tikhonov, who died years ago and whose personal library they had purchased. They asked me to sign the book again.

This afternoon we persuaded Sergei to take us for a walk along the Arbat. He begged us to let him stop at the Post Office to fetch a letter from his girlfriend in Prague. He doesn't trust Gorbachev or *Perestroika*. There was no letter for him, so he was dejected the rest of the day. Along the Arbat sidewalk orators called for the overthrow of Communism; artists sold mediocre paintings.

I just came back to the *Rossiya* after dinner with Azhazha at a private apartment in Moscow where we enjoyed warm hospitality. I asked them if they had heard of a man named Sanarov, well known in the West for his extremely detailed demands for sighting data.

Fig. 1. The Moscow Symposium with Vladimir Azhazha, Jan.1990.

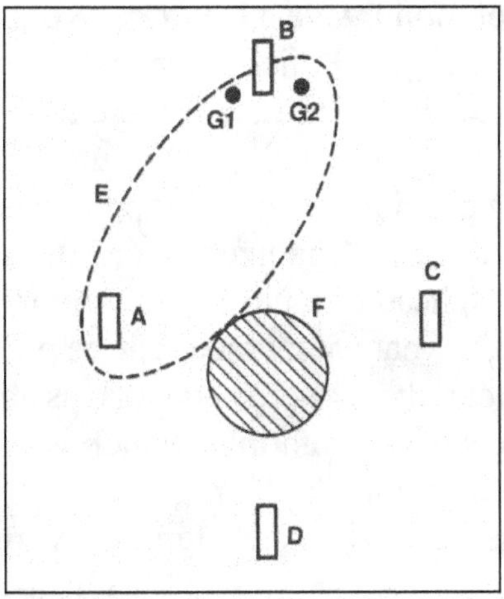

A, B, C, D: rectangular imprints

E: area of flattened grass

F: epicenter, radioactivity level double that of the background

G1, G2: holes fifteen inches deep, vertical and smooth

Fig. 2. Traces noted after the close encounter case in Voronezh.

I detected some amusement around the table. Their evasive answers confirmed they were aware of this "vacuum cleaner" activity.

There was another amusing incident. Sitting in a corner, a young engineer was repairing a personal computer. He was a UFO buff, and in the course of the discussion he assured me that "some French researcher" had pointed out that the probability of a witness making a report varied as a function of the strangeness of that report. He said he'd read that in a book called *The Invisible College*, which he'd gotten in pirated Russian. I had a copy of *Invisible College* in my briefcase, so I autographed it to him as everyone laughed.

My work is known here, often copied and retyped for circulation among interested researchers who cannot find the original books. Someone even handed to me a Russian manuscript entitled *Commentaries on Passport to Magonia,* and melted into the crowd.

Moscow. Friday 12 January 1990.

Martine and I spoke before a scientific symposium on UFOs this morning; in the afternoon I gave a lecture at Novosti before some 400 people, including Czech and Polish journalists. It was set up as a panel with Azhazha and the vice-chairman. But the round table was the most impressive event. We expected a few ufologists; we found 25 scientists, including physicists and anthropologists. I wondered if such a meeting could have been organized in the West. One of the people in attendance was the head of a physics laboratory of the Academy of Sciences. A report on what we learned will be published in the book I am preparing (4) but there were side discussions about the most extraordinary aspects of the sightings, which were given, once again, on condition I wouldn't publish them.

The temperature is –27C. We leave tomorrow for Paris.

Paris. Rue de la Clef. Saturday 13 January 1990.

I traveled back with Martine, who has become a trusted friend. We could not hide our pleasure as we passed Soviet security and found ourselves aboard the Air France jet. In spite of the gentle hospitality of Kazantsev and Zolotov (**5**) I felt relieved as the frozen plains receded behind our wings. I bring back some caviar for my mother for a little feast tomorrow. Maman gets easily tired now, yet she always insists on preparing everything for us, in spite of her 90 years. This may be the last night I will spend here on *Rue de la Clef.*

Paris. Hotel Clément. Monday 15 January 1990.

Friends have taken me to see a short movie, *La Mouette Infernale*, a charmingly disturbing art film that takes place on the cliffs of Etretat. It should cheer me up, but Paris is gray and I am tired: I rest in this little room with the faded wallpaper. I have to fly to Geneva tomorrow for a visit to a factory for high-precision auto parts.

A civil war has erupted in the Caucasus. The Red Army is rolling into Great Karabanh even as the Soviet empire continues to collapse.

Paris. Hotel Clément. Tuesday 16 January 1990.

A bad cold makes me feel sick, my legs wobbly. The trip to Geneva was a nightmare: My cheerful colleagues had not confirmed our appointments and didn't know their way to the company we were supposed to visit. I dragged myself from meeting to meeting all day. Nothing is easy here. Getting people together for a simple decision, or even to sign a routine letter, takes three days or more.

Paris. Hotel Clément. Wednesday 17 January 1990.

To forget my fever I read Le Carré's *Russia House*, which puts me back into the mood of Moscow. Then Janine called from Spring Hill and cheered me up. Soon I will have to get up, ready or not. The advisory board of our Fund meets this evening.

At Laffont, editors are happy with *Autres Dimensions*, selling at a fast rate, so they're drawing up a contract for Janine's translation of *Confrontations*. I paid a visit to our *notaire*, to push along the slow bureaucratic process of buying the small apartment Janine found near the Mabillon metro station, close to Saint-Germain-des-Prés.

Hyde Street, San Francisco. Monday 22 January 1990.

Back home in California: In San Francisco harbor the masts of the Balclutha swing in the sunshine. I relish the dubious pleasure of jet lag, sliding into afternoon sleep with nothing to hold me back.

Peter Sturrock tells me I have been elected to the Council of the Society for Scientific Exploration, and a letter from Aimé Michel brings sad news about his health: "My carcass is often out cold. I just linger there, wasting away in my chair, day dreaming."

Now an Army officer named Ed Dames, one of Hal Puthoff's remote viewers, calls me from Maryland. He says he's a friend of Ron Blackburn and John Alexander: He "has been psychically monitoring a site of paranormal activity" and wants my involvement.

New York. Hotel Plaza. Friday 26 January 1990.

The other evening, over dinner with Bill Calvert, researcher Barbara Honegger said she found out about Jack Vorona's "secret" funding of SRI research through the DIA and knew of the psychic interests of Scott Jones and Senator Pell, "always looking for psychic thrills, afraid of missing out on some extraordinary experience." He took Uri Geller to the Senate and to peace negotiations in Geneva. **(6)**

Barbara suspects that Dan Quayle got the vice-presidency because he had the smoking gun of the *October Surprise*, the pact made by Reagan and Bush with the Iranians to delay the release of American hostages until after the 1980 elections in order to humiliate Carter: "The plan involved a saucer-like, non-lethal craft designed to induce physiological effects, paralyze guards or put them to sleep," she said.

Hyde Street, San Francisco. Saturday 27 January 1990.

Janine's birthday: I gave her a small Russian lacquer box (two lovers under the moon) and we spent this sunny day at home. We both feel signs of age. Janine is worried by pains in her hands. I took her in my arms and told her the plain truth: I want to grow old with her. I will be here with her, caring for her, as long as I can.

New York. Hotel Plaza. Monday 29 January 1990.

Back in New York in a rainstorm, getting ready for a Partners' meeting of our venture Fund with legendary financier Fred Adler. In this morning's *Chronicle* I read that the two French cops (Jean Schmitt and Christophe Garcia) who murdered a student during the 1986 protests will not be doing any time in jail after all. Thus not much has changed since Charonne, even if the socialists now run the government (7).

On the phone yesterday Dr. Christopher (Kit) Green, intelligence expert and former monitor of the psychic experiments at SRI, told me of an interesting incident with General Strudebov, chief of the Soviet General Staff, whom he met at a Texas A&M workshop on disarmament that served as a preliminary forum for the Bush-Gorbachev talks. During a quiet moment at a cocktail party he said, "It's time we turned our attention to a more important danger."

"What danger is that, General?" asked Kit.

"Well, the threat from space, naturally!"

Somewhat taken aback, Kit commented: "I understand that our Star Wars Initiative has caused concern among your people."

"I'm not talking about your Star Wars," interrupted the general with urgency. "I'm talking about the threat posed by extraterrestrials."

"What was that all about, that talk about extraterrestrials?" Kit asked the interpreter the next day. The fellow looked embarrassed.

"Please do not pay any attention, our General drinks too much..."

Kit and I agreed this behavior matched the surprisingly intense official interest in the subject I had noted in Moscow.

"It occurred to me that it would be difficult to get together a group of similar calibre if we had to do it in the States..." I told him.

He disagreed: "In the classified world we have people studying the metallurgy of titanium, analyzing the composition of various UFO samples using magnetic resonance; you could find experts studying UFO photographs, and the FastWalker project is being revived at Lockheed. They're finally taking a look at unusual signals. The problem is their arrogance: They're sure they can solve the problem. Another flaw is bigotry: When I meet some of these folks, the talk turns to religion. That's the only question, after a few beers."

Montréal. Hotel Shangri-La. Thursday 1 February 1990.

Yesterday was spent in Manhattan with Fred Adler, reviewing investments with my partner Chaban-Delmas before flying to Canada for two days with tech companies.

Then I called Professor Jean Baudot who once invited me to join the computer science faculty at the *Université de Montréal.* Nearly 60 now, he teaches linguistics. He told me I'd made the right decision, back in 1967, not to move to Canada. He recalled the strikes in the 1970s, and demonstrations by radical groups that had no regard for research work, wasted time.

Hyde Street. Monday 5 February 1990.

Dr. Richard Niemtzow called from Texas with his impressions of a meeting on "abduction trauma" presided by psychiatrist Rima Laibow. About 40 people were there, including some physicians like Paul Tyler, but no expert in treating the medical effects of UFOs.

"The group had no idea of methodology," Richard noted. "When someone mentioned they had access to witnesses' blood and urine samples but didn't know where to send them, Rima yelled, 'Send me the goo!' implying she'd analyze it."

"It won't do any good to send you the goo," Richard told her, "if you have no baseline to evaluate the results. That's what happened with the French gendarmes, in Cergy-Pontoise (**8**)..."

Hyde Street. Thursday 8 February 1990.

Silent typewriters, empty offices, workstations with flashing displays that read "Out to Lunch" in a feeble attempt at humor; I had a depressing experience at SRI this afternoon. Dr. Ed May told me the parapsychology project had run out of money; the five remaining staff members are looking for jobs. The DIA project monitor, Jim Salyer, has been recalled. Nobody was paid this month.

This debacle happened as a result of two things. First, cuts in the Defense budgets consecutive to the breaking out of world peace erased the money earmarked for remote viewing research (1.25 million dollars for 1990 alone). Second, the Special Access Program run by the Army out of the New York office of SRI under Ingo has faltered. The work became so sloppy that the Inspector General of DIA issued a scathing report. Jack Vorona has been pushed out into a position that will lead to his retirement. The other "sugar daddy" of the program, General Rapmund, left the Army months ago. Ed's only hope is with Congress, with possible support from Sam Nunn.

We went on to discuss Hal Puthoff's energy research. Ed May is skeptical: The Casimir force may not explain super-electrons, he said. As for the stable state of hydrogen, Ed believes the fundamental issue is the quantization, not the stability of the electron's orbit.

Hyde Street. Monday 12 February 1990.

This was a curious day, starting with a private financial lecture by Fred Adler delivered in dictatorial style. Much of the afternoon was spent with microbiologist Dr. Moshe Shifrine, the discoverer of a process that grows cultured truffles, and our colleague Dan Tolkowsky, legendary founder of the Israeli Air Force, now head of the Athena group in Israel. Shifrine has a teen-age son who is a keen student of history. He was thrilled to collect Dan's signature.

At four o'clock Ed Dames came to my office for a quiet talk. Ed is 40 or so—short, blond, with much eagerness and enthusiasm. He comes from the East coast remote viewing operation, a classified psychic team that claims to have successfully tracked Qaddafi into the desert and studied abductions: "We even found strange creatures showing up in our data-base, or as the Russians say, our *Thesaurus*."

Thinking they dealt with inter-dimensional events, the team decided to come talk to me. The data points to a mesa outside Los Alamos, so Ed Dames wants us to go there in May with Dr. Ron Blackburn, a senior Lockheed physicist. Sensing my skepticism, Ed said:

"It may be hard for you to believe it, but the data just accumulates without anyone in charge. No single case demonstrates hostile intent, so it doesn't fall under anyone's mission. In the seventies there were projects like Aquarius and Majestic run by AFOSI, but they only aimed at finding out what civilian researchers like you knew about the subject. They were hushed up because the Air Force isn't supposed to spy on American civilians..." I looked at him and laughed, thinking that Bill Moore had told the truth after all, that night in Lyon, when he said he'd been hired as an informer to report on private researchers like me.

Hyde Street. Sunday 18 February 1990.

Janine and I went to Spring Hill on Friday through a spectacular rainstorm. During the night, when I got up and lifted the drapes I saw the snow quietly falling over the bushes and the tower. In the morning it was a faëry vision, deep white cushions resting on the bushes with their red berries, snow over the dark fences. A large branch fell and brought down the phone line. Then we lost all power.

Hyde Street. Friday 23 February 1990.

Once in a while it's nice to clarify some little puzzle, even if the big mysteries remain. Over lunch today the enigmatic Colonel Ron Blackburn decided to come clean with me in anticipation of our trip to New Mexico. Ron gave me his impressive biography, with sanitized entries entitled "Achievements in the field of national security." He'd co-founded what I jokingly nicknamed the "Secret Onion" group and co-organized a national panel on UFOs. In the first case, his co-founder was John Alexander; in the second case, it was none other than Kit Green, who never told me about this.

Back in Paris our purchase of the Mabillon apartment closed after much correspondence, telefax and calls with *Monsieur le Notaire*. After all these years we finally have a home of our own in France.

Hyde Street. Monday 26 February 1990.

In two weeks screenwriter Tracy Tormé, producer Bob Weiss and I will be in Las Vegas for conversations with television reporter George Knapp. Universal has made the arrangements: We have been promised a contact with a mysterious witness named Bob Lazar who claims to have seen Aliens at Nellis Air Force Base and Area 51.

Colonel John Alexander came over for dinner yesterday. We spoke of non-lethal weapons of the sort Mr. Payan had investigated in France (**9**). "Should the US offer them to Gorbachev to put down the revolts in Azerbaidjan? Will the day come when they will be used in the US?"

Spring Hill. Saturday 3 March 1990.

Janine has given me a fine stereo for the tower library: Now I can listen to Hildegard of Bingen while indexing cases. The people of the Dark Ages knew something powerful I try to rediscover inside myself, a mode of meditation I find intimately comfortable. These thick walls seem to know it too, our quiet pond, and an infinity I want to probe.

Last Thursday we saw Dr. Harary, my gifted friend from the SRI project. Keith and Darlene have settled in San Francisco in an area of trendy bars and art shops that lost much of its veneer when the AIDS crisis hit. It is becoming lively and fashionable again.

In a recent letter Joe McMoneagle urges me to use caution following Ed Dames' experiments. On the demise of the SRI remote viewing project, Joe adds: "If you see Ed May... well, pat him on the shoulder and buy him a cup of coffee, he'll probably need it." (**10**)

Hyde Street. Sunday 4 March 1990.

Confrontations causes a storm because I refuse to blindly follow the dogma of abductionists. The latest magazine of the pro-UFO CUFOS group is a hatchet job, with my picture on the cover: *Where Vallee went wrong!* The photograph dates from 15 years ago and that seems appropriate: These people have remained stuck in time. They are also wrong about hypnosis: One of the 20-odd abductees I have been quietly studying has made a shocking discovery, of a deep forgotten trauma. Now she wonders if her molestation as a teenager might have led to her false memories of UFOs rather than an actual sighting.

Hyde Street. Monday 5 March 1990.

At the *Perfect Recipe* Ron Blackburn confirmed Major Ed Dames was arranging to meet us in New Mexico for a night drive to hunt for

Aliens. I asked Ron about his involvement with Roswell. He assured me he knew a man who did radiation tests on the crashed material:

"It was amazing. He had a piece as large as this room, and he could lift it with one hand! The fellow is afraid to talk about it."

"Where do you think that material is now?" Blackburn shrugged:

"It could be anywhere. Since the Iran-Contra affair the folks in Washington don't take any chances that a Congressional staffer might stumble on the truth. It's all been farmed out."

Monterey. Hotel Hyatt. Wednesday 7 March 1990.

Janine is with me at this conference of the American Electronics Association. Over dinner at the beach home of Barbara Honegger we swapped information on real and fake UFOs she learned about during her days at the White House, including correlations between actual (but covert) projects and the wild claims of zealots like Bill Cooper and John Lear. One of the "Alien" projects is called *Snowbird,* a cover for a real project called *Redlight.* In *Snowbird* the government reportedly built a saucer and flew it as a disinformation drone for the release of the American hostages in Iran during the failed attempt at rescue organized by Jimmy Carter. The date was 24 April 1980. The Reagan-Bush camp sabotaged the rescue, she said, secretly negotiating with the Iranians to delay the release until after Carter was booted out. Snowbird may have used a large drone over the embassy, allowing intrusion by US commandos.

Barbara once asked a woman abductee if the beings who took her might have been human. She blurted out,

"One of them did tell me he was with the Air Force!"

"Why didn't you mention this before? It could be vital!"

"Frankly, I didn't remember it until you asked me that question..."

Barbara knows another woman who found out under professional therapy that she had not been abducted to a UFO at all; instead she had been taken to a house in San Francisco, where her supposedly "Alien" abductors also turned out to be humans as they removed their fake faces in front of her. That description sent chills through my bones, because it was one of the scenes in my novel *FastWalker*.

Monterey. Hotel Hyatt. Thursday 8 March 1990.

Janine and I had dinner with a warm and generous woman, the Russian-born psychic Larissa Vilenskaya, resplendent in white embroidered silk. I had brought the Voronezh papers for her to review, as well as *Commentaries on Magonia* by Emil Batchurin. She gave me a summary translation, including a remarkable episode in which a woman was seized by black hands attached to an invisible body. I have in my files a similar 1950 Loire episode.

Las Vegas. Hotel Mirage. Saturday 10 March 1990.

In the lobby of the Mirage Hotel wrinkled women from Iowa wearing butterfly glasses ogle bronze statues of mermaids who offer their youthful breasts to the wind, buttocks barely swimming above the foamy waves. The white tigers of Siegfried and Roy live in this castle-like structure while the volcano in front is a grand structure, wonderful in its decadent debauchery of fake rock and palm trees.

"This is as close as most people will ever come to experiencing adventure," comments my friend, producer Robert K. Weiss as we make our way through the crowd at the slot machines.

Last night scriptwriter Tracy Tormé met us for dinner with George Knapp, the cheerful television journalist who broke the Lazar story. He was with a real estate appraiser from Las Vegas, a burly man who wore glasses with a thick mount, knew the jargon well, speaking fluently of antiprotons and gravity amplifiers. He saw himself as Lazar's manager: "Lazar's story is worth many millions of dollars," he told us enthusiastically.

Las Vegas. Hotel Mirage. Sunday 11 March 1990.

We did go to Channel 8 to see Knapp and there was Bob Lazar, a brand-new portable telephone at his elbow, sitting at a folding table in the back lobby. We spoke for an hour and came away convinced that we'd been thrust into a puppet show.

After the interview Bob Weiss wanted to drive north towards Area 51. As soon as one leaves the main highway to Salt Lake City the road becomes straight, the monotony broken by wild rock formations on either side. This is the road to Ely, used by big trucks hauling goods and produce. Two hours north of Vegas we seized our last chance to refuel and turned towards Tonopah. The sun had already set behind the western peaks and a full moon was rising behind us.

On the way we told stories and joked with Tracy's blonde girlfriend while we tried to find a decent radio station. Bob only came up with a fire-and-brimstone show, Mephisto cursing born-again Christians.

The turnoff came suddenly in the moonlight: a dusty, wide trail that shot straight down the range and up the first row of hills. Behind the mountains the map showed a wide array of gunnery fields and Air Force installations, including the test base at Nellis, Dreamland and, if Lazar told us the truth, the secret Alien hangars at S-4. At a turn of the road a guardhouse loomed ahead with a tall pole for surveillance equipment. Two men in fatigues came towards us, pleased with some diversion from their boring job. They informed us we had trespassed on military property, took our identification inside the post and escorted us back down the hill.

Any disappointment we might have felt evaporated in the warm atmosphere of the Little A'Le'Inn, a prefabricated shack in a dusty parking lot, ready to be blown off by any gust of desert wind. Inside were bearded characters swapping UFO stories against a background of posters showing bald Visitors with big eyes.

The café sells T-shirts with the picture of the Stealth fighter, and assorted medals. The guest book is filled with names of Japanese journalists. We caught the *Billy Goodman Happening* on radio, another enthusiastic show for Alien believers. He was interviewing British author Timothy Good who bravely fielded idiotic questions like "How do the Aliens brainwash American kids?"

Later we met an investigator who revealed that in real life "physics expert" Lazar was part owner of a Nevada brothel. The man was visibly scared to discuss the situation. There are rumors that government folks picked Lazar as a result of unspecified events. Perhaps the main question is not to know what all this is supposed to reveal, but what it is designed to hide.

Hyde Street. Thursday 15 March 1990.

Whitley Streiber called me from New York, incensed at an outrageous review of my book *Confrontations* in the CUFOS magazine: "We always knew these guys had been co-opted into the disinformation story," he said.

Whitley is coming to the same conclusion I do: Somebody in Washington concocted a fairy tale about captured Aliens and spreads it within the Intelligence community and the UFO believers.

"Something provocative is going on; it comes from a group inside the Government, with links to the crazies, the extreme religious and political Right: It feeds the fantasies of the folks who believe in demons and harbor insane, deep-seated fears!"

Spring Hill. Saturday 17 March 1990.

My architect friend Bill Calvert just attended a meeting at the Berkeley home of Arthur Young, who played Bob Lazar's "secret revelations" tape to the assembled elite of New Age San Francisco. Arthur also displayed the Billy Meier dubious pictures from Switzerland (**11**). Engineer Ron Hawk, psychologist Jean Millay and entrepreneur Henry Dakin were there, dazzled by these alleged psychic revelations.

"The audience seemed charmed by Lazar. Many wanted to get copies 'to show it to their friends.' Why do I have the feeling that I've just seen a glib actor do a breakfast commercial? The Berkeley crowd was your basic aging space cadet, not much skepticism…"

Here at the ranch I have tried some tentative experiments to probe the nature of reality and time: I believe the mind and the multiverse are linked through undiscovered pathways. I remember our lovely friend Eve Berni, back in September 1987, visiting the tower when it was still caught in the scaffoldings, telling us how she shared in our dreams. In the quiet night of the forest, drawing from the unique information assembled here, can we build a singularity that will manifest a higher level?

2

Mabillon. Sunday 25 March 1990.

A milestone: A special place waiting for us, our own apartment. This is a special journey; a return to Paris of old—a genuine time loop.

As the plane got closer to the French shore a few lines from Jose Maria de Heredia's poem to his daughter (**12**) kept coming into mind:

El dia que tu naciste
Nacieron todas las flores...

("The day you were born, all the flowers were born…") surely the most delicate and profound description of the feelings of a father for his child, the sweet sorrow and silent joy of getting older and watching one's family grow. I could not hold back warm tears as I thought of my precious daughter at school in snowy Colorado. So, I pulled the blanket over my head to hide those tears from Janine, who would surely wonder if I'd gone crazy.

The taxi drove down deserted boulevards, passed *Saint Sulpice,* holier than thou in the early gray of Parisian laziness. Nothing moved around *Saint-Germain-des-Prés*; our new neighbors were busy dunking their first croissant of the day into their *café-au-lait*. We stuffed our suitcases into the elevator, eager to see the apartment.

Annick's magic wand had touched everything in the place. There wasn't much Janine's sister could have done for the ugly wallpaper, the dismal fabric on the bedroom wall or the brownish kitchen paint, but we found the new bed all made up, curtains at the windows, small tables with nice lamps, a phone in working order, two armchairs and a television set: We were home. All we had to do was hang our clothes, wash off the jet lag, and resume our Paris life as if we had never boarded the Queen Mary in 1962, as if we had not gone off to Texas and Chicago a quarter century ago; as if we had never fallen in love with San Francisco's luscious hills.

It was hard to realize that we'd spent Sunday watching the daffodils bloom at Spring Hill; or to recall that Friday was Manhattan, the Plaza, a walk to Times Square to see *The Hunt for Red October*, meetings with the wise Dan Tolkowsky and Fred Adler's team, power lunch at *La Brasserie*, a run up Madison to see financier Shel Gordon; Then Janine leaning softly against me in the cab to Kennedy. In Paris we visited my mother, bravely recovering from the death of her sister Louise. She smiled mischievously about her encounter with the Protestant minister:

"How can anybody still believe that there is a *Bon Dieu*, in this day and age, with all the horrible things we see on television?" she asked the pastor in his dark and smelly little apartment, "and if we have to have religion, why are there so many churches, always fighting?"

He invited her to sit down and discuss theology: "There was an armchair in the corner but it was so run down that I feared I would crash to the floor if I sat down. So I took a hard chair and he told me, 'Madame, you would be far more comfortable in the armchair,' but I replied, 'I'm not old enough to sit in that armchair.' He looked at me carefully and concluded, 'That is true, Madame, you are quite right.'" She still laughs about it. After all, she won't turn 90 until September.

Mabillon. Tuesday 27 March 1990.

Paris is cold and gray, with brief interludes of unsatisfying sunshine. We had an afternoon drink at *Le Rostand* with astronomer Pierre Guérin, about to retire. He faces that prospect with a mixture of relief and horrified febrility. He frequents various clairvoyants, whom he drags into his research. The same evening we had dinner at *Brasserie Lipp* with Joël Mesnard who takes over publication of *Lumières dans la Nuit*, the most reliable UFO magazine in France.

Mabillon. Wednesday 28 March 1990.

The Paris Book Fair was held at the *Grand Palais* yesterday. Several writer friends were there. Simonne Servais was signing her book about De Gaulle (**13**). Jimmy Guieu wore a splendid red jacket, next to sociologist Pierre Lagrange. Guieu held court, surrounded with a fierce team of tough-looking disciples of the "Short Grays."

A man named Alain Boudier, whom I had first met in Hynek's office back in August 1975, re-introduced himself. Hinting of secret contacts, he said he'd run a division of Roussel-Uclaf in Vienna and an operation of ELF in Germany. He believes every saucer crash story, is sold on Majestic 12 and is certain Hynek was a CIA man.

"And what about the Mahatmas?" he asked me suddenly, catching me off-guard, "What do you think the High Initiates are doing?"

Mabillon. Saturday 31 March 1990.

Janine has bought a fine desk with a leather top. I sat there and watched the towers of Saint Sulpice turning pink in the morning sun.

I spent the afternoon in a stuffy meeting room listening to amusing factions of French ufology. Madame Francine Fouéré, a forceful white-haired woman in her 60s, delivered a moving eulogy of her husband: a philosopher, wise man, collector of odd facts and founder of Gepa, the first group of serious UFO investigators in France (**14**).

A young man forced his way forward and said: "It's been revealed that 17 nations have signed a secret treaty with the UFO beings..." Catcalls covered his voice. Mme. Fouéré told him to be quiet, the Horrible Truth notwithstanding. I met atmospheric scientist Patrick Aimedieu and researcher Jean Sider, a serious man in his 50s.

We also reviewed the critical Cergy-Pontoise case of 1979. Investigator Marceau Sicaud introduced me to Gérard Deforge who had been the teacher of Franck Fontaine, the supposed abductee, at the *Parc-aux-Charettes* school which I had attended years before. I asked about Fontaine's background: as a child he was a mediocre student but posed no discipline problem, Deforge said.

Boudier and I sat at the nearby bar. He told me that a French doctor was once approached by "the Americans" to analyze some cells he concluded were extraterrestrial, he assured me, a story I had already unsuccessfully tried to check.

This morning I spoke to Gordon Creighton in London. He believes a hidden force is enslaving mankind by pretending to be extraterrestrial, just as in the 1800s it spoke for spirits of the Dead.

Mabillon. Friday 6 April 1990.

On Monday my colleague Gabriel Mergui and I were in Ghent, near Brussels where we saw an interesting biotechnology company. The founders are from Plant Genetics, which first succeeded in transferring portions of the insect genetic code into plants, thus developing seeds for agricultural products that needed no fertilizers.

On the Paris-Brussels, in the refined luxury of the restaurant car, our table companion was an official of the World Bank busy with loans to Poland and Hungary, newly liberated from the Soviet rule.

We continue to settle our Parisian base. My brother and his wife came over. We had pastries bought on *Rue de Seine*, then went with them to see *The Shadow Makers*, the sad story of the atom bomb.

At today's Board meeting of Photonetics, a company near Versailles, I spent an exhausting afternoon of arguments around the table. They make fiberoptic gyroscopes and industrial lasers but their markets are constrained by the French government and they compete against giants that can crush them financially.

Mabillon. Sunday 8 April 1990.

All the little frictions, the iniquities, the absurd principles embedded in the system become obvious again after just two weeks in France. They overwhelm the charm and magic of Paris. My spirits are not helped by asthma, inflammed by the flu, which flares up in painful fits of coughing and a drowning sensation like a foretaste of death.

On the positive side I met with François Louange and Jean-Jacques Velasco of CNES at Fleximage, a smart technical company in a street with a delightful name: *Rue de la Brèche aux Loups*, the "street of the wolves'passage." Louange, a satellite imaging expert for French intelligence, develops civilian applications of the technology based on novel software. He used a late-model workstation to show me the port of Long Beach caught by the Spot satellite, as ships in the channel illegally unloaded their pollutants... He agreed to digitize three oversize UFO negatives I'd brought back from Costa Rica.

Much of the discussion had to do with the renewed interest of the

French Air Force: Velasco recently gave a briefing to a Colonel who pledged support. Yet Louange and Velasco are convinced there's no genuine UFO research within the French structure.

Spring Hill. Saturday 14 April 1990.

The hillside was bursting with obscene life when we drove to the ranch upon our return: dandelions and weeds in an embrace with flowery bushes in an advanced state of intoxication, delicate irises of pale purple and deep orgiastic violet, apple trees in bloom, tall grass everywhere. I peeled back the pool cover, bringing into sunlight a swarming biological experiment where every form of life seemed to thrive: insects and tadpoles among disgusting bacterial cultures, and four toads that looked up at me with reproach in their eyes when I swept them into my net for a trip to the grassy hillside.

The library was quiet and cool, the books lined up in the multiple light of stained glass. This tower is sealed in silence, anchored to a mildly interesting planet hurtling towards constellation Hercules at 12 miles per second, toads and all.

"What shall we do now, Master?" asked the four of them in unison, mocking me as they stared from the bottom of the filter. They had found their way into the pool again, fallen in, and of course they had been swept back into the trap. I offered them a stick, which they grabbed one at a time, and I jettisoned them over the wild bushes. Surely they will return, obedient Familiars they are.

Hyde Street. Monday 16 April 1990.

Over lunch again with Colonel Ron Blackburn at the Gatehouse in Palo Alto he revealed that the "Secret Onion" group started in 1985 in the classified tank located in his basement at the Lockheed Skunk Works (**15**). Colonel John Alexander had brought him a list of the people for the inner circle. They divided the world into layers of concentric trust and ability. John introduced Blackburn to Ed Dames.

Blackburn and I have firmed up our plans to travel to New Mexico on May 4th, up to the high mesa—supposedly to meet some Aliens.

Detroit. Tuesday 1 May 1990.

The Hubble telescope is in orbit now, looking at the universe with an order-of-magnitude improvement over terrestrial astronomy. For the first time a telescope of great power is looking up at the stars rather than down at the pitiful bickering of armies and politicians.

Chicago was the first stop on my author's tour for *Confrontations*, with memories of Allen Hynek in Evanston and of tender, happy times with Janine and Olivier on Bryn Mawr Avenue.

Sunshine in Detroit. The Omni hotel looks over a little train and the river. Four interviews today, then I fly on to Washington. At every opportunity I state on the air that the military must have a lot of data in their classified files, but the real UFO secret may be the fact that the government has no clue how those things work.

Hyde Street. Thursday 3 May 1990.

In Washington I stayed at the Madison and had a free evening, but I recognized little of the once-familiar area. Huge buildings going up everywhere are destroying any human feeling. I walked many blocks into the darkness, increasingly dejected.

Time to start packing for the mesa: mountain shoes, a heavy parka, a compass, small camera, notepaper, sample bags. If something does happen and we decide to tell the world, can we explain why we picked this place and date without compromising *Grill Flame* (**16**), at a time when even the people who closely follow parapsychology are convinced the project has long been disbanded?

Española, New Mexico (Chamisa Inn). Friday 4 May 1990.

Ron Blackburn is as tall as I am, younger by a couple of years. He walks stiffly and expresses himself hesitatingly without moving his head, his lizard eyes scanning in a subtle, disquieting way.

We established our base of operations near Los Alamos.

"I'm convinced the government is working on UFOs," he told me.

"What are the chances some witnesses are being fooled by special effects developed for psychological warfare?" I countered, thinking of cases like Bentwaters in the UK or Cergy-Pontoise in France.

"They're pretty good," he admitted. "Suppose you shine a weak infrared laser into people's eyes; it won't hurt them but may induce a hallucinatory state. Experiments have been done where you send a microwave beam through someone's brain; you pick up the transmitted energy pattern. You can influence people this way, even make them hear things. Holograms have been used, too."

Ron once developed magnetic UFO detectors at Kirtland Air force base. They were stolen when he moved. "The president of the moving company came in person to tell us our crates had been opened and burglarized, right in the locked and patrolled area where his company kept customer items. The only things taken were my devices. That has to mean something, don't you think?"

In the evening Ron and I drove to Abiquiu, home of artist Georgia O'Keefe. The weather up in the mountains was stormy, with rain and snow on the higher peaks. Ed Dames and his crew arrived tired from their first reconnaissance trip, driving a big black Jeep covered with mud from headlights to tailpipe. We had to wait for the roads to drain. Ed's companions were two other remote viewers, Mel Riley and Dave Morehouse, a Special Forces guy built like a linebacker. After a couple of hours spent comparing notes we put on our heavy shoes and climbed back into the Jeep. The roads were still impassable; the four-wheel drive vehicle slipped from side to side.

"Why should I worry?" I thought as we almost crashed, "I'm in a big Jeep with three Army guys and an Air Force colonel…"

Eventually our leader gave up the attempt to reach the top. Ed and his buddies still believe there's an Alien race there, but evidently they were very shy that night. The sky cleared up but I only saw a lone shooting star. Ed assured us the Army's remote viewing project was continuing. They count on Fred ("Skip") Atwater for support.

Española (Chamisa Inn) Saturday 5 May 1990.

John Alexander lives in a beautiful adobe home in a new subdivision north of Santa Fe. In his living room the nine members of the fifth meeting of the "Secret Onion" core group (and the first one where I have been invited) sat around the long table. The first day of the meeting went well, considering the confusing agendas and the fact that some of us were privy to the nature of Ed Dames' experiment going on secretly 40 miles away, while others were not.

Kit did not come for various reasons he enumerated in a letter. He stated that the phenomenon was "robust" and had strong physical effects on people. He added that delusion often struck unsophisticated witnesses but also, occasionally, the "best and brightest." Surprisingly, in a reversal of what he had often told me, he stated the Government was involved "appropriately, legally, and fairly" through a black analytical program.

Hal described his research in a crisp one-page statement of his current physics model. John Alexander spoke of parallels between UFOs and near-death experiences, which also involve a multi-dimensional reality. Contrary to Kit, he never found a secret government "Box" for UFOs. Scott Jones was next. With his tanned face, white hair and soft eyes, he was the epitome of the wise New Age philosopher. His interest began in the 40s, in Naval Intelligence. He looked for "the Box" too, and found none. He met Dr. Leo Sprinkle who convinced him that he may have had some personal experiences with extraterrestrials. He now works for a newly created "Human Potential Foundation" created by Senator Claiborne Pell.

Scott also told us about conversations he's had with Rabbi Korf, a conservative Republican who was close to Richard Nixon in his hour of greatest stress. "May I ask you a theoretical question?" the Rabbi began as he broached the UFO subject with the President. "What would be the consequences if we knew that Aliens existed?"

"The question is not theoretical," Nixon is said to have answered…

The next presentation was by Bob Wood, a summary of his involvement on behalf of the Douglas Aircraft Company. In 1967 his boss asked him to look at UFO electrical charge characteristics and to try to duplicate some of the observed phenomena. They spent half a million dollars on a secret three-year study, experimenting with gravity control, looking for "the giant discoveries of future science." They started from a modified ET hypothesis, with a paranormal component supplied by Jack Houck. Physicist Stanton Friedman was one of the technical people on the project.

Ron Blackburn gave the Lockheed viewpoint. When he joined the SkunkWorks at Burbank he worked with a scientist named Paul Tyler who encouraged him to investigate UFOs from the point of view of "energy, consciousness, and form—where form is negotiable." Ron believes that Roswell was a true crash, with bodies.

Dick Haines followed Blackburn. He said he'd become interested while doing perception experiments at NASA-Ames in the 60s in support of spacecraft docking. He first looked at UFOs as illusions, but later became convinced they were real. The subject is a non-issue at NASA because the SETI folks under Carl Sagan feel threatened by the prospect of serious work on UFOs upsetting their models.

Professor Robert Jahn, Dean of the engineering school at Princeton, and his assistant Brenda Dunne, said their interest had grown out of man-machine anomaly research. Echoing Gordon Creighton, he said: "The problem with UFOs is that somebody is creating reality for us, and we don't know who it is."

He went on: "Einstein once said that we should stop worshipping the concepts we create. So we must ask, is there a wave mechanics of consciousness?" In Jahn's opinion, consciousness behaves as a wave that interacts with the environment. It diffracts, refracts and resonates, has access to all of time and space. (A good definition of operating magic, I noted.)

"Could there be a consciousness that is shifting the mean point of the human system, altering our statistics in subtle ways? All it would take is to create an experience that changes a few individuals."

Indeed most UFO witnesses are changed in subtle ways. What I saw in 1955 has changed me, and in turn my work in this field has changed others; also true for Aimé Michel and for Allen Hynek.

"In the 1976 Tehran case, the weapon system on the jet turned itself off as soon as the pilot *thought* about firing at the UFO..." continued Bob Jahn. This triggered a discussion on psychic effects. Hal mentioned Pat Price's experiments affecting the function of a magnetometer: "The various parts have consciousness," Pat Price used to say. "I can only produce the effect when I get these parts to agree to help me." Another psychic, Duane Elgin, felt that the magnetometer "was aware of him."

Dick Haines wants to pursue contact experiments, building devices that would allow the Aliens to respond to our questions. We had dinner at Maria's, a Mexican restaurant in Santa Fe. John's wife Jan met us there, a warm and articulate New Age woman.

Hyde Street. Sunday 6 May 1990.

This morning, as we had just packed our suitcases, Ron Blackburn reached out dramatically to the telephone in his room, carefully took it apart "in case someone had an infinity device plugged into the line," and we reviewed yesterday's ludicrous expedition.

Back in Santa Fe the conference fell apart. Senator Harrison Schmidt never showed up. Our flip charts filled up with the same wishful thoughts and pointless projects every ufology group has drawn up, a morass of routine proposals. Bob Jahn kept calling for academic projects. Dick Haines slipped me a note: "I give up!"

The only interesting item was the presentation by Bob Wood of the work Douglas Aircraft had performed secretly in the late 60s. "We had a data collection van," he said. "We moved it from mountain top to mountain top in an attempt to detect and track UFOs. We also had two laboratory experiments going, one to study rotating magnets, the other to influence gravitation. Stanton Friedman did the literature research. We stayed in contact with Jim McDonald. We conducted witness interrogations: They led nowhere. Finally my management asked me how I would ever know when I got where I was trying to go, and I couldn't answer, so they closed the project."

"And why didn't you contact Hynek and me at Northwestern in all that time?" I asked abruptly. "We had the only global database."

Bob was taken aback by the question, so I went on: "You must realize that when this kind of covert study is done, other researchers in the field, if they are not dumb, become aware of it and pull back their data. The result is a chill on your own research, not progress."

The people around the room seemed stunned. Blackburn said that was "a damn good question" while Bob Wood answered that the study had been secret, labeled as "Douglas private."

"But the secrecy was your undoing, it led to your failure," I said.

As in the old days with the Air Force, I didn't feel the group was ready to hear about the research I planned to undertake, so I only made peripheral comments about data structures and my experimental program at Spring Hill.

As our plane took off on the way back, Ron Blackburn pointed to a series of tall towers under the airplane. "Those are the electro-magnetic pulse testing facilities I built for the Air Force," he said. "Thousands of volts flow between those towers."

New York. Le Méridien. Friday 11 May 1990.

The papers report the unceremonious ouster of Craig Fields as head of DARPA. Connie McLindon, now director of information systems at NSF, says that Craig misread the climate of the Bush administration. The media argue he should never have had such power (**17**).

Another day of live interviews: Radio hosts are puzzled. "How come no one reports those things over the big cities?" they ask me. Phone lines light up at once, filled with the voices of people reporting personal sightings in Chicago, Detroit, and now in NY.

In Boston, WBZ organized a live television panel on *People are Talking*: An articulate woman abductee from Strieber's Communion Foundation, a woman who believes the Aliens have implanted a device in her arm, a MUFON representative, a fellow from Unarius who's in psychic contact with 33 planets, astronomer Steve O'Meara of *Sky and Telescope*, and a psychiatrist who explains everything as sexual repression. A cute bimbo in a very short pink dress followed him everywhere, patting down his hair for the camera.

The two skeptics poured sarcasm on the unfortunate witnesses. O'Meara asked me to sign his copy of the book, and the psychiatrist told me he was moved to meet someone who had worked with Hynek, so I managed to make friends, except for the stiff Unarian, firmly in league with the Ascended Masters, who spoke to no one.

Hyde Street. Saturday 12 May 1990.

In glorious sunny New York yesterday morning, I had a rare privilege, breakfast uptown at Fred Adler's apartment, a block away from Central Park. He was relaxed, in white tennis shorts and a white shirt.

We sat before a table loaded with healthy foods, orange juice, yogurt, slices of banana and fresh strawberries, toast and coffee.

"If I was five years younger," said the financial tycoon, "I would go and live in Paris. As you know, I am a Francophile. I believe that France has a great opportunity to emerge in a leadership role in Europe after 1992, no matter what people are saying about the imminent greatness of Germany. I could be a factor there."

He overestimates the influence he would have over traditional French structures, torn by political skirmishes among the socialists, worn down by the exercise of power. Adler does know this, and he finally concludes that New York is more pleasant than any place in France, "when you know your way around," as he surely does.

I had to admit there was nothing wrong with life on a magnificent morning like this, in an apartment that occupies the entire 14th floor of a skyscraper, surrounded with gouaches by Fernand Léger, drinking fresh juice served by a stylish, silent maid. Fred feeds two little white dogs. The nanny brings him the 6-month old kid he has adopted, a happy giggling boy. The next hour is private tutoring for me in the mysteries of finance. He tells me to kill the Metricom deal.

Portland airport, on the way to L.A. Thursday 17 May 1990.

Having finally reached Major Ed Dames, I learned what happened after we met at Los Alamos: "We'd taken you and Ron to the wrong mesa, that's why we saw nothing! The next night we saw a large UFO in the West." I think Ed Dames and his associates are losing their sense of perspective, like everybody else.

In Seattle yesterday I met astronaut Ed Gibson who's just written a novel about space. I teased him about the fact that Soviet cosmonaut training acknowledged parapsychology. He said that it would be a long time before NASA came to the same point. Now I am in the friendly city of Portland where life consists of "shades of gray."

Spring Hill. Saturday 19 May 1990.

After the bright lights of Los Angeles television studios I savor the peace of our library again. I went to ABC with Barbara Hershey of

Right Stuff fame (she told me she saw weird lights over Edwards Air Force base when they filmed that movie) and I took live questions from viewers with "Sonya" on CNN, but I'm glad that trip is over.

Janine and I spent the afternoon in the observatory tower, charmed by the heavy, steady raindrops over the roof. This evening I called Hal Puthoff, our first conversation since the meeting in New Mexico. He confirmed John Alexander had gone very high to get the Secret Onion funded: "He briefed the head of Norad, the head of the Space Command, the top guy at SDI, all three and four-star generals, all had given him the green light..."

"Yet he was suddenly removed," I pointed out.

"John was in charge of Directed Energy Weapon work for the Army, over a billion-dollar budget. When they suddenly decided to reassign him, he got mad and quit, then he heard Los Alamos was looking for someone at the Defense Initiatives Office. True, he doesn't know a lot about UFOs, but he's a sharp fellow."

"So where do we go from here?"

"Three possibilities: One, we discover a super-program somewhere and connect with it. Two, we find that there isn't one but our own project is encouraged; so we build instrumented sites like you and Blackburn were planning, we accumulate institutional history, archives on the phenomenon, we wait for a bigger effort."

"What's the third possibility?" I asked.

He sighed: "The null hypothesis. No funding. Zero progress."

Hyde Street. Tuesday 22 May 1990.

Robert Wood of McDonnell-Douglas tries to refute my "five arguments against the extraterrestrial theory"--clinging to the first-order belief that we deal with actual Aliens from some remote planet. He explains the overly-numerous encounters by the fact that several civilizations must be visiting us. He does add an interesting comment about the McDonnell research of the early days:

"I much regret that you and I did not make mutual contact in 1968-70. Allen always had so much going on, and he was more interested in developing "proof" than figuring out how they work. Carl Sagan got wind of our project before the AAAS Symposium and called me up to find out about it with the possibility of contributing a paper. I told him that it was obvious that UFOs were real (I didn't waste any time trying to prove that) and that our McDonnell-Douglas angle was to figure out how they worked. Sagan never called back."

If I'd been able to contribute to McDonnell's study I'd have advocated a diametrically opposed approach: quiet, frugal long-term research with little money, no government input and only contact with reliable witnesses, avoiding cases heavily featured in the media.

Hyde Street. Wednesday 30 May 1990.

Psychologist Arthur Hastings and his wife Sandy came over for dinner last night. Catherine was here with a friend from Colorado and a visitor from Paris, so Arthur had a warm public for his magic performances and his impassioned descriptions of channeling.

We discussed the powers of the mind. Arthur pointed out that people often tended to decrease their intelligence level in response to their environment and that it always took a conscious effort to raise it back up. He used to do an experiment with his Stanford students: get them to visualize that their IQ was 20 points higher, and decide how they would change their lives if they commanded such genius. They discovered that the brilliant changes they mapped out as a hypothetical game were well within their reach in real life.

Air Canada flight to Montréal. Friday 1 June 1990.

When I left for New York the airport TV monitors showed George H. Bush and Gorbachev exchanging greetings in Washington.

Last night Whitley Strieber and Ann joined me for dinner at the Manhattan Ocean Club. He's grown a mustache and changed his glasses in order not to be recognized on the street. We went back over his meetings with "The Visitors." Budd Hopkins had biased his expectations by indoctrinating him before hypnosis, leading him to expect a horrible experience and those Aliens with big black eyes.

An Intelligence agent, a contact of Bill Moore, has assured Whitley that the crashes really happened: "Why is their story always so bad?"

Whitley asked me with humor. "They've been telling the stupid Roswell tale for so long they need to update it periodically!"

Yet when he asked Brigadier General Arthur Exon about his tenure at Wright-Patterson, the old man confirmed the Air Force had indeed dragged in some material that had fallen from the sky over Roswell: "It was titanium and some other metal they knew about, but the manufacturing process was completely different," he said.

The other metal was nickel, forming an alloy called Nitinol, the first "memory metal" developed at Battelle by the team of Howard Cross in the late 40s. Another general, George Schulgen, who led Air Force Intelligence, penned a secret memo on October 30, 1947 about "unusual fabrication methods to achieve extreme lightweight."

When we discussed his feelings towards the Visitors, Whitley got emotional, as if he had another family far away; he actually missed them. Ann testily pointed out there might be psychological explanations to his feeling that way.

Toronto Marriott. Monday 4 June 1990.

I just learned of the death of Bob Noyce in Austin, at only 62. One of the luminaries of Silicon Valley, a founder of Fairchild and Intel and one of the early investors in my InfoMedia company ten years ago, he suffered a sudden heart attack. He played tennis the previous day, had a swim. A test two weeks before had disclosed no ailment. The media don't cover the story: This man changed our lives, but the public is much more fascinated by the fact that singer Michael Jackson has just suffered a bruised rib during a dance rehearsal.

Hyde Street. Tuesday 5 June 1990.

Dick Haines tells me John Alexander's agenda is the development of non-lethal weapons. When Dick speaks about the spiritual benefits he derives from the Bible, he feels an otherworldly force: "Our world has never needed prophets as much as it does today," he says.

Next week I'll meet Kit in New York. He tells me he's reached radical conclusions over the last three months. The government is taking care of the right problem, he now believes: "The evidence is solid." Yet I've often heard him complain about the "flaky data" …

Then my friend Ralph, a slender young man with long hair, mustache and glasses called from Berkeley with alarm. "Someone's life is in danger," he said. "An air traffic controller at Edwards AFB says MJ-12 is vectoring saucers from space over the desert!"

Hyde Street. Monday 11 June 1990.

A new asthma crisis hit me last Wednesday, on top of a cold. Janine had to rush me to the hospital, panting and shuddering. They took X-rays, diagnosed acute bronchitis. An orderly pushed my bed into a room. I only returned to the ranch yesterday, pumped up with cortico-steroids and antibiotics. I had to call Kit to cancel.

At the hospital I was aware that I could die of this. The available drugs against asthma depress the immune system and counteract inflammation, decreasing the effectiveness of the treatment against infection and making the issue uncertain. Patients have been killed by such respiratory infections that flared up quickly out of control, most recently Jim Henson, creator of the Muppets. Yet I was glad to discover there was nothing but a great peace within me, a new friend in my soul. On Sunday, when the drugs took effect, this feeling was still in my mind, that my life was in order and that I was free to leave this world. I would take with me one last glimpse of our hills beyond the tower, *et un prénom de femme*, as Jacques Brel used to sing.

Oxnard. Saturday 16 June 1990.

Sailboats under our window. The French scientific mission has gathered students from the Western States, the consulate staff and representatives of major French firms. I gave the keynote speech, my voice still shaky from last week's illness. This afternoon we'll drive down to Hollywood to join my friends Bob Weiss and Tracy Tormé.

Hollywood. Roosevelt Hotel. Sunday 17 June 1990.

A white gray day over L.A. We had dinner at *Musso & Frank* and strolled on the boulevard. Hundreds of motorcycles congregated under the close watch of cops. Girls in little more than panties were clinging to machines and riders alike; punks stared provocatively at everyone and tried hard to look menacing.

During an afternoon meeting at Bob's temporary offices at Warner Brothers (he is filming *Trickhouse*) we did a walk-through of my *FastWalker* story with Tracy who was equally distracted, busy with a miniseries for another studio and with *Star Trek* projects. We are still without a script, so the studio is about to kill our project.

In Las Vegas I'm told Lazar has been found guilty of offenses related to the Honeysuckle brothel. One hears hints of a criminal environment. Back in Gulf Breeze, people come out of the shadows, stating that UFO models were found in Mr. Ed's attic and that the saucer story was concocted and passed on to ufologists... So much for the "final proof," another public fiasco.

Hyde Street. Monday 18 June 1990.

Colonel Blackburn was striding across the parking lot when I arrived at the *Perfect Recipe* in Palo Alto this afternoon. He handed me a historic paper from the second meeting of his group, dated 1985. It proposed a compartmented scientific approach, with a small research team composed of Peter Sturrock, Allen Hynek and myself receiving funds (some $150,000 for my own part of the research, although I was never consulted about what I would do) for specific phases of activity. But it also contained an absurd map of alleged UFO centers, bases and hypothetical "entry points" at Mount Shasta.

Tonight, Whitley Strieber called, pleased with our dinner in New York. He suggested that I meet with a senior Senate staffer, Richard D'Amato, convinced there was illegal Intelligence activity involving UFOs, but "The spooks will circle the wagons as soon as they notice outside pressure, just as the Nixon thugs did at the time of Watergate and friends of Oliver North at the time of the Iran-Contra scandal." D'Amato has been on the Senate staff for 16 years.

"This could be dangerous," Whitley told me. "D'Amato will only speak to you on condition of secrecy, he doesn't want anything to do with ufologists." Whitley adds that Falcon (Bob Collins) has met with Senator Bill Bradley, "a man with a spin."

Washington. Hotel Madison. Thursday 21 June 1990.

The muggy summer has hit the East Coast. There must be some days of clement skies here, however, because Connie McLindon drives a blue Mercedes convertible that creates ripples of admiration among the parking attendants. I hadn't seen her in years, so we spent a leisurely dinner catching up on the adventures of her former boss Craig Fields, the computer networking efforts of the National Science Foundation, and the current whereabouts of Vint Cerf and Bob Kahn, Doug Engelbart and Lynn Conway. Connie has kept her sharp eye and her keen sense of humor:

"None of this technology actually works," she said cheerfully, sipping white wine. "We spend taxpayers' money sending people to complicated seminars where Harvard professors puff themselves up and talk about *mis-interoperability* and the *failure of paradigm congruence!* Why doesn't anybody just come out and say frankly that computer networking is a mess?"

Later the same day.

"You must be Jacques Vallee. I'm Richard D'Amato." The Counsel for International and National Security of the Senate Appropriations Committee is a solid man in his early 40s, at ease in the magnificent setting of hand-painted ceilings, soft red carpets strewn with gold stars, and Presidential portraits. Senators gave a touching picture as they sat with constituents in the grand dining room: a group of young women from some College, old supporters from a town back home...

D'Amato, who has read *Confrontations*, told me he was upset at the Intelligence community: "These guys have been hiding their UFO data from the legislative branch for years; they behave as if they ran the country. They only come before us to get the appropriations for their secret projects, like their latest discoid platforms, although they're not authorized to fool the American public, or to create hoaxes or UFO simulations using taxpayers' money, *as they do*. I intend to find out what's been going on."

"Are you thinking of new Congressional Hearings?" I asked him.

"Not in the sense ufologists talk about Hearings, as if they were a panacea. You can't setup such a process to find out the truth. In this town you must find out the truth first, and THEN you hold the Hearings. *You have to catch the fish before you go fishing!* That's what we did with Watergate and Iran-Contra. In both cases we dragged in super-patriots who thought they were above the law."

I told him about Jim Irish, the closest I ever came to find a man who had been part of a large, secret UFO data-gathering operation. I had once taken Kit to meet him, but there was no follow-up.

Mabillon. Saturday 23 June 1990.

It was a strange feeling to arrive in Paris alone, my key in hand. I took care of urgent business, carrying Janine's translation of *Confrontations* to Robert Laffont and going on to Fleximage with the large-scale Costa Rica UFO negatives. François Louange will digitize them next week on his satellite image reduction machines.

Since April our love nest has been redone, painted and papered in soft gray with blue flowers and puffs of white foliage. Again, that odd feeling sweeps over me, that we could bring our lives back here and never spend another day in America. A few phone calls would dispose of what we own. I would miss the morning light over the Bay and the blessed nights at my tower observatory but not the bustle of Silicon Valley or the roughness of Manhattan, the fake sophistication of Washington, or the dazzle of Hollywood.

This morning I went to the Boul'Mich for breakfast in the alternating drizzle and pale sunshine. I walked back along the quay admiring the sundial on the headquarters of the Paris police with its Latin legend, *Fugit Tempus, Stat Jus*: Time flies, Justice remains. Well, maybe. Recently a cop who was arresting a petty crook on Place Saint-Michel held the man down on the sidewalk. He pointed a gun at his head and abruptly, for no reason, blew the fellow's brains out in plain sight of the crowd: *Stat Tempus, Fugit Jus*.

Mabillon. Sunday 24 June 1990.

It was raining on the church of *Saint-Germain-des-Prés* when I met Martine Castello for dinner. We reminisced about Russia: "It was like a dream," she said, "sometimes I wonder if it really happened: the characters right out of Dostoievsky, the secrets they shared with us, which we can't publish."

I asked about Martine's recent trip to Spain. "There's a link between Ummo and the extreme-right group of *Fusion,*" she reported. The French disinformation machine is working overtime: Two writers who have never studied UFOs published in *Science-et-Vie* magazine the absurd idea that the Belgian flying triangles, seen by thousands of people, were nothing but the stealth F117 aircraft…

Now an accordion plays old French tunes under my windows. I had lunch with Maman, worried about the health of her sister Huguette. We strolled in the sunshine along the Seine, looking at books. She complained about recent celebrations in Paris: "It's always De Gaulle this, De Gaulle that, you should have seen it! As if people shouldn't be looking forward, instead of wasting their time with old stuff!"

She observed that the taste of food had changed for the worse in France: "The bread and croissants used to be so much better! They say they use butter, but it's a kind of industrial butter designed for bakeries. It just doesn't taste the same as what I recall as a child. And do you know what my baker told me? He doesn't remember his parents ever making white bread! He says, "the bread we sell you today is white, isn't it?" But it has nothing to do with what we used to eat... They mix different kinds of flour to increase shelf life. Even what they call *brioche* doesn't taste like what we had."

This remark struck me. We take it for granted that our technology keeps improving conditions for the largest number of people, another myth. There's a whole universe of quiet grace, a luxury of small things we may never recapture, like the taste of that wonderful white bread even the poorest people used to eat, a taste I remember well.

Mabillon. Wednesday 27 June 1990.

Pierre Guérin forgot our breakfast appointment. He was all confusion and apologies: "I've got family problems. I just got back from La Rochelle... Wait for me; I'll jump on the bus..." He arrived ten minutes later, returned to me the Costa Rica photograph that he had measured, finding a discrepancy in Dick Haines' estimate of the object's size. He was most excited about his impending meeting with a French

Intelligence agent sent by Aimé Michel.

"When will you write your own book on UFOs?" I teased him.

"Once I'm retired: They won't be able to do anything to me..." **(18)**

Pierre states, "GEPAN was never meant to do research: the real work is in the military. Sepra is a cover, set up by Hubert Curien."

At noon Alain Boudier picked me up and we drove over to his apartment in Sceaux. We met stage hypnotist Danny Dan and a serial contactee named Jacques Carter, from Nice, who says he was picked up by a beam from a UFO as early as 1940. Danny Dan described his research in Africa, where natives told him they had watched a small entity coming out of a flying object. They carved a fine statue of it for him. He showed it to me: It stood about three feet tall, with a very large head, thin lips, and two small breasts.

Mabillon. Thursday 28 June 1990.

Pierre has met with his French *barbouze*. The man had many questions on the socio-cultural impact of the UFO problem, if it were to come out into the open: How would the scientific world react? he asked. He implied that many political leaders worried about the belief in UFOs getting out of control, but he may be fishing for the opposite data: *What would be the effect of making up such information?* He also wanted to meet me, but Guérin, eager to keep the contact for himself, didn't tell him where I was. Just as well.

Whitley writes about secrets in *Majestic*: "When the history of this era is written, it must certainly be called the Age of Secrets. *Public knowledge has degenerated into a form of entertainment...* Official secrets are the snare of modern life. If you don't know them, you're helpless. If you do, you're trapped."

Paris. Charles de Gaulle airport. Friday 29 June 1990.

This morning I met with Gilbert Payan for breakfast at *Le Départ* on place Saint Michel. He was still fuming about a new book by physicist Jean-Pierre Petit. Payan thinks that Ummo is a brainchild of the KGB, designed to steal advanced ideas in science. Like Martine, he suspects a connection to LaRouche's *Fusion* group, one of the KGB's operations in the West. "They're financed out of Berlin, a place where money can just appear out of nowhere." He seemed astonished when I told him that MHD (magneto-hydrodynamics) was known in the US, long before Petit's research.

While the UFO field stagnates, my professional work moves forward. Not only did we advance the status of five investment investigations, including a potential buy-out of Daisy Systems (**19**) but *Groupe Siparex* agreed to launch our second EuroAmerica fund: "We like to work with you," they told me.

Hyde Street. Tuesday 10 July 1990.

Long phone conversation with Kit, who heralded a major change: The "best" analytical minds are digging into UFO data, he said, mostly aerospace and technical people. "Small mesh, sensors of all kinds. A lot of strange things are not so strange when you expand the bandwidth," he said: "Bright people with good access, not impressed by standard explanations." He used to think that no really secret project could exist without his awareness of them. But he was wrong, he admits. Kit now thinks that UFO material was recovered but he observes "a large body of consistent, unusual data from a small number of squirrelly people. It looks like multiple sources of consistent information, when in fact there are only few sources of inconsistent data." What does that all mean?

Hyde Street. Thursday 12 July 1990.

Another lunch with former White House assistant Barbara Honegger. In her recent vindication a Federal Court decreed her source innocent of perjury. The man had exposed the deal for weapons made in Paris between the Reagan camp and the Iranians in exchange for a delay in releasing American hostages, the famous *October Surprise* of 1980, a meeting attended by Bill Casey in person. At the trial, the Bush Administration sent Intelligence officers to testify *under oath* that the meeting at Hotel Raphaël never took place. They were proven to be lying; the media didn't care. What does that say about the chances of a similar exposé in the study of UFOs?

Barbara spoke about her tiredness, loneliness and fear as she assembled, correlated and published that evidence.

In the morning Martin Cannon joined us. A young man with a black mustache and a decisive flair for investigation, Martin tracks the extreme-right background of UFO groups. I was impressed by his knowledge of the "I AM" cult and the followers of Dorothy Martin alias Mrs. Keech alias Sister Thedra, the woman who accompanied George Hunt Williamson on his quest for the mythical *Monastery of the Seven Rays*. He speculates that George Green, the financial backer of Colonel Stevens, is linked to the Samizdat group in Canada. The neo-Nazi links go all the way back to Hermann Oberth (**20**) and his promotional efforts for George Adamski in the 1950s.

Kit doesn't believe the phenomenon involves non-human consciousness. He still attributes it to delusionary states of mind. Isn't that in contradiction with the new statements about hardware?

Albuquerque. Airport Inn. Friday 13 July 1990.

Janine and I have finally met the mystery man of American ufology, Paul Bennewitz, although Martin Cannon had just told me it was impossible to reach him. We spoke to Bennewitz for three hours. His wife Cindy, a pleasant, quiet woman in her early 60s, opened the door of their white two-storey townhouse in the Villa Serena community, surrounded by a white wall like a fortified town. In the Bennewitz home the medieval theme is heightened by a collection of swords and books about ancient warfare.

When Paul came down the stairs I noted his blond hair and his high-perched eyebrows. He is more than a little paunchy, but he has a good face, with deep lines and feverish eyes. His fingernails are long and his thumbs curve back away from his hand. He showed signs of nervousness, trouble controlling his trembling.

"I haven't given any interviews in the last five years," he told me, "but I wanted to meet you because I'd heard about your research; I knew that you were working alone, as I do."

Paul and Cindy have lived in the house for 10 years. They have three sons. The eldest now runs Thunder Scientific, the company Paul founded 25 years ago. It first developed solid-state humidity sensors, for which he holds six patents, and precision instruments sold to the military and aerospace companies. They fly on the Shuttle and the Hubble telescope. Thunder Scientific, from which Paul retired two years ago, has grown into a million-dollar company.

In 1979 Paul decided to get serious about this research after working with ufologist Jim McCampbell. He developed electronic instruments that he pointed at the sky. "I must have spent about $250,000 on this," he said. "I started picking up magnetic interferences. I could tell how many ships there were."

"I'm told those interferences could be ordinary emissions from Kirtland Air Force Base, rather than UFOs," I interjected.

"No way! The pulse facility gave signals at a high power level, but in a different range. I've been involved with radio frequency evasive maneuvers, I know what to look for. What I started picking up were video images. Those aliens have several bases. I was able to confirm this, with my own airplane. I took pictures at Archuleta."

"You'd expect these objects to show up on radar," I objected.

He shrugged: "They go too fast for radar; they just look like noise, glitches. I made a presentation to those tower operators; I showed them pictures of a 10-foot saucer under the wings of an airplane that was taking off, and they'd never seen anything like it. I filmed one at Dulce from 30 feet away (Figure 4 p.87.) It burned me, that's why my eyebrows are seared. You can only see them when they stop to look around, every five or ten miles. I've learned how to watch them. There are over a hundred over Albuquerque every day."

"How come people don't see them? Or take clear photographs?"

"They cloak themselves. They can look like clouds."

"Where do you think they come from?"

"Scorpio, Capricorn, Orion, Zeta Reticuli, all over. They fly through hyperspace. They come here to take what I call human life essence: ovum, sperm. They kidnap, they kill people. One boy was taken by the Aliens and drowned in a tank of water."

Bennewitz sensed our disbelief because he added: "They use a hexagonal design for their tanks. Each one has a human in it. It's filled with blue oxygenated water that's swirling."

"So... How do we know this really happens?" I asked Paul.

"It's a long story... I made the mistake of my life when I started working with an abduction victim from Cimarron, Myrna Hansen. She was hypnotized by Leo Sprinkle."

"I understand you've also met with Dr. Hynek?" I asked.

"Only once. He came over for dinner, a nice man. He said a curious thing: 'Before we discuss anything, I want you to know that I believe in psychic abilities,' he told me." (Note)

"Where did the notion of the Dulce base come from?"

"It started with Gabe Valdez. He was worried about animal mutilations. He felt the perpetrators came from outer space."

When we told Paul that we had to go back to the motel and would be back after lunch, he carefully unlocked all the deadbolts on his door and let us out. Janine and I just had to breathe some fresh air.

The second meeting lasted for two and a half hours. Paul must have decided we were all right, because he opened his library and we were allowed upstairs. The back wall of his study holds two bookcases with such titles as *UFO Crash at Aztec* as well as the *Book of Urantia*, *Oahspe*, Jim Hurtak's *Keys of Enoch* and my own *Invisible College*. Between the bookcases was a pleasant painting of trees and horses in a field. The back wall held two large closets. The one on the right had some shelves and a safe containing Paul's photographs. In the center was a big desk with an oversized Bible, two lamps and a microscope. Behind his chair was a working table with papers, more lamps and records, and on the wall a map of the moon and one of the night sky: The study of a well-organized researcher.

Paul setup a screen against the back closets. For the next couple of hours, he showed us film after film of indistinct objects that could have been anything—blurs and rainbows and exaggerated blobs of blown-up grain where he saw all manner of fantastic spacecraft.

(Note) According to Greg Bishop (*Project Beta*. NY:Pocket Books, 2005), in 1981 Allen Hynek was induced to deliver to Bennewitz a computer that AFOSI (or the CIA?) had rigged with deceptive software to make him misinterpret the classified signals he picked up as garbled communications from Aliens. In a conversation with Bill Moore, Bennewitz later said he had assumed the program Dr. Hynek gave him had "been modified by the Aliens themselves" to facilitate his communications with them…

Albuquerque. Airport Inn. Sunday 15 July 1990.

Flooded expressways, cars stalled in two or three feet of water, uprooted trees, leaves and mud strewn across the roads: that was the scene downtown Albuquerque as we drove back from the Bennewitz home at nightfall. This morning the sky is blue but the papers report twisters, kids swept away by the storm, electrical failures and men blown away from their motorcycles by lightning.

Later the same day. In the plane flying back to California.

"The day after Easter, the Celestials took Jesus Christ from his tomb," Paul told us. "They flew his body to New Mexico and buried him in the pyramid of Eden where the three Eves are resting, one of them being none other than Isis!" Paul's only evidence for this is in a large jumble of rocks he's photographed from his airplane. He sees sculptures there: Sarcophagi, hieroglyphics, statues, mysterious shadows, evidence of an observatory built 40,000 years ago…

Paul Bennewitz is a nice man. It is impossible to interrupt him, much less to contradict him. I didn't know whether to laugh or cry.

Men are puny in the American Southwest, yet one feels in such intimate contact with infinity in the thin air of the High Desert that anyone could be impelled to become the interpreter of that dream, to give it formalism in the shape of complex instrumentation. As the plane took off I looked down at the awesome landscape and I thought I saw what spiritual needs Paul's strange theories fulfilled.

Spring Hill. Sunday 29 July 1990.

The white dome of our observatory now rests on top of the tower at Spring Hill. Soon I'll be able to resume quiet research on the metastructures of the phenomenon. In the meantime, the world plunges into weirdness: Six soldiers have deserted sensitive intelligence posts in West Germany to fly to Gulf Breeze, the new hotbed of ufology, where they reportedly hoped to kill the Antichrist and fly away in spaceships. They are Christian fundamentalists who believe Jesus will pick them up. There would be Armageddon, starting with war in the Middle East. They were on their way to New Mexico (**21**). They are now held at Fort Benning, Georgia.

Someone has rummaged around my friend Fred Beckman's car and dragged out old papers from under the seat, spreading them over the dashboard. His binoculars and a radio set were pulled out, but nothing was stolen. The car was still locked. A warning? Fred told me he was in touch with a network of fringe ufologists loosely tied to CIA analyst Ron Pandolfi but he left the connection very vague (**22**).

Washington. Hotel Madison. Thursday 2 August 1990.

Kit met me in the bar of the Madison last night. Our long-postponed conversation covered his insight into government projects, current claims by ufologists, and a follow-up on Brazil. Kit still denies there's a genuine UFO phenomenon. Perhaps only those who have experienced it can grasp its implications? He agrees with my case analyses, but he draws conclusions diametrically opposed to mine:

"There might just be a very few real occurrences," he says, "That Brazilian stuff sounds like rumor amplification, sheer mythology."

"What about the unexplained cases? Thousands of them," I insisted.

"Natural effects we haven't encountered yet. And clever hoaxes."

That made no sense, so I prompted him to clarify his letter to the Los Alamos group, stating that the government "had things under control." Before answering he ordered a cup of coffee and some apple pie, adding cheddar cheese on top of it. He said it was an old Wisconsin custom. I needled him, saying it was disgusting.

"I never had ice cream on my pie until I got to Colorado as a student," he countered with a wink.

"That must have been a happy day for you!" I teased him again.

When the waiter departed we turned to the serious stuff. He told me what had changed his mind about the secrecy issue. "As you know, Jacques, for a long time I have claimed that in my position I would have had to know of secret projects on this topic. Even if they didn't tell me the contents of 'the Box,' I would have had to know there was a box. Between Hal and you and me, and the wide network of contacts we represent, we should have heard something. Well, that was pure hubris on our part. I know this because of something that just happened in an unrelated field, a project I've just been invited to join. Not only had I never heard of it, but it involves people I thought I knew well. It also involves five levels of clearances above my own. And I had a clearance above top secret."

We let the conversation die while the waiter served our coffee and Kit's abominable cheese and apple pie, then he went on:

"When I was indoctrinated into that project, (which I should have been invited to join years ago, by the way, because it fell exactly in one of my fields of expertise) the briefing took place at a large facility that the government operates. The first meeting was a psychological orientation, before they would tell me anything else...

"You'd get a badge at the first desk and sign a book, then you would go to a second desk and receive a second badge, and so on five times, and you would not even get through the front door unless you had a top-secret clearance. The fellow who came to fetch me and take me into the briefing room was a man I had once hired. I had no idea he was involved in anything like this; with a budget in the billions. Even the codename is classified within its own level; it doesn't appear anywhere. There's no way for anyone to know of its existence, until someone invites them inside."

Kit admits he's shaken. No wonder he now develops a respect for government secrecy that borders on awe. We discussed the possible location of a super-secret *Alintel* (**23**). He dismissed the 1987 report by Howard Blum about a secret group. Blum's book simply alluded to John Alexander's and Ron Blackburn's proposed project I have nicknamed the *Secret Onion*. It went nowhere.

"There's also a rumor about something called Joint Task Force 6, and about Dale Graff setting up an interagency working group, but it was never given any responsibilities," he said.

"Someone told me it was buried under Jack Vorona's budget. He never knew about it," I interjected. Kit agreed energetically:

"Right! I went to see Vorona. His shoulders dropped when I mentioned UFOs and he lowered his head. He told me, 'They never let me in on it!' very sadly and dejectedly. Vorona is leaving DIA for a job with military vehicles."

"What about Colonel Hennessey? Bill Moore mentions him as the top guy above Doty, the man giving orders to Falcon."

"I spoke to Hennessey; he swore he'd never met Doty or Moore."

"One of these days there will be an 'Alien Intelligence Agency,' as in my novel, and it'll be staffed by moronic technocrats," I joked.

"I thought I'd found it once," he answered. "I had a tip that there was this office in the Pentagon, 5G47, where the UFO project was located. I went there, and they had a perfectly good explanation for what they did, low-level observables. Until one day I was relaxing with a friend who used to be in the Carter administration, so I asked him about 5G47 and he said, 'Well, that's the UFO office!' Just like that. He had old Pentagon phone books but we couldn't find that office listed. We eventually found it in a 1967 phone book. It has been kept out of subsequent editions. I went back and I had three briefings with those guys. They do Stealth and drug interdiction. Their low-level observables are plain old anti-drug aircraft."

"That doesn't mean there's no UFO project," I pointed out.

"Of course not. I have another source, an insider who tells me he's seen hardware and bodies. But it's always the same story. There are claims of evidence on the side we don't have access to," he said drawing a vertical line on a napkin and writing an exclamation point on the left, "but there is no evidence whatsoever on this side." He completed the drawing with a question mark to the right of the line.

Hyde Street. Monday 6 August 1990.

Dr. Rima Laibow, current arbiter of alien abduction speculation, came for dinner tonight. She stormed about the bumblings of Budd Hopkins, Leo Sprinkle, and the others. She described a videotape in which Sprinkle interrogates Judy Doraty, who originated the idea of underground vats with human parts stirred up by Alien monsters:

"I could swear it's Sprinkle who is hypnotized," she said. "His head is lowered; he speaks in a low, dreamy tone. The woman is all business, vivacious, talkative. At one point she seems ready to cry, then she opens her eyes wide, takes a handkerchief and runs it carefully over her eyelids, and checks it to see if her Mascara is running… Is that deep hypnosis? I've done hundreds of sessions in therapy, and I've yet to see my patient check her make-up."

Rima believes there are "cult multiples," people who have developed artificial multiple personalities or were given certain wackinesses, that can be controlled throughout their lives. It's an important idea.

Hyde Street. Wednesday 8 August 1990.

After the opening of the Society for Scientific Exploration (SSE) at the Palo Alto Holiday Inn I had dinner with Hal at Stickney's.

"Kit believes that 'Colonel Phillips' in Howard Blum's book is actually Dale Graff," I said, reporting on our conversation.

"No, he's a Colonel at Wright-Patterson," answered Hal. "Collins, who is Condor, met him when he worked there as a consultant. Graff did sponsor some of our work on remote viewing. Blum's book has all the right elements—with the wrong story! There was never a project Aquarius in remote viewing."

"How did you meet Collins?"

"Henry Monteif brought the two of us together."

"Who is Falcon?"

"There is no question that Agent Doty is Falcon, even if he now tries to imply he's only a conduit to the real Falcon."

"Who is Hennessey?"

"Hennessey is head of security for Stealth."

I had to let the implications sink in. "By the way, Hennessey claims no interest in UFOs whatsoever," Hal continued.

"Who was paying Bill Moore, then?"

"Presumably he was paid by Doty, but there is a Mister X behind all that, who's never been identified. Mind you, there was only one meeting in Washington: I organized it. I brought Scott Jones, Condor, Falcon, and Moore together. There was no meeting with Senators. We told Doty he'd better produce something solid. He gave us an official-looking document that turned out to be another fake."

"What about the six soldiers from Augsburg who recently defected and were arrested in Gulf Breeze?"

"You don't know the half of it," sighed Hal. "They were members of an INSCOM unit. They were not headed for New Mexico but for the spot in Texas where my facility is located! They had a computer disk, filled with scientology stuff. Someone warned me of an attack to discredit us. Imagine: remote viewing, UFOs and Antichrist all wrapped into one! They were simply crazy Fundamentalists."

At the SSE I met again with sociologist David Swift and with Brendan O'Regan, whom I hadn't seen in years. We discussed Lazar and Hans-Adam Liechtenstein. "I went to Vaduz and the Prince told me about your conversation," Brendan said. "I'm getting used to visiting the same places as you, trailing you by a few months..."

Rima Laibow told me a surprising anecdote. At the dinner following the first Abduction Trauma meeting, the Prince reportedly said that he'd been briefed by the KGB, the CIA and NATO Intelligence. They told him people were being "taken" from every country.

Hyde Street. Friday 10 August 1990.

The SSE is a group of middle-aged academics with gray hair, beer bellies and good intentions. Last evening in Peter Sturrock's garden we discussed lofty subjects with Yervant Terzian who is Carl Sagan's boss at Cornell, Bob Jahn, dean of engineering at Princeton (who once saw a UFO in Florida but never reported it) and Jean-Jacques Velasco, whose paper I read at the conference.

He argues convincingly that crop circles are caused by a novel directed energy weapon.

As we left we passed a van parked on the sidewalk and were harpooned by an inventor who showed us a strange energy machine powered by a magnetic flywheel.

"I've come here because of you," he told me as his wife snapped our picture next to the strange contraption. "We've seen you on TV."

"What does this do?" I inquired, pointing at his machine.

"It develops free energy."

"Does it run your van?"

"No," he confessed without batting an eye, "but it could."

Spring Hill. Thursday 16 August 1990.

On Sunday Jean-Jacques Velasco came over to our house with his family. He gave me a copy of his correspondence with Russian "Professor" Silanov who has researched the case in Voronezh.

Catherine has arrived from Boulder. We drove up to the observatory, the car loaded with books. She helped me install the dome onto its ring of rollers.

On Tuesday night we met members of a local Pagan group: Dan Stewart, a gifted writer for their magazine *The Green Egg*, invited us for the Dark of the Moon.

Spring Hill. Tuesday 21 August 1990.

We drove across the creek on the dusty dirt road that leads to Dan Stewart's house, half a mile away, to meet Pagan leader Otter Zell who emerged from the woods with a dozen witches and warlocks from the *Church of All Worlds*. We had coffee and pizza and Janine's special almond cake. Otter Zell lives with his two partners, Morning Glory and Diane, on a beautiful 55-acre parcel called *Annwfn*.

The group included a white-haired lady, an Indian woman and blonde Diane with her other boyfriend and her punk son. Eona was the hostess with a fellow who used to work at the ranch, Dan Stewart, and half-a-dozen others in complex relationships.

It was a feast, a fun evening. We spoke of flying saucers, unicorns and mermaids; we formed a circle and sang "the Blood of the Ancients." A witch sprinkled everyone with duck charm, and then we drove home across the wooden bridge.

Hyde Street. Sunday 26 August 1990.

Over dinner at Ghirardelli Square, Fred Beckman confided, "I was 58 years old yesterday. I never thought I would get to be so old. You might say I've completely wasted my life..." I tried to cheer him up; I brought up photography, about which he has great credentials, and music, which he delights in explaining to me in spite of our differences: "You listen to Hildegard von Bingen," he says, "but me, it's Mahler I love, all gloomy trombones and cavernous bassoons!"

Paul Bennewitz sends me a friendly letter listing what he believes are the locations of Alien bases in New Mexico, "for my eyes only."

Today a man named Armen Victorian called from England. He'd gotten my number from "Mrs. Page of *Fusion Magazine* in Montréal."

This turned on red lights, because I don't know any Mrs. Page. *Fusion* is linked to Lyndon LaRouche and I'd been warned that a strange Englishman was contacting ufologists. The caller, in perfect English with a touch of Mediterranean accent, started going down a list of topics that included Alien autopsies, various doctors (he mentioned a "Dr. Crowley",) Navy work on ESP research and my own work in Brazil. He told me I should research Von Papen.

Spring Hill. Wednesday 29 August 1990.

Unfinished business: mailing lists, book catalogue, the observatory, a painted glass window in the library, swimming... My new panel shows Mélusine (**24**). Bill Calvert and his daughter Elena visited us, discussing the Taliesin architectural experiment and Frank Lloyd Wright, and the threatening war in Iraq. I have yet to recompile the sighting files from Russia and the medical injury cases from Colares.

Spring Hill. Thursday 30 August 1990.

Pilgrimage to Covelo, an isolated spot in the Northern California paradise: we drove up the mountain road to Round Valley, one of nature's quiet marvels, gate to the realm of Yolla Bolly. Twenty years ago, we made that trip with our children, battling a rainstorm over the precipices of the Eel River in a Wagnerian tumble of rocks. We'd watched a bright double rainbow embracing the valley below us. Today the river was dry. We had a pleasant picnic in the shade.

Spring Hill. Friday 31 August 1990.

Our forest is filled with bird calls; blue jays pick at the ripening figs, the neighbors' dogs keep bringing old tennis balls for me to throw. Diane Darling has elegantly described the region in *Green Egg* (**25**):

"The land itself is wooded hills and small meadows. Trees are mostly medium-sized Douglas fir, madrone, buckeye and manzanita, with black- and tan-oak. In the spring it grows rare and beautiful wildflowers such as lady's slippers and fawn lillies, as well as milkmaids, shooting stars, wild irises, pussy ears, mariposa lillies and golden fairy lanterns. Black tail deer, foxes, raccoons, porcupines, jackrabbits, flying squirrels, bats, newts, skinks, swifts, hawks, ravens and owls also live here, not to mention several species of delightful harmless snakes and the beautiful Western timber rattler."

Hyde Street. Sunday 9 September 1990.

The newspapers report that Manly Palmer Hall died on August 29, at age 89. Born in Canada, he moved to Los Angeles in 1919.

Today Rear Admiral Houser, the president of Harvest Systems, one of our companies, invited us for brunch at the Saint Francis yacht club. Paul Baran was there, as well as a cross-section of Silicon Valley nobility. The fog rolled in over the Golden Gate as racing sloops cut into the wind just outside our windows.

Sheraton Grande, La Jolla. Tuesday 11 September 1990.

Hal Puthoff, Kit Green, and I spent last evening together in this great hotel near the Pacific. My excuse to convene our meeting was a review of high-tech projects at IRT, a company in which my fund has invested. We compared notes about MJ-12 rumors. Kit assured us there once was a real "Majestic," but it was only concerned with surviving a nuclear strike. Ralph Blum's book *Out There* claims that the CIA's Domestic Collection Division investigates U.S. UFO cases.

"That's all true," said Kit, "except that since 1977 that group has been called *National* Collection Division. The Agency isn't supposed to have any domestic operations."

"In your letter you said you thought there was a black program..."

"That's right, I'm sure it's handled appropriately. In my days there wasn't more than one case a month in the classified reports. Now there are several per week; sometimes they go up to the President."

He used to have a drawer full of intriguing stuff at the Agency in the form of photographs, films, reports, tapes; he threw it all away when he left. So the fact that information is collected doesn't mean that it's being studied. Then we spoke of the Belgian wave, and of an article in *Paris-Match*, with F-16 radar pictures of alleged UFOs.

"Within a 100-mile radius of this hotel several companies make black boxes, 'DURFUMs' that can put spurious echoes on any radar screen," I said. "It turns out the Belgian pilots never saw a UFO; the French long-range radars didn't see a UFO; people on the ground never saw a UFO... and the French Air force doesn't even believe the Belgians had those two jets there. Is everybody playing games?"

San Diego airport. Later the same day.

After a full day of technology review our private discussion came back to Blum's book. The leak may point to Pandolfi at CIA: "They'd asked him to investigate the Augsburg business, the six soldiers," Kit said. "It's getting more and more weird. The messages on classified terminals came out of a secure network..."

"Then it can only be one thing, the Agency counter-intelligence guys, messing with their brains," said Hal.

The conversation returned to the topic of secrecy. As an exercise Kit asked us, on a scale of zero to ten, what was the probability of existence of a hidden government project?

He reiterated: "I am sure there is active collection, handled appropriately. I'm not interested in infiltrating my own government."

Question two: "Are UFOs physical objects, like coffee cups?" I answered that the objects that made the ground traces in Trans-en-Provence and Valensole certainly were. They also agreed. On the question of the existence of biological entities Kit gave a high score. Hal and I were much lower. The research needs to go on.

Hyde Street. Thursday 13 September 1990.

Janine and I spent last evening with Keith, Darlene and Dr. Margaret Singer, a 69-year old psychology professor at Berkeley, an expert on cults. She scoffs at current journalistic stories of satanic ritual killings and molestations: "Hypnotherapists are trained very badly, if at all," she told us. "Often, they reach a point where their patients are well enough to fend for themselves, but they don't recognize it's time to let go of the therapy. They pick up on details: 'Did you ever see men around you, wearing dark robes? Did they carry candles?' They allow the patient to come up with invented fantasies."

I called Leo Sprinkle in an attempt to understand Myrna Hansen's abduction case. He confirmed meeting her twice in New Mexico with

Bennewitz. Paul first treated him as a hero. The second time he was suspicious, carried a gun, and accused Leo of being a CIA agent.

Hyde Street. Tuesday 18 September 1990.

As we sat in the sunshine at the Gatehouse in Palo Alto, Dr. Edwin May told me that yesterday had been his last day at SRI.

"I feel so much lighter!" he said. "My exit interview was interesting. My department manager said he'd never believed in what we were doing; he was sure there was nothing to that psychic stuff. What a time to pick to reveal such pent-up hostility! We went through the lab where so much happened over the years. Do you realize that was the first time he'd seen our facility?"

The good news is that Ed will be able to restart the project with an $8M budget for three years at Science Applications, Inc. This came about because Senator Cohen (Republican from Maine) instructed Jack Vorona and Dale Graff to find a way to continue the research.

Tomorrow I'll pack up a few manuscripts and fly from the madness of America to the weirdness of Europe. Janine is taking *The Misfits* to read it on board. I carry Céline's *Voyage au Bout de la Nuit*.

TGV Atlantique. Tuesday 25 September 1990.

The train speeds on the way to Nantes where I hope to close a complicated investment in Sangstat Atlantique, the French subsidiary of a breakthrough immunology research firm founded by a French doctor, Philippe Pouletty (**26**). The company will be based at the organ transplantation center, one of the largest in Europe. Four law firms are involved, egos are flaring, phone calls are made in the middle of the night, and lawyers who earn $300 dollars an hour are calling one another idiots and fools. Fortunately I carry a power of attorney signed by Fred Adler, like a license to kill. It will enable me to cut through their silliness in order to get the financing completed.

Air France flight to Geneva. Friday 28 September 1990.

Last night Janine and I celebrated Maman's 90th birthday in the elaborate setting of *Le Procope*. She was as cheerful as a schoolgirl.

"I want to live!" she said with enthusiasm.

Over dinner at *Café Trinité* on Wednesday Marie-Thérèse de Brosses told me Jean-Pierre Petit's son had died. People think he committed suicide, perhaps by staging an underwater accident.

Everyone who knows Petit as a brilliant physicist is torn between a feeling of sympathy for him and dismay at his bitter reactions.

Marie-Thérèse now leaves for Siberia, where she will spend a month with Kaznacheyev, said to be studying brain waves, UFO abductions and remote viewing in Novosibirsk. She grew up near Pontoise at the Château in Ennery, a village I know well. Small and delicate, with short blond hair, she is full of energy and driven by certainties that remind me of journalist Linda Howe.

Bayeux. Saturday 29 September 1990.

Looking at the gray sky through the lace curtains of Annick's apartment, I daydream, an old volume of fairy tales next to me. I spent the afternoon with the two sisters, exploring antique stores, perusing dusty books in Bayeux and Caen. Annick's proud farmhouse in Brunville has been sold to an English family: Thus, old memories fade, even if gestures and smiles, books and certain expressions often come to remind us of other rainy days spent looking at the gray sky of Normandy, through other curtains of lace.

The larger world, too, has suddenly swiveled into an uncertain future. The crisis with Iraq spells war before Christmas. The Soviet empire has caved in, Germany is reuniting.

History is gathering a funeral wreath for the grave of the Millennium.

A year ago, there seemed to be no limits to creativity, no obstacles to freedom. Academics speak of the triumph of democracy. Today the Dow Jones has collapsed below 2400. Even Switzerland shivers:

Yesterday in Geneva a prominent financier, Mr. Barbey (a director of Guyer-Zeller Bank of Zurich, one of our investors), invited me for lunch at a restaurant overlooking the lake.

He spoke of new concerns for Europe, its diminishing prospects for industrial creativity.

Martine led me through cobblestone streets to lunch in the dusty enclave of *Bibliothèque Nationale*: glass rotundas, old bookstores.

Mabillon. Tuesday 2 October 1990.

This afternoon - such a luscious autumn day! - Janine and I walked along the cliffs that overlook Port-en-Bessin and the shores of Arromanches with Annick and Michel. A golf course now runs over the old German bunkers. At midnight Germany will be reunified.

Mabillon. Thursday 4 October 1990.

A financial crisis looms over France. My colleagues are worried as major Paris brokerage houses quietly go out of business: "The financial community is covering up, of course. Larger institutions are quickly buying up those that fail. But this can't go on much longer..."

Yesterday I had to fly to Geneva again, but I came back early enough for dinner with researcher Joël Mesnard. He mentioned that three men-in-black with pasty faces and fierce looks visited him once. Today I had lunch with two other ufologists, Jean Sider and Alain Boudier. The latter rambles about bases on the moon and Billy Meier's fakes. Sider is more serious. He spoke of a Dr. Visse, of Saint-Pourçain, who was a mineralogist before he turned to biology. In that role he was part of an archaeological expedition in the 50s, to a region between Syria and Lebanon. A rumor claims they found Alien traces.

Mabillon. Friday 5 October 1990.

About to retire, Guérin told me J.P. Petit once saw a saucer over La Javie while camping in the Alps. Three years ago, as he researched Ummo in Spain, "visitors" are said to have come into his motel room "to operate on him" but his roommate saw nothing. The next day he claims he found a small probe, a red dot on his shoulder.

Lyon. Hotel Roosevelt. Monday 8 October 1990.

Yesterday, through rain and sunshine, we escaped in a rented Renault to Ivoy-le-Pré in the Berry region for lunch with biology professor Rémy Chauvin and his wife in their château. At 77 he remains filled with original ideas, from detection techniques based on butterfly scents to the study of ant colonies. We spoke of Alien biology. He explained to us why intelligence has no obvious need of a humanoid body. He has studied birds capable of sewing leaves together, adding, "When we want to do some really fine work, we use pincers that look exactly like a bird's beak."

He also mentioned octopuses easily opening bottles with screwtops to remove food. It was accidental for higher intelligence on earth to develop from primates: He wouldn't expect Aliens to look like us.

Spring Hill. Saturday 13 October 1990.

It finally rained here. Now the earth is resting like a woman content, the warm wind caressing her hillsides. On Monday Olivier leaves for Paris, looking for a change after more than eight years in San Diego. I encouraged him to seek new opportunities there.

When I called her in Arizona last night, Mimi Hynek was moved, happy that we thought of her. I assured her that I took good care of all the books and documents Allen had entrusted to me.

Hyde Street. Wednesday 17 October 1990.

Universal has just bought the movie rights for *Alintel*. This doesn't mean they'll make the movie, of course (**27**). Scott Jones called me to report on his recent trip to China, where he met five leaders of local UFO groups. They suspected him of hiding something ominous: "Given my position on the staff of a Senator, they felt I must know everything the U.S. Government is doing."

Chinese ufologists gave him some metal filings from an object, which turned out to be an aluminum alloy, like several of the samples I have recovered. They made no claims about bodies.

Spring Hill. Sunday 28 October 1990.

A letter from Vladimir Azhazha confirms that Editions Progress will publish *Dimensions*. Dr. Chevtchenko, of the Russian Academy of Sciences, has begun the translation.

Applying the "signal grabbing" technique I learned from Ingo I pursue my experiments at the observatory amidst the golden glory of a perfect day. The structures of the phenomenon are slowly revealing themselves. I think I understand why our physical theories failed.

Now Fred Adler calls and asks me to manage his West coast portfolio from his Menlo Park office on legendary Sand Hill road. Olivier, who now lives at Mabillon, tells us it's raining hard in Paris.

Hyde Street. Thursday 1 November 1990.

Dr. Ed May settles down at SAIC. His budget includes one year for planning "the next step in parapsychology." One of SRI's former clients, Joe Angelo from the Air force, plays a new role on the team.

Halloween puts excitement and controversy in the air. This afternoon I passed a small group of Pagans assembling before City Hall, outnumbered by cameramen and cops. They looked formidable in their purple capes, while Christian forces converged on the City in a futile effort to exorcize the celebrations.

At a coffee shop on Polk Street a tall man with a green face and short white skirt gave out candy to roving bands of Chinese dressed as Batman or Mickey Mouse. Down the street a Christian orchestra played church hymns at the door of a gay bar in futile protest. A transvestite in a costume complete with boots and an extravagant hairdo walked past them, dragging a slave in full leather face mask at the end of a leash, just another night in San Francisco.

Hyde Street. Sunday 4 November 1990.

I have caught the KGB in a little UFO hoax: A landing took place in Cuba in 1968; Soviet Intelligence was called in to see the traces and the witness, unconscious for 15 days after firing machine gun rounds at the craft (**28**). When he finally woke up he drew a picture of what he had seen, but the picture released to the public is a fake, a carbon copy of another case shown on Russian TV six years earlier. That case, in turn, was a carbon copy of an old Italian sighting. The KGB has kept the real drawing for its files and released a hoax.

Yesterday we walked in the woods, opening a new path. "Don't you think that solitude, or rather loneliness, is the truest and deepest state of the human mind?" Janine asked. One of the few things in which we disagree: I reach my deepest levels when I am with her.

Spring Hill. Sunday 11 November 1990.

The California elections have passed, with their parade of paradoxes. People are confused about environmental proposals. One of the results is that the developer who owns the timberland north of Spring Hill can now cut all his redwood trees--unless we stop him.

Our friend Diane LaVey drove up with us Friday night, bringing a comfortable outfit for the country and letters she wanted us to read. We enjoy her recollections of life with Anton, the lion Togare, and the acolytes and sycophants who made up the unique atmosphere of the Black House on California Street where she spent 24 years. Her humor shows in the fantastic episodes when she took the appearance and the personae of several women to fool Anton's followers into imagining an entire organization around him: there was Lana the Brunette, Sharon Hansen the little goody-two-shoes, and Mistress Greta the dominatrix. There was even John M. Kincaid, who wrote in the *Cloven Hoof*, but nobody could ever meet him...

Sipping tea by the fire out of witches' cups we spoke about the people we used to know and the people we used to be, with Mussorgsky's *Song of the Flea* playing in the background.

Hyde Street. Wednesday 14 November 1990.

The Parapsychology Research Group has shrunk to only 25 people, and a rather sad group it is; they repeat experiments that have been done dozens of times with the same tantalizing expectations and marginal results. Businessman Henry Dakin, who pays for all that, dozed off during the proceedings. A 'shamanic' woman smoked a few puffs of dope before a presentation about her "power world."

Olivier writes about demonstrations in Paris, his hope of finding a job. Tomorrow I leave for Michigan and Washington. Janine is off to Boulder. The smell of rain makes me feel nostalgic and moody.

Ann Arbor. Sheraton hotel. Thursday 15 November 1990.

This is my first visit to Ann Arbor, which evokes memories of the Hillsdale "Swamp Gas" case. From the plane all I saw was flat countryside, brown smog over Detroit, green zones that might be cemeteries. When we came lower I realized they were golf courses. Country clubs and cemeteries fit in the same category for me.

I work hard on this Diary. I don't want to wait until I am old to write, as many authors do, a polished account of their supposed greatness. I still have productive years ahead, I must use them to detect and correct my mistakes. Seeing what I have done, how I have handled the challenges and opportunities of life, forces me to define who I want to be while there is still time.

Menlo Park. Monday 3 December 1990.

I saw my colleagues again in New York: a board meeting of Photonetics and a long strategy session with Fred Adler. Now, in my office on Sand Hill road, I share in the vague sense of dread that lingers in California like the long gray clouds I see over the ridge. Perhaps it has roots in the AIDS epidemic that marks this generation, perhaps it was last year's earthquake, or the financial debacle. Discouragement finally hit home with the crisis in the Gulf. I'm glad Olivier is now in our Paris apartment with a European career ahead of him. Our clever daughter graduates this month from Boulder.

Spring Hill. Friday 28 December 1990.

Record cold has hit the West Coast. From Seattle to Monterey many people have spent Christmas bemoaning power failures. A pale sun is trying to shine. Yesterday was spent breaking the ice of the pool, restarting the well, patching a broken water pipe and directing a bulldozer to clear a new road into the back of the property. Workers are rebuilding the "Condon" septic tank behind the cottage. I have named each of our four septic tanks after prominent skeptics: Schatzmann behind the studio, Klass near the house, and Menzel at the foot of the tower.

Hyde Street. Wednesday 2 January 1991.

In California for the holidays, my friend Gretchen tells me sadly that Bill Murphy, companion in research, died last year. I begged the universe to make a special place for Bill, and to allow him to get a little closer to that pure knowledge we had sought together.

Now an interesting phone conversation with Brendan O'Regan, just returned from London, reveals that Hal Puthoff's CCT technology has proven difficult to apply and that Ken Shoulders plays a personal game: investors went away disappointed. Our physicists at IRT Corp validate Hal's condensed charge phenomenon as real, but they doubt the zero-point energy theory.

Paris. Hotel Madison. Wednesday 9 January 1991.

The world plunges ahead towards a Middle East war whose consequences are unpredictable while the Eastern block continues to disintegrate. Gorbachev has sent tanks and helicopters to put an end to Lithuania's move towards freedom. The Western economy is freezing in the expectation of another oil price shock.

The *Boulevard Saint Germain* is dark, windy and wet. The Seine has filled her banks. Business is slow. All I see of Paris is the gloomy mood of winter, but in this tiny intellectual nucleus, theaters and cafés remain alive, students chat eagerly with blonde tourists they hope to seduce, and treasures are still found in dusty bookstores. In the background, nostalgic songs: *Tu viens me dire bonjour, au coin d'la Rue du Four... Il n'y a plus d'après, à Saint-Germain des Prés...*

Paris. Hotel Madison. Friday 11 January 1991.

Last night I had dinner in a fine apartment on the *Ile de la Jatte* in Neuilly, home of a senior executive of the BSN food company. The head of research for Hofmann-LaRoche was with us. They wanted to tell me about their personal UFO events, unreported, of course.

Following the current political turmoil is like watching a bad film. Yesterday's dreams of democracy for all and the proud orderly march into a new world order, all that is gone. Most of the earth has only a vague, distorted idea of what democracy is, anyway. Every cop in Paris wears a bulletproof vest; police barriers are erected in front of every sensitive embassy. As war threatens, journalists stare sadly into their cameras, Iraqi diplomats argue, and blue-suited men in Washington express polite pessimism. Helplessly, ordinary folks like us can only recoil in private horror.

Hyde Street. Thursday 17 January 1991.

Our flight home landed a few minutes before the deadline for the war against Iraq. It was a somber trip, every passenger lost in his or her own thoughts, and the crew obviously concerned about terrorism. The imminence of bloodshed is around us like a spreading epidemic.

At a Silicon Valley board meeting, as we exchanged best wishes for the New Year, Admiral Bill Houser expressed hopes that the military operations might force Saddam Hussein to beg for mercy. I left with an eerie feeling, driving up that Peninsula where much of America's modern armament has been conceived, past the Blue Cube that controls the spy satellites in the northern hemisphere. Suddenly the voice on the radio broke into the program with the news of Saddam's missiles falling on Tel Aviv. The traffic around me became tense, drivers oddly staring ahead, cars moving like robots in an atmosphere that reminded me of the night of the earthquake, with a similar fear of what we would find at the end of the road.

Spring Hill. Sunday 20 January 1991.

Yesterday I got through the busy circuits and spoke to Dan Tolkowsky in Tel Aviv. He calmly reviewed the Board of IRT and joint investment projects. The Israeli Air Force (which he founded) has called up his son Gideon. Here the sky sparkles with throbbing constellations. Orion is reflected in the darkened pool, and the dome atop our tower glistens with the silvery glow that marks the infinity of mind. Never has mankind seemed more unworthy of those gifts.

Spring Hill. Saturday 26 January 1991.

Hal Puthoff has run into a case of journalistic exaggeration. An article in *Omni* (**29**) gives him credit but describes him and Ken Shoulders as energy wizards: In 10 years, cities may be powered by the energy of the vacuum! Hal never said anything so outlandish.

Today the sun is bright in the cold air. A plume of blue smoke rises up from the cottage chimney into the bare trees and an invitation comes to speak at a scientific congress in San Juan next month.

Hyde Street. Wednesday 30 January 1991.

New debunkers have appeared in Russia, while Scott Jones brings back physical samples of UFOs from the Soviet Union with great fanfare "to have them analyzed by the CIA."

"Most of the researchers we know are zealots at heart, and religious nuts," Kit says. "But there are other things going on. Ever heard of Eric Walker, president emeritus of Penn State University? He claims that Aliens have indeed been recovered and taken to Wright-Patterson… You'd be in awe of the man, dean of engineering at Harvard, co-founder of the Academy of Engineering and of Sciences, chairman of the Defense Science Board, former head of the JASONs, science adviser to the President, former chairman of TRW,... it goes on and on. He stated that four live Aliens were retrieved. We studied them, they learned our language. We allowed them to blend into the population..."

"What's Walker's field of research?" I asked, stunned.

"Sound waves, applications of acoustics. He founded the Navy's underwater sound laboratory. He was also a co-founder of the Institute for Defense Analyses, and a member of the H-bomb team. In one of his books he writes that citizens don't necessarily have the right to know what government scientists are working on."

Kit went on: "He still has an office on campus, so I went to see him. I made it clear I had an official portfolio and clearance to talk to him. He asked me two questions: *Why I was interested* and *why I thought the information should be made public*. I told him my interest stemmed from concern about misinformation circulating in the media and that I wasn't sure the data should be made public. Those must have been the wrong answers, because he flatly refused to confirm or deny that he had made the comments in question, or written the letters. But I'm sure he wrote them."

"What else did he tell you?"

"Damn little. When I asked what could make him change his mind he said, 'Bring me a letter from the President, instructing me to talk to you about that stuff, and I'll call the President to make sure the letter is from him.' So I said, 'Perhaps those letters that are circulating over your signature are not really from you, perhaps they're forgeries?' He wouldn't discuss it, and would I please leave his office immediately? By the way, he frequently travels to Russia. He was a close friend of the late Armand Hammer."

Hyde Street. Monday 4 February 1991.

A new witness, a woman named Julia has sent me a dramatic letter. Janine and I visited her yesterday. She told us the very prospect of recounting her experiences was very distressing.

Julia is a 40-year-old woman with black hair who looks like singer Linda Ronstadt. She overcame her reluctance to talk to me after reading *Messengers of Deception.* She began: "About August 1968 I used to go to a certain bar in Baton Rouge where a couple of singers were performing. The man, Duane Yates, was especially talented; he could sing with the voice of any singer the public requested. The girl gave her name as Linda Clark…"

After Julia had gone into this bar a few evenings with her boyfriend, the performers sat at their table. "Did you feel compelled to come here? Do you even know who you are?" they asked.

The man had pale skin and white hair but wasn't an albino. He had no wrinkles or bodily hair. He told them "the time had come." Julia looked into his eyes, they were "terrifying and wonderful," but his touch felt reptilian. Somehow, he knew all about her childhood.

"Are you ready to carry out your destiny?" he asked. "Are you willing to help humanity when the time comes?" The con.

They went over to the woman's apartment; music was played in the dark. They felt they were floating. The session seemed to last only a minute or so, then "Duane" turned the light back on and told them "their third eye was open now," and that "the Intelligence will be able to speak to you in your sleep."

Back on the street Julia and her boyfriend realized that hours had passed. They felt elated, with a lot of energy. There was a second session later, to "open them up to the future." But at no point were they asked to pay anything; no money was exchanged.

It would be easy to conclude that she is delusional, but her story matches a pattern of sectarian indoctrination with which we've become familiar: Duane hinted he was from Sirius and that his companions had bases on Venus and the Moon; that Christ lived on Venus. Their mission was to teach people like Julia, according to a structure with nine levels. *When they reached the ninth level they would be taken to an underground location near Las Vegas; they would contribute to a New Age. They would board flying saucers*.

No part of the "teaching" was ever written. Supposedly a device had been implanted and activated inside their bodies.

I asked Julia if she had actually seen UFOs. She only saw lights that would move as if answering mental commands. She was instructed not to tell anyone: People were not ready… "They" prepared a new order. If she divulged any of it "they" would take drastic action. She began to have many dreams: She was aboard a UFO, going under the ocean. She was told her subconscious would register this information and would know how to use it.

They kept her on a strict vegetarian diet: no sugar, eggs or cheese, "down to nuts and seeds." She lost weight. This diet supposedly "cleaned the body." She slept a lot. Another part of the philosophy was abstinence from sex. She was supposed to write her experiences in a private journal mailed to the "Station of the Cosmic Light" in Las Vegas. As she recounted the experience for us she was shaking.

I wanted to review Julia's early years. As a child, she frequently climbed up to the roof of her house: She would call "come and take me away!" to the sky. There was a tragic accident when she was three and her sister Teresa was four. As they were left by themselves a man led them to a beach. She vaguely remembers a bright light in her face. She recalls falling backwards. The two girls were naked when other people came onto the scene. The stranger tried to escape by swimming away with her sister; Teresa drowned.

Julia has three younger sisters and two children who have reported unusual incidents such as a light at the window, vibrations, and a strange hand. Last year she saw a doctor at Kaiser who found a lump in her throat and diagnosed an advanced thyroid tumor. She was operated on a medullar carcinoma but they were unable to get all of it. "Were you exposed to radioactivity 20 years ago?" they asked her.

Julia believes there is a "base" near Yountville, close to the Carmelite monastery, in an area of abandoned gold mines.

Hyde Street. Sunday 10 February 1991.

Sweet warm days already herald the spring but there isn't enough runoff in our creek. California is in the fifth year of a drought. Yesterday we drove over towards Potter Valley to pat the unicorn at Otter Zell's house and to see Morning Glory again, a warm woman who lectures about Gaia and the Goddess.

Up in the tower Janine helps me classify my correspondence. What will I do with all the letters my sophisticated readers are sending me? (Note) Another world is lurking just beyond the dense borders of our perceptions, and sneers at the coarseness of our thoughts.

On the plane to Puerto Rico. Wednesday 13 February 1991.

The Mideast war occupies all minds now, with bloody nightmares and dreams of glory whipped up by the media. I am reading *Operators and Things* (**30**), a striking account by a young schizophrenic woman who was lucky enough to overcome her condition. She used her experience to develop insights into her mind.

Sociologist Pierre Lagrange has sent me an analysis of my work and the French scientific mission has invited me to meet French Cabinet member Hubert Curien next week (**31**).

Janine tells me we should sell the ranch. I felt a sudden chill. "Nothing stays," she said with sober realism, her hand on my arm. "We'll be moving through, you know." But isn't that precisely the only value of our lives, to capture instances of permanence?

Hyde Street. Saturday 23 February 1991.

I return from Puerto Rico with a briefcase full of reports, having met a group of UFO investigators led by Jorge Martin and a professor of

----

Note: In 2017, thanks to an invitation from a major US University, I reorganized all my files into three major categories (ABC for Analysis, Background and Correspondence) and shipped an initial batch of 32 large boxes to be indexed by their librarians and used by graduate students.

The data will be embargoed for ten years to preserve the privacy of my correspondents and of the many witnesses I have interviewed in their homes.

pharmacology named Tomas Morales Cardona. I made myself understood in Spanish, well enough to argue with my new friends.

Janine has the flu, an excuse for us to huddle in bed as we follow the unfolding horror of military events in the Middle East.

Yesterday I did have lunch with Hubert Curien, the French minister of research. He said with a friendly twinkle in his eye that he'd seen my books. "Are you still interested in the philosophy of science?" he asked. I told him it was my job, as a high-tech investor, to make sure that I knew not only cutting edge researchers but also those who were ten, twenty years ahead... even if they sound crazy.

Anaheim. Tuesday 26 February 1991.

Yesterday, during the long drive from Ojai, psychologist and abduction researcher Maralyn Teare told me that Prince Hans-Adam and Robert Bigelow, a Las Vegas developer, had joined forces to provide Hopkins and Jacobs with a $200,000 grant to determine "how many Americans have been abducted." The result is chaotic: with the prospect of a bundle of dollars, anger rises among ufologists, egos are bruised, data gets corrupted or covered up.

I am in Anaheim for Nepcon, the major electronic manufacturing trade show. Hundreds of robust American entrepreneurs are in attendance, fighting to establish their products, close new sales, sign contracts. I admire the agile pick-and-place robots doing their magic.

New York. The Plaza. Thursday 28 February 1991.

Tonight we discussed the future of Eastern Europe over dinner with Pierre Simon and his wife, editor of *Politique Internationale*, whom I had last seen at our meeting with former Prime Minister Raymond Barre in Lyon. Tomorrow I will visit Synaptic Pharmaceuticals, one of the leading research groups on neurotransmitters, notably serotonin (**32**). Tomorrow night, happily, I will be back with Janine.

Spring Hill. Sunday 10 March 1991.

IBM scientist Marcel Vogel died of a heart attack a month ago. He was 73 years old (**33**).

Our neighbor the land speculator plans to cut the redwoods to the north of us, threatening the slopes, digging a road that encroaches on a corner of our land. Those are the aggravations of life in the country. Yet Spring Hill is magnificent and the observatory is secure. I have posted a stellar map in the dome, a present from Olivier. My experiments here continue through increasingly focused mental states, building on remote viewing and precognition. I compile a catalogue of information singularities (in the sense of Wolfgang Pauli) to probe synchronicities. Beyond the design of UFO databases I am mapping out a three-level software architecture from which I hope to force the multi-pattern phenomenon to emerge through AI.

Orion surveys the tower, dragging Sirius over the pond. My confidants are the giant beings of the forest, the redwoods that were here before the Spaniards ever set foot in California. They teach me how to think of life and reality, not from the perspective of a puny human life, but with the scope of centuries.

3

Lyon. Hotel Pullman. Thursday 21 March 1991.

Spring Equinox. The European Venture Capital Association holds a meeting in France's second city: Fine speeches are made. Monsieur Raymond Barre, former Prime minister, smiles like a benign uncle saying reassuring truths about the brilliant destiny of the bureaucracy the government has created to secure its own continuity.

Sailing along the Rhône on board the *Hermès* as we dined with entrepreneurs and financiers, I admired the region as Château St. Jean and splendid Abbeys glided silently beyond the river. The orderly life of the French bourgeois takes its course behind elegant windows. It looks clever—and boring. In this sheltered world little will change.

In Paris Janine, her brother Alain, Catherine, and I had a warm reunion with Olivier and his girlfriend, and dinner at a restaurant overlooking the boulevard, all shiny and neat after the rain.

Lyon. Hotel Pullman. Friday 22 March 1991.

Investors in venture capital display an interesting cross-section of professional experience, a discrete, mature group. The fine dinner at the Paul Bocuse restaurant last night was congenial, yet I heard a number of my contemporaries comment that "life is a sad joke." I do not share such feelings, I find life increasingly exciting as I get older.

Bayeux. "Les Vikings." Saturday 23 March 1991.

Annick's new house retains the flair of her old Brunville farmhouse, with more convenience, yet the deeper charm cannot be recaptured: the subtle power of many generations haunted the old place. Today we enjoyed a Norman lunch and dessert of *tord-goule* (a kind of rice pudding) and *confiture de lait*. A cold wind is whipping the flowers Annick has planted in her expectation of spring, too early.

Yesterday afternoon I went to Laffont to pick up *Confrontations*. I took the first copy to *Rue de la Clef*, where I found Maman in good spirits, although preoccupied by the disposition of her two sisters' estate. She no longer has the incentive to paint and fears she's lost her skills in drawing. Yet she was as sharp as ever in conversation. She complained her building would soon have an elevator, a lot of dust and noise for nothing. "Others will use it if they want to," she bragged indignantly. "I'll go on taking the stairs, of course."

I went out to chat at *Intersigne* with Alain Marchiset, rare book dealer and esoteric scholar who spoke of the follies of men. Many discoveries were foreshadowed by visionaries who came too early to be heard, he said, like Paracelsus. Similarly, Antonio Snider had described continental drift 50 years before Wegener (in *La Création et ses Mystères Dévoilés*, 1859). As for Neper, the illustrious Scot mathematician, he invented logarithms to facilitate his astrological computations. I was never told about this at the Sorbonne.

Paris (Mabillon). Monday 25 March 1991.

My colleague Gabriel Mergui drove me to Inria in Rocquencourt, for a meeting with its director, Dr. Alain Bensoussan. I was amused as I recalled how, 23 years ago, I had made the long bus trip from Paris in hopes of landing a job with this newly created software institute. A guardhouse has been added but the old barracks are still standing.

The atmosphere is as depressing today as it was when I visited the place in 1968: Computer science research is not a priority for France, in spite of all the fine speeches. The lack of vision is obvious.

London Heathrow. Tuesday 26 March 1991.

A visit to a financial software company in the City left me with time for lunch at Hotel Russell with Gordon Creighton, distinguished diplomat for the Crown, editor of the best UFO magazine today. He remains smart, incisive, humorous, and most considerate towards Joan, who tires easily, suffering from emphysema. We had lunch at the magnificent Carvery, now a buffet with few waiters. Joan was disconcerted when she had to get up to refill her plate: "Things are not done in the proper English manner any more," she said.

Angers. Sunday 31 March 1991. (Easter)

On a well-deserved vacation we began an expedition to medieval relics and the historical roots of my mother's family. Olivier and his Japanese girlfriend discover this part of France with amusement.

The five of us drove off towards the Layon, a modest stream lazily flowing through pastures and vineyards. In Passavant we had no trouble finding the massive fortress. It overlooks a small lake formed by a dam on the river. We saw some beautiful vaulted rooms in a state of disrepair and a modern structure appended to the tall keep. The current owner gave us a tour. Her grandfather had bought the dilapidated property, she explained, finding the deep cellars suitable for his wines. There are legends about buried treasures, but how likely can they be? My mother's ancestors left Passavant centuries ago to follow the hardships of the Huguenot life in Switzerland.

We stood on the platform at the top of the fortress as our hostess explained that we were at the border between French Anjou and English Aquitaine: "Passavant has often been synonymous with frontier," she said. "The other castles built by your mother's family stood at the threshold of Lorraine and Franche-Comté, or on the borders of Burgundy. Here you can see three lines of defense. Obviously many knights and guards lived inside these walls."

On the stone ledges were carved holes where sentinels used to play tic-tac-toe, as Centurions already did in the days of Caesar.

Angers. Monday 1 April 1991.

We drove North of Angers today to visit Challins-la-Potherie. Janine had fond memories of summer holidays in the romantic castle. Later we hunted for an ancient megalithic site and found a small hill in the middle of a vast round valley, with a beautiful white quartz stone raised at the top, an obvious power site where several other needles of rock were lying in pieces, perhaps toppled by the irate priests of a more recent god. The white stone was a marker, aligned with others on distant hills. We paid a visit to a tall menhir hidden in a hollow.

The impression that stays with me is of the wind in the *bruyères* and the grass on the knoll with the white stone under the tormented sky, so full of interrogations--a true sky of Brittany.

Mabillon. Wednesday 3 April 1991.

This morning I met with Velasco at *Le Départ*. We discussed the slow progress of ufology in France and my trip to Moscow but he was disappointed with the Russians: "Vladimir Azhazha has written to me, as you had encouraged him to do," he said. "But he didn't provide much information. As for Silanov in Voronezh, the CNES can't get anything from him that makes any sense!"

Velasco smells a fish in the Belgian "flying triangles" affair. Why is the military so eager to cooperate with the amateurs of SOBEPS? He thinks the objects are rigid dirigibles that move over one region while the ufologists are being flown elsewhere by the friendly Belgian Air Force. Here in Paris the CNES-GEPAN group is becoming a political football again among scientists like Dr. Pellat who would love to disband it and Perrin de Brichambaut who would reinforce it.

This evening Janine and I went to Vanves for dinner with Alain Boudier. He'd invited researchers Jean-Luc Rivera, Jean Sider and

Joël Mesnard. Hypnotist Danny Dan was there again. Boudier said Velasco claimed the flying triangle of November 5th, 1990 was only a re-entering Russian rocket, raising accusations of censorship.

Mabillon. Thursday 4 April 1991.

Marie-Thérèse de Brosses, investigative journalist and esoteric researcher, has an apartment in Pigalle, filled with intricate wonders. She showed me tiny skulls carved out of the knuckle bones of dead Tibetan monks, and told me of her plans to travel to Asia.

"Did you review Alexandra David-Néel's experiences?" I asked.

"I met her, you know, a long time ago, thanks to Jean Giono. We had dinner together. She already was a very old woman. She looked at me with her little eyes that didn't miss anything. She picked up some seeds and closed her hands over them, making a sort of ball with her fingers interlaced. Within minutes there were little green shoots pushing out between her fingers. But neither Giono nor I had the presence of mind to pick them up and analyze them."

Marie-Thérèse was disappointed by her recent trip to Siberia. Like Jean-Jacques Velasco, she was fed up with everything Russian, including Kaznacheyev: "They're unreliable; their sources don't exist and nothing is documented!"

Mabillon. Friday 5 April 1991.

Yesterday Ernest Hecht, owner of Souvenir Press, whom I'd missed in London, invited me to join him for breakfast at *Deux Magots*, where he was holding court. He was in Paris for the Book Fair. He said he was ready to publish *Revelations* in Great Britain.

Last night we had a family dinner at the *Burning Bush* with Maman, to whom we brought pictures of Passavant and a case of wine from the *Coteaux du Layon*. Catherine and I walked her home.

I'd taken time off to dig into the collections of folklore stories at the *Bibliothèque Nationale*. Once there, I also looked up references to Passavant and found several interesting facts: There was a Jean-Charles Passavant, born in Frankfurt in 1787, who became a well-known philosopher (**34**). He was taught by Schelling in Munich, then studied physics and natural science, and made a living as a doctor in Frankfurt. He aimed at nothing less than founding a system that would bring together Catholic and Reformist views of the world.

He also tried "to infuse new spirituality into science." What impressed me was the list of his books:

- *About Human Freedom Compared to the Deterministic System* (Frankfurt 1835)
- *About Magnetism, Somnambulism and Demonology* (1821, 1837)
- *On the Immortality of the Soul* (1843)
- *On Consciousness* (1850)

He also published a theory of the future. He died in 1856, at age 69.

Hyde Street. Saturday 6 April 1991.

The luxury of flying home together radiates through layers of tiredness. The phone machine held 19 messages. Luisah Teish had called with her incomparable voice, "I love y'all... You've connected me to so many places in the world...." Keith spoke of the murderers of researcher Scott Rogo: their motive was simple robbery, he said.

Kit called. He wanted to spend several hours and talk, in some quiet place, "about stuff... I now think you were right all along," he said.

"Well, that's a big surprise!" I laughed. We will meet next Friday.

Hyde Street. Wednesday 10 April 1991.

Rima Laibow is looking for someone to head up a new research project on UFOs. Rumor has it that the money comes from Scott Jones, who has obtained some $300,000 from Rockefeller and the Claiborne Pell Foundation. I declined, the context isn't right.

Reading producer Julia Phillips' depressing autobiography (**35**) I stumble on her memories of *Close Encounters*:

> "First we needed to acquire the rights to the expression, which had been coined by a sweet wacko named Alan Hyneck (sic) in a primer called *The UFO Experience*. Hyneck had once been the head of a government project called project Blue Book, a secret study under the aegis of the Air force designed

to debunk reported UFO sightings. I always figured these were sightings of machinery we were testing secretly. Who'd want to visit us? I wondered."

The number of errors in that paragraph is striking, even if Julia confessed she was stoned when she did that movie. She got Allen's first and last name wrong, he was never head of Blue Book, and the project was not secret: another lesson from Hollywood.

Hyde Street. Friday 12 April 1991.

Kit and I spent most of the day together. We discussed spread-spectrum technology and the *Communion Letter* in which Whitley Strieber writes: "*The so-called UFO-ologists are probably the cruellest, nastiest, and craziest people I have ever encountered.* Their interpretation of the visitor experience is rubbish from beginning to end. The abduction reports that they generate are not real. They are artifacts of hypnosis and cultural conditioning."

We went out for a sandwich at Ghirardelli Square and walked around Fort Mason. Kit has now contacted six cabinet-level people, including former CIA director William Colby. All said, "drop it, we don't understand the statements that were made to you about captured hardware and beings, people must have lied to you."

Kit now believes I'm right about the control system, "but it's human." He recently met a four-star general at a desert location who confirmed the existence of a secret UFO project. Later, Pentagon types who didn't know about that contact tried to mislead him, attacking his clearances. He was shaken by it, although he emerged from the ordeal with a letter from the CIA director: "*Dr. Green is empowered by this office to inquire into any matters that he chooses to investigate.*" He speculates he's too independent to be recruited by the Cabal and shown "the hardware," assuming there is such a thing.

The UFO phenomenon is a major enigma of contemporary science: it encompasses fundamental problems and their solutions could benefit humanity. Yet academic scholars ignore it, politicians won't touch it and religious groups recoil in saintly horror.

Spring Hill. Sunday 14 April 1991.

Our apple trees are in bloom. We took a walk into the woods this afternoon, and found a lovely bed of leaves and moss that was so inviting and well hidden that we lingered there in the soft sunshine before walking back across the prairie.

Los Angeles. Monday 15 April 1991.

Janine phones me about a letter from Prince Hans-Adam, a clever restatement of the first-order "Alien visitation" hypothesis, in a style both relaxed and precise. He seems certain that the truth will soon be found. Yet I hear that Hopkins and Jacobs are over their heads in their survey. Unable to spend the funds given to them by the Prince and Robert Bigelow, they allocated $125,000 of that money to their pet projects, only $75,000 being allocated to the survey.

After spending the afternoon with the founder of Isocor, an electronic mail and data interchange company **(36)**, I drove to Beverly Hills where Jeremy Tarcher received me at his house among Japanese puppets and African masks. He'd read *Forbidden Science* (Vol. One) with interest, but he turned it down: The subject isn't current enough, he says, since the text stops in 1969; his distributors are skeptical. They find I have "the best name in the field" but they add, "Not even Dr. Vallee can alter public apathy about the subject."

"Your diary is frustrating, although very readable," he said. "Time and again I found myself drawn into a story that turned out to be a tangent, or an episode that gave me hopes of finding out *The Truth* at last, only to be disappointed. You should highlight the major issues, describe what the main characters look like, make us feel that we know them. Some of them are never heard from again! There are too many; prune the minor figures... So many trails lead nowhere…"

But life is like that, I said. Polished *Memoirs* only betray the truth.

Hyde Street. Friday 26 April 1991.

Brendan o'Regan's inquiries with his favorite "high-level sources" have convinced him that the Air Force does have knowledge of recovered disks. He speculates they are kept as museum pieces that no one has figured out. Brendan, who now sports a black beard that throws his bright blue Irish eyes into sharp relief, is fascinated by wealth and power. The most interesting part of our discussion had to do with medicine: the Noetics Institute continues to amass information about "spontaneous remission," notably the healing of cancer. Bill Harman is still there, as is Edgar Mitchell, who denies ever saying anything about mysterious structures on the moon.

Brendan kept urging me to develop a proposal to be funded by Laurance Rockefeller: "That'd be too bad, if you didn't pursue this research while Hopkins and Jacobs end up being the most visible people in the field. The worst drives out the best."

I replied I had no interest in competing for attention with them.

Hyde Street. Sunday 28 April 1991.

A Pagan feast in Mendocino County: we bought a gift for Otter Zell, a French book entitled *La Licorne* featuring a picture of Lancelot, one of his wonderful creatures. Morning Glory and Diane Darling arrived from a fair in Ukiah with their latest baby unicorn.

This is a warm and erudite group, capable of discussing biology and archaeology, physics, and crop circles, UFOs and cattle mutilations, as well as ancient history, mythology and witchcraft lore, long into the night. We paid a visit to Fluffy the python at Diane's house. There was a full moon over the hamlet; we felt we'd found real friends in Mendocino County at last.

Spring Hill. Sunday 5 May 1991.

Yesterday I installed my refractor in the dome, in preparation for buying a larger instrument. It is a fine World War One artillery telescope, given to me long ago by my uncle Maurice. Unfortunately the sky covered itself with haze and I could only train the lenses on a pale blurry disk of Jupiter. Standing in the warm wind at the top of the tower we watched the pond come to life: a turtle swims up to gobble up smaller things, bright fish glitter briefly in the light, swarms of tadpoles line the banks. A new generation of blue jays and hummingbirds go about their business all around us; bees and wasps, inquisitive and menacing, disturb my work.

I've found out that Richard Doty worked for Hennessey until 1985. He was honorably discharged a couple of years later, left Air Force-OSI and took a lowly job in New Mexico, keeping connections and clearances alive. "When I went to see him he was fully briefed on who I was and what my access was," said Kit. "The altercation I had in DC a few months ago was with Hennessey, distorting the record."

"So he's still with the Stealth program?"

"Yes, but the program has gone through several names. It used to be called 'low observables,' then it became deeply classified and Hennessey was made head of physical security for all Air Force black programs. Now it's under Stealth."

"Where does that leave Doty?"

"Doty claims to be in contact with the manager of a program doing reverse engineering of UFOs. He once made a phone call and then took Moore and Shandera to a place where they actually saw a flying saucer land, close to Sandia." I had to chuckle: "Very impressive! But if you wanted me to make a fake saucer land in the desert, I don't think I would have too much trouble doing it," I said. Kit agreed: "Shandera wasn't fooled; he thought it was a pure Hollywood job."

Paris. Hotel Madison. Sunday 12 May 1991.

Periodically life forces you to sharply reconsider priorities, and this is such a time. When my doctor told me that my latest bout of asthmatic bronchitis wouldn't prevent travel, I took the chance and boarded the flight, a bad decision. For the next 10 hours I coughed and cursed under what was left of my breath as my friendly neighbor, who happened to be the president of Raychem, tried to engage me in a conversation about artificial intelligence. I lacked even the strength to answer him. I nearly panicked over Greenland, hours away from emergency help. Today my chest is still congested. I must regain strength: There's an investment committee with Fred Adler on Wednesday, and visits to technology companies in Paris. Now I watch an admirable ancient music concert on television, a Spanish broadcast

Fig. 3. Janine with Otter Zell "Ravenheart" and live unicorn, Feb. 1991.

Fig. 4. Paul Bennewitz claimed to have caught this super-fast UFO over a "secret base" in Dulce, New Mexico. He did not actually see any object.

that fills my eyes with tears. I want to work at the highest level my mind can reach, and let everything else slide into the garbage. Men like Fred Adler and Dan Tolkowsky have given me the toughest standards I've ever had to meet. Money represents one measure of achievement but I feel contempt for those who view it as the sole standard. Even Fred Adler is driven by other forces: the passion for innovation, technical excellence. Why else would he let me invest in improbable medical ventures, when we could be making so much money in conventional deals?

Paris. Hotel Madison. Monday 13 May 1991.

During May the French take many days off to celebrate Victory, the Ascension of Christ, and then Pentecost, all the while marching behind red flags through the routines of socialism. Yesterday I was having a quick lunch with Olivier at Mabillon (he and his girlfriend still use our apartment to save money, while I stay in hotels) when police sirens interrupted our conversation. The Royalists were making a laughable show of depositing flowers at the feet of the statue of poor Joan of Arc. Riot police intervened, just in case.

Paris. Hotel Madison. Thursday 16 May 1991.

A pleasant night of warm springtime. Shutters closed, windows ajar, drapes thrown open. Women giggle, people make calls to lovers, bits of intimate conversation drift up and down the narrow courtyard. I find easy sleep, breathing deep again. Janine calls from Spring Hill. We speak of love.

Paris woke up today with its first woman prime minister, Edith Cresson, who succeeds Rocard. Martine Castello hints that Cresson is Mitterrand's mistress, Elisabeth Antébi denies it... (Women rightly accuse men of sexism, but they are the offenders in such rumors.)

Over lunch at the Colbert, Martine told me about a crisis at the missile base at Albion five years ago. A UFO was detected on radar. Two jets were sent up and reportedly vanished: No crash, no fragments. The Air Force sent up two drones and blew them up so they would have some debris as evidence of a mid-air "accident."

Paris. Hotel Madison. Tuesday 21 May 1991.

Aimé Michel's strong voice and sharp mindfulness reassured me when I called him, although he complained of increasingly long idle periods in an armchair, unable to write because of the pain in his hands. His concern about Aliens: Do "they" intervene in history?

When I asked what he thought of Guérin's theories he said, "Guérin needs to believe that the Government knows everything. I disagree: all the evidence I've seen points to them being a bunch of *crétins*, incapable of grasping this type of problem except when it threatens their power, or their greed."

Yesterday afternoon Marceau Sicaud, Father Brune, Franck Marie and Gérard Deforge came here for an all-afternoon discussion of paranormal topics. It was a delight to meet Father Brune, a warm, jovial man with obvious sincerity and humor. The phenomena he described center on voices from "Beyond" that he ascribes to the same entities manifesting through "turning tables" in the last century.

"But tell me, Father, do they know something we don't? About life, about the cosmos, about human destiny, about science?" I asked.

He shrugged: "No, they really don't seem to know much more than we do," the good priest admitted somberly. But then, what are they?

Marriott Hotel at Dulles airport. Wednesday 22 May 1991.

A funny incident took place at the airport. A federal officer stopped me when she saw my name. I dreaded wasting time in Customs.

"Are you the writer?" she asked effusively, and as I mumbled that I was, she went on: "I've read your stuff! I've seen two UFOs, one in Texas and one in Arizona..." Behind us, a line of puzzled travelers was becoming impatient. Now I am on my way to the SSE Council meeting at the University of Virginia. I'll meet Bernie Haisch, the editor of the Society's Journal, for the drive to Charlottesville.

Charlottesville. Cavalier Inn, the same day.

Prince Hans-Adam funds Hal's energy research but when it came time to invest another $1.25 million he stalled, telling Hal that he was afraid of the consequences. Is the earth a jail planet? Are extraterrestrials prepared to ruin anyone who helps humanity get into space? He believes Aliens will make sure we don't get out of line.

Mike Swords tells me that Bob Bigelow and Prince Hans-Adam funded John Mack's survey of abductions because they're certain it will sway intellectual opinion: The similarities among cases will be overwhelming, he assures me. Another hopeful speculation, in my opinion: opponents will be quick to point out that the methodology is flawed, and Hopkins' practice of hypnosis unconscionable.

United Flight to San Francisco. Friday 24 May 1991.

Flying back from Washington, where I just met for three hours with Richard D'Amato at the Senate Appropriations Committee. When I told him about Kit's investigations he agreed the three of us should get together before he did anything about Doty. Since our last discussion he's met with Timothy Good, George Knapp, and Bob Lazar. He also mentioned Heineman, former CIA officer and now an independent consultant who may have access to UFO data. "What that stealthy group is doing is a felony," he pointed out. "For a government employee to knowingly disseminate false information to the public is an offense that should send him to jail. The Government can't spend appropriated money on projects that Congress doesn't know about; it's an even greater offense if they spend private money to do it."

"That raises the question, would the President be told the truth?"

"Worse, it raises the question of who is running the country. If the men who sit in this chamber cannot find out about such a project, we are no longer in a democracy. Is a private contractor, a Battelle or a Lockheed, deciding the fate of the nation? Whatever that secret project, it must be controlled by an incredible level of fear, because nobody dares talk about it. I find no leaks anywhere."

Hyde Street. Friday 31 May 1991.

Now that I manage the West Coast office for him, Fred Adler has put me on several Boards of his portfolio companies, in addition to those I supervise for Euro-America, a genuine (but perilous) compliment.

In Hollywood Joe Dante is off on a new project and Bob Weiss has doubts about *FastWalker*: "We don't have a strong enough script."

Hyde Street. Thursday 6 June 1991.

Hal has received a polite response to his letter of 14 May to Eric Walker suggesting a dialogue about UFO propulsion. Walker replied he was impressed with Hal's research on zero-point energy and relativistic models of anomalous phenomena, but he added, "You will learn very little from spending much time on what you call 'some of the more bizarre claimed observations in the UFO field.' It seems to me that other approaches would be much more fruitful."

New York, Kennedy Airport. Wednesday 12 June 1991.

Thunderstorms are moving into the area, delaying flights. Yesterday in Washington the weather was hot and humid when Kit dropped me off at National Airport after four hours of intense conversation with D'Amato. I had introduced them to each other at the Madison, having reserved a quiet, private table in the back of the restaurant.

We ordered coffee, pancakes, toast, and the discussion began.

"I know where I've heard your name," said Kit. "You were involved in the review of the SRI psychic work." Richard explained that he was now funding the project himself, had actually written the research into legislation, and was hoping to get it signed before July. He didn't know to what extent Kit had been involved. Neither did he know that I had been cleared for *Grill Flame* and trained by Ingo Swann. So we spent the first hour catching up on psychic research and its impact within the Intelligence community.

"There's a man at your old shop who's negative on the whole thing, namely Ron Pandolfi. Do you know him?" D'Amato asked.

"Sure I know him, I hired him!" answered Kit. "I can tell you why he may be reluctant to buy into the whole thing. He's had problems with the data provided by Dale Graff, at DIA."

"Well, Dale too is negative sometimes," D'Amato observed.

"I know where his hesitations come from. Some years ago a bunch of us were involved in an operational remote viewing situation when we tracked down a Russian aircraft that had crashed in Africa," Kit went on. "Dale Graff ran the project. It worked so well that he was awarded the Director's Intelligence medal. The day he was supposed to receive it, he'd already boarded the plane at Wright-Patterson when Lou Allen, his commanding general, pulled him off suddenly. Someone had told Allen that the psychic slept with the project leader, and had gotten the information the night before."

"Was that true?" asked D'Amato.

"Hell no! Nobody had any idea where that plane had crashed. So you can see why Dale was upset."

"There seems to have been no end of obstacles for that unfortunate project. Everybody has tried to kill it. That's a damn shame."

"I stopped it once myself," Kit said. "When we did physiological monitoring of the subjects during remote viewing, they occasionally got into extreme states, with blood pressure going wild and massive endocrinological changes, even though these subjects were never under medication or drugs. One day I was visiting the project. One of our best subjects ever, Pat Price, was supposed to track me while I drove to a site I would select by a random algorithm. I ended up in a little chapel. I remember bending over baptismal fonts, a hexagonal thing. I drove back to SRI and found Pat in a dangerous state, close to a coronary. We got him stabilized and he said, 'don't ever do that to me again, there are certain places I can't go to.' He'd described the place with precision, but he never realized it was a church. I knew right there that the project was starting to violate every rule about the use of human subjects, and I had them stop the work."

"What happened to this fellow Pat Price?"

"He died a few years later, in a Las Vegas hotel room. His body was taken to a hospital. Within minutes a man showed up with Pat's full medical file. He put it under the nose of the physician. The doctor wrote "Coronary" and closed the file, didn't bother to check. We never found out who that man was!"

"Did you ever ask the psychics to look into the UFO problem?"

"Many times. Pat Price assured us there were bases on earth. He produced a map with four locations; we checked them carefully. They were technical facilities. One of them, in the French Pyrénées, was a government project, but it didn't involve anything out of the ordinary. Pat said he saw women there; it was an assembly plant with female workers. We never got beyond that." (Note)

"Well, we're hoping to get the project restarted under Ed May," D'Amato said. "I expect to fund it at $2 million a year for at least two years. There's only one fellow who opposes it on religious grounds, a man named Speister. But he's got no right to stop it."

"You don't have to be afraid of Pandolfi doing anything to stop it, either," concluded Kit. "He may be reluctant to accept every claim, because the project has gone through cycles of remarkable anecdotal results and wild unproven claims. Dale Graff was supposed to provide the briefings and reports, but that wasn't strong enough."

The Puerto Rican waitress came to refill our cups. D'Amato went on, more eagerly: "What about crashes? Have you looked into them?"

"I've been told to go see various authorities that will get me initiated. I've visited two previous directors of the CIA, John McCone and William Colby, and Professor Eric Walker. You should read his autobiography, *Now it's my turn*."

"What did Bill Colby say?"

"He gave me advice. He said, go back to the people who sent you and tell them you're worthy of their confidence. And if they still won't tell you what it's all about, drop it!"

"Why do you think he said that?"

"He thinks I'm being used. He told me, 'Not many people can come and talk to me, face to face. They want me to know they exist'."

"It works like a Brotherhood, then. What are the parameters?"

"Ah, that's an interesting question," said Kit, perking up. "I think they belong to a project but it's a small project, not a big one."

"It's a small project made to look like a big one?"

"Yes. And it's hidden away in a contractor's basement somewhere, not in the government. And all the Brothers, come to think of it, are people in their seventies, older gentlemen."

(Note) The location was supposed to be Monte Perdido, on the Spanish border, at 42°40'N and 0°02'E, 50 meter from the ridge, facing West by Northwest. My maps don't show anything there, so coordinates may be off.

I silently wondered where they had been between 1939 and 1945.

"What is the initiation process?" I asked. "In the Mafia, you'd have to kill somebody to qualify."

"Apparently you get invited to go into the desert, near Sandia in New Mexico, and there you see your first UFO," Kit answered. I recalled what he had told me about Bill Moore. But that UFO was a cheap special effects gadget from a Hollywood backlot.

"I heard the MD in the Brotherhood passed away recently, I was supposed to succeed him," Kit added. "Somehow it didn't happen."

"You must not have passed the test," said D'Amato. "How do you think the information works?"

"You'd better ask Jacques," said Kit, "he's the expert on that."

We spent the next half hour discussing control systems, and my observation that the information arrow always seemed to be directed inward like a retro-virus, not outward.

In summary: The secret project is illegal, it isn't within a Government agency. It is small, it generates high-level "leaks" designed to infect the research community with false data, and the cover makes it look bigger than it really is: not bad for one meeting.

After our quick lunch D'Amato left in a hurry to get back to the Hill. Kit relaxed, ordered more coffee and told me, "I know where I've heard of him at the Agency. He's got a good reputation but he's typical of all those Senate staffers, who think they know everything. The world just doesn't work that way."

We spent the rest of the time talking about crop circles. There is a Government Enigma group that checks with botanists. To Kit's surprise, none of them had heard of the phenomenon. I told him about the French finding that the British were experimenting with beam weapon calibration from low-observable dirigibles.

Spring Hill. Saturday 15 June 1991.

This evening we plan to observe the conjunction of Jupiter, Mars, and Venus, a magnificent *ménage à trois* in the Western sky that will not occur again for a couple of centuries. The weather is pleasant and I feel happy, healthy. I haven't had asthma since I have followed the new treatment prescribed by a French doctor during my last trip.

Over lunch with Dr. Ed May in Menlo Park yesterday he confirmed the progress of the SAIC project. Lunch with Ed is always a joyous experience. He wants me to pursue my idea for the generation of random, unique target scenes that require no human coding, thus avoiding uncertainty in judging remote viewing. He would reconcile the second law of thermodynamics with the reality of precognition.

"I think causality is stochastic," he said. "Therefore we can have psychic phenomena without violating known laws of physics. When I digitized various scenes we used as targets, and computed the Shannon entropy, I found it directly correlated with success in remote viewing. That suggests that you were right in talking about information singularities in the event universe. But it also means that we can design better experiments."

He took me to see his new offices above Kepler's bookstore, an amusing location for a classified research center. "I'd heard one couldn't tell a book by its cover," I joked as the elevator took us to the third floor. "Apparently that also applies to the whole bookstore."

The offices house safes and an electromagnetically sealed remote viewing lab. From this place one can see our old SRI buildings beyond the quaint little Menlo Park train station.

Now a friend of writer Jimmy Guieu named Roger Rémy calls from Albuquerque, talking about advanced propulsion. Could I consult with him? I am no expert in plasma physics, I replied.

Hyde Street. Monday 1 July 1991.

Hal Puthoff works on vector-scalar potentials, which theoretically provide a way to develop an undetectable source of energy. You could walk around the transmitter with a probe and never find either a magnetic or electric field. But if you put a wire around it you'd generate a current. He's been working on a theory of such potentials for years, and only recently built a detector to his specifications, so that the effect can be demonstrated. He claims to have evidence of a range of energies similar to the electromagnetic spectrum, but not detectable through the existence of a field. If true, this opens the way to a new mode of looking at the cosmos, searching for intelligence.

Spring Hill. Saturday 6 July 1991.

The last three days at the ranch have been idyllic. At nightfall we linger in the pool and watch the stars—red Antares burning high over our pasture, and a little diamond-shaped constellation rising in the east over the pine trees. An occasional satellite brings the genius of man, or his folly, into the scene as we discuss the future.

I have an old book about the region: "The climate of all of that section of Mendocino County, that lies eastward of the Coast Range, is simply perfectly delightful. Here the sun never shines but to gladden the face of nature, and to make the valleys paradisiacal, and a happy and lovely spot for man to locate his habitation, and to build homes that he and his children may enjoy in unalloyed measure..."

On the Fourth of July our Pagan neighbors came over from Potter Valley, bringing fireworks and magazines. Otter Zell and Morning Glory, Orion and Dan Stewart quickly stripped and jumped into the pool, after which dinner was served with two jugs of local wine. Our artist friend Morgane has decided to come and live at Spring Hill, using the studio to pursue her painting projects.

Spring Hill. Sunday 4 August 1991.

Keith and Darlene have just left us after a day filled with discussions of parapsychology and abductions, a walk in the forest and many cups of good coffee. The observatory is an ideal place to sit and talk, a mysterious cell at the edge of the darkness and a perfect site for experiments with time and mind. We heard the cry of a mountain lion, and when we walked into the woods today I found the scattered bones of a deer it must have surprised on the path. The night in the upper chamber was sweet and profound. Janine and I woke up several times, only to gauge the time by the grayness of the sky, her head warm with dreams against my shoulder.

In the morning I called my mother, as I usually do on Sundays. She told me, in a remarkably steady voice, that her sister had died: *Huguette est décédée hier*.

"The end of an era," remarked Janine—the last of the Passavant spinsters, women who lived through two world wars with stubborn perseverance. My aunts insisted on surviving in the kind and obsolete world of their meekness, so gentle and absurdly "nice" they once grated on my young, rebellious nerves. My brother explained the medical circumstances. No tears: we pretended to be responsible men handling a stressful situation with competence. It is curious, and sad, that we can only talk to each other like this when someone dies.

Spring Hill. Tuesday 6 August 1991.

The observatory has taken shape as I begin a new review of causality and information physics. Under the dome the electrical installation is complete, with red lights to read star maps and a shortwave radio for universal time signals. Shelves hold optical accessories, filters, cameras and the mounting hardware for the astronomical computer. There's a hot plate in the lab and a small refrigerator, a gift from Mimi Hynek; we could survive comfortably in this tower if we had to, but the region is not at peace: local developers stir up new arguments; people fight bitterly over a small creek, a dirt road, a displaced marker. No one knows where one ranch stops and another begins. The price of redwood escalates, a fact blamed on ecologists, because supply has dwindled with every new regulation. Agents are now getting $500 to $800 an acre for raw land, $1,500 for timbered land.

Catherine has repaired our wooden gate and painted it red. She saw two fat rattlesnakes she nicknamed Silvia and Silvester.

Spring Hill. Thursday 15 August 1991.

Our architect friend Bill Calvert is with us for a couple of days. He's helped me modify the fork of my new 11-inch Celestron telescope to install a guidance system. As we relaxed around the pool he told us about Gurdjieff's influence and about his recollections of life around Mrs. Frank Lloyd Wright, who had a strong dislike for Dr. Puharich.

Spring Hill. Friday 16 August 1991.

Diane has won her lawsuit against Anton LaVey, so she gets half the value of the Black House. Anton didn't bother to come to Court; he simply delayed the whole process. Anton has 60 days to comply, a sad ending for a once intrepid philosopher of darkness.

The *Kirkus Reviews* have published a piece about *Revelations*:

"Vallee does unglove the heavy hand of military intelligence in many cases, while at the same time exposing the absurdity of others, including Budd Hopkins's best-selling alien-rape reports. So what's left? A host of genuinely mysterious cases, e.g. the 1989 Soviet Union sightings, and the spirit of rigorous scientific inquiry that Vallee urges they be subjected to... A forceful and refreshingly iconoclastic study that, for all its good sense, will likely add up to only a cry in the alien-infested UFO wilderness."

Hyde Street. Saturday 17 August 1991.

As we slept in the tower last night a strange incident took place, possibly a first result of my experiments. In the middle of the night Janine saw a peculiar dot of bright light, four feet away in the general direction of the bookcase. It was surrounded with black swirling smoke that delineated a circular form. She moved her eyes away, noting it didn't follow her gaze. When she looked back she found the orb again in the same position. I slept through the incident.

We drove home early, taking a lazy route. We have decided to sell the Hyde Street Victorian house, and to move to a condo in the City.

Hyde Street. Sunday 18 August 1991.

Dennis Stacy has sent me an extract from *Explorer of the Universe* by Helen Wright, a biography of astronomer George Ellery Hale for whom the Mount Palomar telescope was named:

"An odd thing happened during his visit (to Menton on the Riviera). One night, when he was sitting in his room, out of nowhere a little man suddenly appeared, and soon was advising him on the conduct of his life (…) After this, his first visit, he came often, in many widely scattered places, until he became almost a mascot. Hale rarely spoke of these visitations."

Other noted writers and scientists have had similar experiences, notably E. T. A. Hoffmann.

Hyde Street. Sunday 25 August 1991.

Bloodshed in Russia: an extraordinary period has come to an end, a week of horrors and turmoil with its cargo of betrayal, murder, suicide and tragedy. I am reminded of the words of Tom Belden as we walked down the corridors of the CIA, describing the world as a group of thugs playing pool aboard an ocean liner pitching among the waves... "*and at any time, any player has the right to kick the table...*"

Hyde Street. Thursday 29 August 1991.

Yesterday I was in L.A. to tape the Ron Reagan show with astronaut Buzz Aldrin. Phil Klass was there so I had a surprisingly pleasant dinner with him at *Musso and Frank*, well-known hangout of the movie crowd. He tried to impress the waiter by telling him we had just "done" the Ron Reagan show. Since most of the diners in the room spent their life on stage, the waiter was not moved.

Klass thinks Richard Doty alias "Falcon" (together with his bosses) is responsible for the current insanity. He reminisced about the Lear family. When he was 17 John Lear rented an acrobatic plane in order to impress his father who was building a new jet in Switzerland. He crashed near their large mansion outside Geneva.

Hyde Street. Tuesday 3 September 1991.

Kit's phone is disconnected. He told me that someone was harassing him: "I'm not sure who is doing it, or why. They filmed us during my trip to San Francisco, when we walked near Ghirardelli Square."

"Big deal," I told him. "You didn't reveal any secrets to me."

"They just want to show me they always know where I am."

The fellow he'd noticed near us tracked him in L.A. the next day.

Kit has been testing the French hypothesis about crop circles, using different waveforms to hit the nodes of cornstalks.

"At 5-minute exposure Velasco's hypothesis makes sense; there are biological effects. We suffuse the nodes with plastic to document the results, and after a calibrated burst of energy we take out thin sections. The beams are composed of microwaves."

Los Angeles Airport. Friday 13 September 1991.

When I called Kit today he told me someone had snapped his picture at Boston airport. This reminded me of Fred Beckman's adventures: a woman photographed him at a restaurant, and later the galleys of *Revelations* I had entrusted to him were stolen from his car.

In a few days I will be meeting my business colleagues and our investors in Paris to review our strategy in the midst of a recession in Europe and a lingering slump in the U.S. The Dow oscillates around 3000. In spite of this uncertainty Janine will put our Hyde Street house on the market. Her intuition is right, as usual: the time has come to unburden ourselves of that fine Victorian structure. All we need is a smaller, functional place. Janine dreams of a simple two-bedroom apartment, high above the city lights.

Whitley Strieber advises me to "get out of the business":

"You're only exposing yourself to attack from idiotic ufologists. The phenomenon provides a very different angle once you're out."

Mabillon. Monday 16 September 1991.

Paris was hot over the weekend, making the air stale and sticky. When we wake up in the middle of the night we hear the drunken songs of people coming out of the discothèques and the rumble of cars returning to the suburbs. There's a lull of an hour or so, then the city wakes up with a big jolt and the machine lurches forward.

Angers. Hotel de France. Sunday 22 September 1991.

Our press conference before business journalists is done, Fred Adler has flown back to his Manhattan lair, and our investors are pleased with what they heard. Now Janine and I are off on a short holiday.

Yesterday's skies were full of the light and the warmth of summer as we climbed back up the old keep of Passavant castle with my dear old mother. At 91, she scampered over the tumbling stones without hesitation. The owner gave us another erudite lecture while we stood on the upper terrace and the wind rose from the plains below. She showed us the grand old rooms inside the tower.

If it hadn't been for our exploration of Passavant we would have missed the Tapestry of the Apocalypse in Angers, which we visited almost by accident. Maman said it was the most beautiful thing she'd ever seen. It is surely the grandest in the genre, even if the *Lady and the Unicorn* at the Cluny packs more mystical power.

Janine is happy here. She looks the way I knew her 30 years ago, with her demure white sweater, her hair cut short.

Sarlat. Tuesday 24 September 1991.

Passing through Blois we visited Lusignan, an old dream of mine. We stopped at the marvellous site where the Mélusine legend was born and saw the nearby stained glass museum. This morning we left the ugly suburbs of Poitiers under the rain. In Angoulême the sun came out, but the city looked decrepit and tasteless.

For my birthday (I am 52 today) we had lunch in a modern château with butter-colored walls and ugly modern paintings of red lobsters and green apples. After Périgueux we found winding roads under slanted rocks, caves everywhere, the peaceful Vézère, proud castles on every hill. Sarlat is a medieval dream of gorgeous loggias, gargoyles, narrow passageways and stone arches where the rich spirituality and healthy lust of the 15th century linger in the darkness.

Europe is rocked by demonstrations in Piedmont and in Tuscany calling for independence, bombs in Corsica, murders in Ireland, war between the Serbs and the Croats, and an ugly famine in Moscow.

Tours. Friday 27 September 1991.

We left the medieval town, driving towards Padirac and Rocamadour. The rain came down in buckets, bringing back memories of that France of narrow roads I had so often seen through blurred windshields, little dead towns engulfed in blackness, bleak landscapes. Our short trip to the depths of central France has shown us a sadly deserted countryside. Our hotel is located in a stately mansion that has been cut up into a series of rooms with weird shapes and high ceilings: it looks like the set of a play. I dreamed of the days when our children were young and woke up in tears.

Mabillon. Tuesday 1 October 1991.

We're back in Paris after our brief excursion. Yesterday Janine and I had coffee with Guérin, more nervous and irritable than I had ever seen him. He never listened to anything we said, simply ranting and raving about ugly Aliens.

This afternoon I met again with my French publisher, Mr. Robert Laffont. He was seated in a recliner, looking weak and tired. He invited me to pull up a chair next to him as we discussed *Revelations* and my Russian book. I was surprised to find that he'd actually read every word. He commented, "Your books are too lucid. Rational books never sell as well as the fake ones."

It is wonderful to be next to Janine, in Paris again. We talk softly of our plans, and sadly of our memories, of the people we've lost.

London. Intercontinental hotel. Thursday 3 October 1991.

Is this really London, this clear city, sunny, warm and cheerful? Many countries, from Poland to Spain and Italy, are represented at the *Financial Times* investment conference I am attending here, all worried about the same things: jobs and technology.

United flight over Iceland. Saturday 5 October 1991.

Old volumes are getting expensive in London, 60 pounds for a copy of D. P. Walker's *Spiritual and Demonic Magic from Ficino to Campanella* published in 1958 by the Warburg Institute. At Souvenir Press, Ernest Hecht was in a joking mood. The bookstore downstairs has taken the same appearance as Hecht's own office, with piles of books in every corner, a lovable scene of literary chaos.

Now I am flying towards the Arctic, reading Martine Castello's latest book and watching the glaciers of Iceland sliding into the Atlantic. A correspondent of mine urges me to investigate the elves...

Minneapolis. Tuesday 15 October 1991. Whitney hotel.

I have just spent two days in Manhattan, where several of my press interviews were cancelled because of the media's fascination with a

Senate debate on sexual harassment. It hinges on the size of the penis of a Black candidate to the Supreme Court, challenged by his former assistant Anita Hill. Amusingly, the trial takes attention away from the confirmation hearings of Robert Gates for the top job at the CIA.

In New York I met with Dan Tolkowsky and Fred Adler at the latter's current office near the PanAm building. Now I am in Minnesota, where people wear parkas and hats and say sensible things.

Hyde Street. Sunday 20 October 1991.

Disaster has struck the Bay Area again. A large section of Oakland is burning out of control, bathed in a light of Armageddon that turns the sea deep grey-green, the sun orange, the sky brown: people are stunned by walls of flame that quickly swallow whole city blocks.

We drove home with somber thoughts: the alleged "witness" of Gulf Breeze fame and Navy physicist Bruce Maccabee threaten me with a lawsuit (**37**), mad at my finding that the author of alleged UFO pictures was a convicted forger. I'm reminded of Whitley Strieber's admonishments about ufologists.

Spring Hill. Saturday 26 October 1991.

My daughter has joined us again at the ranch in the warm coziness of autumn. The air smelled heavy with rotting apples and wet leaves. She lit a log in the fireplace. When night fell, all the timeless pleasures of home and the approach of Christmas were in the air.

We found a note from Morgane: "It's been a wonderful healing time! Lots of interesting visitors, you'll see the bear prints in the pool's plastic tarp, bent trees, bear poop sample for good scientific evidence of what bears eat (apples). Also found this dead alien."

She has just discovered potato bugs. I'd never realized how much these horrible, yet harmless insects looked like the "Visitor" on the cover of Whitley Strieber's *Communion*.

Hyde Street. Friday 15 November 1991.

With the help of investigators in Florida, I have gathered documents to rebuke any legal action. Not only is the Gulf Breeze hoax clear, but

Fig. 5. With my mother at Angers castle, September 1991.

Fig. 6. With planetary astronomer Pierre Guérin in a Paris café, Sept.1991.

I actually understated it in *Revelations*. The alleged witness had been sentenced to three concurrent terms of five years in jail, not for joyriding but for forging bad checks. I can confidently go to Court, according to my publisher's amused lawyers, but it would simply be another nail in the sad coffin of ufology. Why bother?

Yesterday in my office in San Bruno I briefly discussed UFOs with Dan Tolkowsky, one of the finest minds in finance. He said there was certainly something there, but was it a scientific problem?

After this conversation I met Kit for lunch in Fremont for the first time since our conversation at Aquatic Park. He'd been shaken up by recent events and there was an edge of fear in our conversation. He has come over to my view that we are faced with two distinct, interrelated phenomena: there are true UFOs "as real as coffee cups," but there's also an Undercurrent that exploits the expectation of extraterrestrial visitors. (I wrote as much in *Messengers of Deception,* back in 1979.)

Kit is busy investigating the case of journalist Joseph Daniel Casolaro, a free-lance writer found dead in a motel bathtub. The body was hurriedly embalmed on orders of local cops without the family's permission and against police procedures.

Casolaro connected the case of a software company called Inslaw with the Iran-Contra scandal, BCCI laundering of money for CIA, drug dealers and terrorists, and the "October Surprise" (**38**).

We also spoke about Brazil. Why were the Brazilian reports kept from the U.S. Government, he wonders? Or were they?

"I should have received them at the time," Kit says. The only explanation is that somebody is watching: "There must be a pre-existing structure that intercepts such cases." Now we are starting to learn something. (Note)

Spring Hill. Saturday 16 November 1991.

Is it another echo from my consciousness experiments, imperfect as they are? I woke up twice last night, both times in the middle of a

----

(Note): The revelation, years later, that *National Enquirer* journalist Bob Pratt was a CIA "asset" in Brazil throws new light on this comment.

dream where I was working with Allen. Morgane thinks that Dr. Hynek is helping my work "on the inner planes." The old connection is certainly there in the recesses of my mind, and deep in my heart.

My research is now concerned with erecting (or rediscovering?) a methodology that integrates synchronicity and time with Ingo's teachings in remote viewing and long-neglected traditions stating that the records of the past and the future are equally available.

Hyde Street. Monday 18 November 1991.

Deep, heavy sleep. I am at peace now that the trilogy (*Dimensions, Confrontations, and Revelations*) is complete. Some ufologists, predictably, are incensed: "You will be excommunicated by the Primates of the Church of Nuts-and-Bolts!" warns one reader. But independent researchers write they are electrified by *Revelations* because it blazes a trail for their own work.

Janine reads the early Journals, amused to come to this passage: *my desk is finally clear and I'm eager to leave the UFO field...*

"Here you are, 30 years later, telling me the same thing..." she laughs. I reorganize my field investigation files as I go through hundreds of folders packed with photographs and tape transcripts.

Yesterday Olivier married his girlfriend in the 6th *Arrondissement*.

Hyde Street. Friday 6 December 1991.

Yesterday Janine and I took a sentimental trip to Dr. Jim Harder's house on top of Hilgard in Berkeley to meet Soviet ufologist and air force researcher Marina Popovitch. The house is perched up at the end of a series of steps cut into the hillside. Many years ago we had lunch there with Allen Hynek and Dr. Luis Alvarez.

Harder was relaxed and friendly. He'd invited a geologist (who kept falling asleep) and the daughter of Rusty Schweikert, who didn't seem to know why she was there. Marina engulfed me in her arms and gave me a big kiss. She showed us her slides, including a picture of alleged dead Aliens in Russia that didn't fool us. Janine giggled all evening, accusing Marina Popovitch to be in love with me.

Hyde Street. Sunday 8 December 1991.

Bill Calvert, Regina and Elena have come to see us at Spring Hill. Morgane was there with her cartoons, fancy cooking and stories. On Saturday Otter Zell brought his whole Nest: Morning Glory, Orion, intense Dan Stewart who has just published our interview in the *Green Egg*, and Diane Darling with Gary, dressed in Renaissance costumes. We spoke of unicorns and hypnosis, psychic surgery and high cuisine, Aliens and gnomes.

The Plaza, New York. Tuesday 10 December 1991.

Manhattan is clear. I spent the day with Dan Tolkowsky, who had many new questions about UFOs. He also wanted to know if I had ever been threatened. He maintained that the phenomenon may be beyond the range of science. I reminded him about many phenomena that people once thought intractable, now reduced to science.

At the meeting of Synaptic Pharmaceuticals, I thought about that as I listened to Dr. Eric Kandel, the Columbia University pioneer on neurotransmitters, debating cures for temporal lobe epilepsy.

Dan got lost on our way back, so we spent an hour circling the George Washington Bridge. Eventually we found ourselves in Harlem, and it took a hilarious conversation in my broken Spanish with a Puerto Rican who drove a beat-up Chevy to get us back to the FDR drive. To make up for losing his way Dan invited me to dinner.

"What would the Israeli Air Force do if it was faced with a UFO report?" I asked him. "Probably assign it to two analysts, one from Operations and one from Intelligence," he replied.

Hyde Street. Sunday 15 December 1991.

Handwriting expert Ted Widmer has analyzed a recent letter from Dr. X, finding him psychologically stable. "He's independent, a nice fellow, easy to get along with, but he'll surprise you because of his strong need for privacy. He lacks long-term energy, you wouldn't want to be his partner in business. You'd end up doing all the work."

Ted had attended the bankruptcy hearings of Anton LaVey. He found him the perfect image of a con man, all in black, along with his new consort Blanche Barton.

Dan Tolkowsky writes from Tel Aviv, “I finished *Revelations* on the return flight. It's fascinating, the story of that witness, Franck Fontaine, in particular.”

Spring Hill. Friday 20 December 1991.

This is Solstice Eve, full moon racing in a field of dark clouds shredded by winter winds. Morgane will spend Christmas with us here. A good, productive year is behind us.

Now I learn of an interesting close encounter that took place on 25 February in Bath County, Kentucky. A farmer named Billy Goldy and his employee James Carpenter saw a disk flying from the northeast at about 100 feet altitude. It moved toward some trees in a hollow, turned on its side or unfolded until it looked like a bright aluminum circle flashing “the brightest blue, green and yellow lights” they had ever seen (Fig.7). The lights. Always the lights.

Spring Hill. Wednesday 25 December 1991.

Peaceful days and nights by the fireplace carefully tended by Catherine, Christmas carols on the radio. I work well here. We have not listened to the news for days, so it is a call from my mother that told us the news of Gorbachev's resignation. The Soviet Union is no more: people are rejoicing everywhere. The end has come for an inhuman system collapsing under its own weight.

4

Washington, D.C. Friday 17 January 1992.

“Stagnation” best describes the planet as the year begins. The U.S. economy has failed to recover from last year's debacle; IBM just recorded its first year of losses; millions are out of work, and the number of AIDS patients has passed 200,000 in the US alone.

Every hazy day hangs as if waiting for news that never comes. Yugoslavia experiences a tragic turmoil that may foreshadow an even greater problem for much of Europe. People fight over food in Moscow. As usual, the Middle East peace talks are breaking down; the young are throwing stones on both sides. The Foundation for Mind-Being research, a New Age group, notes accurately, “In our cities and on our streets we see pervasive evidence of despair, frustration, and alienation.”

Madison Hotel, Washington. Saturday 18 January 1992.

With great sadness, Janine has just read to me over the phone a letter from statistician Michel Gauquelin's sister Martine:

“I know all the friendship and the esteem that my brother Michel felt towards you. This is why I take the liberty to write this letter to you, against his last wishes. My beloved brother is no more, since the night of last May 20th, when he decided to take his own life.”

I felt a sudden heaviness, knowing what would follow.

“Michel committed suicide by using barbiturics, swallowing nearly 300 pills of Mogadon. We do not fully understand his desperate, yet lucid gesture. Perhaps it was caused by a certain solitude he felt, but I believe other stressful factors combined: his endless fight of 45 years to get his results and his novel research recognized; constant arguments with certain scientists.”

Poor Michel Gauquelin! He was under relentless, dishonest attack from academic skeptics, furious because they couldn't find fault in his planetary correlations. We had urged him to leave France and move to America, where I could get him a job. He regretted ignoring my advice, but I never thought he would sink to such despair.

Hyde Street. Thursday 23 January 1992.

Guérin complains that Aimé and I ignore reports of crashed saucers and dead Aliens. I don't ignore them, there may be crashed UFOs, but we don't have the hard data. Now a good review of *Samizdat*, my book about Russian UFOs, appears in the *Kirkus Review* calling it "an intriguing example of *glasnost* in action and an important document opening up rich new veins of exploration."

Hyde Street. Tuesday 28 January 1992.

A letter from Aimé Michel states, "I can testify about Hynek. When I went to his place in Evanston there was a congress in Yerkes, so I travelled with him in his car. A marvellous trip. As it frequently happens with me, he felt in confidence and spilled everything about his private life, his childhood, his marriage, his religious beliefs, his professional troubles, his kids, his quasi-mystical experiences, the Rosicrucians… Hynek was one of the most sincere people I have ever met in this stupid ufological world."

Bob Wood of McDonnell-Douglas confirms this. Bob doesn't believe the rumors about Allen's supposed "insider" status.

Aimé goes on, "One of his sorrows was to have lost you, because of his own failure to find something interesting enough for you in the vicinity. I consoled him the best I could... Your idea of publishing your memoirs is excellent. I remember your fat notebooks. Unfortunately, you will not stop the crazies..."

The U.S. is standing down the bombers and dismantling its nuclear arsenal, as the former Soviet republics are also doing. I only hope that these actions are not caused by the fact that the military has secretly achieved something even worse than nuclear bombs. Many UFO sightings I get turn out to be caused by human craft capable of extraordinary maneuvers, new flying platforms undergoing tests.

Hyde Street. Sunday 2 February 1992.

Teish spent the weekend with us at Spring Hill. I am fond of Luisa and I admire her sharp intelligence. She supports my experiments to deal with the information universe and interrogate its foundations.

Over lunch with Fred Beckman on Friday I told him about the Journal. I handed to him the two fat spiral-bound typescripts: "I'm giving it to you to get your frank comments, but even if you had no comments I'd give it to you as a friend."

Nantes. Friday 14 February 1992.

This is the first week of long meetings and hard work. I spent time at BNP and Banque Elkann. Let no one tell me that there is no money in France! Later I went up to *La Défense* for a pleasant lunch with Olivier, discussing everything from computer networking to his plans in Japan. I told him about this Journal, asking him to review it.

The next day, more meetings at Photonetics, who have sold their fiberoptic gyroscope to Northrop. I travelled to Nantes with Dr. Philippe Pouletty, to attend a test of Sangstat's anti-rejection drug. I spent part of the afternoon at the side-viewing arm of a large Zeiss microscope, watching an extraordinarily skilled surgeon stitching the aorta of a donor mouse heart to that of a live one, a demonstration of steady hands and precise use of needle and thread.

Today I got up early to reach Efi Arazi, the founder of Scitex (**39**) and to confirm that we would invest in *Electronics for Imaging*.

London, Hotel Russell. Friday 21 February 1992.

At a meeting yesterday with Richard Hooke of British Aerospace (which makes the *Harrier*) I told him "If we can make a jet fighter that flies backwards, and if we can perform a heart transplant on a mouse, we can do anything... we're only limited by our ability to manage creativity and to understand markets." But we are also hampered by the obsolete cultural barriers of Europe.

Gordon Creighton tells me the *Flying Saucer Review* doesn't have an office any more and all the early documents are in storage:

"As you recall, Charles Bowen's wife was very much against our subject. She destroyed a lot of documents, as Mrs. Girvan, wife of the previous editor, had also done. I rescued a few papers, like the letter of subscription from the Chinese Academy of Sciences..."

Gordon has read David Jacobs' forthcoming book (**40**) but disagrees with him, the beings involved are not real Aliens, abductions are caused by entities that only pass themselves off as extraterrestrials, he said, an opinion close to mine.

Now I'm eager to catch the flight home.

Hyde Street. Thursday 27 February 1992.

Fred Beckman commented on my manuscript today: "It's very hard," he said, "combining your Journal with the more recent stuff. Your book takes me back to many emotional things..."

As we walked over to the restaurant by the Bay we halted to watch the white-billed coots playing in the mud at low tide. "People will probably remember all the wrong things from your book, like who you were sleeping with in Paris. But it will be fascinating for those who really care about the history of the phenomenon."

He reminded me of what Jung said in his own book, that he had an ominous feeling about flying saucers, and that he had only had that same feeling once, in 1933, about the rise of the Third Reich.

"The Jungians are trying to sweep his book under the rug, as if Jung himself hadn't said it was the most important thing he'd ever written! In some anthologies it's not even cited...Yet I have that same feeling he did, that something terrible will happen."

He also reminisced about travelling with Hynek and the funny embarrassments that created, like the time in Paris when Allen decided to take pictures of the new rubber-wheel *métro*. An irate woman across the track, seeing this character in checkered jacket, Tyrolian hat, and Texas silver dollar tie, aiming a stereo camera towards her, called the cops and tried to have Dr. Hynek arrested. Or the time when he was introduced to the Lord Mayor of London and immediately thrust a cheap tape recorder under his nose, asking him to "say a few words for the people of Chicago..." Or the time when he visited the House of Lords, where he spoke at the invitation of eccentric old Lord Clancarty and decided he had to take a picture of the Thames River. They nearly broke the august windows when they tried to open them: The frames had been kept shut for 400 years and were coated with dust and grime.

Then Fred started to talk about music, his favorite subject. In my Journal he was surprised to find that I liked Varèse, whom he'd met, and that Janine and I had been guests at Pierre Schaeffer's home.

Hyde Street. Sunday 1 March 1992.

Spring Hill was all pink trees and white flowers this weekend. Gossipy frogs give us nightly concerts. We observed Jupiter through the new telescope, with its four major satellites. When humans observe a galaxy, is the galaxy aware of us watching it?

Otter Zell has introduced us to computer expert Adam Rostoker, an OTO practitioner. Adam is a big teddy bear, with great scholarship of everything concerning Crowley, Jack Parsons, and Robert Heinlein. In his big bus pelted by the spring rains, where the faulty generator was causing the lights to blink, Adam printed out a draft of *Whence came the Stranger*, which he gave me (**41**).

Adam would not reveal to me who the current OTO leader Hymeneaus Beta was. "Alpha," who was McMurtry, died in 1974. Adam was surprised that we'd known him, as well as Regardie. As a child he remembers some remarkable visions, including little men. He believes his mother became sick and died as a result of UFO events in their neighborhood (in Lunenburg, MA.). When he grew up he took up computing and ran the Comdex computer show.

Hyde Street. Tuesday 10 March 1992.

Lunch with a naval officer, a friend of high-tech executive Steve Millard, who works with Paul Baran. He described two UFO incidents: the first one was seen from the cockpit of a jet fighter in the seventies. He was flying from Nevada to Point Mugu one night when he and his radar officer saw 8 lights below them, looking like brush fires, yet they kept up with him until he veered towards San Diego. In the second incident he was flying from Majorca to England and was in the vicinity of the French coast when he saw a silvery disk far above him, crossing the sky very fast. He estimated its altitude at 80,000 feet and its speed at 5,000 mph.

"To whom did you report it? Who debriefed you?" I asked.

"I wouldn't be in command of a nuclear aircraft carrier in the Navy of the United States if I had ever reported this to anybody," was his answer. He is not aware of any channels for such observations.

How can one claim that the Pentagon has an all-pervasive program to secretly gather UFO data? Here I am, listening to UFO reports from a rear admiral, and the military never got that information.

Abduction believers are meeting in a room rented from MIT, so they call it "the MIT meeting about abductions," as if the Institute had anything to do with it. The committee is made up of Hopkins' followers, with a few psychologists thrown in to appear objective.

Hyde Street. Friday 20 March 1992.

Last week I had lunch with Guy Snodgrass, former special assistant to defense secretary Jim Mattis, considered one of the best pilots in the U.S. Navy and former commander of the Dambusters. He told me he'd never seen the UFO topic in any budget.

Janine has just returned from Ukiah with two offers for our properties there. We're fed up with the absurdity of a state government that encourages over-reliance on welfare in the guise of assisting people. The social system destroys what is left of their identity without providing financial support to those in genuine need. Abuses are built into the system: We've had to evict tenants who didn't pay the rent while using their apartment as a hothouse for growing pot, making thousands of dollars a week while receiving welfare checks and relying on free state attorneys to fight eviction.

Spring Hill. Thursday 26 March 1992.

I have secured a document confirming that the CIA simulated UFO abductions in Latin America (Brazil and Argentina) as psychological warfare experiments. On Tuesday aerospace researcher Morvan Salez met me in Burbank. I gave him the Fleximage digital tapes of the Costa Rica photographs before going to dinner in Hollywood with

Bob Weiss and Tracy, who told us that the abduction miniseries had run into problems; John Mack insists the Aliens are good guys who came to save us, while the plot takes a negative twist in Hopkins' sado-masochistic mindset. They are on unfriendly terms. Now Aimé Michel writes of the death of Yves Rocard, father of the French A bomb.

Spring Hill. Saturday 28 March 1992.

The countryside has emerged from winter dressed in emerald green, the grass as tall as our windowsill. I am trying to read Jacobs' *Secret Life*. The author appears obsessed with what he views as a massive Alien invasion, his analysis is no longer balanced.

Hyde Street. Thursday 2 April 1992.

On Tuesday night Keith Harary came over. He told me of a time when he was driving back to his dormitory at Duke University and saw a huge ball of light go down into the building. His roommate had an out-of-body experience at the same time.

Yesterday I had lunch with Ed May, who still works closely with Dale Graff of DIA. They've now run four subjects, including Keith and DelMonaco. He is pleased with the data. Ed also said that Puthoff's Institute in Austin had funding concerns, "Like many millionaires, Bill Church recently lost a lot of money in the stock market," he said, "and Hal keeps everything too damn secret."

I am reading *The Transmigration of Timothy Archer* by Philip Dick, one of his best books, ironically more readable than his science fiction. I think he was wrong about Bishop Pike's psychic experiences (**42**). Like many sci-fi writers, Dick missed the reality of the paranormal, except when it came over and hit him, as in *Valis*.

Ann Arbor, Michigan. Thursday 9 April 1992.

A meeting of Peter Banks' National Advisory Committee of the University of Michigan has brought me to Ann Arbor. Astronaut Jim McDivitt is with us. This evening Peter told me he'd recently seen French science minister Hubert Curien; my name came up again.

Northwest flight from Detroit to SF. Friday 10 April 1992.

On the way back I spent an hour with Kit at the airport. He was eager to discuss Hal's involvement with Gordon Novel, who says he's been "brought into the government conspiracy," with no proof of it.

Novel reportedly asked Hal to mount a zero-point energy device on a flying craft that came from the Roswell crash. Hal is convinced this is the big break. Novel has given him a description of a material called titanium aluminide, allegedly from the Roswell saucer. (There is indeed such a material, manufactured by Northrop Aviation.)

Kit offered information from his own sources: "We have analysts looking at FastWalker records, photographs, MJ-12 documents, the whole bit. Yet I've never seen anything biological that was anomalous, and you've never seen anything in the system sense, and Hal had to admit he hadn't handled any crashed material... so there's still no hard evidence." But I do detect anomalies in my databases.

Something abruptly changed about five years ago when the fake MJ-12 documents came to light and the Roswell case was revived. The media campaigns hyping the "crashed saucer" business date from 1980, launched by newspapers controlled by Moon and K-CIA.

Thus, there are two new factors: anonymous sources from inside the government that plant well-designed hoaxes, and high-level officials like Eric Walker who refuse to deny such leaks. As an information scientist I have to regard the channel as more important than the message. The whole conundrum stinks of disinformation.

Spring Hill. Sunday 12 April 1992.

An electrical failure has forced us to drive to downtown Ukiah for lunch. Morgane came with us. We went off to Mrs. Benson's Cookies like kids on a lark, and then we drove up to the well-hidden Russian orthodox monastery where we admired the icons.

Paris. Tuesday 21 April 1992.

The sun has returned after a period of gray, humid weather. I found Olivier suffering from bronchitis and my mother locked in a strange nightmare. The death of two of her sisters has filled her apartment with objects loaded with acute sentimental value.

A long talk with me over lunch made her feel better; we even found some items she had misplaced. But at 92, with her generation vanishing, she is faced with a level of worry it is beyond my power to alleviate.

On the train to Manchester. Saturday 25 April 1992.

Yesterday I spent a pleasant evening with researcher John Spencer and his team at the Bufora research group. I met Ken Phillips, read his statistics, and was introduced to Ralph Noyes, a British civil servant retired from the MoD, a specialist in analytical studies. Now this train passes Castlethorpe, under indifferent wispy clouds.

Manchester. Hotel Britannia. Sunday 26 April 1992.

Rainstorms and happy sunshine alternate over this surprisingly ebullient, at times boisterous city. Yesterday at the celebrated University of Manchester Institute of Science and Technology I spent an interesting afternoon with Jenny Randles, elegant in a purple skirt and jacket over a pale violet blouse. Crop circles were among the topics eagerly discussed over dinner in a noisy bar; everybody downed large quantities of beer as discussion turned to pleasantly paranoid stories of Alien implants.

No matter how hard they try, these English restaurants always smell of dishwater, even in this fancy, gold and blue Victorian hotel. I am reading *Phantoms of the Sky* by David Clarke and Andy Roberts, one of the sanest books I have seen for a long time on this bizarre topic (**43**). It contains a nice picture of Allen Hynek investigating luminous phenomena at Hessdalen, Norway.

Paris. Mabillon. Monday 27 April 1992.

In Hoffmann's *Elixirs du Diable* I find this fascinating passage:

"What we are used to calling dream and imagination may simply be the symbolic knowledge of *the secret thread that traverses our life,* holding all of its phases securely together. But anyone who thought that he might use such knowledge to snap off the thread and confront the obscure power which controls us, should be considered as lost."

Paris. Mabillon. Thursday 30 April 1992.

Fred Adler stormed into town yesterday: The Concorde had engine problems over the Atlantic and turned back to Kennedy. He finally landed at dawn aboard a second Concorde and was in mean spirits.

Ignoring our gourmet lunch at the Warwick hotel he ridiculed the French, bad-mouthed the Germans, thundered against the Japanese and boasted that he was about to spend $300,000 of his own money to promote Ross Perot's presidential bid. Fred even caresses the dream of running for the Senate. That would shake things up…

On the United flight to California. Saturday 2 May 1992.

A happy, carefree crowd was buying bunches of fragrant *muguet* and enjoying yet another day of idleness when I went to lunch near *Porte Dorée* with Gabriel and his wife. I found my older brother relaxed, warm, and more caring than I had ever known him. He reminisced about the times of my early childhood, mentioning some events of which I was never aware: he described the terrible blow to our parents, in 1940, when they lost everything they owned, the unspeakable horror of finding their home destroyed by the Germans. It had burned at such a temperature that metal objects had been fused together. He recalled their distress when a sad little train—an "omnibus" that stopped at every village—finally deposited us on the platform in Villedieu-les-Poëles at two o'clock in the morning, our mother carrying me helpless in her arms. Maman was never accepted in Normandy, where our father's family treated her like a foreigner. She responded with suspicion and contempt of everything Norman.

Next, he spoke of his medical career: "When I started at Necker hospital," recalled Gabriel, "we had one director, one business manager, and a personnel coordinator. Now there are no less than six directors, middle managers by the dozen equipped with fancy computers they don't understand, and a maze of offices that sponge up most of the available money while clinicians and researchers are condemned to fail, with minimal resources and a nightmare of red tape. I've never been as happy as I am now, in retirement. I wonder how I was able to go there every morning, all those years."

Later, speaking with my friend Elisabeth Antébi, she recalled meeting Philip Dick about 1964. She'd made a documentary with five science-fiction luminaries, including Asimov and Spinrad. She'd even taken Dick to Disneyland, a trip he recalls in one of his books: "He was the strangest and the most gifted of all," she recalled, "a man with mediumistic abilities."

She also remembered her own visits to Fred Adler in Manhattan. They had discussed the paintings in his office; one showed a huge sand dune where some passing explorer had left footprints, leading where? Perhaps he was just over the horizon now, short of his goal, dying of thirst like an unlucky entrepreneur running out of cash? A philosophical reflection on the life of the innovator.

Elizabeth says Europe becomes a huge bureaucracy, incapable of achieving anything except wasting large amounts of money. My brother, who politically stands firmly at the other end of the spectrum, has reached the same conclusion about faceless bureaucrats in Brussels. Where is the democracy they promised?

Over the phone from California Janine tells me of violent riots in Los Angeles, an ugly upheaval that followed the absurd verdict exonerating the cops who had beaten up Rodney King. In San Francisco, Market Street stores have been looted and shops vandalized. A curfew is in effect.

In contrast Paris has been comfortable and peaceful all week, even under these rainy skies. Every morning I go buy the paper at the foot of the statue of Diderot. An old beggar draws shrill, mournful wails from a saw blade at the corner.

5

Hyde Street. Friday 15 May 1992.

Caltech researchers have just discovered magnetic material in the human brain (**44**). Geobiologist Joseph Kirschvink is quoted as saying, "We don't know what the magnets do, or where they hide in cells." Could they also be a factor in dowsing? Or in the effect of electrical current on cancer?

I've returned to California eager to resume my experiments at the ranch, extending Ingo's techniques, expanding on the theoretical concepts of "addressing" I'd demonstrated to him, which led to the invention of coordinate remote viewing (but the information science angle was never pursued at SRI). Janine and I drove up to Spring Hill with our long-time friend Hans Rasmussen. It was also an opportunity to renew an old friendship, to swim for the first time this year, and to continue the tests of the telescope.

Hyde Street. Tuesday 19 May 1992.

The media continue to be flooded with absurd images of hypothetical Aliens. It seems Americans are being taught what "They" look like and what we should expect from "Them." The *Intruders* TV miniseries is so bad it reminds me of Arthur Koestler's remark, in a letter to me, about contactee experiences that felt like "badly told dirty jokes." Witnesses get exploited by one side and ridiculed by the other, while research opportunities go to waste.

On the plane leaving Dallas. Wednesday 20 May 1992.

Dallas was a mess of thunderstorms today, with massive traffic jams on the vast freeways that were built to do away with traffic jams. This is Ross Perot's town; all conversations center on his bid for the presidency, but much has changed in Texas since the days of heady affluence. I remember visiting Trammel Crow in this city over 10 years ago and feeling awed by the limitless power that emanated from his world of big dreams, vast as a Texas sunset.

The board of IRT (**45**) met in the conference room of the Southland Corporation, thanks to the hospitality of John Thompson. He is a true gentleman, an accomplished executive who at one time was worth two billion dollars. He has seen his fortune wither to "only" some 200 million when he lost his 7-11 empire to the Japanese. The skyscraper stands as a marble relic, an anachronism.

Washington. Hotel Madison. Thursday 21 May 1992.

For once the weather is perfect here, a fine spring night. America scrutinizes its ghettoes for answers to the problems of riots, poverty, misery, and greed. Those in power make hypocritical speeches about the decay of moral values, all the time violating those same values. They look reproachfully at what people do in their bedrooms, but they refuse to talk about the obscenities in their own banks.

The Interop Show, devoted to the art of computer networking, strikes me as much by its confusion as by its technical maturity. Twenty years ago, when we made history with the first Arpanet demonstration at the Hilton in this city, all our machines were connected through a single node: It was a miracle when anything worked. There was a single electronic mail system, its messages flowed freely. Today there are hundreds of machines, their reliability taken for granted, but the software has become a jungle ruled by incompatibility of modes, formats, languages, codes, packets, and protocols in spite of all the hopeful talk about "interoperability."

Washington. Hotel Madison. Friday 22 May 1992.

Another fine spring day in Washington; wild flowers are growing out of every vacant lot littered with old Coke cans, used hypodermic needles and broken recliners tossed out the back of pickup trucks. In contrast, much of the downtown area has been "renovated." Now it is properly antiseptic, with uniform brick and concrete walls where little hotels and funky mom-and-pop stores used to flourish. Surveillance cameras watch every lobby from every angle. Human nature has been denied or channeled into marble hallways leading nowhere. Some day all of America may look like this.

Yesterday I enjoyed a friendly lunch with Colonel Charles Halt, the former base commander of RAF Bentwaters near Woodbridge in Suffolk. We met at the Key Bridge Marriott. I learned details about the curious events that took place there ten years ago, a landing witnessed by the troops, but I remain cautious about his interpretation. We disagreed politely.

Today my main meeting was with Richard D'Amato. He arrived on time, ebullient and dapper. He commented gleefully on the media circus. "This city thrives on chaos," he added. "The abduction miniseries on TV has put people to sleep, but Senator Pell remains fascinated by UFOs." There's a group within the American Federation of Scientists that investigates "mystery planes" of the Belgian type.

Dick is convinced those are human and the project that makes them, illegal: "No money was ever appropriated for it. Intelligence groups like AFOSI continue to cover, distort, destroy data, and generally make it impossible for Congress to find out what's going on." I told him I could understand how a rogue group could keep the lid on data in the U.S., but what about other nations?

Spring Hill. Sunday 24 May 1992. (Memorial Day)

The mail brings messages from witnesses whose lives are affected, cases that elude our grasp. Fred Beckman rightly observes "a sort of religious fervor, engulfing the whole business now." The largely biased Roper poll report sponsored by Bigelow and Liechtenstein has been mailed to 86,000 psychologists.

Flying from Seattle to San Francisco. Wednesday 3 June 1992.

This is my favorite flight in the whole world, over the Cascade Range. From Mt. Rainier that brings back memories of Kenneth Arnold, the route follows a stupendous line of snow-tipped volcanoes all the way to Oregon, Crater Lake, and South into California with Mount Shasta and Mount Lassen, which remind me sadly of my good friend the late

Bill Murphy. My venture work provides interesting challenges but more importantly the opportunity to help research save lives. I just spent most of the day at the University of Washington discussing radically new brain imaging.

Hyde Street. Monday 8 June 1992.

On a brief visit to Phoenix last week I was shown the full extent of the APRO files. Paying a visit to Mimi Hynek, I found her cleaning pottery shards. The CUFOS desert expedition to New Mexico was a failure: "We found nothing at Roswell," she said. We discussed abductions. She told me she once experienced hypnopompic imagery of an earth sphere; she felt that she went inside, but she drew no conclusion about anything psychic. She recalled how she used to fight Allen about parapsychology, something she now regrets.

"Allen's files for the period 1970 to 73 were missing from the Center after his death," she confided to me. "His office was ransacked. I'd returned the key to Northwestern. His drawers at the new observatory were found open, papers scattered everywhere."

The next day I had an early breakfast with her by the pool. The temperature was already up to 75 degrees, birds were fighting in the orange trees.

Mimi fondly remembered our last visit, "Allen came alive when you were here with Janine, he really perked up."

Hyde Street. Tuesday 9 June 1992.

Last night Janine and I had dinner with Dan and Miriam Tolkowsky at *L'Escargot*. They invited us to visit them in Israel in late summer.

Kit reports that he just spent two days in New Mexico with Rick Doty (alias Falcon.) He concludes: "Every person, except two (Doty and you), of the dozens with whom I have walked closely enough to have (a) a professional judgement, or (b) a clinical-medical judgement, are either losing it scientifically, analytically, or mentally."

He's decided to "follow in my footsteps and stay away from the mess," he says. But why this deference to Doty?

Princeton. Nassau Inn. Wednesday 10 June 1992.

Another meeting of the Society for Scientific Exploration (SSE) is assembling. I have invited William Corliss and Hilary Evans as speakers tomorrow. Among recent letters was an elegant one from Liechtenstein, responding to my article critiquing abduction research, and a courteous note from François de Grossouvre inviting me to come and talk to him, handwritten on stationery of the Presidency with the sub-heading *Comité des Chasses* (Hunting Committee), a most elegant cover for a sophisticated master spy.

Over dinner with Dean Radin, Bernie Haisch with his wife, Hilary Evans and Ed May, we had a debate about crop circles, apparitions, the Dead and (when Dr. John Derr arrived) earthquake lights.

That old novel by Philip Dick, *The Man in the High Castle*, remains on my bedside table. I can identify with his main character, the writer Hawthorne Abendsen, who has guessed a secret about the alternative reality and is deathly afraid of being right.

Princeton. Nassau Inn. Thursday 11 June 1992.

Hardly characteristic of New Jersey, the weather was balmy tonight as I walked down Nassau Street for dinner at *Lahiere's* with Robert Bigelow. A tall, tanned outdoor type with a Burt Reynolds mustache, he was wearing bright new basketball shoes and a brown and black shirt. He believes in Roswell and crop circles but doubts Meier. He wants to know where the soul goes after death: don't we all? He plans to give money to the Society. Hearing this, Bob Jahn and Charlie Tolbert immediately enlisted him as a member.

Bigelow explained to me that he owned 3,500 apartments in Las Vegas (with a 20% vacancy rate at the moment.) Born in 1944, he strived to make enough money to be able to sponsor research in parapsychology, but he has new doubts about Dave Jacobs and Budd Hopkins, who "get carried away," he says.

Velasco is here with his eldest son. He still argues the Belgian triangles are dirigibles with the propulsion system located on top. He says the Belgian air force is playing games and confirms that the celebrated F-16 radar records published by *Paris-Match* are fakes: the

French Air Force has no trace of a UFO over Belgium that day, and the over-the-horizon radar didn't paint two fighters there, either.

Jean-Jacques remains convinced that the French observations of November 5th were caused by a massive satellite re-entry. Here I don't agree: Too many observations have been recorded of a dark triangle with well-defined lights. Not to mention my own sources: an ambassador and a member of the Academy of Sciences.

George Hathaway is also in attendance. He told me he had built a spectroscopic analysis camera under the sponsorship of Prince Hans-Adam. He offered to loan it to me if I ever had a case of continuing sightings. He's already taken it to Gulf Breeze, with no results so far.

Hyde Street. Sunday 21 June 1992.

John Alexander called tonight to invite me to yet another conference on abductions. I have no desire to attend, but this led to a friendly chat about the recently-concluded "MIT conference" organized by John Mack and paid for by Bigelow and Prince Hans-Adam.

"You didn't miss much," he said. "There was zero independent thinking. There were more abductees than researchers among the 150 people there, and cases were restricted to those that fit the Hopkins-Jacobs pattern. Skeptic Bob Schaeffer was right when he pointed out that the nature of these cases depended on the investigator, obviously a bias at the source. There was a cat fight at the dinner table when one of Budd's groupies was challenged about the abduction memories related to child abuse," John recalled with a snicker.

Hyde Street. Monday 22 June 1992.

I am hoping that D'Amato, as a Senate staffer, can make the secret Battelle "*Pentacle Memorandum*" available to the research community. The copy I have is stamped SECRET, so it can't be published in the absence of declassification. He told me he needed that copy, that it was historically important. I could mail it to him via "any mechanical method that included a way to trace it."

This way I can discharge my responsibilities as a loyal citizen, and leave it up to him to publish it, he has the proper clearances. If I sent the document to the Executive Branch (the Air Force or the FBI) or reported it to SRI, the bureaucracy would make sure it never saw the light of day. Dick is going to Europe following a hearing in D.C. with Donald J. Atwood, the DOD's number-2 man, who professed ignorance of anybody building flying triangles.

Spring Hill. Wednesday 24 June 1992.

In the tower, having assembled books and souvenirs of Allen Hynek, I reviewed memories of our work. His presence is more vivid than ever. When I replayed a lecture taped at Stanford in 1974 his knowledge and humor came through again. I wondered how he would deal with the absurd rumors and shameless exploitations that deface the field today, fueled by some of his own followers.

In a book that comes from Allen's esoteric library **(46)** I find this poem by Longfellow, *The Legend Beautiful*:

In this chamber all alone
Kneeling on the floor of stone
Prayed the monk in deep contrition...
Suddenly, as if lightened,
An unwonted splendor brightened
All within him and without him
In that narrow cell of stone...

Allen, who spiritually considered himself in the Rosicrucian tradition, as I do, although not through membership in any group, had placed a marker on that page.

Spring Hill. Sunday 28 June 1992.

Listening to Allen's Stanford conference again I became aware of two factors. First, he was too eager to be liked. Strength or weakness, this manifested in his preoccupation with entertaining his audience. He had Stanford laughing at his jokes and UFO cartoons, so much so that they kept on laughing when he shifted to serious discussion, quoting dramatic letters from concerned witnesses. People thought the gentle joke continued and they kept giggling.

Allen wasted an opportunity to sway that influential academic audience. People went away relaxed, seeing Allen as a competent astronomer and nice guy who surely wouldn't be joking like this if he felt there was something profound to that UFO business.

Patchy gray skies were rolling over Willits when we started driving towards the coast this morning with Morgane. We went on to Mendocino, the landscape alive with dark clouds and salty wind. We had coffee near the Masonic temple, with its haunting statue of *Time and the Maiden*, and then the rain started coming down in squals.

Hyde Street. Sunday 5 July 1992.

Last night I found D'Amato's formal response on my fax machine:

This is to acknowledge receipt of a document sent by you via Federal Express, dated January 9, 1953, classified SECRET... The document has been placed in appropriate storage in the Senate.

I am relieved as the Cross letter is finally released, validated and available to researchers. There's nothing more anybody can do to deny this, although assets among UFO groups like CUFOS may again be used to try and minimize its impact. (**47**)

Albuquerque. Doubletree Hotel. Sunday 12 July 1992.

Midnight at the MUFON UFO conference. A senior member of their group discreetly called my room to say that "beyond Hopkins' hostility towards you there's wide underground support for your position that current abduction research is a lot of garbage."

Roger Rémy came over today with Jean-Luc Combier, a plasma physicist at NASA-Ames. Roger wants to build a novel propulsion and energy generation system. He used to be part of a French group that included Barjavel, Guieu, Carrouges, and admiral Calteix, head of Mensa France. Rémy also met Marcel Vogel of IBM as a result of their common interest in electromagnetic waves for plant growth.

Vogel had been asked to examine bits of supposed Alien hardware and tissue samples by "someone in Intelligence circles who didn't want to go to a University for such work." It showed evidence of *frittage*, he told me, where molecules are squeezed, but not fused over large sections in a way reportedly impossible for the time... The *frittage* technique is used to meld ceramic structures with other materials.

Hyde Street. Tuesday 28 July 1992.

Janine and I just came back from Phoenix where I visited a software company, and again spent the afternoon with Tina and Brian. Tina related how she'd met Allen in 1982 at Corralitos observatory. He had told her, "Don't come over if you're not bringing a bottle of red."

Again, we saw the APRO files in rows of filing cabinets, many of them still taped shut. The data for the years 1948 and 1949 was missing; there was no file on Roswell. Many of the drawers only contained clippings (labelled "Features") but others were full of data.

Hyde Street. Thursday 30 July 1992.

I spent yesterday with Fred Adler visiting companies and learning more about the early days of Silicon Valley, the crisis at Intersil and the momentous rise of the semi-conductor industry. We attended the shareholders meeting at EFI, where the Board decreed the public offering. The technical revolution is booming, with a breakthrough in the sophisticated handling of digital images.

United flight to Paris. Wednesday 5 August 1992.

Since I had just received the first copies of *Forbidden Science,* I gave one to Fred Beckman over lunch at the Marriott. He proceeded to tell me about his friend Ralph and his involvement with a woman who calls herself "Wendy." She reports being forced by several men to travel to Las Vegas, and now claims to be an Alien hybrid. She "proved" it to Ralph by displaying large black eyes--much too sensitive for her to submit to an examination, of course!

Ralph is charmed by the ET woman, to such an extent that his wife now threatens to leave him. I told Fred the story pointed to a crude fabrication involving special contact lenses. Whether she is a disturbed woman, or a hired actress, is the only question. There is an interesting similarity with the latest Hopkins story where a woman he calls "Linda Napolitano" tells of a weird abduction in Manhattan.

Briançon. Saturday 8 August 1992.

On a well-deserved vacation in France I am reading *The Ghost of 29 Megacycles*, which describes electronic communication with the Dead. I find it unconvincing, even under John Fuller's gifted pen.

My brother says he reads my books with interest but remains skeptical, people simply erect a legend and then proceed to ignore all the facts that don't quite fit, he says, adding, "This research cannot be understood without reference to myth, like Apollo's apparition at Delphos as a ball of destructive fire, which helped put an end to the worship of the Goddess and ushered in a male-oriented mythology."

Now we have drawn the drapes in our room, Janine has bought some fruit and yogurt for a frugal dinner. I am spreading maps of the mountain: tomorrow I must find my way to the summer retreat of the most mysterious witness in France, Pierre Gueymard alias Dr. X.

Ceillac. Sunday 9 August 1992.

This is the highest valley in Europe ever inhabited by man. We did find Pierre and his second wife Suzanne with her children. They took us on a spectacular excursion during which Pierre and I discussed the hidden meaning of fairy tales. He was particularly interested in *Le Petit Poucet*, the story of Tom Thumb:

"Tom Thumb is the prototype for the individual Seeker for truth, lost in the forest, in the darkest night," he pointed out. "Tom Thumb is smart, careful to document his way, even though he doesn't know where he's going, by dropping little white pebbles along the path. He climbs a tree, thus *rising above* all confusion, and he *sees the light*. But once he has come down from the tree, he doesn't see the light anymore. However, *he knows it is out there*, and he walks towards it *through the darkness*. The light comes from a house. But of course, it is the house of the Ogre, *who will devour him* if he isn't careful."

Tom Thumb represents the alchemical journey, the confrontation with evil and the triumph of light over darkness. It is also the story of scientific research. This Journal is my own trail of white pebbles.

Ceillac. Monday 10 August 1992.

We drove into the valley and up to Aimé Michel's aerie today, a breathtaking trip over needle-shaped turns and twists overlooking precipices. Way down, the lake was sparkling in the evening light.

We found Aimé in the stone house where I had spent a night 20 years ago. He was sitting at an old wooden table loaded with books. He got up slowly, as his infirmities permitted, and picked up our conversation where we had left it years ago, quoting Einstein who had said of flying saucer witnesses, "These people are seeing something real. I don't know what it is—and I don't care."

Ceillac. Tuesday 11 August 1992.

Pierre spoke to us of the three methods for the Great Work: the *Voie Humide* (Wet Way), the *Voie Sèche* (Dry Way, faster but dangerous because of possible explosions,) and the *Voie Sacerdotale*, or Priestly Way. The alchemical symbol of man is a triangle with two horizontal lines, dividing it into (1) a base that is the body, (2) a middle section for the spirit and (3) the apex or top section of "salt," the divine soul.

After our trek we took our hosts to dinner at *La Cascade*, overlooking a high waterfall, where we ate some very tasty wild pig.

Pierre Gueymard is an initiate, whatever that means. His adventures are mind-boggling in their irrationality: Did the Aliens heal him of skin cancer? Pierre has been deeply affected by contact with a man, or a group that suggested the expectation of UFOs. The main sighting in Sisteron in 1968, becomes suspect in this light.

Mabillon. Wednesday 12 August 1992.

Gueymard told us a funny anecdote about General Stubbelbine and Rima Laibow, who came to France recently. Pierre didn't tell her much. She rushed through a hypnotic session with him because she had to go out and buy black garter belts: "The General likes it!"

Today we drove to Briançon and took the train back to Paris. Aimé Michel told me how delighted he was to read *Forbidden Science*:

"You've changed my mind," he said, adding: "I thought I'd never be interested in the subject again. You're the only one who followed the proper method, but much hard work is yet to be done. One would have to record all the details, of all the cases, an enormous job... You've turned out a real writer's book, *un livre d'écrivain*. Your description of May 68 is the first sincere account I've read. And your relationship with Janine makes me cry, the marvellous balance you two have found, when I think of all the broken families around us."

He continues with reflections about France, "You ought to read De Tocqueville's book about *Les Abus de l'Ancien Régime;* it describes the France of today to perfection, all the stupid privileges, and the intellectual arrogance. In France revolutions never change anything; they simply shore up those aspects of the old system that are falling apart. In order to succeed in such a system, you have to respect appearances absolutely, an actor playing a comedy. Your mistake, at Shell, was to assume they'd hired you to solve real problems!"

Nantes. Hotel de France. Thursday 13 August 1992.

This afternoon Janine and I took the new TGV to Brittany. At a local bookstore I bought *Les OVNIs et la Tradition*. The author takes me politely to task about *Passport to Magonia*, not being close enough to Tradition. Whose tradition? Ufologists usually attack my thesis because it places too much value on medieval stories...

After the Sangstat Medical board meetings we'll drive on to Brest for a symposium on future pharmacological applications of algae.

Nantes. Hotel de France. Friday 14 August 1992.

A phone message tells us that we have an offer to buy our Victorian house on Hyde Street. Now Janine is sending and receiving complicated legal faxes, counter-offers. I attended an all-day meeting of the Sangstat Board with Professor Jean Dausset, the French Nobel

Fig. 7. Close encounter in Bath County, Kentucky on 25 February 1992
Credit: *Herald-Leader* and witness Mr. William Goldy.

Fig. 8. Janine with Dr. X and Suzanne, Ceillac, August 1992.

Prize winner who discovered the HLA factors that control the immune system's rejection of foreign graft. In the evening we went to the sound and light show at *Puy du Fou* with Philippe Pouletty, Gordon Russell of Sequoia Ventures and Vincent Worms of Paribas.

Le Figaro anticipates the imminent end of Mitterrand's reign. They describe his inside team, including an amusing reference to "a gentleman-farmer with a somewhat faded look, as courteous as he is enigmatic, François de Grossouvre, officially charged with managing the president's hunting domains. In reality, he is the well-informed confidant of a *Président de la République* who never hunts (**48**)."

Brest. Le Quartz. Monday 17 August 1992.

We just had an excellent dinner in a typically French provincial apartment with researcher Renaud Marhic and the group that edits *Phénomèna*, one of the best new magazines in the field.

Renaud told us that Prévost, one of the main protagonists of the fake Cergy-Pontoise abduction, was still in Brittany, suspected of minor offenses. As for Fontaine, it seems he genuinely never knew where he had spent the famous week (**49**).

Our friends believe the Belgian objects are unexplained, but I still suspect they are American platforms being tried out by Nato. As for the case of November 5th, 1990, it could not have been a satellite reentry: Mirage jets took off after the object, and the French High Command suspected an attack (**50**). As for Velasco, he was uninformed about a recent case near Istres where an object was sighted, and counter-measures fooled French interceptors, so it seems that the French military continues to keep important cases away from researchers at CNES, for their own good no doubt.

Brest. Hotel Continental. Tuesday 18 August 1992.

Janine and I went to the Technopole where sailboats were gently rocking in the waves under the gray weather. We saw the *Charles De Gaulle* nuclear carrier under construction. The region is making a big effort to retain its industrial base, centered on shipbuilding.

Today I met with representatives of five small companies, including a group based on Ouessant Island, in touch with Japanese seaweed experts interested in food and cosmetic applications; tonight, we will meet Jean-François Boëdec for an early dinner.

We feel blessed with sweet love--mixed with nostalgia, and hope.

Brest. Hotel Continental. Wednesday 19 August 1992.

Jean-François Boëdec confirms that the French military has sighting files it isn't showing to anybody, including CNES. We discussed the Pontoise case. He recalls seeing some forty military men at the site, in the cabbage field, even before the gendarmes had filled out their report. *Who had called them?* "It was like finding myself suddenly in the middle of a war, the very day after Fontaine's disappearance."

It rained hard as we drove from Landernau to Huelgat, through the *Monts d'Arrée* and the Black Mountains. Quimper was filled with crowds that fled the stormy beaches. Economically, Central Brittany is dying. Many properties are for sale, the price of houses has dropped. English families are eagerly snapping them up.

Saint Malo. Thursday 20 August 1992.

The road was still battered by the storm and the landscape vanished behind a watery veil when we left Brest. It rained hard until Saint-Malo greeted us in a milder mood: in the medieval town center (*Intra Muros*) we found a bookstore on the hill where we could hide when thunder struck again. We read dark Breton legends while the storm rolled by. I feel restless here. Janine is ill at ease too, because this region had a strong place in her mother's life. She regrets paying little attention, as a child, to the stories she heard about places with bitter names like Roscoff and Tregastel. I wanted to buy a Breton flag but Janine doesn't like it, all black and white like a death notice.

Bayeux. Friday 21 August 1992.

The sun finally came out when Annick and Michel came to meet us. They took us to the sculpted rocks of Rothéneuf that Janine recognized from her childhood. They turned out to be much smaller than the gigantic figures she recalled. We drove on to Normandy where things were happy and quiet. This trip leaves me disoriented, however, unsure of my future direction. I would like most of all to curl up with a book, or simply to fall asleep, and let the winds that come from the Atlantic soothe my anguish.

Mabillon. Saturday 22 August 1992.

Janine is so pretty when she sleeps! And me, privileged to be with her, able to stand guard as she rests. Today we're going to Fontainebleau for lunch with the Mesnards, steadfast in their careful documentation, which they publish in *Lumières dans la Nuit*.

United flight to California. Monday 24 August 1992.

Amusingly, Joël and Hélène Mesnard call Alain Boudier *Agent Triple Zéro*, a reference to his boast of secret government contacts. As we sat down for lunch on the lawn behind their house near Fontainebleau a black helicopter flew over, prompting more jokes.

When I called her to say good-bye, my mother told me she loved *Forbidden Science*, which she read until four in the morning. Like Aimé Michel, her first comment was about the fact that Janine and I had stayed together all these years, how rare that was, how precious. Rémy Chauvin, very warm, promised to send me his manuscript on trans-communication to help my research at Spring Hill.

Hyde Street. Monday 31 August 1992.

We have a serious offer for this house, from a Japanese architect. Janine and I are ready to move on, a healthy turning of the page as both of our children are leaving. Fred Beckman has just reached the age of 60 and feels depressed. As his belly becomes increasingly rotund and his hair whiter, his neck becomes shorter and his head stoops more into his shoulders, so that he looks more and more like one of those angry 18th-century composers he likes so much. His wonderful misanthropy and his dark sense of humor are intact.

Fred had gloomy news of Ralph, still entranced by Wendy, his dark-eyed extraterrestrial hybrid paramour. The woman packs two loaded guns and a mean temper. This she-Alien had once been attacked by government agents and one man-in-black, all of whom she promptly gunned down. The fact that none of this actually happened is not a deterrent to the story among ufologists. Fred believes that a certain "consultant" to Ford Aerospace is involved in the charade.

After an ophthalmologist pointed out that Wendy's lenses didn't quite cover the whole eye (after all, she's only a hybrid!) Ralph finally conceded that she was a fake, much to the relief of his wife. Yet he rented a hotel room for her in Berkeley and told researcher Lindemann she made him experience incredible orgasms even when she wasn't there, long blissful spasms. Fred is struck by the parallel I draw between the Wendy episode and Budd Hopkins' alleged abduction case involving "Linda Napolitano" in Manhattan. A private investigator was hired by Hopkins who didn't like his negative findings about that story, so he just ignored them.

Reactions to *Forbidden Science* continue to pour in. After Peter Sturrock, who commented warmly, Ray Fowler has written to me that "without (FS) your books were akin to unconnected key events... it provided me with further insights into the life and behavior of our deceased mutual friend, Allen Hynek."

Hyde Street. Wednesday 2 September 1992.

Brendan O'Regan has passed away. Keith, who just broke the sad news to me, says Brendan died of AIDS.

A tall, distinguished man came to my office today. He looked like a senior executive and said he sold OCR equipment, but he didn't visit any other office in the building and wouldn't leave his card with my secretary. Was that visit related to a letter I recently mailed to *Monsieur de Grossouvre?* Do these FBI guys think everybody is stupid, or crooked? Why don't they just ask direct, honest questions?

Spring Hill. Sunday 6 September 1992.

When we woke up in the tower this morning, surrounded with precious books and the wooden carvings that fill the upper chamber,

Janine remarked again that this room, as happy as it was, always made her think of death - her mother's, mine, her own. Perhaps that is so because the tower was conceived as an interface between this earth level and a higher world of spirit, I told her. But then it should evoke joy, not sadness, she replied.

I recently saw a quote from the Indian *Laws of Manu*: “When the householder observes that his skin is wrinkled, and his hair is turning white, and when he sees the son of his son, it is proper for him to retire to the forest...” But I have not yet seen the son of my son.

When we visited him last summer Janine told Aimé Michel, “You’re in a nice place here.” He replied sardonically: “Oh yes, do you know what's just on the other side of this stone wall? It's the village cemetery. Most convenient, to shorten the final trip!”

Hyde Street. Monday 7 September 1992. (Labor Day)

Maman was enthusiastic over the phone today when she commented on *Forbidden Science*, although it made her cry, “especially the beginning, of course,” she said. But part of the book worried her: “If you publish it in French, you should tone down the things you say about De Gaulle,” she remarked with a smile in her voice. “After all, he was a general; you're only a writer.” I was also pleased to receive a nice letter from Mark Rodeghier, a rare friendly word from CUFOS.

Hyde Street. Sunday 13 September 1992.

We just signed an offer on a spacious condo Janine has found in Pacific Heights, with enough room for an office and library.

At Spring Hill autumn is spreading gold over everything. Last night I took photographs of Saturn with the C-11 and started designing a video system. Then I attempted experiments in trans-communication, following Rémy Chauvin's instructions, with negative results so far.

Hyde Street. Thursday 17 September 1992.

The French TV news show Mitterrand coming out of Cochin hospital after an operation for prostate cancer while traders at the *Bourse* try to cope with the upheaval in European currency markets caused by rate differentials between Germany and the rest of the world. Interest rates are being ramped up at the worst possible moment.

Dan Tolkowsky asked me how I would vote on Europe if I were in France. I told him truthfully that I always supported the idea, but in the present case I was negative for two reasons: first, what is being created in Brussels is a huge, gray bureaucracy composed of individuals nobody knows, second, there has been no word about the real cost of managing all this.

Hyde Street. Friday 18 September 1992.

On the phone with Whitley Strieber yesterday I brought up the curious new abduction scenarios that have recently appeared, with "Linda Napolitano" on the East coast and Wendy on the West coast.

"The problem is that Hopkins has a slippery mind, he believes anything," Whitley said. "The real phenomenon is a moment of epiphany, an effect that lacks logical continuity. We have no words in our human language to describe such constructs, tangible to the senses but important only in terms of mental experience. These beings do go into the physical, in some way. They create odors; they design an appearance of reality."

No medieval demonologist could have described it better.

Hyde Street. Tuesday 22 September 1992.

A new journal called *Syzygy* contains an interesting article on the influence of Cagliostro on modern magical groups. The author, Massimo Introvigne, points out the links between Randolph's Brotherhood of Luxor (**51**), the OTO, and other adepts of the "wet way" of initiation centered on sex rituals that may have begun with the Indian, Iranian, or Gnostic movement. He adds that in Europe such rituals passed from the Gnostics through the Cabalistic currents of the Middle Ages and the Renaissance, and into occult organizations, particularly those of 17th-century Germany.

The methods described by Introvigne take us back to Gueymard's reference to a "Dry Way" and a "Wet Way." In lower magic the practitioner evokes entities such as the Holy Guardian Angel. In modern times these entities have merged with extraterrestrials. In higher magic it is the biological transformation of the practitioner that is at stake: The body of man is believed to have a material base and a "part of light" or spirit that must be liberated.

In the "wet way" or rituals of Osiris the spirit, *pneuma,* is identified with the semen. Magicians supposedly meditate under colored light during ritual sex to create an immortal "body of glory."

Hyde Street. Friday 25 September 1992.

Janine is back from three days in Charleston, where Alain celebrated his 50th birthday. Now it's the last-minute frenzy before we leave for Europe and Israel. We're expecting Carol Ruth Silver with the signed papers for the sale of this house. Dinner with our daughter at *Just Desserts*: The Castro district gets ready for Friday night fun, bars are full of revelers and music; the bookstores are lit up.

Paris. Place Saint Michel. Monday 28 September 1992.

I am on my way to Saint Denis where I will meet Christian Fayard, the president of Siemens France. Paris alternates between sweet, fresh sunshine and rain while we move from heavy slumber and vague awareness of time through the haze of jet lag. Next is Tel Aviv where we will spend a week, returning before Yom Kippur. Fred Adler will meet us in Paris as the circle of formal presentations of our new venture fund to the financial press begins again.

Maman had valiantly organized a dinner at *La Hucherie* last night. Gabriel came over with Jeannine. Our mother gave us her recollections from the opening days of the Second World War: I was 8 months old when we left Pontoise. Gabriel remembers the gloom of the train trip to Villedieu but, oddly enough, he has no recollection of how he came back a few months later. My magistrate father stayed in Pontoise. The French army had blown up the bridge to slow down the Germans, so he was given a pass to take a ferry across the Oise River. He used to dine with the District Attorney, a *Monsieur Lasborde*, in Saint-Ouen l'Aumône. He slept at his house, since our apartment had burned down. The two of them ran what was left of the Court system. Later, when the region was evacuated, the Tribunal closed down and its archives were transferred on a horse-drawn cart to a secret shelter in Vendôme. My father then took his bicycle and rode all the way to Normandy to meet us there.

Discussing all this we ate a simple meal of fish followed by an excellent dessert. But once she got home Maman decided her two sons must have felt insulted not to have more substantial food on their plates, and she wept all night because she had not insisted on a bigger meal, appropriate to the occasion.

Herzliya. Thursday 1 October 1992.

M. De Grossouvre, to whom I spoke briefly two days ago, will be on his way to Morocco when I come back from Israel so I'll miss him, but he told me, "I do want to discuss your works, which interest me..."

We began the trip with breakfast on the Mediterranean shore at the *Dan Accadia*, just North of Tel Aviv. Janine has bought me Tom Robbins' *Skinny Legs and All*, about the silliness of religious fanaticism, Jews and Arabs, Jezebel, and the sexy rites of Astarte.

Herzliya. Friday 2 October 1992.

The laboratories of Zoran in Haifa, which I visited yesterday, make high-power chips for image processing. In the afternoon, along with Gideon Tolkowsky, I went to ART where another team of computer scientists is inventing methods for handwriting recognition for computers that will have no need for keyboards.

Today: leisurely breakfast, then I read Tom Robbins on the deck. A container ship streaks along the horizon. A backhoe builds a marina for wealthy yuppies from Tel Aviv. Last night I visited the offices of Athena Ventures on a residential street.

Dan Tolkowsky kindly took us to Jaffa for a fish dinner on the edge of an ancient pier. One of the world's oldest cities, an Egyptian harbor, later used by Phoenicians, Greeks and Romans, Crusaders and pilgrims, Jaffa is filled with the memories of a hundred wars.

Jerusalem. Later the same day.

We went through the little streets of the Jewish quarter before the shops closed for Sabbath. We bought a small Aladdin lamp for our daughter and had lunch at a tiny stall that served shish kebab; Janine bought some tasty grapes for dessert. In the old Jewish center we saw an ancient cistern, part of a remarkable complex.

The Lot Hotel. Saturday 3 October 1992.

We drove to Qumran today, then on to Masada, and floated in the salty Dead Sea. What were the zealots of Masada and Qumran if not a fundamentalist cult? These cults gave rise to Christianity through the intervention of Saint Paul: Did he misuse their teachings when he offered his own interpretation of Jesus' life?

Night had already fallen when we drove back through the suburbs of Tel Aviv. We admired extraordinary salt formations that might have passed for Lot's petrified wife. The sunset over the Judean desert was magnificent.

Herzliya. Sunday 4 October 1992.

Electronics for Imaging (EFI) went public last Friday at $12.75, three times what we paid for the stock, our investors can be happy.

Over the centuries, men have come to Jerusalem for many reasons, but never, as I did today, to discuss transgenic chickens. I just visited a biotech company that proposes to develop such animals, and heard their plans. Later we spent time at the Hadassa Medical center.

Ben Gurion airport. Tuesday 6 October 1992.

We're waiting to board the plane to Paris after very thorough security checks. Yesterday an El Al cargo plane crashed on takeoff from Amsterdam, so everyone is on edge: there are disturbances in Jerusalem and the Gaza strip. Yom Kippur begins this afternoon.

Yesterday I was able to visit Mercury, Medicano, and especially M-Systems, a new generation of memory based on "flash" technology.

Mabillon. Tuesday 13 October 1992.

More meetings as soon as we landed. Paris is gray, sticky, moody, worried. We explored the flea markets of Alésia and *Porte d'Italie*, came home for coffee and went out again to hear pieces for trumpets and organ at *Saint Julien le Pauvre*.

Yesterday I visited the CEPH biotech center (**52**), under the guidance of Nadine Cohen, a doctor trained in Jerusalem and San Francisco. She gave me a crash course in DNA sequencing.

On the flight to San Francisco. Friday 16 October 1992.

After a busy day of company visits including a trip to Pontoise to see InferOne (**53**), I had a drink with Gabriel Mergui and Professor Daniel Zagury, an expert on AIDS who explained to me the mechanisms of the immune system that are disabled by the HIV virus, which he contributed to characterize.

A heavy malaise is felt in France as the latest American crisis washes over Europe's shores. Banks are thrown out of balance by their unstable real estate portfolios. The French financial community used to be a well-ordered game among gentlemen, a fine *jardin à la Française* with no overt scandals, few questionable deals and fewer surprises. Now personal attacks and public humiliations are frequent.

Spring Hill. Saturday 17 October 1992.

The ranch is dark. This community remains in crisis, decimated by drug addiction. Ufology, too, is in turmoil: Keith Harary, at a symposium on abductions, was horrified at the abuses of hypnosis. He asked: "How can something so bizarre be so depressing?"

Mimi Hynek acknowledges *Forbidden Science* with a nice letter: "Naturally I was absolutely enthralled by it. There are many things you describe that I knew about only partially and was puzzled by, especially since I was some years behind Allen in acceptance of the phenomenon of UFOs, as you know... I hadn't realized the intensity of Allen's alternate hope and discouragement in those years."

Hyde Street. Sunday 25 October 1992.

Fred Beckman tells me Ralph is recovering from his affair with the Wendy hybrid. The black Alien eyes, as I'd tried to tell them, were indeed contact lenses, probably obtained from the *Narcissus* research company that makes "designer eyes" for actors. What is curious is the involvement of a Ford Aerospace consultant. Wendy has multiple personalities and may be under this man's control. Coincidentally, a number of "private investigators" have recently appeared in the UFO field. Fred thinks Wendy is simply a test subject in a government mind control experiment, part of what I call the "undercurrent."

Yesterday we sailed around the Bay with Aryeh Finegold and his staff from Mercury Interactive, one of our most promising firms.

One of my correspondents aptly observes that ufology is turning into a new religion: "Every nascent religion requires relics, even if they are only pious frauds." It also requires martyrs like Jim McDonald, and pilgrimages like Roswell.

Hyde Street. Sunday 1 November 1992.

We went up to visit the new apartment again. With surprise and delight we saw a hummingbird hovering over the balcony as if waiting to welcome us, fifteen floors above the street.

Planning the move, I have disposed of three large crates of letters from readers that would have been excellent raw material for somebody's dissertation on the UFO mystery and society's reaction to it. I can hear future scholars cursing me, but where am I going to find the space for all this? No University has any interest in it.

Yesterday afternoon Janine dressed up as a medieval lady and we went to a Halloween party at Hans and Ana's Van Ness apartment. Afterwards we roamed through the Castro district where the "Clinton girls," a group of gay men in drag, were mocking President Bush. We ended up listening to techno music with our daughter.

Dick D'Amato has returned from Belgium where he met with Colonel De Brouwer, a "very interesting fellow." Dick's conclusion, again, is that the triangular objects are very plain human craft.

San Bruno. Tuesday 3 November 1992.

In the course of a review of a business plan about a new pharmaceutical company I found a need to call Kit for technical advice, after which we got on the subject of abductions, notably Hopkins' Linda Napolitano case in Manhattan. He told me he was getting data from eight people connected with it. "It's highly polarized," he said: "Half of them say it happened, but their descriptions point to delusional syndromes known in the literature. The other half are secret service people or police officers. They find the stories inconsistent. It's a mix of delusion and deception. The abduction as described by Hopkins never happened."

The presidential election results came in as I drove around the streets of Los Angeles tonight, looking for a quiet place for dinner in the balmy fall weather. I heard Perot concede defeat, and then George Bush congratulated Bill Clinton: the Reagan era is over.

Hyde Street. Sunday 8 November 1992.

Kit has faxed over 14 pages of data on delusional paraphrenia that he believes accounts for the Linda case and most abductions. I do not follow Hopkins and Jacobs, but I don't believe things are as simple as Kit assumes. I pointed out to him that the psychiatric material fails to account for the contagious nature of abduction reporting and the fact that even scientists and doctors often undergo a conversion when exposed to these stories.

Kit responded that the professionals who believed the stories all started out with a predisposition: "Your picking up on the contagion aspect is prescient," he added.

Hilary Evans has sent me a thoughtful commentary on *Forbidden Science*. Noting that "One thing which emerges is the abiding 'Frenchness' of your attitude to life, with all the tendency to adopt literary postures, and the relapse into philosophy at the first opportunity," he found the book rich in revelations, but he was struck by "the simple-minded *naïveté* of those early years when it seemed reasonable to take witness reports at face value and when the social forces were unguessed at."

He finds this the saddest part of my Journals, the evidence that every individual has a private hobbyhorse: "Your book provides a perspective within which to evaluate current happenings. I came back from my travels to find awaiting me your package enclosing the documents on the Linda Napolitano case. I dare say it will end up as inconclusive as the Roswell fiasco, the Gulf Breeze fiasco."

Hilary writes that if one person were qualified to get an answer, it would be a scientist, preferably not American; someone "who managed to prevent his involvement blinding him to alternative impossibilities, who could investigate reports of landings seemingly by nuts-and-bolts extraterrestrial spacecraft and still entertain the possibility that their nationality of registration was Magonia..."

He signs, "With kind regards to Janine who lived it all beside you."

Hyde Street. Sunday 15 November 1992.

A meeting has taken place with Scott Jones in Falls Church, to plan a new approach to the President for the release of UFO data. Laurance Rockefeller has given him $250,000 to get things organized when he left the staff of Senator Pell but Scott, concerned with spiritual issues, doesn't know much about actual sightings.

In the afternoon, at the law offices of Sandground Barondess near the Beltway, I met Dick Farley, an investigative journalist and former Cousteau assistant who prepares a briefing paper for what they call "the Rockefeller Initiative." He has been tracking my work.

Hyde Street. Tuesday 17 November 1992.

We spend our last night at Hyde Street amidst memories of friends who visited us here, of Janine's mother, of Allen Hynek and Mimi. We feel weights being lifted from our life as we pack up boxes, throwing out or giving away old gadgets. With the sale of the house our financial burdens are getting lighter.

Last night, in the new apartment we simply call "Hummingbird," we felt we were hovering on an ocean of lights as we looked over the splendor of the Bay.

Falls Church, Virginia. Friday 20 November 1992.

Laurance Rockefeller wishes to meet me along with John Mack to discuss his approach to the Clinton administration, so I am back at the home of Scott and Johnnie Jones on Shady Lane. Scott feels that he may have had an abduction experience as a child: Leo Sprinkle once regressed him to the age of one, when he almost died from pneumonia. Hypnosis did not uncover anything but subsequent *rèverie* caused him to recall a gray being covering his little body with his hand and healing him. He now attends a circle of abductees where another member recalls "meeting him on board."

Over dinner we discussed the uses of remote viewing. Scott has had the same experience with Ed Dames as I did in New Mexico, with an added twist: when the Jeep emerged from the desert at 7 am, they staggered into a coffee shop for breakfast. Two New Mexico highway patrol officers were watching them, and one of them was Richard Doty. Scott thinks it was a coincidence. I certainly don't.

United Flight from New York. Saturday 21 November 1992.

Scott Jones and I were picked up by a limo for the leisurely drive up the Hudson Valley to the family compound near Tarrytown where Laurance Rockefeller was waiting for us, a distinguished man in his mid-70s. He dropped names casually, mentioning his friendship with Melvin Laird, who sits on the *Readers' Digest* Board with Mary Rockefeller.

Professor John Mack, whom I was meeting for the first time, is tall and gangly, in his early 60s. He walks with an uneven gait, one shoulder raised higher than the other. I found him sharp and intense, a classic east coast intellectual with easy access to the media and influential thinkers. He was accompanied by Pam, a smart assistant involved in his hypnotic regressions. All his UFO information comes from Hopkins and Jacobs. He seems to take it for granted that Space Aliens are routinely abducting his patients.

Laurance told us he felt the time was ripe for a major announcement from Washington about the extraterrestrial presence, and he was going to make it happen. George Bush should have made the revelation himself, but Clinton was now in power, he observed.

"Who could help us get the word out?" he asked. "Senator Sam Nunn is supportive; the Truman Agreement is no longer valid..."

In previous conversations Melvin Laird had thrown cold water over Laurance's ideas by reminding him that satellites were often mistaken for UFOs and that NORAD had never found solid data.

Fingering his Countess Mara tie, which he wore over a plain blue shirt, Laurance said it was time to legitimize this research, that the government should state that this was a serious issue. I stressed it would only work if no exaggerated claims were made. "Larry" then spoke of Dr. Detlev W. Bronk, associated with Rockefeller University, who wrote a report on the UFO question. He kept coming back to the idea that a change in atmosphere should be promoted now that the Cold war was over, the military cover-up no longer necessary. I strongly agreed and pointed out that the President would likely delegate the issue to Al Gore, so I volunteered my OTA contacts again as possible links to the new Vice-President, but they insisted to get to Clinton himself (**54**).

When Scott proposed a conference in Washington, to coincide with Disclosure, featuring the Dalai Lama, the Pope, and Billy Graham I thought "Scott is dreaming," although I heard all the right words: "Mobilize the world to understand the phenomena; bring data together; involve major science centers; motivate researchers."

John raised the debate a notch by stating it was our role to "heal the split between science and religion that had arisen in the 17th century" and that the UFO phenomenon could cure this malady. Recognition of it, he said, may be "the next step in the maturation of our species." He has discussed this with Thomas Kuhn, who cautioned against the seductive use of such big words.

Time for lunch was approaching, so we strolled through the estate, admiring the Mexican art on the walls. In the greenhouse Laurance picked up a small jade tree and presented it to Mack.

Along the way I had a private talk with John, who asked if I felt the phenomenon was "ominous." He is puzzled by the cases when his patients would simply go out in the evening and return a couple of hours later, having seen flying saucers. "Why can't you or I have this kind of experience? What is special about them?"

Kit would say they're typical paraphrenics. Who is right?

I asked John just how much he'd used hypnosis in his professional work. To my amazement he answered that he'd only studied it for one week in medical school 25 years ago, hadn't used it in his psychiatric practice, and relearned it from Hopkins (!) to research abductees. When Scott asked him how he could accomodate these studies on top of a busy schedule at Harvard, Mack answered, "Abduction research has blown everything else out of my life."

Lunch was soup, salad and a simple sandwich. When Mary Rockefeller joined us we spoke of the current woes of Russia and the problems of Europe, then we returned to the meeting room where a bright fire was lit. Beautiful French doors with their view on the lawn created an atmosphere conducive to lofty conversation, but we achieved no breakthrough. The Rockefeller jet was waiting at the local airport to take Mack and his assistant back to Boston. John looked every bit like the distracted scientist when he came back five minutes later: he had forgotten to take along the precious jade tree.

The limo drove me to Kennedy after dropping off Scott Jones. If the "Rockefeller Initiative" is just another well-intentioned move by a few idealists, then it will fizzle out. John Mack brings intellectual muscle to the party, combining his intensity with the Rockefeller money and power, the Harvard name, and the media connections. Yet high-level premature exposure could simply scuttle the research.

John Mack, whom I liked and respected at the first contact, made me uneasy because he reminded me of Jim McDonald. Like Jim, he is obsessed with the subject. He met Laurance in 1983 at a disarmament event. That contact must not have led to much, however, because Mr. Rockefeller didn't remember the occasion.

Part Fourteen

HUMMINGBIRD

6

Hummingbird. Sunday 22 November 1992.

In the morning Nob Hill emerges from its delicate darkness, shaking the fog draped around its cornices. Later the soft sunshine comes through, silver clouds race south, blue haze rises over the eastern hills, and eventually the glory of noon takes over.

Our new home is a delight we keep discovering. There are ships at anchor on the Bay, Alcatraz dreams of drifting out to the open sea, faraway Berkeley stretches like a kitten.

This was our first day at Hummingbird. We took it slowly. We spent time opening boxes, sorting out clothes, hanging paintings, assembling bookcases, finding the best place for each little treasure. Now the Transamerica Pyramid is aglow; the majestic city rests.

We're inventing new traditions: evening coffee by the orient window, the better to watch the sun reflected in the skyscrapers that glow pink and orange with blinding flashes of fire in the glass panes of the office towers. The Bay turns deep blue as light gets sucked out of the landscape, shadows lengthen, lights are turned on, neon glows, rows of sodium lamps outline the avenues.

Charles Musès writes about *Forbidden Science*, "You have never forgotten that poetry was always the primary prose." He adds, "You are right about the majority of esotericists. They do not, as you do, wish to combine intelligence, love, and fact. I call them the three H's: Head, Heart, and Hand, plus the all-important fourth: The Harmony between all three."

Hummingbird. Wednesday 25 November 1992.

Fred Beckman wisely suggests that abductees studied under hypnosis should always be asked if they've ever been hypnotized before, and if ordinary human beings appeared on the scene. He is still intrigued by the Wendy case: she once appeared on a TV talk show as a multiple personality patient. Fred recognizes her as the woman who gave him a come-on at a local diner, uncrossing her legs and making eyes at him, then snapping his picture and running away. She recently tried to get Martin Cannon involved in the same way. She may be a recruit of some Federal black program, a pawn in the *undercurrent*. Who are these people? When I came home I held Janine in my arms and told her I was fed up with such silly games. “Let’s go to Spring Hill,” she said, “we'll plant daffodils along the driveway, you'll forget these ugly people.”

Spring Hill. Saturday 28 November 1992.

Catherine and a friend joined us at the ranch for Thanksgiving dinner. I’m reading Evelyn Waugh's *Ordeal of Gilbert Pinfold*, for the second time. There are still clusters of yellow leaves on the trees, frogs in the pool, and a wonderful smell of rotting apples around the observatory. Last night I swung the C-11 towards Mars, but there was too much moisture in the air for good viewing.

The best thing about Spring Hill is that blissful feeling among the redwoods, with leaves underfoot and the rustle of branches and the movements of small animals. Suddenly, clearly, I know there will be plenty of time for the most complex tasks; there will be resources whenever needed. Sounds are hushed, dark branches filter the sun with reverence. We did plant the daffodils.

Hummingbird. Monday 30 November 1992.

I have been listening to taped lectures by a abduction “expert,” a woman who speaks to small groups of believers, hinting about the horrors of the experience. Her subjects cry and whimper as they claim to recall atrocities committed by Aliens who torture them and brand them with impunity. Following the lead of Hopkins and Jacobs, she has found dozens of such victims. The impact of her own obsessions on their imagery is obvious from the leading questions she plants into her interviews. The parallel with the witchcraft era with its forced sadistic “confessions” is becoming clear.

Hummingbird. Thursday 3 December 1992.

In town for an anthropology meeting, Professor Douglass Price-Williams came over to our home last night. Along with him, Keith and Darlene Harary were our first dinner guests at Hummingbird. We touched on many subjects, from shamanism and the study of cults to the development of the UFO mythos in America.

Today I received a letter from a 67-year-old man, Edward A. Dudgeon. A reader of *Revelations*, he exposes the infamous "Philadelphia Experiment" in which a ship was rumored to have vanished in 1943 (**1**): "I was on a destroyer that was in Philadelphia at the same time as the *Eldridge DE 173*. The whole story is a bunch of bunk... We had the same equipment on our ship as the *Eldridge* did. We were with two other destroyers and the *Eldridge* on shakedown in Bermuda and returned to Philadelphia... We had things put on board that were secret at the time as they were all new developments but now would be considered primitive..."

So this is one of the mysterious "sailors who vanished" in the wild tale that UFO books have made legendary. I have just spoken to this gentleman. The ship was made to "disappear"—not from our universe but more prosaically from the sensing devices of German magnetic torpedoes, a process that was secret in 1943. I won't have a chance to meet him until I get back from France where I'll visit the Bertin Company to assess their work on the human genome. (**2**)

Mabillon. Sunday 6 December 1992.

Cold rain glitters over car tops and makes the smooth pavement shine like black leather. I went to *Rue de la Clef* this afternoon for coffee with my mother. My nephew Denis arrived with his wife and their daughter Olga, whose birthday was being celebrated.

Paris. Café Le Départ. Tuesday 8 December 1992.

An engineer from Bertin came over to pick me up this morning for the trip to Evry where we visited the *Généthon*, a remarkable medical center for the deciphering of the human genome where twenty "multiblotter" robots process DNA in search of the nature of genetic diseases. With the talent of Dr. Daniel Cohen, using the money raised from the French public for muscular dystrophy, and four years of hard work by gifted engineers, another step has been taken towards the Holy Grail of modern biology, the mapping of the genome, giving access to a level of knowledge not even dreamt of 20 years ago. Whether we have the wisdom to use it is another question.

It has rained the whole day. The countryside looked like a muddy swamp, big black trees twisted in the grayness like swaying kelp. The factories on the horizon resembled sunken liners.

Mabillon. Thursday 10 December 1992.

Nantes, where I visited the research hospital on behalf of Sangstat Medical, was feeling the first bite of winter. The evening before I left Paris, I was nostalgically walking around the old medieval streets behind the Châtelet when I noticed a tall, elegant silhouette in a cape, a black hood over her head. I gathered up the courage to approach her. It turned out she was simply enjoying the walk home after her daily swim at the public pool on *Rue de Pontoise*.

"You look very mysterious in that cape," I told her, "a figure from another era." She seemed to like the compliment.

After one look at me she must have concluded that I was harmless, because she allowed me to buy her a cup of coffee at a bistro on the boulevard. She threw back the cape, revealing a charming young woman. We walked around the *Marais* near the stronghold of the Templars, invoking a mystical flame that never died.

Hummingbird. Monday 21 December 1992.

Fred Beckman called today. He said Ed Dames was upset because I wouldn't give him my new home phone.

"Come on, Fred," I joked, "Ed Dames is a military remote viewing expert; he ought to be able to locate me psychically anywhere!"

"You want me to tell him that?" he retorted.

"You tell him whatever you want. I don't like all that craziness. Have you heard that the Greys were transponding to Earth through the Face on Mars?" We both burst out laughing. John Mack believes the Greys are good guys. Fred loves the weirdness of it all. I don't.

Hummingbird. Monday 28 December 1992.

We are back from a four-day stay at Spring Hill. Diane LaVey accompanied us. Anton has managed to get another Court hearing set for April, she told us, so the sale of the Black House is not yet effective. His attorneys use every trick to delay execution of the judgment. She recounted these troubles with emotion, but Spring Hill had its healing effect. We walked up to the waterfalls; she leaned happily into the mossy embrace of a grand old tree.

Hummingbird. Friday 1 January 1993.

It takes so little to derail the brain! I came back from the hospital on Wednesday, after an operation on my sinuses (on December 29.) In the recovery room I had a long, nightmarish "bad trip." My brain was wallowing in deep despair about itself, the future, prospects for old age, disease, money worries, and my standing in the community, as if that was something worth caring about.

Hummingbird. Tuesday 5 January 1993.

Keith and Darlene came over last night for a glass of champagne and stayed till two in the morning. Keith complained about the psychic project spending $3M a year on dubious magnetic experiments. Secrecy limits Ed May's progress, poisoning communications.

Reminiscing about the old days at SRI, Keith told us how he once bumped into a well-dressed man who came out of a door under the stairs, which he'd always assumed to be the janitor's closet. Hal confided to him in great secrecy that the door in question led to a classified area, a SCIF (**3**) that extended under the parking lot.

Later the same day.

It is through a message from Perry Petrakis in Aix-en-Provence that I just learned of the death of Aimé Michel.

Hummingbird. Sunday 10 January 1993.

Rémy Chauvin tells me that Aimé died during the night of 27 to 28 December, without pain. He'd commented he'd lived long enough. He simply allowed himself to move on. "He once told me that he'd never understood what he was doing on this planet in the first place. I kept pointing out how respected he was, but he dismissed it all," said Rémy.

Our conversation drifted to the phenomena of transcommunication. Among various experiments with a tape recorder, Rémy tries to contact friends who've recently died, with meager results. He called out to Aimé and only got a few sounds on tape. We went on discussing the Absurdity factor, which Rémy acknowledged as a fundamental parameter. He recognized it in UFO manifestations, a remarkable parallel to the absurdity of psychic phenomena, and reminded me that the lives of mystics were filled with irrational episodes.

"The Church has censored these events, they seem ridiculous! They put away Joseph of Cupertino, forbidding him to see anyone for four years, because the phenomena were so extraordinary. But you'll find the same absurdity in natural evolution."

He gave me one example among many, the reproduction mechanism of the orchid. I recommended to him Theodore Flournoy's old book about *Psychology and Spiritism*, my current bedtime reading. Flournoy lived in an innocent age when he could still hope to see Freud's novel psychological theories converge with a serious study of paranormal human abilities.

Aimé's funeral coincides with the time when I was sinking into the deepest sense of despair I have known. What I want to leave behind, as a tribute to him, is this Journal, because other minds like his will come along. It's essential to describe the facts as we know them, along with the mistakes we keep making. Aimé discovered how transcendence extended to the physical world. He was waiting for the connection while doubting that mere mortals were capable of it.

Through the tears in my eyes I can see San Francisco below. The storm has passed. All is bright: the blue and white sky, the silver Bay. Mankind is waiting for something that never comes, an insight coiled within us, unacceptable to our mediocre brains.

Hummingbird. Thursday 14 January 1993.

Fred and I reminisced over lunch about our departed friend and drank a sad toast to him. He now leans towards the dubious theory that most abductions are staged. He probed me about my impressions when I met the Hills, and their relationship with Dr. Simon. (4)

A letter from Melvin Laird, Nixon's secretary of defense from 1969 to 1973, to Clinton's new Pentagon chief Les Aspin has gone out on behalf of the Rockefeller Initiative. In our latest phone conversation John Mack and I wondered why Laurance always insisted on going "to the top." In science you have to build consensus from the bottom. The issue might become political, in which case all hope of a sane outcome will be lost. Peter Sturrock tells me he won't sign any letter. I agreed but I suggested supporting the Rockefeller Initiative anyway.

Hummingbird. Friday 15 January 1993.

John Mack called today to invite me for dinner at his home on February 10th, when I will be in Boston for the AAAS. He's also inviting Dr. David Pritchard and a Harvard astrophysicist who recently mentioned higher dimensional realities as one of the likely future breakthroughs in science. John and I discussed the wisdom of the Rockefeller strategy. The letter from Melvin Laird to Les Aspin requests to "open the files of the classified aerospace programs."

Hummingbird. Friday 22 January 1993.

On Tuesday I saw Ed May and I was happily surprised to find that Larissa Vilenskaya had joined his project, so we went to lunch together. They just returned from Moscow. People there don't know what's forbidden any more, so they've shown them many curious things, including geo-magnetic effects in psychic performance.

Last night I had dinner with Linda Howe (at the Gatehouse in Palo Alto). She came over with her usual intensity and a briefcase filled with papers, copies of my writings she had annotated, and a fat manuscript for me to review. It covers crop circles, cattle mutilations and abduction reports recalled without hypnosis—prompting Hopkins to dismiss them. "In his perverted logic," she said, "if it's not recalled under hypnosis, an abduction story can't be true!"

One of her observations concerns the crop circles. She said the CIA had descended on the English fields since my conversations with Kit on the subject and hinted Pandolfi may have sent George Winfield along with Rosemary-Ellen Guiley, Robert Irving and Owen Lewis.

"They come straight from Langley," said Linda. "The group also includes Dan T. Smith and a Dr. Schnabel." I can't verify any of it.

Spring Hill. Saturday 23 January 1993.

We drove up last night with Teish, who wanted to get away to work on *Carnival of the Spirit*. The rains of the last three weeks have left the place rich with new creeks along every path and waterfalls in every gulley. Venus is high in the sky, very bright, while Mars rises, blazing in the east. There's a spirit of the place at Spring Hill, a *genius loci*, watching over this land. Most of the time it is stern, gloomy, forbidding; then we feel overwhelmed, cut off from humanity. At other times the spirit is happy, smiling, benevolent, open to us.

Hummingbird. Wednesday 3 February 1993.

A woman I will call "Mathilda," who claims to run a company in Vancouver, has written to me, asking what amount of funding I would need "to facilitate the research mentioned in *Dimensions*?"

"What business are you in?" I asked cautiously.

"I sell environmentally safe technology to Asia; I've been asked to bring technology to Australia. I can raise funds for all that, you see." "Why are you interested in funding my research?" The answer was evasive, "I can't tell you the whole thing over the phone. Back in 1984 five Australians had information but it was suppressed..."

I told her I would follow up with her when I returned from France.

Sheraton New York. Tuesday 9 February 1993.

An exposé of J. Edgar Hoover is being broadcast on public television. It boldly claims that the FBI and the Mafia had a common interest in getting rid of the Kennedys 30 years ago. Gordon Novel, the New Orleans electronics expert involved in Hal's current research, has testified against Hoover's character and his Masonic connections.

I spent the day with Jean-Jacques Chaban-Delmas and my French financial partners from Lyon. Fred Adler was as sharp as ever.

Dr. John Mack has just left word he'll meet me at Cambridge hospital tomorrow. We'll have dinner at his house.

Boston. Thursday 11 February 1993.

John was waiting for me in his office, room 242 on the second floor of the Macht building. There was still snow on the ground.

Mack's office is small and cosy, with an old wooden desk, a closed bookcase with his award-winning book on T. E. Lawrence (*A Prince of Our Dysfunction*), a Tibetan scroll, and several paintings. On the wall is another award recognizing him as past president of the Association for Political Psychiatry. Mack is a courageous activist who has been involved in peace and disarmament.

He spoke about the stress he felt, in part because he shares the abductees' sense of mystery and urgency, and in part because colleagues are critiquing him so vehemently. We went to the Charles Hotel for a drink. He lost his way in the streets of Cambridge in the heat of our discussions. He told me that his wife didn't share his conclusions and that Carl Sagan had attacked him in print in an article for *Parade*. He'd naïvely assumed that his initial burst of publications, together with the television miniseries, would blow the subject open. Now he realizes that nothing has moved in spite of his notoriety. I could have told him this two years ago.

I asked him about the dubious case of Linda Napolitano (alias "Cortile") and found to my surprise that he'd become consumed by this research, to the alarm of people around him: when we got to his house it was obvious that his wife Sally, a warm and well-adjusted brunette who is able to cope with the challenges of academic life and an activist husband, didn't buy the ufological catechism.

Professor David Pritchard, a tall physicist who reminds me of the rugged good sense of Bill Powers, came over with his wife. He was wearing a white shirt, white jacket, and no tie. We were joined by Dr. Rudolph "Rudy" Schild of Harvard, a leading expert on gravitational lenses who confirmed what I had published about the interdimensional theory, even though he didn't buy my UFO arguments. Pritchard showed me the details of an alleged "implant" he's been studying, which only reinforced my skepticism. Kit assures me that most implants are simple material, not mysterious technology.

Pritchard spoke critically about hypnosis and the Linda case, but when Sally dared to suggest some abductees may be delusional, John flew into a sudden rage and put her in place in a severe lecture delivered in an icy tone "to clear the bullshit." This demolition of his wife in front of his guests was in contrast to the congenial atmosphere we had admired in John's grand old house filled with Japanese artefacts and sculptures: the Macks lived in Japan for two years (1959 to 1961) when he was in the Air Force. There was a fire in the fireplace and their big dog Digger ran around, making friends with us, but we remained embarrassed by this outburst.

After dinner Pam Kasey, John's smart assistant, drove me back to the Sheraton. She was eager to know whether I thought that Budd Hopkins was being setup in the Linda case, and whether John might be exposed to attacks designed to discredit him. I told Pam I was surprised to see him embrace Hopkins' and Jacobs' dubious brand of hypnotism. But John has very limited knowledge of hypnosis, contrary to what people assume.

Mabillon. Tuesday 16 February 1993.

As soon as we arrived in Paris we had to struggle with typically French practical problems, like a full day without water and two days without heat because of some complication in the basement.

Over lunch at the *Bon Saint Pourçain* I discussed professor Rocard's interest in parapsychology with publisher Thérèse de Saint-Phalle. She's a personal friend of his son Michel Rocard, former prime minister and presidential hopeful.

The professor never loved him because he suspected him of being the son of Louis Armand, the French economist who was his wife's lover.

A technology that uses a cardiac patient's own tissue to make heart valves has been submitted to us. One of the surgeons showed me how simple it was to make such a valve, over the sink in his kitchen.

Then I spent an hour discussing esoteric matters with expert bookseller Marchiset, who sold me the rare, curious writings of Maria Naglowska, the sex priestess of Montparnasse in the Thirties.

Mabillon. Sunday 20 February 1993.

The cold sky was clear yesterday, so we went to *Rue de la Clef* and took my mother for a walk to Notre-Dame. She was wonderful. She complains that she cannot stand as straight as she once did, and she has to wear old shoes because of pain, yet she was able, at 93, to walk with us all the way. She even plans to start painting again.

Today we drove deep into Berry for lunch at the castle of Ivoy-le-Pré with Rémy Chauvin and his wife.

His current thesis on trans-communication involves the idea of an *égrégore*, something like a psychic ocean of the Dead where souls might be merging.

Mabillon. Tuesday 23 February 1993.

Visits to Thérèse de St-Phalle and Simone Gallimard today highlighted the contrast between these two *grandes dames* of French literature. Thérèse is concerned with Bosnia, the savagery of the Serbs, about which Europe does nothing. Simone Gallimard was as dry as ever, on guard as if I had come to steal her teaspoons. The red room on *rue de Condé* hasn't changed. From the lobby one still has a fine view of the *lieu d'aisance*, the toilet at the end of the corridor; the same books are in the display window as five years ago.

I met again with genetics pioneer Dr. Daniel Cohen yesterday to discuss plans for the financing of a new multiblotter, a DNA sequencer and novel genetic instruments.

Hummingbird. Monday 1 March 1993.

Back in California we learn that a Texas cult worships a fellow named David Koresh who thinks he's Jesus. They've been doing battle with the police and federal agents, killing five of their assailants. Clinton and Janet Reno don't seem to have learned anything from the Peoples' Temple debacle, because we see tanks being unloaded from a huge aircraft.

Don't they understand that these folks believe the end of the world is imminent? Why don't they hire someone who understands cult psychology, like Margaret Singer, before they kill more Americans?

Hummingbird. Sunday 7 March 1993.

On Friday Peter Sturrock and I had a conference call with John Mack. Things don't go as smoothly as Rockefeller had anticipated. Secretary of Defense Les Aspin has answered Melvin Laird's letter with a courteous but short "I will look into the issue when current events are less pressing," or words to that effect. He will "examine the aerospace archives..." But the real stuff may be elsewhere.

Last night at Spring Hill Janine and I tested the new video system to scan the nearly full moon and we spotted Jupiter and three of its satellites, a beautiful sight.

Carl Sagan's article in *Parade magazine* rebutts the notion of Alien abductions. He points out that medieval men and women experienced something similar and that extraterrestrials would have to be scientifically backward to perform absurd biological operations as reported by Hopkins. Sagan borrows both of these arguments from my *Passport to Magonia* written 25 years ago. Ufologists had refused to listen. Now they have no choice but to hear Carl Sagan say the same thing in a much more antagonistic voice than mine.

San Diego. Windham hotel. Thursday 11 March 1993.

Over lunch in Mira Loma with Ed Dudgeon, the former Navy electrician who served on a destroyer commissioned at the same time as the Eldridge, of *Philadelphia Experiment* fame, I learned he was familiar with the classified equipment she carried, counter-measures "making ships invisible" … to German magnetic torpedoes (**5**).

Aviation expert John Andrews met me for dinner. John couldn't account for the Belgian triangles, and he'd never heard of the curious dark green triangle as described by one of my correspondents, who saw it close to the ground (**6**).

Hummingbird. Sunday 14 March 1993.

Last night Janine and I had the pleasure of meeting George Kuchar, a reader of mine and colorful underground filmmaker who teaches Cinema at the Art Institute. George has had experiences with strange lights and an even stranger man in black who claimed to be his cousin and took his photograph. When George checked with his mother he learned he had no such cousin. I have enjoyed George's program, including his brother's classic *Sins of the Fleshapoids* filmed in 1965, followed by *No Such Thing as Gravity* and the 1962 *Creation of the Humanoids*, a favorite of Andy Warhol's.

A magazine has started to publish the declassified text of the *Pentacle Memorandum* (7), leaked through George Knapp.

Hummingbird, Thursday 18 March 1993.

In his book on *Style and Idea*, which Fred Beckman has lent to me, composer Arnold Schoenberg writes, "Man is petty. We do not believe enough in *the whole thing*, in the great thing, but demand irrefutable details. We depend too little upon that capacity which gives us an impression of the object as a totality containing within itself all details in their corresponding relationships. We believe that we understand what is natural; but the miracle is extremely natural, and the natural is extremely miraculous."

Schoenberg adds: "The more exactly we observe, the more enigmatic does the simplest matter become to us. We analyze because we are not satisfied with comprehending nature, effect, and function as a totality and, when we are not able to put together again what we have taken apart, we begin to do injustice to that capacity which gave us the whole together with its spirit, and we lose faith in our finest ability — the ability to receive a total impression." He gives as an example his first hearing of Mahler's Second Symphony, which moved him to extreme excitement. Later he analyzed it critically, only to realize that he could not account for the overall impression the work made on him.

Hyatt Regency Irvine. Tuesday 23 March 1993.

My venture capital work continues to absorb me. We are firming up plans to visit financial firms in Japan and Singapore next month.

Psychotherapist Maralyn Teare shares my unease as we see John Mack follow Hopkins, beating abductees into submission to his ideology with the fervor of Inquisitors forcing witches to confess.

"When Mack and I were with the Dalai Lama in India, it was clear the trip was setup to convince him of the abductionist viewpoint. Mack even played a tape for him of a woman recalling such an agonizing experience. The holy man seemed annoyed. He finally grumbled, 'We've always known there were demons...' "

Hummingbird. Thursday 1 April 1993.

Janine's reaction to the Journal (Volume One), now in final form: "Do you know what the most amazing thing is about all this? It's that you managed not to go crazy!" But it is to her that I owe my sanity, because her love always counted above everything else, stronger than any dream of faraway planets or Alien girls with fake eyes.

Dick Farley speculates that someone is playing with the interface between the human mind and the phenomenon, manipulating reality for nefarious purposes: Was the Linda abduction scenario designed to embarrass UN Secretary Perez de Cuellar?

Hummingbird. Sunday 4 April 1993.

Last night we attended a reception for Silicon Valley venture capitalists at the San Francisco Symphony, followed by an evening of Bach that highlighted the massive new organ at Louise Davies Hall.

When I called John Mack to tell him that Sturrock and I would send separate letters to presidential science adviser John Gibbons he became upset. "That means we're falling apart," he said. "We're not working as a team any more."

7

Tokyo. New Otani Hotel. Friday 9 April 1993.

The wind spreads cherry blossoms around us like snow and the cool, soft weather invites us to explore. I feel intimidated by this metropolis of thirty million people spreading from horizon to horizon, yet the transition from California was surprisingly smooth. Otoguro-San, a financial correspondent of my French partners, received me with great courtesy yesterday in his small conference room in the Akasaka sector while Janine visited the Palace with Olivier.

Two years ago eight people shared these offices, including three managers from *Crédit Agricole*, but the recession means leaner staff and meager business in acquisitions and venture investments. As a result Mr. Otoguro is now alone with one secretary. He took me to a formal restaurant to eat delicate portions of tasty food served in lacquer boxes. It started raining as we walked back through the business district but the clouds had passed by the time we reached our appointment at Yasuda, an insurance company.

Tokyo. Diamond Hotel. Sunday 11 April 1993.

Yesterday, between visits to financial firms I took the subway and went through a maze of nameless streets to the publishing area of the city, the *Jimbocho* sector. Browsing for works on the paranormal was an amusing experience. We found translations of a few UFO books from Vorilhon and Adamski to Hopkins and Brad Steiger.

In the evening we had a fine dinner with Olivier who pointed out the irony of building a traditional Japanese restaurant on the fortieth floor of a skyscraper. The moon, nearly full, was rising all orange, smiling like a weird clown.

Now we have switched hotels. Walking hand in hand through Tokyo in the clean air of spring we found the Diamond, less pretentious, much less expensive: “Only” $200 a night for a simple room with bath. We happily went all over the city again with our son. Cherry blossoms kept falling and the shrine of the emperors was all red and gold. Like tourists we discover floor upon floor of computer games, displays, cameras and camcorders, and the latest generation of everything from robotic toilets to videodisk players with fuzzy logic. Lights and colors are everywhere, providing stimulation for the young crowd. Today we will attend the wedding of Naoko, a charming young woman in my son's new family.

Tokyo. Diamond Hotel. Wednesday 14 April 1993.

The filtered sun blessed the wedding, a blend of elegance, formality, humor, and inspirational addresses by Mitsubishi executives. Olivier was best man and I was recruited to make a speech.

Tokyo is a maze with no street addresses; even my local guide gets confused. When she stopped a cop for directions he had to take off his hat and read the map he had pasted inside, but even then he couldn't locate the building we were looking for. Fortunately we happened to be standing in front of it…

I found Yokohama unforgettable. Otoguro-San took me there on the commuter train that speeds through the metropolis, a landscape where low houses and working-class apartments bearing evidence of grime and hard life soon replace the glamour of central Tokyo. The harbor, site of Mitsubishi Heavy Industries, is a naval construction center with all the charm of the Brest arsenal or the docks at Dunkirk.

The bank where we made our presentation was pure steel and concrete with windowless, mindless offices. But when we walked out under dark clouds I had to admire the seventy-story building of pure beauty towering over us with its angular structures, changing lines at mid-height, and row upon row of windows watching the horizon like the bridge of an aircraft carrier. It must seem easy, from up there, to survey the new universe emerging in China, Vietnam, Indonesia, Malaysia, Korea, Taiwan, Hong Kong...

At the foot of the tower is a four-masted sailing ship used to train officers of the Nippon Navy while a tall, slow Ferris wheel spins vertically, next to the sail-shaped curves of the Intercontinental Hotel.

I am told these developments were products of "The Bubble" that burst three years ago and left the Nippon economy in shambles.

Over drinks at the Intercontinental I watched a thunderstorm sweep over the harbor, low dark clouds erasing the cranes and the bridges and the piers, raising black waves to batter the shoreline, and I was suddenly back into a recent dream of tall unknown towers, high castles, maelstroms at the edge...

I came back to Tokyo Station in the commuter train dashing through canyons of exquisite blinking neon signs among Japanese office workers who dozed off over their newspapers. This journey has a deeper message: I must recapture the vision of higher levels, regain that ability I once had, of reaching beyond human concerns. I know many things, but that knowledge isn't good enough any more.

Singapore. Carlton Hotel. Thursday 15 April 1993.

Ministers of the Group of Seven were arriving under extensive security as we left Tokyo. We flew over the South China Sea in darkness and woke up amidst skyscrapers and banana trees, small churches, mosques, Buddhist temples, and the busiest harbor in Asia.

I had three meetings today, with people who were young, energetic, knowledgeable, well trained, ambitious, and "vibrant." This last word is the favorite term here. Every "vibrant" meeting I attend in Asia deepens my awareness of the opportunities Europe has missed.

At the Raffles City bookstore I even found a copy of *Revelations*.

Singapore. Carlton Hotel. Friday 16 April 1993.

Across a bridge on the dirty, oily Singapore river is the old town where real people live in colorful houses. That part of the city is not "vibrant" at all. The gaps in broken tile roofs have been patched up with corrugated metal. There is mildew over the walls that turn black with humidity. Ferns grow through cracks in the plaster.

The temple of Sri Marianam hoists a weird crowd of gods, goddesses, and sacred cows in various positions of leisure or menace over the decrepit roofs of the old Chinatown. We went in, leaving our shoes in a box on a shelf. Chapels scattered in the yard shelter huge faces of vampiric monsters; others have curtains of delicate silk hiding sexy, well-endowed goddesses, their many arms suggesting simultaneous delights. Monks' cells line the courtyard; men work in the cavernous kitchen; devotees crowd the space in front of the altar where half-naked attendants are beating drums, lighting charcoal, and blowing trumpets to consecrate various implements of the cult.

Farther down the street an Asian market sells everything from dried mushrooms and baskets of seahorses to Casio calculators complete with spreadsheet software. Large decorated fans show ancient god-astronauts battling each other aboard their powerful vimanas. The weather is hot and permanently humid, creating a sense of disorientation and difficult breathing. One can find crocodile meat here, which is supposed to cure asthma, but I didn't try this remedy.

Hummingbird. Monday 19 April 1993.

We are back to the US, a nation caught in the horror of the slaughter at Waco, another abomination in the abuse of power. The extermination of the David Koresh cult, in which law enforcers used gas and armored tanks in an attempt to flush out a handful of befuddled believers in a false Christ, is an atrocious illustration of an advancing illness in American society. Koresh, like Jim Jones, was a self-deluded fool, but his folly doesn't condone the deployment of weapons of war around his refuge, nor does it authorize the Gestapo-like methods of Treasury agents sent by Attorney General Janet Reno and the highest levels of the supposedly enlightened Clinton White House.

It was predictable that Koresh, like Jim Jones, would seek an exit in mass suicide. Defusing the issue by pulling the tanks and the voyeuristic cameras away from Waco would have revealed him as a pitiful, powerless figure. Where could he have gone? There would have been many opportunities to free up his followers once they ran out of food, instead of slaughtering innocent women and children.

Hummingbird. Sunday 25 April 1993.

Winter is long and wet this year. Our Pagan friends suspect researcher Dick Blaisband, a follower of Wilhelm Reich, of upsetting the weather with his cloudbusters. But I am happy in any weather, in love with Janine, and she in love with me.

Scott Jones has kindly sent me a detailed note about a meeting held on April 14th between himself, Laurance Rockefeller, his lawyer and Dr. Jack Gibbons, science adviser to the White House. The meeting lasted only 25 minutes as Gibbons "professed no knowledge of the field. He declared himself an agnostic. Laurance only got his attention when he told him he planned to communicate personally with the President on the subject," Scott added.

Hummingbird. Wednesday 28 April 1993.

Dr. David Pritchard has refused to cosign John Mack's proposed letter to John Gibbons. "I tend to agree with Condon's statement that further study of the phenomenon is unlikely to result in scientific advance," he stated. I am sending my own letter to Scott Jones, with copies to Sturrock, Rockefeller, Pritchard, and Mack, offering my services as a *Friend of the Court* if and when the government seeks to make an overall assessment of the scientific problem:

"In the past I have twice testified at Hearings chaired by Congressman Al Gore, and my position on the reality of UFOs is well known to OTA and the Congressional Research Service, where Dr. Gibbons worked for many years. Therefore I am confident that he will feel free to call upon me if he sees a need to hear my views."

I spent the afternoon at the Dolby laboratories, watching selected film segments in his high-technology theater and listening to his new six-channel digital system, which uses a chip from Zoran, one of our companies. The arrogant venture capitalists in attendance showed their childish side: all they did was to brag about their home stereo system, and how much they had paid for their sub-woofers.

Hummingbird. Thursday 29 April 1993.

Until recently one could argue before the technical community that lack of funding had hampered UFO investigation. This is no longer the case. In the last few years UFO advocates and abduction researchers have had large sums at their disposal: Grants for digs at Roswell, funding by Mr. Bigelow and Prince Hans-Adam for the Roper survey, financing of conferences, the meeting in Cambridge, and current abduction studies, reach well over half a million dollars. This doesn't include monies given to the Fund for UFO Research.

Any scientific panel reviewing the field will have a right to ask what has resulted from such spending. The answer is: very little, and it isn't even accessible in a form that permits independent assessment.

Hummingbird. Sunday 2 May 1993.

A nice surprise: a delightful letter from Lilian, a friend from our Belmont days who has "devoured" *Forbidden Science*:

"It is just the sort of book I was hoping you would publish some day. It is honest, personal, evocative, and fascinating (...) I was surprised and impressed with your honesty. I hope there will be a sequel... I hope you and Janine are well and happy."

Indeed we are. Janine and I delight in our new neighborhood, the restaurants, the bakeries, and the funny shops of Pacific Heights. The sun shines over the city, the wind a soft brush on your hair.

Paris. Mabillon. Tuesday 11 May 1993.

I stopped in New York on the way to France, again visiting Synaptic Pharmaceuticals with Dan Tolkowsky. He still doesn't believe UFOs can be studied scientifically; it challenges the methods of science and its very nature. "That's a good reason to study it," I countered. "There are other examples, after all, like neuro-transmitters..."

We attended the EFI road show on Wall Street, preliminary to the Initial Public Offering. I saw Joe Blades at Ballantine. The sun was shining; the Columbus Street fair was filled with color and song.

Belfort. Hotel Boréal. Saturday 15 May 1993.

Another studious vacation, exploring the eastern part of France where my mother's family had its roots. The landscape is of flat monotonous plains and a tortured gray-white mass of heavy clouds.

At Passavant-la-Rochère, near Plombières, the site is similar to what we'd seen at the older Passavant castle site in Touraine. Only two guard towers remain, atop a wall that overlooks a small river. A glass factory in a property once deeded to "*our noble squire Simon de*

Thyzac" by Charles de Beauvan, sire of Passavant in 1475 is still in existence today, the oldest such establishment in France.

We came back towards Belfort to have lunch in Champagney. All traces of a Passavant castle have disappeared there, but the women at the inn told us there was a hill by that name just beyond the railroad station. Again it was a steep slope overlooking a secluded lake. Next we drove to Baume-les-Dames. This particular hill of Passavant, the third one in the region, was crowned by an old church built over the ruins of the castle, probably with its very stones.

Thérèse de Saint-Phalle urges me to write a personal book that would establish me on the French scene as a "Thinker." As if the French didn't already have too many thinkers... No matter: we fly back to the West Coast this weekend, my work completed. Yesterday I suggested to my partners to raise a second Euro-America fund.

Spring Hill. Saturday 22 May 1993.

Returning to Spring Hill in an explosion of flowers, a rosebush even blocking the doorway. We drove to Laytonville to order another water tank in order to build up a reserve for the summer, then we had a quiet lunch in Willits. A peacock has appeared on the ranch. He looks at us with suspicion as he picks his way gingerly across the courtyard.

I will be able to observe Jupiter in all its glory tonight.

I think back about our trip and I muse about writing a book about European history as seen through the various Passavant generations spanning ten centuries, in France, Germany, Belgium, America…

Hummingbird. Tuesday 25 May 1993.

Today my brother came to see us, on a U.S. vacation with Jeannine. Although they had to rush back to their hotel to join their French tour group for dinner, we did spend a few relaxed hours together.

A journalist who has followed the Ummo affair for years, studying the anonymous letters supposedly sent by Aliens (**8**), now has definite proof that a man named Jordan Peña was the sole author of the hoax that fooled ufologist Antonio Ribera, French physicist Dr. Jean-Pierre Petit, and many others: "In the first period (the 60s and 70s) he typed the reports by himself. During the 80s a lady did it for him. The relationship was sado-masochistic, she being the mistress."

A meeting was held last month at Farriols' home and a letter from Jordan Peña was read, explaining everything, but Ummo adepts refuse to believe Jordan's confession...

Spring Hill. Sunday 30 May 1993.

Rain has started again, heavy white clouds drag their bottoms among the pine trees across the canyon. Janine lit a fire and we did a bit of brush clearing in the rough weather.

Vancouver. Thursday 3 June 1993.

The approach to Vancouver airport discloses a peaceful, green suburban landscape, gray hills, and the gray waters of the Pacific. I flew here to visit an electronics company, an opportunity to cautiously follow-up on my contact with Mathilda, the woman who wrote to me, proposing to "fund my research." The city is attractive and lively. It hasn't suffered from the recession as much as the rest of Canada, enriched as it is by Chinese immigration and Hong Kong money. After my meeting with the executives of the new company I walked around the waterfront and visited its bookstores.

Mathilda met me at the Meridian. She used to be a professional model. She is petite, with black hair, about 40. She works with art galleries but has also been involved with aircraft manufacturers and hi-tech projects in Asia. In the confusion that surrounds this beautiful woman with the enigmatic past, odd questions were posed:

"Why didn't we go back to the moon?" She asked me. "Were we prevented from doing it by extraterrestrials?"

I stayed on guard, keeping thoughts to myself, my answers short.

Vancouver. Friday 4 June 1993.

Mathilda doesn't know much about UFOs; she leaves me puzzled. Why and on whose behalf did she contact me? Clearly, she was tasked to assess what I knew. She has an association with wealthy, unnamed Texans with wide interests; she dangled their support, but I am too old to fall for that: Why don't they just call me? I told nothing to her about my research, or the experiments at Spring Hill.

Hummingbird. Saturday 12 June 1993.

Roger Rémy, who called from Albuquerque, is busy designing a space plane that could reach 10 km/sec (36,000 km/hour) using plasma thrusters and a novel fusion reactor. I raised the UFO question with him and found he no longer thought that the Pentagon had obtained anything tangible through reverse-engineering.

I retain huge respect for Kit but we had a curious phone conversation last Wednesday. We haven't met since our discussion at the Detroit airport over a year ago. We last spoke on the phone on November 3rd following insinuations by a shadowy "Armen Victorian" that Kit, Hal Puthoff, and Pandolfi were keeping too many bizarre secrets.

"A year and a half ago I started a project to check into what you'd told me about Northeastern Brazil," Kit began, "but I'm not finding what I thought I'd find. I've gone after forensic data, but what came back correlates strongly with military operations instead."

"What do you mean?" I jumped, surprised at this introduction.

"At the most important sites you mentioned, namely Belèm, Parnarama, Sobral, and Fortaleza, there were indeed some medical events, but did you know those sites were co-located with aerospace facilities, second only to the French spaceport at Kourou?" (Note)

"All this is close to the places where the medical anomalies occurred. Three of the provinces have a medico-legal institute with good files, just like a County medical examiner's office in the States, so I sent people with a forensic background looking through every medical archive. In the area there are mutilation murders, were you aware of that? People see magical attributes in them. The Indians in the area never go anywhere alone."

"Indians? What Indians?" I thought to myself as I heard this. This made no sense. Most people in Parnarama are not Indians. I've seen

(Note) At the time of Project Prato in Colares (1977) there were no sophisticated aerospace facilities in the area. Even today there is only one major launch facility in the Brazilian Northeast, the Alcantara Launch Center, but it is 500 kilometers away from Belèm, where our investigations were centered.

young girls go off to hunt alone, a rifle on their shoulder, and kids play in the bush all the time. Yet Kit now dismisses all Brazilian sightings as “a colocation of military bases with unusual medical incidents, high-level verbal reporting of deaths and illnesses and attribution of magical causes to normal things.”

In other words, he thinks there may be something a bit strange in all this, such as an environmental agent linked to aerospace activity, but certainly no UFOs. Here we run into intellectual analyses ignoring local conditions, the intense complexity of the cultures and social differences between medical researchers in big city hospitals and their mosquito-bitten colleagues in the bush. There are no aerospace facilities near Parnarama, a hamlet with no paved roads, not even any bridges to cross the river. Kit’s speculations don't begin to explain the *chupas* or the three months of low-flying UFOs recorded by the Intelligence task force at Mosqueiro.

Kit then argued that Pandolfi's interest in crop circles was peripheral to his real work, that he’d never gone to England, and that George Winfield’s trip was irrelevant: “That crowd make all sorts of claims, including that lady crop circle researcher, just because she had lunch with Ron once.”

“Then what do you think the crop circles are?” I insisted.

“Infrared and microwaves combined, as you once showed me. The guys at the Department of Agriculture have chambers where they're begun experiments of their own. I've satisfied myself that it was physically possible to do it, at least with hydrated grain. Some engineers over there in England are having fun.”

So at least we agree on that: he’s come around to the conclusion Velasco and Payan reached a year ago, based on their own lab work.

“What do you think now, about the phenomenon?” I asked Kit.

“My ideas have changed dramatically in the last two years. There's a fascinating system here, which is not military, not government. Pandolfi doesn't have access to it. There may well be actual UFO technology somewhere but I think the business is simple.”

“Is Pandolfi fooling around with the crazies? Why? There's real data he could get if he wanted to,” I insinuated.

Kit's answer surprised me: "*He gets the most real data there is! The chief science adviser to the French project came to see him secretly, the guy who oversees GEPAN.* The British ministry of defense's chief scientist also spent two days with him. He gets all their data."

Still, that CIA office may be only the tip of a very strange iceberg.

"The phenomenon is not ultra-dimensional or psychic," Kit went on. "It's not amenable to traditional analysis but it's not magical either. I haven't really discussed UFOs with Ron. He keeps sending me stuff but we haven't talked about the subject for a year and a half. He's seen the imaging material from spacecraft, all the data. He knows the objects are real and not electrical gremlins. Three years ago the Director appointed him to get all the briefings and follow the subject. He goes back and forth to Brazil. But he doesn't know what the System is, and how it's managed."

There were so many contradictions in that statement that I didn't even try to sort them out. It sounded like a recorded speech.

"You have to understand that mere curiosity has never granted anybody access to a closed system, in the whole history of Intelligence. *The only way to gain access is to provide value. Then you start getting stuff back.* So yes, Ron does spend time going around requesting information about "The System," but he never gets it. He thinks UFOs are just another enigma, as there are so many in our field, rich in superficial technical data, but meaningless. He thinks the private sector only has soft data. He's a physicist. UFOs are not his main job. In fact, he's coming over here tomorrow to talk about non-destructive testing. That's his real expertise, acoustic resonance scattering. UFOs are something fun he does when he's ready to close his office. And he didn't go to England. I know this because he didn't even have a passport until two weeks ago."

"Then how did he get to Brazil? You said..."

"He didn't go to Brazil, he sent people there; he got data from there. And it had nothing to do with UFOs."

What am I supposed to do with all these contradictory claims?

"If he thinks ufologists are crazy," I went on, "why is he becoming so visible in their community? Why does he even talk to them?"

"People beat a path to Ron's door. He gets all sorts of pictures, videotapes. You should see his office! There's a whole culture building up around him. He's a very bright guy; he feels obligated to listen to the crazies, but he knows that what they say makes no sense. He's got a reputation as open-minded. He's got one assistant at CIA who does nothing but screen UFO data."

Kit went on: "Whenever ufologists come to him with data he triggers extensive background investigations, using the resources of his office; he gets their banking records, he sets up telephone taps, I've never seen so many background checks. He wants to know why they're coming. He doesn't think there's a mystery; he just finds recreation in oddities."

That doesn't add up to a picture of someone who is open-minded, I thought, so as I hung up I was even more puzzled than before.

Fortunately a hot summer day fills Polk Street with light and lively people. There's a street fair with food, jewelry and mediocre art, pretty and fun. But the fellow who runs the mailbox service made a point of apologizing to me today. As if to underline Kit's statements, he told me that most of my mail always arrived after everybody else's and was often left in the outside box. The mail usually gets delivered by 9 am, but mine only arrives at noon. Why should my mail be delayed by three hours? Perhaps I've been thinking too much about the government's puppets, but the connection was unavoidable.

Hummingbird. Monday 14 June 1993.

Janine has read about my conversation with Kit. She was incensed. She thinks the Spooks are trying to use me:

"They contradict themselves all the time; don't you see they lie to you? The stuff about Brazil makes no sense. What did they know about it before your book *Confrontations* revealed where the events happened, the places and the names? Why do they rely on people who don't know what to look for? You remember the fishermen you and I spoke to there, and 10,000 photographs from Colares, bought up by unnamed visitors? Why didn't CIA track them down?"

She is right, of course: none of that makes sense. It shows absurd reliance on a system that consistently leads government agencies astray. I have seen it at work at ARPA, and in the SRI psychic project. Janine put down my notes, curled up on the sofa and said, "You're the one who first told them what the crop circles were, remember?"

Would the Agency spend so much time on Brazilian UFOs, if they had real data?

The same goes for Hopkins and Jacobs: They haven't found the real data, or they'd be asking a different set of questions.

Spring Hill. Sunday 20 June 1993.

Last night Jupiter reigned in a moonless field of stars. Janine and I spent the afternoon spreading red rock around the junipers to keep the weeds away. In the library I filed dozens of new sightings. I have the nicest readers in the world, they are my teachers. So I called Linda Howe who remains one of the most dedicated researchers in the field. She's studied recent cattle mutilation cases where the flesh has been cut with high heat, leaving serrated edges to the wounds.

She gave me another view of Pandolfi: "He runs a special project with an interest in crop circles, the paranormal… Rosemary keeps sending faxes to him. She and Dan Smith introduce themselves as "working for the CIA." They ask questions like: How can Christians help in the coming Apocalypse?"

The religious obsession again.

Hummingbird. Monday 21 June 1993.

Fred Beckman has called me with alarming news. He'd been in the hospital with a sub-cortical stroke (an ischemic episode) linked to high blood pressure. He hadn't paid attention to the headaches he suffered a couple of weeks ago. When the stroke hit he was temporarily paralyzed on one side, but he seems to have recovered.

I keep finding more contradictions in Kit's statements. If the study of UFOs is something Pandolfi only does to amuse himself at CIA, what do they talk about when the head of the French UFO research project comes over? Or his British counterpart? Would they spend so much time on Brazilian incidents, sending agents with medical training to study old archives, if they had hard data?

If there is nothing to the UFO question, why does the CIA appoint someone as the central point for UFO information?

But if there's something to it, why appoint someone who sneers at the data?

Beverly Hills. Wednesday 23 June 1993.

Los Angeles is in the midst of a Stage One alert: we drown in hot yellow smog. That didn't stop 10,000 people from coming to the Hilton to learn about what the organizers smartly call the new ICE Age: Information, Communication, and Entertainment. This event, organized by Jonathan Seybold, heralds the disappearance of many dinosaurs. John Sculley, just ousted as CEO of Apple, showed up in a bow tie, gave a demo of the Newton PDA and painted a wide overview of digital futures. He was followed by an IBM type who gave an equally ambitious, yet incompatible picture. Soon we'll have 500 channels of interactive television through a "set-top" box. It promises to "give the citizens more control over their lives," of course, and where have I heard that before?

What kind of control can they have over 500 channels of trivia enforcing pre-structured behaviors, feeding advertisement to hypnotized crowds?

Beverly Hills. Friday 25 June 1993.

Still upset about my conversation with Kit about Brazil, I had to talk to someone who knew the ground truth so I went to see Pamela de Maigret, who lives on Bundy drive in fashionable Brentwood Heights with her husband Hervé. She laughed at my predicament and told us real-life stories over a glass of champagne. The fiancée of my long-term friend Steve Millard joined us for dinner.

Pamela is the real thing, not an occasional tourist like those CIA guys. She recalled her days as manager of a mining project deep in the Amazon, when she stumbled upon German encampments and became entangled with Israeli agents who were chasing neo-Nazis.

"Of course the US government has only vague ideas about what goes on: the mysteries are deep and the cultures complex," she said.

Dinner at Musso & Frank last night with Bob and Margaret Emenegger. They are so worried about the recent riots in Los Angeles that they've installed a big steel gate to protect their home. Bob drives a little red Maserati that must be worth as much as the house. He's found out that Air Force Colonel Robert Friend was the physicist who designed the device used to spray bacteria over San Francisco in the 1940s, before he ran Project Blue Book. The experiments, which probably sent to Heaven a few elderly citizens with weak lungs, were intended to test models of biowarfare…

Hummingbird. Friday 2 July 1993.

Rumors continue to swirl around Gordon Novel, supposedly raising money for Puthoff's Austin lab (**9**). Hal called me because Pandolfi wanted him to get "the most interesting incident" he knew of. Hal told him it was my report from Colares, adding that I had private information I wouldn't publish. Pandolfi is going to Brazil after all—allegedly for an energy test, magnetism affecting car performance.

Hal said he now had three engineers doing tests with a physicist from Northeastern University while preparing a paper for *Phys. Rev.* with our common friend Bernie Haisch (**10**).

Hummingbird. Thursday 8 July 1993.

Dr. Ed May invited me to dinner with Nataliya Lebedeva, a visiting Russian psychic researcher, so I went back to his SAIC office in Menlo Park, now sponsored by the DIA. It is located two floors above Kepler's affluent and fashionable bookstore. Ed's sponsors have trouble with an employee deeply involved in the remote viewing program. On a trip to Moscow she compromised several Russian scientists whose involvement in psi was confidential.

Russell Targ, Peter Sturrock, and Larissa Vilenskaya joined us with Lebedeva who spoke at Stanford on biological effects of ELF and EHF waves. Sadly, Russell told us that his doctors had given him six months to live, which he will dedicate to "exploring his own psychic realities and powers." (**11**)

Over dinner I gave a copy of the Pentacle letter to Sturrock. CUFOS has published a whitewash of the role of the CIA and Battelle Memorial Institute, even attacking my release of this document: someone with influence over CUFOS wants to minimize the impact of the disclosures it contains.

They even suggest I fabricated it!

Spring Hill. Friday 9 July 1993.

Tonight I plan to observe Io's occultation by Jupiter and to continue my private development program.

Spring Hill. Saturday 17 July 1993.

Catherine drove up with us last night. We went swimming and she regaled us with many stories. These long peaceful talks with my daughter delight me. Saturn is not yet visible, but Jupiter shines brightly over the western ridge, and we may have a chance to observe it tonight. There are fishes, frogs and birds everywhere. Little green apples fall into the blue pool with a happy splash. Like a "familiar," the neighbor's mischievious young raccoon follows me everywhere. He looks like a burglar with a mask around his eyes.

Spring Hill. Tuesday 3 August 1993.

A drive to Fort Bragg: purple flowers everywhere. Janine and I admired the seascapes of Jenner, returning through Willits where artist-cowboys were carving huge redwood Grizzlies with chainsaws.

Yesterday Adam Rostoker came over for dinner and spent the night in the guest room. Adam has served as a green beret and a Special Forces fighter with a high-security clearance from NATO, where he served as a courier. A member of the OTO, he now devotes most of his time to Crowley's "magick." We agreed there must be both a real UFO phenomenon and a separate government mind control experiment, an *undercurrent* turning some abductees into victims of post-hypnotic suggestions. But why? And *cui bono?*

Hummingbird. Sunday 15 August 1993.

I've just read with astonishment that the Willamette Pass photograph, one of the few photographic cases I would have taken as genuine, has been exposed as a hoax. **(12)**

My mother tells me that the French are depressed by bad economic conditions and continuing scandals. The suicide of former Prime Minister Pierre Beregovoy has left people stunned.

In San Francisco we're working hard, with a break to hear the Chanticleer group singing Gregorian hymns at Mission Dolores.

Spring Hill. Sunday 22 August 1993.

Janine saw the brown bear just beyond the retaining wall last night, less than ten feet away. We have gotten used to various noises outside our window when the deer come to nibble at the pear tree and taste the grapes, but this was far more dramatic, two huge furry legs and a big shape bent over the arbor. The beast ran off, shattering two boards of the fence as he retreated into the forest.

Last week I met in Menlo Park with a ufologist named Larry Hatch who is compiling a fine catalogue of UFO sightings. I have made little progress on my own files. I'm ashamed of my laziness and complacency when I consider poor Jim McCampbell in bad health, Fred Beckman without a job, financier Jim Pelkey in horrible pain (**13**) and handicapped people who would happily trade places with me.

Hummingbird. Monday 23 August 1993.

We drove to Healdsburg yesterday to interview a witness of the *Winery Frog* case (**14**) who wrote to me after reading *Confrontations*. Mark Uriarte joined us, bringing his collection of UFO photographs. He told us of an episode that took place when he was in the Air Force in Utah: "Another agency" had come and taken over an Air Force helicopter. They painted it black, loaded it into a big transport plane and took off. An officer erased all mention that this helicopter had ever been in the Air Force's inventory, and he did it so well that he was commended. A superior officer explained to Mark it had to do with UFOs but refused to say anything else. Was it used as a decoy? Fred says any sighting after 1980 has to be suspect.

Hummingbird. Wednesday 25 August 1993.

NASA has lost the Mars Observer, much to the dismay of ufologists who hoped the mission would prove the reality of their ludicrous Face on Mars. Over lunch with Ed May at his SAIC lab, I met again with Larissa and Joe McMoneagle. D'Amato has put in only another $500,000 into the project, which won't last long. One of his "discoveries," a Russian general named Savin who supposedly has 200 psychics working for him, turns out to be a man Dr. May met in Moscow. (**15**)

Hummingbird. Sunday 5 September 1993.

We spent last evening in the Mission district with filmmaker George Kuchar and his equally gifted twin brother Mike. An underground video theater on Valencia was showing *In Advance of the Landing* (**16**), a gentle view of the expectation of space visitors. Also on the program were excerpts from contactee Meier's fake UFO movies and a ludicrous, yet oddly touching feature by the Unarius Society where Madame Norman, alias Archangel Uriel, was displayed in her dazzling robes over a background of stars, muscular UCSD students dressed up as Egyptian warriors, and swirling purple galaxies (**17**).

Linda Falorio, a gifted Pittsburgh psychologist, sends me a splendid *Shadow Tarot* for the exploration of the tunnels of the Qlithoth (**18**). Her words resonate with images of caves, worlds within worlds, forbidden passages under the visible universe of the soul.

New York Sheraton. Wednesday 8 September 1993.

The weekend was spent helping our daughter move to a new apartment. I worked on the older Journal with renewed amazement at events I'd pushed out of my mind. I pity those who never review the details of their follies and the thrill of old insights. Then I had dinner with the IRT Board at the Union Club on Park Avenue, "the oldest mens' club in the city," as our chairman is fond of pointing out.

New York Sheraton. Thursday 9 September 1993.

Power breakfast at the Regency with a partner at Oppenheimer. The shareholders meeting of IRT followed. The world, seen from New York, seems easy to grasp.

Janine has already flown off to Paris. When I called her she was having lunch with her sister Annick in our little kitchen that looks at Saint Sulpice. They leave tonight by train through Munich and Vienna, on the way to visit Budapest.

New York. Kennedy airport. Friday 10 September 1993.

Intelligence expert and brilliant writer Michael Levine and his wife Laura Kavanau spent the evening with me. I shared with them my disgust about the silly games played by the government around the study of UFOs, the fake "revelations," false leaks and CIA puppets.

Michael cautioned me to stay away and reminded me that those who ran the Intelligence services of the world have had no controls placed on them for decades and therefore behave like wild animals.

He once exposed corruption throughout the IRS and was rebuffed for it by politicians who didn't want to touch the mess. Another time the CIA freed up the drug lords he'd just arrested in Colombia, and put them in charge of the country.

Mabillon. Saturday 11 September 1993.

The plane landed in Paris on schedule. The mail had brought a historical monograph about the village of Passavant near Baumes-les-Dames, an excuse for a surprise visit to my mother. On the way I bought a *demie-baguette* at a bakery near the *Arènes*. I didn't know the new door code, but she saw me from her window and rushed downstairs without using the new elevator "because it is too slow."

In spite of the economic crisis Paris is in a naughty mood tonight. People congregate in cafés where loud music is playing, they rush into dark clubs or argue at street corners.

Mabillon. Sunday 12 September 1993.

Joël Mesnard and Guérin remain captivated by saucer crashes and dead humanoids, an obsession that reminds me of my limo driver in New Jersey, convinced that the government kills the space creatures who come innocently here, from a world that has no sin, no poverty, no war. This concept has acquired the force of a religious dogma.

Students are back in force all over the Latin Quarter, ready for another year at the Sorbonne. On the sidewalks where textbooks are sold and bought in the mean, cold wind I forced my way through their boisterous ranks. In body and soul I still love Paris, but this is no longer where new thoughts are born. A lot of knowledge sits here on library shelves, but it is not operational knowledge of the kind I see and touch every day in Silicon Valley.

George Kuchar's movies have been selected for a show at the Pompidou Museum that I visited before going back to *Rue de la Clef* for the 12th birthday of my nephew Adrien.

Mabillon. Friday 17 September 1993.

The French economy is catching another cold. Peugeot, Air France and Bull all cut thousands of jobs yesterday in what they euphemistically called their "social plans." Yet France has a lot to offer that is unique and brilliant. Yesterday I was in Nantes again with the board of Sangstat. We argued about the protocol for our medical trials, to be conducted on kidney transplant patients. Dr. Dausset who, at 77, carries the authority of his Nobel Prize in medicine, spoke about the proper use of skin grafts.

Later, as we walked over to a restaurant along the uneven streets of the old city, he leaned on me to steady his step and I had a chance to ask him about details of the procedure. He rolled up his left sleeve to show me a series of paler spots on his forearm:

"How do you think we learned so much in such a short time about HLA factors and the immune system?" he queried.

Janine calls me from Vienna, delighted with the city's beauty. She comes back tomorrow, and we'll travel together to Provence to resume our investigation of the Dr. X case (**19**).

Sisteron. Hotel Tivoli. Thursday 23 September 1993.

A storm fired up and cracked all night over the awesome rock of Sisteron. Torrents of rain washed up the whole region. The previous two days, however, had been warm and pleasant, with filtered sun and fine views of the Durance Valley.

We celebrated the equinox with a memorable trip to the probable site of ancient Theopolis, a ghost city that my friend Roger Corréard has located near the rock of "Dromon" along the old road of Roman Prefect Dardanus through the narrow passage of *Pierre Ecrite* that relates his exploits. From an ancient chapel that hides a crypt of Mithra one can see the hills of St. Géniez. Even more impressive is the evidence of sizeable ancient ruins in an area that hardly feeds a few shepherds today.

Roger Corréard, a 63-year old erudite ladies' man, keeper of mysteries, and self-appointed Guardian of Forgotten Secrets, took us along steep slopes to another Roman *Via* that archaeologists have neglected to investigate.

A former French sailor, Corréard delights in bringing this ancient landscape and its subtle energies back to life.

It rained all day, a soft and quiet rain that put a silvery glow over the Citadelle and puffs of white above the Thor, where Pierre Gueymard's wife Eliane still lives in the house where her husband, "Doctor X," saw his double disk and met a mysterious contact. I called her using the phone number Pierre had given me some 15 years ago. This is a happy country where such things endure: the number was still good, although Eliane now lives with another man. Delighted to hear we were in town, she invited us to dinner.

"The good thing about all these divorces," remarked Janine "is that we get to double up the number of our friends!"

Sisteron. Friday 24 September 1993.

Janine bought a bottle of wine for Eliane. The rain finally stopped, leaving the creeks full in their banks and the roads muddy. We had a quiet lunch in Forcalquier, where all the shops were shuttered between noon and 3 pm, as if the current economic crisis that sweeps Europe could pass unnoticed in this sleepy town. There is talk of closing down the observatory whose big silver domes shine above the woods.

Avignon. Saturday 25 September 1993.

We spent a long evening with Eliane Gueymard in the famous house high above the Durance. I remembered her well, a vivacious and pleasant woman, an energetic little blonde with hazelnut eyes who welcomed us warmly. She was shocked to hear of Aimé's death.

I felt something odd in the house, the same sense of living outside time we experience at Spring Hill. We went to the place where a strange man allegedly appeared to Pierre Gueymard and caused him to be "teleported" to Paris. Eliane only confirmed the events as far as she experienced them: he did leave his car but never came home to meet his friends, Jacques Dragon and his wife. She made up excuses for him. He called later, saying "I don't have time to explain, I'm in Paris right now; tell our friends I've had a problem with the car..."

She recalls the time when Aimé and his wife spent the evening with them. Pierre suddenly announced "*They* were there!" Aimé rushed outside but saw nothing. In the morning he announced, "I know how to get the proof..." as he walked up towards the beehives, only to stop halfway up the hill and return crestfallen: "This never happened to me before, I've forgotten what I was going to check out ..."

After this episode Aimé gave up. He told Gueymard, "These events were meant for you, nobody else can understand them."

The parallel between the Dr. X case and Whitley Streiber is striking: "Presences" in the house, no confirmation by the wife, strange electrical phenomena, and no proof beyond the skin mark.

Eliane mentioned her own researches in the area. A shepherd knew where to find Roman artifacts, ancient oil lamps. Eliane gave us one of the charming sculptures and a lampshade covered with flowers.

Mabillon. Wednesday 29 September 1993.

Before returning we had a brief meeting with Vincent Gueymard, son of Dr. X, who now works as a technician. The mysterious triangular skin mark doesn't reappear any more.

We have reached a stage in life when many of our friends are in their mid-50s to mid-60s and are already retired. Some did it by choice, like Annick and her husband; others by following the rules, like my brother, or by an accident of life, like Eliane's new companion: divorce left them without the energy to fight a daily professional routine. Others, like Fred Beckman, are simply too bitter or proud to restart.

What strikes me is the vacuum in these people's world. They are still young, they should be able to go on.

"L'obligation de se tenir soi-même compagnie est une épreuve à laquelle nombre de cerveaux ne résistent pas," wrote French psychiatric pioneer Gatian de Clérambault,"The obligation of keeping company to oneself is a test many brains do not survive."

Mabillon. Friday 1 October 1993.

This morning I joined Fred Adler at the *Plaza Athénée*. He was dressed for the weather in a gray raincoat and a hat that made him look like Satan in person with his fine evil features, his beak-like nose and piercing, greedy eyes. He showed no sign of jet lag as he reviewed his older European fund before skeptical investors who'd lost money in his ventures. He went on to analyze the state of the financial world, prospects for novel technologies and the impact of Clinton reforms.

When he was done one of the investors said, "Mr. Adler, all of us here are impressed with your grasp of the issues. But we would like to know when we're going to get our money back."

To which Adler answered drily that the performance of a venture fund was determined by its date of inception (as evidenced, he added, turning to me, by the success of our newer fund) and that as a professional "he never cried when investments went down or smiled when they did well." He added that, with patience, the investors might still end up making money. They didn't believe him. (Note)

Now it's raining again in Paris, winter is at the door. We're packing our suitcases for the return trip to California tomorrow.

Hummingbird. Sunday 3 October 1993.

My greatest treasure: your hand in mine, as we fly across the ocean, as we walk in the streets of Paris, or as we sleep in California.

Home again: we woke up early, turned on the news, and we were riveted to scenes of riots in the Moscow evening. Yeltsin's tanks

---

Note: Under Fred Adler's guidance I successfully helped turn around three of the five remaining companies: We made money, and the skeptical French investors lost theirs.

converge on the city. I can imagine the pain of the Russian people, when I recall my brief stay three years ago. I was fortunate to go there just as the régime was allowing some openness and before the disintegration it triggered had engulfed the social system. Profiteers were already taking control while teachers and scientists sank into poverty; hungry old people now lose their dignity by begging in the streets while mafia bosses and oligarchs buy Rolls-Royces. I feel like the village idiot in *Boris Godunov*, crying of impending chaos.

Hummingbird. Wednesday 6 October 1993.

Lunch with Fred Beckman. We discussed the continuing wave of UFOs over nearby Clear Lake and the abduction enigma: is there a backdoor to the subconscious? Has someone found a way to influence minds, to project hallucinatory experiences? Is that why the CIA encourages its puppets to turn up the heat of paranoia in an already-bizarre field? Have they secretly restarted MK-Ultra?

Roger Rémy, who called from Albuquerque, has been involved in high-technology briefings at Edwards, in particular at the Philips Lab hidden in the mountains in the eastern part of the base, like a monastery. "We say our prayers every morning, and we have visions every evening," one scientist told him **(20)**.

The Air Force is interested in his research on RF plasma confinement, including its application to antimatter-matter interaction for propulsion beyond the solar system. Roger works with Jack Schmidt, eager to get the US to return to the moon to mine Helium III before the Russians can do it in alliance with Japan.

Spring Hill. Saturday 16 October 1993.

There's a sense of the closing of a cycle in Silicon Valley. Harvey Lehtman, who worked with me at SRI on Doug Engelbart's team, told me that McDonnell-Douglas, when they bought Tymnet, had acquired both our old software and Doug himself. When they let him go, Stanford had him for a while on condition that after two years he would become affiliated with one of the departments; typically, he found himself unable to work with anyone. He could have embraced the Internet communities that his vision had anticipated, but he won't recognize his own children.

He keeps insisting that "it's all wrong."

Doug's personal life reflects his career.

After the fire that practically destroyed his Atherton home, he argued bitterly with the contractor. A long lawsuit followed, during which he kept living in a house that was mostly a pile of ashes and burnt timber.

Today, after lunch with Paul Baran, I was shocked to hear an obituary of astronomer Karl Henize on the radio. He died at 67 on an expedition to Mount Everest, of sudden respiratory failure.

He was carrying a cosmic ray experiment to 21,000 feet. His wife gave a moving appraisal of his life that made me cry.

Hummingbird. Sunday 17 October 1993.

A thoughtful letter from Michael Levine:

"Whether UFOs portend a new religion, a universe in which we are holograms in some maniac's computer game, or the existence of parallel dimensions, from the point of view of investigating the government's role in the phenomenon it doesn't really matter. What does matter is that the phenomenon is real and that it has a powerful, mind-altering, controlling effect on us walking-around humans, and that is the kind of power that no organized government on the face of this very paranoid earth could resist using …"

He goes on to provide possible questions behind the CIA's puppet show that is harassing ufologists:

"What are the psychological and physiological effects? Do percipients become more vulnerable to suggestion? *What can they be made to believe?* To what extent could they be manipulated? Can sightings be associated with religion in a way that would control a population's propensity for war?

"There are many such questions the intelligence services would want answered about the possible use of paranormal phenomena as both a weapon and a tool for control..."

He concludes:

"It's a process that by necessity involves the creation or fabrication of ufological experiences of all types..."

Hummingbird. Sunday 24 October 1993.

On Wednesday night I went to Hollywood for the *Vicki Show* with Scotty (James Doohan), other *Star Trek* actors, and two abductees.

Now Gerald Askevold writes with sad news about our friend Thad Wilson, diagnosed with brain tumors while Keith Harary tells me that Jim Salyer, the DIA man who was the eyes and ears of Washington at the SRI psychic project, is dying of intestinal cancer.

Doug Engelbart attended our Silicon Valley gathering last night, somewhat emaciated, looking more than ever like an old bird with an aquiline beak. Bill English, creator of the first mouse, who now works for 3DO, was there too, as well as my former colleagues Jake Feinler and Charles Irby. Many attendees were between jobs, or working as consultants with troubled companies like Apple.

Hummingbird. Saturday 30 October 1993.

We just attended a dinner of the Santa Fe Institute, where a boring academic gave a very bad overview of Complexity Theory.

One of our companies, Mercury Interactive, went public at 13 dollars a share yesterday, closing at $18.50. That means that the $900,000 I invested on behalf of our Fund have now turned into significant gains. Coming after the success of *Electronics for Imaging* this means we are assured of returning to our investors far more than their initial funding. We are creating new value as we create new jobs. The money we earn is not money we are taking from anybody. The fund generates new opportunities. Why is it so hard for Europeans to understand this?

Hummingbird. Sunday 31 October 1993.

We had a Mexican Halloween dinner with George Kuchar. I went up to his apartment dressed as a white unicorn, sending his poor black cat into a frenzy of terror. "That cat never gets out," said George in mock apology, "a big rush of adrenaline is good for her."

He showed us a funny little film about extraterrestrials called *Orbits of Fear* and a couple of short subjects from the Art Institute, where he teaches cinema. I presented him with a robot movie. There were vampires everywhere. Formidable nuns in various states of undress spilled out of every bar, mustaches twitching with excitement.

Hummingbird. Tuesday 2 November 1993.

At a biotechnology meeting today I heard Dr. James Watson, co-discoverer of the Double Helix of DNA, urging the select audience of scientists: "We should not simply look good but do good, even if we have to say things people don't want to hear" and he urged us "never to accept mediocre research," a lesson we would do well to apply to the paranormal field.

Hummingbird. Thursday 4 November 1993.

Yesterday I had lunch with Dr. Udi Shapiro of the Weissmann Institute. We visited the e-mail conference in Santa Clara together.

In his latest newsletter (**21**) skeptic Philip Klass confirms that Dr. John Gibbons, Clinton's science advisor, did ask the CIA for a background report on UFOs. What he received instead was a 10-page summary prepared by Bruce Maccabee: Roland (Ron) Pandolfi, "a physicist in the Directorate of Science and Technology," had passed on the request. Klass makes the fair point that if the government had really recovered a saucer at Roswell the Science Advisor would know about it without having to be told by a consultant.

Spring Hill. Saturday 6 November 1993.

A call came this morning from Dr. Michael Chevtchenko who was in Boston for a conference. He told me that his translation of *Dimensions* would be published in Moscow early next year.

Janine and I had dinner with Dan and Miriam Tolkowsky at *La Gare*, then we drove up North in the dead of the night. Spring Hill has turned to gold in our absence, fallen leaves everywhere. Tonight I plan to point the C-11 towards Draco, and hunt for comet Mueller.

Occult intrigue: I just read of new troubles at Amorc, the U.S.-based Rosicrucian order. After the death of Ralph M. Lewis in 1987 and his replacement by Gary Stewart, the latter was accused of entrusting their monographs to a man linked to Reverend Moon. Stewart was replaced by the son of French Grand-Master Raymond Bernard.

Pittsburgh. Friday 12 November 1993.

Pittsburgh was nice when I arrived on a "due diligence" trip for Accuray Systems, a robotic surgery company I plan to support if I can verify their technology. I had dinner with Linda Falorio and her companion. Linda is a powerful visionary, a daring soul exploring what she calls "the psychic tunnels underneath reality," the forbidden paths of the Qlithoth that "rule the darkness of the soul." At age five she saw ten tall beings bending over her bed. They were not especially scary, she told me. She hasn't seen them since.

Today I met with a neurosurgeon at Shadyside hospital. Between two brain operations, still dressed in operating room greens, he explained to me his plans to test the oncology robot developed by Accuray.

Hummingbird. Friday 26 November 1993.

Mike Levine and Laura came over for lunch today. Janine had prepared a simple feast of delicate shrimp, crisp chicken *crèpes* with rice, and hazelnut cream with chocolate biscuits that melted in the mouth. Mike told us why he didn't think the government knew much about UFOs, *even if they have recovered some hardware*.

"You can't imagine what idiots these people are, even at the top of the big agencies," he told us. "I've worked with the CIA; I've been undercover with them in dozens of places. It's all politics. Big secrets are being entrusted to unreliable fools. They haven't got a clue what the phenomenon is. They're just exploiting it."

Mike is a big, powerful man with great warmth and presence. Laura is sharp, gifted, and proud of her genius father who was instrumental in sending humans to the moon. But Mike is burning out on the lecture circuit. Telling people the truth about the drug war is nearly impossible, just like fighting for recognition of the paranormal. The public demands to be fed dreams and fairy tales.

"The U.S. has lost the Constitution; our legal government has been taken away from us, yet nobody wants to hear it. People go on as if nothing had happened. They dismiss me as another conspiracy buff."

Mike has reached the same conclusion I have, that some recent UFO incidents were staged by special effects.

La Jolla. Thursday 2 December 1993.

Janine and I finally met writer Maurice Chatelain. He lives in a nice green house overlooking Mission Bay in Northern San Diego with his son Thierry, an artist. Maurice has survived a stroke and prostate cancer. He told us he'd started publishing his research in 1975 after leaving NASA when Apollo was over. He still corresponds with Jimmy Guieu and with Lapierre, a man who works in Marseille and feels he's in contact with beings he amusingly calls *Les Voisins du Dessus*, the Upstairs Neighbors.

Hummingbird. Sunday 5 December 1993.

A pall of desolation and grief hangs over the Bay Area today. The body of little Polly Klass, a 12-year old girl kidnapped from her Petaluma bedroom two months ago, has just been dug up near the innocent town of Cloverdale.

Driving back from Spring Hill this afternoon we were shocked to see media trucks with satellite dishes along with police vans near a field that bordered the highway, a piece of land cordoned off by yellow tape. The scene was chilling.

On Monday I got a friendly call from Tracy Tormé, who had attended a "confidential UFO meeting" at Crestone, organized by Tom Adams and a few ufologists.

I had been invited but declined. Much of the time was taken up by arguments with Dr. Stephen Greer who crashed the party, bringing a group of women who claimed they had made five UFO sightings along the way.

The Aliens had even entered Greer's cabin the previous night!

"I've been allowed to remote-view inside the saucers," he said.

Dr. Greer is an emergency room physician in a small Southern town; he reportedly charges people $50 a head to go up a hill and watch UFOs. His group, C-SETI, claims thousands of members.

"Now you understand why Vallee won't come to UFO meetings," Tracy told the group, "they always degenerate into a circus."

Santa Barbara. Monday 13 December 1993.

In San Diego on Wednesday I had a pleasant breakfast with Peter Banks, one of the four engineering Deans who are part of the Advisory board I've assembled for IRT. He's a member of the Jasons, working on global warming and on "classified things having to do with space." Freeman Dyson is one of them.

"If you ever look into UFOs, I'll be happy to brief them," I said.

"We did discuss it one year," he replied. "Our conclusion was that there wasn't any solid data that could be used to justify a study…"

Today I attended the Autogenics Board meeting, held at the magnificent Biltmore hotel, built in Spanish style, framing the Pacific with its stone arches. Afterwards I had coffee with Maralyn, delightful and smart as usual. She unfairly described the Society for Scientific Exploration (SSE) as "a sad group of gray, tired men."

Hummingbird. Friday 24 December 1993.

The driveway to the ranch is covered with frost while a dusting of snow adorns the mountains of Yolla Bolly to the North. The library feels cold and lonely. We walked the six miles to town in the crisp, fine winter air, discovering streams and ponds along the way. Our little world is in order: Olivier and his wife are spending Christmas in Bayeux while Catherine is with us tonight. Teish came over, dressed in magnificent leopard robes, slim and trim, full of stories. We discussed her manuscript of *Carnival of the Spirit*.

Hummingbird. Monday 3 January 1994.

In the coming year my fund will finance Udi Shapiro, who leaves the Weissmannn institute this week to launch a "virtual meeting" company called *Ubique* on the Internet. But there is so much turmoil, horror and butchery in the world that I am ashamed of our happiness: Aimé Michel died a year ago, and even our walk through the crisp, quiet forest yesterday was tinged with a sense of irreparable loss, the inability to retain life itself as it flows through one's hands.

Today, over lunch in San Mateo with Jim McCampbell we discussed his interest in sacred sites and energy research. Jim recalls meeting with Prince Hans-Adam and telling him he should contact Dr. Ishofon and Hal Puthoff to learn about their physics experiments. Soon afterwards George Hathaway, a consultant for the Prince, did obtain enough information from Ishofon to duplicate his gravity tests, and Puthoff got money to continue the work.

Jim revealed that Bob Wood never got anywhere with the McDonnell-Douglas secret study, closed down in the early seventies. The project did hire private investigators to profile witnesses. The files are still in St. Louis:

"The CIA has been gathering all that data, and it's still doing it, using the infiltrated UFO groups as channels," he added.

He doesn't believe the government has answers in spite of all the secret files, illegal informers, and classified shenanigans.

Hummingbird. Tuesday 4 January 1994.

Kit called me today from GM Labs in Michigan. We exchanged good wishes and talked about the soap opera of ufology: "The topic has taken a further psychotic turn," he said. "There's been a change, even within the government. I've developed a model of the contagious nature of this craziness."

"It reminds me of what we saw in the Sixties and Seventies with LSD," I said, "mythology oozing out of secret government projects, first infecting government people, and later the general population."

He disagreed: "That's not a good model, because the appeal of LSD was highly selective; it touched only a subset of personalities, while the UFO ideology spreads much more like a virus that infects everybody. We've got a fascinating paradox here: On one side, I'm more convinced than ever that there is a real research project that has to do with something as physically real as coffee cups: a small, very focused, very secret investigation run by real scientists--but I still can't find it. On the other hand, there's this whole fabricated world..."

"It's a virtual reality construct," I volunteered.

"Exactly. My model of it assumes a slow cerebral disease, a virus of the nervous system. It affects one's ability to think."

Michael Levine had warned me about exactly that.

Hummingbird. Friday 7 January 1994.

The world of technology has caught up with the vision we launched twenty years ago when I founded *InfoMedia*: Even the *New Yorker* now features articles explaining e-mail or hyping computer communications. The Weissmannn Institute is busy trying to patent a form of collaboration software my team had already developed in the public domain in 1973. At one level I feel elated because it turns out we were right, so right! At another level I see imminent human obsolescence, a world about to be shattered by digital technology.

I believe I may have about 15 years of active development ahead of me, time I can use to help research along, even if events and gossips, rumors and bizarre relationships continue to churn up the evil cauldron ufology has become. I was mistaken in associating this delusionary process with marginal elements of society. In the last three years I have met powerful people caught up in what can only be described as a gross deception, ignoring every rational attempt to deal with the facts. Nor is the new ideology as innocent or amusing as many observers think: someone who signs simply "a friend" has faxed over to me stunning information shattering the Bob Lazar fairy tale. My anonymous correspondent is terrified of the criminal connections, a woman's death, events that were never solved.

The reality of an *undercurrent*, actively driven from Washington, is becoming increasingly obvious. The enigmatic Dan T. Smith is setting up meetings all over the Bay Area, again claiming direction from Pandolfi. He dangles money and rumors, arranging luncheons with people, taking their photographs, taping conversations. He claims that Robert Frosh (former NASA boss, now at GM) ran a secret UFO study at the Johnson Spacecraft Center in the mid-1970s along with Kit, using microwaves to study their effect on human behavior.

Spring Hill. Saturday 29 January 1994.

Yesterday I had breakfast with Keith and his friend Steve Leibholz, a Philadelphia scientist who used to serve on the review board of the

SRI parapsychology project. Leibholz told Keith that the UFO subject was taboo in "serious" government circles.

We had a happy visit by Annick and Michel, celebrating Janine's birthday with us in the City, accompanied by their Norman friends.

Hummingbird. Friday 4 February 1994.

Kit urges me to meet Dan Smith: why is he pushing me into this mess? Should I mention that Smith spreads the rumor that Kit was involved in MK-Ultra and "isn't somebody on whom you should turn your back?" Those games are too subtle for me.

Today Laurance Rockefeller and Scott Jones finally briefed the President's scientific adviser, Dr. Jack Gibbons, about UFOs. Rockefeller is being introduced at the White House by a friend of Hillary, but Gibbons hopes there will *never* be an official request.

A friend, a media analyst, recalls that General Stubbelbine used to be the military link to Willis Harman's project at SRI, in the days when John Alexander and others were dreaming of soldier-monks and the First Earth Battalion:

"It all goes back to those days, Dr. Vallee, to Uri Geller and the Nine, and the contact with Hoova..."

My correspondent thinks there's a crazy plan to spread a belief in extraterrestrials among the American public. He uploaded this serious concern before Phil Lader, Clinton's Deputy Chief of Staff.

Hummingbird. Friday 11 February 1994.

On Tuesday night Janine and I went to a concert given by the Symphony orchestra of Russia: they played Shostakovich's Fifth and Tchaikovsky's piano concerto. Yevgeni Svetlanov was conducting. There were three enthusiastic encores.

Yesterday I visited Rosicrucian Park, taking along a copy of *Forbidden Science* as a gift to their library. I spoke to Grand Master Kristie Knudson who called me "Frater," apologized for being busy, and delegated an instructor to take me through the temple.

The large Amorc facility in San Jose is a beautiful structure. I find something touching in these buildings from the 1930s that were made to look like Egyptian temples, now sitting incongruously in the middle of a Silicon Valley swarming with semiconductor fabs.

Dan T. Smith phoned my office this morning, telling my assistant he was referred to me by "his two good friends Fred Beckman and Kit Green."

I didn't return the call, but I have written to Dr. Jack Gibbons, again offering to brief him during his visit for the AAAS this week.

Hummingbird. Thursday 17 February 1994.

The strongest storm of the season hit us last night, with high winds that made the building vibrate and the big windows hum. Sheets of rain are sliding obliquely over the landscape as I write.

Hail was falling over Woodside this morning. I spent an hour at Buck's coffee shop with Craig Johnson, a famous venture attorney, while at the next table a partner at Accel Ventures was sketching out a multi-million-dollar deal with the president of Symantec. Yet even in the midst of Silicon Valley wheeling and dealing I feel the world shifting into a phase of technical development even more dangerous than the hair-raising rides of the last two decades.

Now Dr. Gibbons' secretary informs me that I'd be welcome to send him any material I thought relevant, but that he wasn't setting up any appointments on the subject. Why am I not surprised?

Hummingbird. Monday 21 February 1994.

I attended Jack Gibbons' keynote speech for the annual meeting of the American Association for the Advancement of Science here this weekend.

An old friend of Bob Chartrand, Representative George Brown, chairman of the science, technology and space committee of the House (**22**) introduced our panel on disaster management, where I spoke on information technology solutions.

Hummingbird. Friday 25 February 1994.

Last night I went to Fort Mason to attend the first in a series of lectures on Wilhelm Reich given by a researcher named James DeMeo. About 25 people sat in the old whitewashed room. What I learned about

Reich failed to satisfy my curiosity. He reminds me of Engelbart, a brilliant visionary whose creativity flourished best in the depth of frustration. He seems very Teutonic, very "armored." As a child he happened to catch his mother making love to his tutor, so he went to his father to tell him all about it, after which his mother poisoned herself. Such events would be enough to send anyone into an obsessive search for the secrets of humanity. For good measure, his father managed to die of pneumonia a couple of years later.

Reich's sexual theories may be as profound as Freud's, but in the end he seems to have simply substituted his own view of what morality "should be" over the discredited concepts of his time.

In our little group of San Francisco sophisticates, several people brought up the narrowness of Reich's definitions of "positive" and "negative" sexual situations, his simplistic identification of homosexuality as a neurosis, and his oversimplification of impotence and "super-potency" (naïvely defined as the sex life of men with multiple partners) as behaviors motivated by the fear of females. Like most theories of sex, this one fails to address the basic facts.

Hummingbird. Saturday 26 February 1994.

John Mack's latest book on abductions (**23**) rehashes common ideas about hybrid Aliens, with the addition of a veneer of academic respectability, the expensive flavor of the Harvard name, and hints of "spiritual transformation of Man" that are sure to resonate with New Age believers. Abductees are now urged to recall their past lives.

Tonight, I got a call from Robert Emenegger: "I've watched the documentary they've put together about Roswell," he told me, "and I thought, 'What the hell, we can do better than that,' so I called Coleman. The Army did have a peculiar balloon at Roswell, with triangular-shaped devices made of molecularly aligned metal for radar. Above that was a device that detected soviet radiation testing in the upper atmosphere. If the balloon burst at 110,000 feet there would be bits of metal all over the landscape, of course."

Anyway, the subject has resurfaced, Bob said: "I'm going back to that stuff that I never thought I'd see again. But where the hell is the supposed A.L. Lorenzo, and where's the film? There's a black sergeant down in Mississippi, a guard affected by the incident. He was dismissed for psychological reasons. I never tracked him down. Now Chartle has given me more names. Let's see... Colonel Jim Hunter, Sergeant Whelan, Colonel Hawthorne, and a man named Howster. I love it: It's the old tease again!"

I mentioned the absurd new yarn of Hynek witnessing autopsies. More disinformation, we agreed, managed from Washington.

"Something like that happened to me too," he said. "I had a meeting at my house with a Colonel Phil Corso, an assistant to General Trudeau who was head of a research unit for the Army in 1947. It seems there were seven labs under Trudeau's management at the time, including Lincoln Lab. He hadn't been interested in UFOs, but in 1947 three things came across his desk: a bad photograph of an autopsy of what looked like Aliens, also a piece of metal that was atomically aligned—that's molecular memory, you know—and a computer chip, and we sure didn't have chips at that time..."

"Certainly not in 1947," I agreed. "What did he want from you?"

"He was a gas bag. If you listened to him long enough, you'd think he won World War Two all by himself. Anyway, all I can do is put together what people tell me... even if it's sheer disinformation."

Hummingbird. Sunday 27 February 1994.

Dr. Richard Niemtzow now lives in New Jersey. He's been transferred to McGuire Air Force Base. As soon as he arrived a couple of abduction cases were referred to him, he tells me, the first one a man who remembers a blue beam cutting him on board a craft, and indeed he has a scar across his chest that cannot be explained as a surgery scar. The other victim is a woman, an Air Force major. Richard is in touch with Admiral Mohr, chairman of the Joint Chiefs under Reagan, who's taken an interest in such cases.

Before packing our suitcases for Paris, we attended a concert of the French National Orchestra under Charles Dutoit playing Albert Roussel (*Bacchus et Ariane*) and Berlioz' *Fantastique*. Then I spoke with Scott Jones who was scheduling a meeting in Washington with various researchers and Dan Smith. I declined to attend: Richard Niemtzow had warned me about the plan, which also involves a

French officer who serves as liaison between CNES-Sepra and US Intelligence: that weird connection again.

Scott also gave me news of the Rockefeller Initiative. The group has now had two meetings with Jack Gibbons. At the first meeting, "which went very badly," Gibbons was plainly embarrassed and irritated to have his office invaded by people who wanted to talk about little gray Aliens. Rockefeller showed him a draft of his letter to Clinton. Gibbons discouraged him from sending it:

"If you forward this letter and he gets excited, my office will be swamped beyond our ability to respond. It would be better to find some other way for me to help you, without energizing the President."

"Well, a number of notorious cases require more data, of the kind only someone at your level would be in a position to obtain."

"I'll be glad to help. Give me an example."

They spoke of the Belgian triangles. That was a bad idea since they don't involve American jurisdiction, not to mention that we suspect a classified human technology. Finally, Scott brought up Roswell.

"Let me look into it," said Gibbons, who wasn't aware of the file from the General Accounting Office about the notorious case. Scott Jones and Rockefeller are walking into a trap, betting everything on that single event on the basis of the publicity it received. If it turns out that no hard data is forthcoming beyond hearsay and deathbed confessions, the entire phenomenon will be discredited once again.

Mabillon. Saturday 12 March 1994.

French publishers make it a point never to be available, while their scornful secretaries say things like: "When did you send your manuscript again? Oh, we haven't opened those packages in the last two weeks. And it was about what, your manuscript?"

I found Simonne Servais idle in her Neuilly apartment. A quirky paragraph in the regulations of the bureaucracy denies her any pension for the 12 years she spent at Matignon and the Elysée, so she has given up the little house she rented in Provence. Is this how the French State treats its most devoted and brightest servants?

We spoke of the sightings by Maurice Masse at Valensole, which we had investigated together. They still sum up the whole problem. Simonne is disappointed with Velasco: "He showed up at a recent television show, bragging that he had proof of extraterrestrial visits, pulling out of his pocket a piece of meteorite," she said, disgusted.

On the famous night of November 5th, 1990, Simonne was driving through Paris when she saw the huge triangle in the sky, lit up along the edges; she had it in view for several minutes. "It looked like the Eiffel Tower on its side," she told me. She wrote to CNES, mentioning her diplomatic status, yet no one bothered to interview her. She got an absurd flyer from CNES "explaining" the event as the reentry of a Russian satellite. She felt insulted, as witnesses often do.

We spoke of alternative medicine, and of the follies of hypnosis in ufology. Now a fancy card has arrived: "Le Baron & la Baronne Jehan de Drouas" (Thérèse de Saint-Phalle and her banker husband) are requesting our presence for dinner on Wednesday with Marie-Thérèse de Brosses and Mr. and Mrs. Odier.

This invitation may be Thérèse's consolation prize for turning down my Journals at Plon.

Mabillon. Sunday 13 March 1994.

The bells of Saint-Sulpice call the faithful to Mass. I love our view of the towers where the forbidden name of Jehovah is sculpted in Hebrew. They remind me of the scene in *Down There* by Huysmans, when he describes the finest carillon in all of Paris. The bells'names are Thérèse (la), Caroline (si bémol), Henriette (fa dièse), Louise (do), Marie (do dièse). The Marquis de Sade and Baudelaire were baptised there; Victor Hugo was married in that church.

The abduction obsession is practically unknown here, says sociologist Lagrange. Hopkins' books aren't translated, and Strieber's *Communion* has passed unnoticed: it was issued as a sci-fi novel!

Last night, dining at *Le Procope* with my colleagues, we spoke about our next Fund. They asked about my retirement plans: Would I ever come back to France? Amused, I said I'd think about it when the next Fund is fully invested--and perhaps the one after that, in fifteen years.

Janine and I visited Roland Villeneuve, who kindly inscribed a copy of *La Beauté du Diable*.

Nantes. Hotel de France. Tuesday 15 March 1994.

Henri Michaux (*Qui je fus*) wrote: "I am inhabited; I speak to Those-I-was, and Those-I-was are speaking to me," as in this Journal.

I took the opportunity of a trip to Brittany for the shareholders meeting of Sangstat to visit writer Jean Sider at *La Bernerie*. I found him dressed in a gray shirt, blue tie and purple scarf, in better shape than the last time I saw him in Paris. He had shaved his head and looked like a kinder version of Aleister Crowley, with glasses.

On the horizon I could see Noirmoutier Island and a heavy band of dark clouds dragging their evil shapes across the water. Jean lives in retirement, an easy stonethrow from the beach. His yellow one-bedroom house is well kept, with a row of pine trees on the seaside and rosebushes in front. He has bookcases devoted to sorcery, fairyland, and folklore. I spent three hours with him, pleased to see there were still a few independent thinkers like Jean on this planet.

After supporting the extraterrestrial theory for 30 years, Sider has understood that the problem was far subtler. Now he compiles lists of medieval abductions, correlating old theologians with modern ufologists. We agree that the cause of both series of phenomena must be a form of consciousness manifesting in physical form. The effect of such intervention is devastating, since it shapes our beliefs.

Mabillon. Thursday 17 March 1994.

At Thérèse de Saint-Phalle's luxurious apartment we met Monique and Marcel Odier last night. He's a Swiss banker in his late seventies, with a background in math and science. His foundation sponsors theoretical work in parapsychology, notably that of Brenda Dunne, and some of Costa de Beauregard's research.

Another guest arrived, brandishing a newspaper he'd brought from Brussels, with color photographs of traces left in a field near Couvin by a gigantic lighted object. The witness is a customs officer (**24**).

As a journalist Marie-Thérèse de Brosses travels from Russia to America and Tibet, she said, gathering weird stories. Skeptics occasionally accuse her of propagating tall tales typical of a "desperate spinster badly in need of a good fuck," as she acknowledges with a wry smile.

Then Francois de Grossouvre's office called, telling Janine he wanted to see me on my next trip.

Hummingbird. Sunday 20 March 1994.

Returning from Europe we found John Mack's latest manuscript and read accumulated magazines, amused by all the hoopla about yet another "impending" Alien invasion.

The skeptics, for once, emerge as a voice of sanity. I watched the sun rise over this fine city as I read some 50 letters filled with sightings and vast interrogations.

John Mack's clear description of the abduction case material was long overdue but I balk at his rehashing experiences that could be analyzed from so many more productive directions.

Like most eminent academics with quick minds, Mack hasn't taken the trouble to familiarize himself with the problem as a whole.

Hummingbird. Monday 28 March 1994.

Last week I helped Udi Shapiro, of the Weissmann Institute, formulate a strategy for Ubique, our virtual conferencing company. I introduced him to Dan Lynch at the hot stage of the Interop trade show in Sunnyvale where his staff was lining up miles of network cables for their conference in Las Vegas. Ubique aims at the same technological achievements as my old InfoMedia, with greater resources and better timing, since networks have now blossomed into a major market. It is fun to be again at the core of collaboration technology.

Spring Hill. Sunday 10 April 1994.

Our neighbor has decided to log the parcels to the North of us, where our water originates. His contractors have put up little flags all over the woods, including a large swath of our own land, so the weekend was spent trying to save the hillside from greedy loggers. We met with the foresters who had been drawing up the boundaries. It was raining, so we slipped and stumbled up the canyon, grabbing hold of roots and rocks, until we located their pink flags at the borders.

As always in the country, it all hinges on where the lines should be drawn. They had missed a unique reference point hidden in the weeds, an old vertical pipe marker with an official surveyor's stamp on top, from which I plan to run my own survey. I decided to drag my old uncle's artillery telescope out into the woods. My measurements show the loggers are illegally encroaching into our land by at least 200 feet—and they know it. The forest took hold of me; it engulfed me and mocked my mood with its majesty. Squirrels ran across my way, making fun of me with my telescope and its awkward tripod. A large buzzard surprised me by taking off, brushing against me while I was absorbed in noting numbers on the base of the scope.

Newsweek Magazine has published a scathing review of John Mack's book: "Harvard psychiatry professor John E. Mack makes only a cursory pass at disbelief before buying the idea that extraterrestrials are filching human sperm and ova in order to create better earthlings. (...) Why couldn't their technology clone humans from the DNA in a toenail, instead of dragging people to the mother ship for bondage and discipline?" (**25**) Those are exactly the points I had tried unsuccessfully to bring up in a friendly way during our conversation with Scott Jones and Laurance Rockefeller. A tougher crowd is hammering them now into the coffin of abduction research.

Hummingbird. Monday 18 April 1994.

The February letter from Laurance to Jack Gibbons said two important things: he agreed not to write to Clinton and offered the services of his foundation to Gibbons, elegantly withdrawing from the scene.

An advance copy of a new, devastating article against John Mack by *Time Magazine* (**26**) drops a bombshell: Donna Bassett, an undercover debunker who posed as an abductee and was hypnotized by Mack, claims that he swallowed her inventions of what she saw in the saucer, billed insurance companies for his "therapy" sessions, followed no scientific protocol, and even failed to get her informed consent.

Next, I picked up *The Economist* (**27**) and was shocked to read that François de Grossouvre had died of a bullet to the brain at the Elysée palace on April 7th.

Ominously, the article refers to the fact that he was "compiling archives on unspecified subjects."

Hummingbird. Thursday 21 April 1994.

My former SRI colleague and wonder programmer Dick Shoup invited me to come and see him at Interval Research, a new Palo Alto think tank where he works on the "Roots of Not," a new concept in logic. This led us to discuss the nature of time, a subject I've been pondering in my consciousness and synchronicity tests at Spring Hill. He sees time as nature's way to resolve logical paradoxes. I love his idea that time gets generated from the resolution of semantic absurdity. It informs my *meta-logic* theory.

Spring Hill. Saturday 23 April 1994.

Richard Nixon died last night in New York. We will never know whether or not there were actual photographs of little Aliens in his office file, supposedly presented to him by the Chinese. He was typical of a well-heeled class that could never grasp how deeply the world had changed, although he played a major role by the recognition given to China. His stupidity in Watergate taught the American people the precious lesson in cynicism they had failed to learn from the two Kennedy assassinations.

Las Vegas. The Excalibur. Wednesday 4 May 1994.

The Interop show is the reason for this short trip. I am spending most of my time with Udi Shapiro of Ubique, and with Dave Crocker whom I hadn't seen in a decade or so. I hear many references to that day in 1972, when the Arpanet made its debut and the astonished world, over two days, discovered the first computer network.

As soon as he knew we were in town, Robert Bigelow cheerfully invited us. We met him at his magnificent offices, a Tudor house enhanced by stained glass, an oversize staircase and two big cats (*Mortgage* and *Taxes*) who took happy poses on various desks.

"There is some synchronicity to your arrival today," he said as we sat around a heavy table in his study. "I've been writing a letter to the three major UFO groups, urging them to meet with me in Saint Louis mid-June, to discuss funding some of their ideas."

We drove over to a fish restaurant for lunch with George Knapp. We compared notes about Russia. George knew Lazar's actual identity: he was born in Coral Gables. The darker rumors simmer.

Spring Hill. Saturday 7 May 1994.

After retracing every step I had taken with my telescope the County foresters sheepishly conceded that my newly-surveyed boundary was the correct one, so we will save our redwoods by pushing their lines some 300 feet to the north.

Janine and I walked up the steep hill to locate their new line of flags, deeper in the forest. The most wonderful mist arose from the redwoods. Using yellow paint, we marked the big trees that line the creek to preserve them once and for all, a nice victory against the corrupt practices of the lumber barons.

Hummingbird. Friday 13 May 1994.

Yesterday Interval Research invited me to give a seminar on UFOs. Computer scientist Lee Felzenstein was there, with about 40 staff members, and Jill Tarter from the SETI Institute.

Federal Records have released to us the official transcript of Lazar's bankruptcy of 1986. These documents open all sorts of new questions, which my attorney cautioned me not to explore.

8

Mabillon. Sunday 15 May 1994.

We landed in France in the afternoon with no thoughts of paranormal events. Our first visit was for my mother and my brother. As we returned home we bumped into Pierre Lagrange taking a walk near the Luxembourg Gardens, and enjoyed a talk with him. We sat at a sidewalk café for dinner with our son until a freak storm swept through with lightning and rain, sending us inside. After the cloudburst Janine and I strolled in the Latin Quarter like two lovers: older, hardly wiser. I carry a vial of tiny granules found in the soil of two landing sites by Dr. Yuri Simakov, one near Moscow, the other in Kazakhstan. I hope to have them analyzed by Velasco's colleagues (**28**).

Mabillon. Tuesday 17 May 1994.

An executive from a French company came over for lunch today, bringing Gilbert Payan, so we ended up talking about microwave weapons and Russian energy research. Payan is close to Monory, a powerful French politician, president of the Senate. He promised to send me a paper about the new weapons, which he said the US had been trying to convince the French to develop for the last eight years.

"Microwave weapons are of two kinds," he said, "those that act against electronics, either frying circuits or confusing them, and those that act against personnel, especially at the alpha frequency. An entire region can be exposed, with the inhabitants rendered confused or sick. The exact effects are debated but not denied. So that's how the joint project developed, about the crop circles."

Payan told me that Poher had become marginalized. "It's tough to fight, all alone, for so long. He's disgusted with the scientific community. He's become stuck in dubious theories."

Intrigued by my references to microwave weapons in *Confrontations*, he asked if I'd gotten the information from Niemtzow who he said was an expert in the field. So that's why GEPAN was so eager to work with him; ufology was just an excuse.

Mabillon. Wednesday 18 May 1994.

The sun came out today, a pretty spring sun that turned everything pink. I walked over to see Thérèse de Saint Phalle. She returned *Forbidden Science* with a thousand good reasons why they couldn't publish it: "Polemical books are the only ones that sell, these days," she said. "Diaries don't, unless they relate to rock stars..."

I took a cab to Albin Michel's offices to pick up a new book by Roussel (**29**), which I plan to read on the way to Toulouse. I also went back to see my mother, finding her alert and cheerful. With the sunshine striking her windows, the whole apartment came to life, emphasizing the fine decor full of color, her creativity evident everywhere. I repaired her malfunctioning telephone and suggested lunch at a restaurant near the Sorbonne. We went there at a slow pace, along flat sidewalks, because she can no longer climb even the low inclines of *Rue Monge*. She was pleased with our little excursion. Next, I went to see Robert Laffont, the distinguished publisher, who wanted to meet with me after reading *Forbidden Science*. He received me in his sparse, dark office near Saint Sulpice.

"I've always had the greatest spiritual difficulty to go across the Seine," he told me with a smile, "so when our new owners moved near the *Etoile* they allowed me to keep this little place."

His windows open onto the intimate garden I have crossed so often.

"At 77 I no longer make the decisions for the company," he said, handing the manuscript back to me, "but I have fought for your work, because you and I are very close in our thinking. I wanted to return it to you in person. The marketing people tell me they can't sell it. It would reach less than a thousand people."

"There's a much larger public that's interested," I pointed out.

"I'll grant you that, but we don't know how to find them." He added: "I'm not a specialist, only a generalist who has gained a wide view of what happens in the world. In your Journal I was deeply struck by two things; first the debacle of 1940, the *Exode*. I grew up as the son of a bourgeois family in Marseille; the world was very simple: We, the French, were always right in everything. This illusion was swept away when France collapsed in a matter of days before Hitler. The second thing was the moon landing of 1969. I was surprised that you said so little about it in your Journal. To me it was a watershed event; we stayed up all night listening breathlessly to every detail. An old idea of God, as a deity concerned with our affairs on earth, suddenly became obsolete that night."

I mentioned my plan to write about entrepreneurship. He shrugged and said the same thing as Thérèse: "The French don't understand venture capital or high technology. They haven't yet grasped how deeply the world has changed. They hear that the economic crisis is nearly over, so they assume everything is soon going to be as before. They mistrust entrepreneurs. The man-in-the street detests him, but so do the bourgeois and the high-level administrators. We have an enormous bureaucracy that preserves the structure. At the top are ENA graduates, people like our Prime Minister Balladur, who've never worked a day in their lives at anything productive."

Toulouse. Friday 20 May 1994.

Our meetings with Fred Adler are over: The decision has been made, to launch our new venture fund, Euro-America-II.

I spent part of the day at a technopole south of Toulouse, visiting biotechnology companies. Janine and I had a pleasant drive down to Montgiscard for dinner with Jean-Jacques Velasco and his wife Danielle. We met him in front of the fine old church of his village and he proudly took us through a tour of his town hall.

After giving Jean-Jacques the granules from Russia we sat down, and we talked about the region and the history of the Cathars. Jean-Jacques'job is slowly turning into a nightmare at CNES. His bosses, graduates from *Polytechnique*, won't let him fire his incompetent secretary. As for Poher, he now works at Aérospatiale in Cannes, theorizing about a bi-stable particle but he doesn't want to publish.

From Jean-Jacques and Danielle's house we could see the line of the Pyrenées. As we contemplated this sight they told us they thought of moving near Bayonne, in anticipation of retirement.

Toulouse. Saturday 21 May 1994.

The shops were still closed in sleepy Toulouse when we left this morning for Carcassonne and a dash to Rennes-le-Château, the notorious site of *Holy Blood, Holy Grail*, where I expected to find nothing but hype and a pale rehashing of pseudo-mysticism (**30**). Instead we were surprised and seduced. *First*, the site is spectacular, an isolated ridge high above a rich landscape of luscious fields and farms. *Second*, the local priest (Abbé Saunière) of the 19th century yarn was a man of taste: his little church is charming. Even the village cemetery is refreshingly simple and mysterious. *Third*, the whole thing does represent an enigma. It has nothing to do with the children of Jesus or the bloodline of French kings, but it does have to do with the career of a creative curate, an eclectic book collector who built a tower to house his personal library and commissioned a statue of a grimacing devil to greet his parishioners at a unique time in French politics. I would have loved to meet this man.

We had lunch at a new restaurant near Villa Béthany. The proprietor came over with the *Livre d'Or*: we were the first clients, so I had the curious distinction of writing the initial entry. Later we drove to the formidable Puivert castle, and we came back through the town of Foix, with its fine tall towers overlooking the Ariège River.

The most magical site was Montségur, reached by a steep 40-minute hike over jumbled rock, straight up to the massive grey-blue walls of the Cathar citadel. The last hundred feet of the ascent are made over marble boulders, broken and polished up by centuries of climbing feet. Janine did it in her city shoes, soon reduced to sandals, the high heels destroyed by the trip to the craggy "pog."

The top of the walls provided a dizzying panorama of precipices hanging from the dreamy, drifting grey veil of clouds. The light was changing, adding to our feeling of disorientation, turning the fields to darker and darker shades of green and plunging the gloomy castle, ruined by the Cathar defeat seven centuries ago, into yet another tragic testimony to the murderous propensities of man, his criminal impulses in the name of religion and everything he holds sacred.

Toulouse. Monday 23 May 1994.

Today is the Feast of Pentecost. France is at a standstill. For the last time as President, Mitterrand climbed up the hill of Solutré for his yearly pilgrimage. Early in the morning a shirtless man had taken position at the top, beating a drum "to contact extraterrestrials."

"Let him play," Mitterrand said. He shook the fellow's hand.

We drove to Albi and on to the medieval village of Cordes. We saw some marvellous books and tapestries wherever we stopped. It was an old dream of mine to make this trip with Janine, her smile as my companion "in mist and stone." I love her more than ever as our life becomes simpler, less confused. Many uncertainties have faded away—along with our youth.

Fig. 9. Cinematographer George Kuchar at Spring Hill, Nov. 1993. George was among many artists and writers who visited the ranch.

Fig. 10. Janine at Rennes-le-Château, May 1994.

Paris. Tuesday 24 May 1994.

This was a full day of work at my partners' offices. Having a free evening I called Jean Sider. He said a UFO meeting had taken place on May 5th at *Club 89*, a think tank of Chirac's party. In attendance were a general, someone from the police, Velasco from CNES, Colonel Vermande who reports to the government, and three ufologists. The meeting was inspired by François Coutaine, the earliest ufologist in France, the wealthy scion of an affluent family.

"He's a very nice old man with obsolete aristocratic manners, *très Vieille France*; he meets extraterrestrials in his garden all the time," reported Sider with indulgence.

Paris. Wednesday 25 May 1994.

Janine and I had dinner last night (at *Muniche*) with Alain Boudier. He told us that several labs in France were at work eagerly studying the photograph I had brought back from Costa Rica, Perrin de Brichambaut and Fleximage among them. He was worried about the fate of his company, Plastimarne, which makes plastic tanks in Epernay. He's been forced to borrow money to refinance it.

Boudier said that Payan suggested that the CNES should demand from *Les Américains* a piece of the material from Roswell. A French general named Pouliquen, attached to the Embassy in Washington, has a mission to establish liaison with the Pentagon about this. Boudier suggested I contact him in Washington to see if I could help.

Hummingbird. Monday 30 May 1994.

We spent part of the Memorial Day weekend at Spring Hill, pursuing experiments and keeping a close watch on our abusive neighbor's logging activities. The hillsides north of our land are littered with cut redwoods that his foresters have already felled along the slopes. Now he is bulldozing new roads to gather his spoils.

On Saturday evening we drove up to Willits to meet with Dan Stewart at the Corner Deli, where a lively little band was playing Middle Eastern music. This had inspired a few ambitious local girls to dress up like Sheherazade for some energetic belly dancing. We came home under a beautiful sky, full of big stars.

Los Angeles Hyatt Regency. Monday 6 June 1994.

The *Digital World* show organized by Jonathan Seybold is under way here. I spent the afternoon at Ann Druffel's house in Pasadena, on quiet Sycamore Street. She was eager to show me Dr. Jim MacDonald's diary, which ends on 26 January 1971. I was moved to hold it and fascinated to see that his Journal and mine dovetailed closely. It confirmed my earlier impressions of Jim: keeping his emotions locked up (he had a hard childhood, with a domineering father who brutalized him,) very hard working, well organized. My perceptions of his relationship with Hynek were accurate, too. But there were new aspects: he was in touch with someone high in government and thought he'd soon know (or already knew?) the truth. He suffered from not being able to share this.

Ann has seen his autopsy report: according to the Coroner, he died about 1 am. If that's true, what did he do between 4:30 pm and 1 am, alone in the desert? His body was found 10 hours after death. To the cab driver who dropped him off and enquired if he'd be all right, he said he was about to meet someone. There's no detailed description of the scene in the police file, so it is unknown whether or not they found other footprints at the spot. There wasn't even any paraffin test that could establish if he had fired the gun himself. Evidently, he was depressed. He wrote suicide notes on the occasion of both of his attempts. The precipitating factor was news from his wife that she felt neglected and that she was going to live with a younger man.

Austin Sheraton. Wednesday 8 June 1994.

The Council of the SSE meets in this city today. I had lunch with psychic researcher Roger Nelson from Princeton to review our agenda after a busy morning and a conference call of the investors in Sangstat Medical, then a follow-up with Dan Tolkowsky in Israel.

Over dinner with Hal I expressed my puzzlement about Kit's apology for his colleagues. Futurist John Petersen, who has done work for the Coast Guard about strategic threats, is a friend of CIA director James Woolsey. He urged him to look for UFO data. Woolsey reportedly turned to Ron Pandolfi, who merely gave him a file of clippings. When he demanded to be shown “the real stuff” he was assured the CIA didn't have any. Such is the unlikely story Petersen was told.

At the SSE reception that followed my dinner with Hal, I spoke to Dianne Cameron, Bob Bigelow, Ron Johnson (who used to be known as “Jerry” Johnson,) and ufologist Bob Wood. Later Johnson and I spent nearly an hour together, discussing classification schemes for UFO reports. He is computerizing the cases for MUFON while working as an engineer on Hal Puthoff's project in Austin.

Bob Wood told me that he, too, had seen the MacDonald diaries, and like me was intrigued by the fact that Jim may have gone into the desert to meet somebody. Over a couple of beers with Bob Wood, as he was changing planes in Tucson, MacDonald once told him “he knew what was behind UFOs” but couldn't reveal the full story.

Austin. Thursday 9 June 1994.

The SSE meeting opened this morning with an interesting presentation on zero-point energy by Hal, followed by a theoretical paper by Bernie Haisch about his interpretation of inertia. I had lunch with Professor Ron Westrum, who recommended reading several stories by Robert Heinlein (**31**) and spoke about manipulation strategies.

Our lunch lasted beyond the allotted time for the conference, so instead of returning to the ongoing session I went up to my room to call various startups, then waited in the bar for the coffee break. I met Robert Creegan there. He’s an old philosopher of science, with a sharp mind and a good recollection of Hynek, the Lorenzens and “the Brits,” Gordon Creighton and Charles Gibbs-Smith. The conversation had just turned to my recent visits to Nantes, where part of his family lives, when a commotion took place in the main hall.

A fellow came out, rushed to a phone and urgently called for an ambulance. We were told that someone had been taken ill, so I went into the room where people stood around with dismay on their faces, the meeting halted. Several members with medical training, notably Dr. Larry Dossey, were trying to resuscitate a figure lying on the ground in the back of the room. The victim turned out to be Ron Johnson, with whom I had spent the previous evening. Paramedics rushed in, a team arrived from the Fire department, heart massage was resumed, things became very tense. Twice they were able to revive Ron, but he finally died and everyone very somberly left the room. He was only 43. He had seemed to fall asleep, with no sign of pain; he'd collapsed on the floor.

Naturally the afternoon session was cancelled, but we gathered again in the evening for a somber excursion on Lake Travis. To me, it brought back memories of our astronomy department picnics in 1962 with De Vaucouleurs, when Janine and I lived in this town. It was very nice to see Adrienne Puthoff and Stanley Krippner there, with Andrei Berezin from Moscow, and other people who spoke about ingenious experiments in every facet of parapsychology.

At that point Robert Bigelow came over and sat next to me. Without any preamble, he said he'd made progress in his meetings with the three major UFO groups, as we once discussed in Vegas. He proposed to fund their research at a level of $250K the first year, half a million the second year, going up in half million steps until funding reached $5 million a year: "I could fund it today at that level if I wanted to," he said, "but as you understand, these people don't have the adequate management structure to spend that kind of money."

He asked what I was working on, and made it clear he was willing to finance independent projects outside the three organizations. I simply repeated my offer to serve as a "friend of the Court."

In the evening George Hathaway, consultant to Prince Hans-Adam, demonstrated his spectroscopic camera in the hotel garage. Thunderstorms cracked outside, shaking the hot Texas sky.

Spring Hill. Sunday 12 June 1994.

We enjoy the ranch again today, walking through the woods where I have flagged a new path up to the ridge. This was a good weekend of hard work on the databases while Pete and his tractor began clearing the new road I'd designed. From the top, about 600 feet above the main house, we can see all the way South to Ukiah. There was a glorious moon a few days past half, as easy to reach as a ripe golden apple. Next to it was Jupiter, where we could clearly see the bands and the four major satellites grouped together, a splendid sight.

Hummingbird. Saturday 16 July 1994.

Last night we met Keith and Darlene at *Good Karma*. Keith has decided to work on a book exposing chronic mistakes and cheating in parapsychology research. Tonight, Peter Sturrock and Dan Tolkowsky are coming over with their wives for dinner with us.

CNN called from Washington as I was leaving my office. *Larry King Live* is going to shoot a special program on the "UFO Coverup" in Rachel, Nevada, where they propose to fly me first-class.

"I've already gone to Rachel," I told the producer, "I have no desire to go back there."

"But we need you, to represent the scientific viewpoint!"

Keith Harary urges me to go on "so people will have a counter-point to the propaganda being fed to the public." But I'd only lend dubious dignity to the wild tales spread by John Lear and Bob Lazar, with Area 51 shimmering ominously in the background.

Hummingbird. Tuesday 19 July 1994.

Over lunch at Orchids today Fred related a new rumor spread by Ron Blackburn about the death of Ron Johnson at the SSE meeting. Blackburn claims that Johnson was losing vast amounts of blood by his nostrils, eyes and ears. I told Fred that none of this happened, but he would rather believe a lurid story spread by Blackburn, who wasn't there, than my testimony as an eyewitness.

I've checked with a doctor who gave me his own data about Johnson's death, putting Backburn's irresponsible claims in perspective. The doctor was in the room and saw Ron die. He even gave me photographic documents and confirmed Ron only lost a few drops of blood from his nose. So why should I trust Blackburn again when he tells me he's handled the hardware from Roswell?

Hummingbird. Monday 25 July 1994.

Accuray Systems (**32**) is out of cash again and no Fund in Silicon Valley will finance it. I need to overcome my own partners' skepticism to get more money to the CEO, Dr. John Adler (no connection to Fred). Tomorrow I meet with Udi Shapiro to sign papers for the launching of Ubique. Such are the turns of the venture business, little companies flourish or die in the winds of change.

I was awake for much of the night, re-assessing my life, comparing my achievements unfavorably to those of others who have seized some of the opportunities I missed. But I do have Janine, warm Janine close to me, Janine who loves me, while the great tycoons and wealthy captains of industry I know have left little but a trail of broken families, divorces, and resentment. Janine, too, works hard, negotiating real estate deals with patience and grace.

Now I learn that the source of the rumor about the supposed "assassination" of Ron Johnson is none other than Dan T. Smith. This episode illustrates of the confusion in the field. Much of it is being deliberately created, to what end?

Spring Hill. Sunday 31 July 1994.

Olivier, on a visit from Paris, came with me to the "Object World" show on Friday. Now my son is back with us at the ranch, surveying the boxes he'd left in storage, sorting out his books, records, pots and pans, shirts and pants, and generally having a good time.

After a long swim in the pool we observed Jupiter, scanned the Milky Way and spoke about the future.

Hummingbird. Thursday 4 August 1994.

When I spoke to him today Hal Puthoff was calm, friendly and informative as usual. I trust him and admire his equanimity in the face of decades of hard, misunderstood work. I told him of my concern with the latest rumors.

He answered: "Yeah…Dan Smith called the Chief of Police in Austin, who said none of that had happened. That didn't stop him."

"What's troubling is the paranoia sweeping the field. The people who flip are among those I thought were sane researchers..." I said, with lingering disgust. Hal wasn't aware of the proposed Bigelow grant to the three UFO groups. He said he kept hearing positive comments about my work. "More and more folks are coming to the hyperdimensional idea, as you've been trying to tell us for many years. Even I might start believing it some day," he concluded with a smile. We'll meet again in Scotland for the European SSE meeting.

Hummingbird. Saturday 13 August 1994.

There were splashes of sunshine all over Mission Street when I moved my office yesterday, to large rooms on the top floor of a funky six-story building South of Market, an area that used to hold the warehouses for the Port and the canneries that once shipped California produce all over the world. Sam Spade could have had his office in our building, straight out of *The Maltese Falcon* and the Barbary Coast: the floor is uneven, and the old green carpet shows some suspicious darker spots. We have a useless but picturesque walk-in safe with steel doors and high shelves where a wholesale jeweller used to store gold watches, topaz rings, and sapphire ornaments.

When I look across Mission Street, beyond the *Red Imperial Palace* Chinese restaurant, I see a brick wall with a faded advertisement for *Carnation Mush*, which must have been a trendy drink in the 30s, adorned with gigantic flowers. Beyond it the skyscrapers of the financial center bristle with parabolic antennas and flagpoles.

Fred Beckman tells me that Prince Hans-Adam has assured Fred Alzofon (who visited him recently in Vaduz) that Perez de Cuellar, now running for the presidency of Peru, had been taken even before the notorious "Linda" case, based on documents received by Hopkins, who believes all this. The documents, of course, are anonymous…

Roger Rémy, who has a lab and his own funding, has met a fellow named Pomanareff who spoke of Russian energy systems: "The Topaz at Kirtland is way behind the one they've built in Russia."

Glynhill Inn, Glasgow. Tuesday 23 August 1994.

The first person I saw when we arrived for the SSE conference was Hal. He reminded me that Norton AFB was more than a repository for old scratchy movies: it once housed a high-level group concerned with the deployment of the MX. In one of the SRI remote viewing tests simulating missile deployment, Hal's team had found the supposedly secret missiles 11 times in a row! Coming after the localization of a downed U.S. plane in Africa this feat of psychic detection created a row between the Air Force and the NSC and played a role in stopping the MX project, so the brass at Norton hated SRI and all remote viewers.

Statistician Jessica Utts told me Ed May was off to Washington again, fighting to preserve his budget. The staff has been laid off and little remains of the SAIC project except a pile of cardboard boxes.

The ambitious super-computer company called *Thinking Machines*, on the same floor as Ed's project, is also going out of business.

Glynhill Inn, Glasgow. Wednesday 24 August 1994.

An animated discussion with Jessica Utts, Walter von Lucadou, Roger Nelson, and a handful of others has lasted late into the night, about the statistics of remote viewing and precognition. The subtlest computations cannot distinguish between these two scenarios of psychic functioning: it may not be possible to tell whether viewers are aware of the future validation of the tests or accessing the site psychically. Similar statistical ambiguities exist in psychokinesis, making the possible role of consciousness in quantum mechanics a very murky subject: if I observe event X, and this forces you to observe X as well (for instance, the spin of a particle,) does that necessarily imply instantaneous communication between us?

Doesn't that mean instead that you and I are not separate minds, and that there is only one form of consciousness?

Perhaps we are both simply selecting data from a universal, timeless state vector, later inventing the history of the universe that leads to that particular set of observations?

Glynhill Inn, Glasgow. Friday 26 August 1994.

The conference has continued with much spirit and flair. I had pleasant discussions with Hessdalen researcher Erling Strand, Paul Devereux, and a woman named Angelika who turned out to be Countess Cawdor, as I found out when I asked where she lived.

"In a 14th-century castle, in the north of Scotland," she said.

"Is it haunted?" I enquired.

"I certainly plan to haunt it some day," she answered pleasantly.

Walter von Lucadou from Freiburg (Germany) thinks that multiple personality disorders are often involved in UFO abductions.

As for Velasco, he's still under a lot of strain, isolated in Toulouse and challenged by CNES management, which hates the GEPAN project and would like to get rid of it.

Mabillon. Sunday 28 August 1994.

Paris is full of books and songs. We spent three hours with Elisabeth Antébi who had read *Forbidden Science* and gave me a thorough critique: she quickly got tired of my anger as a young man, she said. As a reader who wasn't very interested in UFOs (she believes Jungian psychology explains it all) she thought my Journal became boring once I described our arrival in Chicago.

"I have no idea who these people were: Hynek, Guérin, Aimé Michel... They seem important to you, but I fail to see why. Also, your sense of humor doesn't shine through; the text doesn't reflect what I know of you in person."

"Elisabeth," I replied, "when you keep a diary, you don't necessarily feel inspired to write when you're happy. You turn to it when you need reassurance, when you're sad or frustrated."

"True, but you don't really share the deeper secrets."

She leaned back in her chair, sighing coquettishly: "There I go, and now you'll never be my friend again. But you ought to write something more clear, a straightforward autobiography, cleaned up of irrelevant facts and secondary characters."

"Isn't that too easy, to erase all the little things out of life and reconstruct it from today's perspective? Doesn't that betray the day-to-day record?" I countered. She was not impressed:

"The day-to-day record is boring, unclear. Besides, she added with a side wink at Janine, who was laughing at my embarrassment, "You don't talk enough about women, all they mean to you."

Mabillon. Saturday 3 September 1994.

Today we had a fine, enjoyable morning after the rains of Scotland. I went to see Marie-Thérèse de Brosses on *Rue Pigalle* and found her sitting on her sofa in a plain yellow dress. She too had read *Forbidden Science*, so she bombarded me with questions and told me about her recent trips investigating abductions, visiting most of the people in the field, including David Jacobs, whom she dislikes, and "good old Budd Hopkins," who charmed her.

She is smart enough to realize that their hypnosis has zero scientific basis and causes considerable harm, as in the case of "Alice," a woman who was insulted by Jacobs *while in trance* when her visiting entity turned out to be an Angel rather than the mean Alien he expected!

We had lunch on Place Pigalle. She confessed to me she used to see fairies and elves as a child, when she lived with her family at Ennery castle. Her uncle was the exorcist of the Lyons *diocèse*. She stopped seeing little people at age seven when her mother told her it was "something only crazy people did."

She also told me about the "Gateau case." This fellow saw a dark object take off from a field, after which he found some slag-like material at the spot. He was asked to give all of it to CNES, but wisely kept one piece for himself. Velasco later told him it was ordinary slag, but Marie-Thérèse is having the last sample analyzed. (Note)

The military likes to hoard everything, but scientists are not much better, afraid for their reputation. Like me, Marie-Thérèse has expressed interest in the death of General Ailleret. But when she approached a member of her family, a military officer, she was told very sternly "Honey, you'd do well not to look into that business."

Mabillon. Sunday 4 September 1994.

Over dinner at his home last night Gilbert Payan told us the full story of the PK tests done by Crussard and Jean-Pierre Girard (**33**). I asked him about the Gateau sample, which he remembered well. "We did analyze it," he said. "It turned out to be a combination of metals, the result of an odd series of heatings and coolings. But what good is a case like that? No piece of the actual propulsion system is available."

(Note): In the midst of much controversy I obtained fragments of that last sample in December 2017 and analyzed it in Silicon Valley.

Payan argues that an Alien race may live in the asteroid belt, from which smaller ships come, using antimatter propulsion. "That may not explain everything, but in France you have to present a believable theory before academics will deign to look at the data," he said astutely as he drove us back to the Latin Quarter after midnight. He thinks that the Council on Foreign Relations is behind a plot to create a one-world government, along with the Trilateral Commission: the far-right connection again?

Albuquerque. Howard Johnson. Saturday 10 September 1994.

Roger Rémy came over to the airport to pick me up, along with his wife and their four kids. Over coffee at a local restaurant I mentioned alleged residues from UFOs. He believes Roswell is bullshit: the material doesn't match other cases, he said. He met Marcel Vogel about the same time I did, when researching the effect of radiation on plants, in experiments that left his fingers permanently damaged.

"Vogel had a CIA alter-ego named Bob Frechi," Roger told me. "He showed me an actual UFO sample. It exhibited a metallurgical technique called *frittage*, where the molecules are almost soldered together. We can only do that on small samples, even now. Beryllium was involved. There was evidence of high temperatures."

Roger proposes novel technical ideas for plasma generation and containment. He doesn't think much of Puthoff's theories, preferring those of René-Louis Vallée (no connection to me: the man worked on the French neutron bomb). Roger has designs for large-scale electromagnetic weapons, essentially guided globular lightning, to be used against post-cold war targets such as biological warfare sites.

Atlanta. Tuesday 13 September 1994.

At the Interop Show yesterday our news conference about the launching of Ubique and "virtual place technology" was covered by the *New York Times* and the *Wall Street Journal* as the next step in networking, beyond the World Wide Web (**34**). It feels good to be at this frontier again with an advanced collaboration system.

Atlanta is warm, sunny, and clear. This event has brought together some 70,000 middle-aged computer types, mostly male, mostly white, pudgy figures in wrinkled suits. The bus that takes us to the slick conference center passes dilapidated buildings, their windows broken, and empty lots where the poor wander. Some sleep in doorways of boarded-up houses while we drive by with our hi-tech dreams, ignoring the real world, unaware of its distortions. Now we're about to build virtual places for remote presences in elegant software structures that will leverage knowledge around six continents, but nothing is done to bridge the distances that stretch between rich and poor, or between the educated and the illiterate.

Later Dick Farley called to alert me to the recent release by the Air Force secretary's office of a silly white paper "explaining" Roswell as the crash of a secret Mogul balloon. Farley is clever and no stranger to controversy. His articles in the *Baltimore Evening Sun* have earned him the Mark Twain award. He helped Cousteau fight nuclear tests in the Pacific when Scott Jones was on the opposite side, calling the tests harmless: "It's ironic that I ended up working for the man," he said.

Dick also mentioned a 1963 publication by the AAAS on "Space Efforts and Society" with reference to the possible damage of revealing ET existence. Respondents had suggested that Fundamentalists would have the hardest time with this notion. A work called *Second-Order Consequences* by Raymond Bauer (**35**) argued that the discovery of extraterrestrial intelligence would not result in the disintegration of religious believers but *in a breakdown of the intellectual elites, unable to grasp the magnitude of the event.*

Several recent books by Christian writers concerned with the spiritual issues of the UFO controversy now quote my position, notably *To Hell and Back* by Maurice Rawlings, *Unmasking the Enemy* by Blandt and Pacheco, and *War in Heaven* by Kyle Griffith.

An anonymous correspondent claims that many UFO stories are a cover for NRO and other agencies. He found an underground base in Georgia, supposedly a nuclear waste site in the Dawson forest preserve: "There were tunnels, fences all over the place, bunkers, big structures, escape hatches, emergency systems. It wasn't a nuclear waste dump at all! The whole project was black. Lockheed and Westinghouse ran it. There are plenty of those things all over. The public doesn't know anything. *Your problem is that you're right.*"

Atlanta. Ritz-Carlton. Thursday 15 September 1994.

I dreamed of Janine last night, a tender, reliable presence. We may sell the ranch, eventually. I had envisioned a bastion of knowledge, a haven for friends strolling through the redwoods or huddling around the fireplace, debating profound experiments about life and death, mind and science. But the local culture cannot support it.

Friendships are hard to establish and maintain in Mendocino County. Our Pagan friends, creative as they are, too often hover in a fog of drug-induced realities that were inspiring in the heady days of Timothy Leary but build nothing concrete as the curtain falls on the 20th century. My own contribution is elsewhere, in the relentless pursuit of research – calibrated against the judgment of those I trust, including a few honest and knowledgeable skeptics.

Hummingbird. Sunday 25 September 1994.

Dr. Udi Shapiro is in town from Israel, so I arranged a dinner with Dan Lynch, who gave us an overview of the changes affecting the Internet. Later I went to a Stanford computer forum with Don Knuth, Terry Winograd, and Nils Nilsson, names from my academic past.

Yesterday I turned 55. My birthday gifts were the joy of spending the day with Janine and Catherine at the ranch, and a visit by Keith and Darlene. We talked late into the night and scanned the rising moon with the Celestron. We looked at Saturn on the video system, after which we had a long discussion about parapsychology and Warcollier's research. Keith gave us a copy of his new psychology book, *Who Do You Think You Are?*

Hummingbird. Sunday 2 October 1994.

Larry King's "Cover-up" program ran last night. All afternoon they had teased the public. Others in the media have already reacted by ridiculing the field. Perhaps I worry too much: judging by David Jacobs' diatribes in the formerly rational *Journal of Scientific Exploration* (**36**), there isn't much of a "field" here to speak of.

Larry King sat at an incongruous desk in the desert in the company of an expert on Roswell (who isn't?) and a few others. The big mystery was never elucidated. Interspersed with the proceedings were sound bites from skeptics. Carl Sagan appeared sick and drawn. Even the debunking case was poorly stated.

Philadelphia. Red Carpet Club. Saturday 8 October 1994.

The east coast again. I've come here in the wake of the destroyer USS Eldridge of *Philadelphia Experiment* fame: American UFO buffs have long been fascinated by a man named Carl Allen who claimed in the 1950s that the ship had gone through another dimension during a secret experiment involving Einstein. But no one ever met Carl Allen.

"A lot of people have left part of themselves here," Christine said with a gesture that embraced the huge ships at anchor in the vast harbor. Christine is a producer for the Learning Channel, an elegant blonde born in London, daughter of a Navy historian. They plan a special feature about the episode.

"Your father would have enjoyed this trip," I told her while her cameraman filmed the turrets of the USS Wisconsin rising ten stories high. Beyond the Wisconsin I could see the guns of the Iowa; beyond the Iowa were two cruisers, a submarine, a dozen destroyers, many frigates; on the other side of the docks were three aircraft carriers and the John F. Kennedy in drydock.

"This is enough firepower to fight World War Two all over again," I told Ed Dudgeon, visibly happy to be among the big ships again.

The Learning Channel saw my recent study about the Philadelphia Experiment hoax and called. I put them in touch with Ed Dudgeon and rear-Admiral Houser. They even dredged up old Al Bielek (**37**), nearly blind, obsessed with the notion that he fell through time when the Eldridge vanished. The Aliens reincarnated him in the body of a child... The story, as he tells it, would require him to be in two bodies at the same time, but logical details don't bother ufologists.

"We tried not to laugh at the fellow," Christine said. "He was obviously convinced of the whole thing."

Ed Dudgeon regretted writing to me: he considers the Philadelphia Experiment a ludicrous episode. Yet there's a sparkle in his eye while he tells our guide, a Lieutenant-Commander, how the Navy did the de-Gaussing that so amazed Carl Allen, alias Carlos Allende, when he concocted the yarn about ETs and vanishing ships. It was a good day. The sun was shining over the harbor, the channel was inviting, seagulls soared beyond the superstructures of the Guadalcanal. It would be silly to dwell on the story, except for the fact that similar hoaxes are born every day, and that aspiring ufologists of the new generation are re-discovering such tales--and believe them.

People can fall into dangerous spirals over such distorted notions: only two days ago some 50 members of a doomsday cult called the *Order of the Solar Temple* were found dead in Switzerland and Québec. Similar delusions helped precipitate World War Two, when Hitler used the *Protocols of the Elders of Sion*, that ugly hoax, to condone his mass killings of Jews. So this trip feels like a pilgrimage, even if the 18-inch guns of the battleships have been silent for years, and if the *Eldridge* has been scrapped decades ago, secrets and all.

Mabillon. Tuesday 25 October 1994.

"It's when you get old like me that you begin to understand what life really means," my 94-year-old mother told me yesterday, "when things start hurting and breaking down."

She has pains in her right thigh, and her fingers have trouble grasping objects; she walks with a more pronounced forward bend. Yet she pulled out a list of questions and a neat file of newspaper cuttings underlined in red, a collection of articles about the recent tragedy of the Order of the Solar Temple.

She wanted to know about technology, medicine, cellular telephones, and cometary cataclysms on Jupiter. There's a lesson in her enduring sharpness, even though she now has occasional lapses.

Beyond the passion and tumult that we tend to regard as the essence of our lives, a vast landscape of intelligence exists that requires no facile entertainment or superficial gloss. My mother still walks around the Latin Quarter, takes the Métro by herself, runs errands, does her own shopping. Paris is lovely, full of light, dense with soulful tenderness.

When I'm not strolling around I read Otto Rahn's *Court of Lucifer*, a touching book by a young author full of contradictions: he was a Nazi, a mystic and a homosexual. I respect his writing, even if he ended up on the wrong side of history, with a philosophy I detest.

Mabillon. Saturday 29 October 1994.

I have decided to start drafting *Les Enjeux du Millénaire*, a book about the financing of innovation. I walked out to buy notepaper. I love these little streets: *Rue Suger, Rue du Jardinet...*

Dinner with Jean-Francois Deluol, teacher and artist. He urged me not to give up research: "Never stop asking questions, even if you've outgrown the web of intrigue in the field." But why preserve these memories? I am glad my children don't share my affinity for secrecy and magic, even though I think the world is, in the final analysis, a secret place that can only be understood through magic.

The stock of *Mercury Interactive*, the major success of our Euro-America Fund, and my best pick so far, is trading over ten times higher than what I paid for it when I invested in the start-up. Ironically, for the moment, that single fact will weigh more favorably on my professional destiny than any spiritual insights I may have gained.

Now Jean Sider tells me socialite Marie Galbraith came to France recently to ask scientists to petition the U.S. Government in an effort to release supposedly classified data on UFOs. Mrs. Galbraith is a very wealthy lady, a close friend of the Rockefellers. She spoke to Pierre Guérin, telling him that she was on the Board of the Human Potential Foundation. Guérin jumped up with his usual lack of subtlety: "Oh, that's the group run by Scott Jones, that CIA lackey!"

"Scott Jones? I fired him!" she replied, surprised that the Foundation's odd reputation had spread so far and wide.

Mabillon. Tuesday 1 November 1994.

This is the Day of the Dead, so the bells of Saint Sulpice are tolling and the streets are empty, save for a few tourists caught unaware in the dread of the occasion. The sun is out in a cold, blue sky.

This two-week break is good for me. It forces me to dwell on the future. Payan, who has no concept of a scientist who can be a free spirit, told me the other day, "You'd never have the same high position in France, given your open interest in the paranormal."

When I hear people tell me about the frustrations of their lives I remember why I left Europe. As Otto Rahn observed when he retraced Tannhauser's route, "Error purifies those whose will is good and strong." Let's hope this applies to me. After all, Tannhauser himself had long lived and worshipped underground, in the mountain of Venus. Should I take Faust's hand, as he did, and seek "the Mountain of the Gathering at the Farthest Midnight"? (*La Montagne du Rassemblement Au Plus Lointain Minuit.*) Should I revive the flame that keeps burning in my ancient temple?

I had lunch with my brother at Odéon today and walked back with him to Saint Sulpice. We talked about his retirement from the department he ran at Necker Hospital and from his role as a professor of medicine. He left everything there: his books, his publications. He turns down consulting invitations and doesn't read medical journals. He finds his new freedom exciting.

Later I went alone to the Cluny museum to see the *Pilier des Nautes*. It is the oldest monument in Paris, a stela erected by the boat drivers of the Seine who belonged to the tribe of the *Parisii*, in honor of Pagan Gods with horned heads.

On the plane back to San Francisco. Sunday 6 November 1994.

Sipping tomato juice at *Deux Magots* Gilbert Payan, "the man in the shadows," told me that he thought the dwarfish beings at Roswell were artificial biological specimens and that the "craft" had been dropped from a real UFO to deliver a Fourth of July warning to the United States, at their first atom bomb site: an idea worth pondering.

I reminded him that I had entered the field because of Aimé Michel and Guérin, and later Hynek, but I certainly wouldn't enter it now, repelled as I am by the blatant hoaxes and the pseudo-religious squabbles that stain the field.

I showed Payan the Melvin Laird correspondence with Les Aspin, which amazed him. He would have given anything, he said, to keep a copy.

He told me that upon her arrival in France Marie Galbraith had gone straight to the CNES where she was received courteously but learned nothing, naturally.

Hummingbird. Thursday 10 November 1994.

Hans Rasmussen is back in San Francisco, sleeping at Ana's apartment. We share many memories. In the evening Janine and I went to see *The Fiery Angel* by Prokofiev. It was a spectacular show, with a dozen humanoids in tight gray body suits gliding acrobatically on the edges of the stage, manifesting the demons in the minds of the participants. It did seem, however, that neither Prokofiev nor the producers had taken full advantage of the plot. Faust and Mephistopheles made a purely gratuitous appearance in the middle of the story, never to be heard from again, while the debauchery in the last scene, the orgy at the convent, was sadly understated.

On Tuesday I voted for Democratic candidate Dianne Feinstein for the Senate and Republican Pete Wilson for governor of California. France lumbers on from one old man to another, dragging along icons of conservatism that haven't had a new idea since the Fifties.

Hummingbird. Monday 14 November 1994.

Dick Farley and I agree that the extraterrestrial belief functions as a virus, while no genuine global research is carried out.

"The problem is the people, not the Aliens," Farley said when I told him about Marie Galbraith's futile trip to Europe. "By the way, her nickname is Bootsie," he told me, "she's a close friend of Steven Greer, who tells people he's in close touch with the crowned heads of Europe, in turn in contact with the Aliens! He got $20,000 through the HPF, not to mention what he got for Project Starlight, which does PR for the Eschaton…" At least we've gained a new vocabulary.

Hummingbird. Wednesday 23 November 1994.

Researcher Larry Hatch has invited me to Redwood City to review his U* database. It is a great piece of work, over 10,000 screened sightings, all important details summarized.

I bought a copy, and as soon as I came home I downloaded it and showed the graphics to Janine, who remembers well the time we spent screening and cataloging the very first system of this type, over 30 years ago. Larry is a skilled programmer, a graphic designer. Unfortunately, he also chain-smokes and drinks a lot. When I rang at his house in Redwood City he was barely able to walk to the door.

Spring Hill. Saturday 26 November 1994.

Otter Zell and Morning Glory came over last night, bringing a pecan pie, a month-old pet possum, and an autobiographical history of the *Church of All Worlds*. Morning Glory wore a stunning black outfit and spoke of the Fairy Tradition with her usual scholarship.

Otter told us of the time when they were infiltrated by a man from the Secret Service, who revealed his affiliation after he ascertained they were harmless: "He recognized we would never give rise to a new Charles Manson," Otter pointed out. Yet Morning Glory remembers with horror a man named Ng who spent time in their Commune before moving to the Sierra and murdering dozens of victims: "One time he had to kill a sheep, something he'd never done," she recalled. "He came and wept in my lap. I had been raised on a farm, and I had to talk him through his anguish. This guy turned out to be the worst murderer in California history—and a cannibal!"

Hummingbird. Tuesday 29 November 1994.

Dr. Ed May has retreated to his home office inside his beautiful house in Palo Alto, filled with Indian artifacts and parapsychology books. I like Ed for his caustic humor and sheer intelligence. He is running up against the same insane bureaucracy Hal Puthoff battled for many years. After a 6-hour site visit, Dick D'Amato cut Ed's budget from $2 million a year to $500,000, displeased with DIA. The contract has now moved "across the river," as Washingtonians say about the CIA.

Over a Mexican lunch Ed told me a Senate staffer had badly exposed Savin, the top man in Soviet parapsychology, while Ed's project was trying to quietly map out the connections among their labs. He also participated in a meeting at which a Russian psychotronic expert spoke about interfering with the brain's circuitry to "cure" psychological defects, a subject of keen interest to CIA.

"Pandolfi is the one who told a journalist about our project," Ed reported. While in Russia he was shown an Intelligence report on "foreign" parapsychology. He couldn't find any mention of SRI: "It's in another report that I can't show you!" the Russian said.

Everything is changing again in Washington. Old Senator Pell is being replaced as chairman of the Foreign affairs committee by Jesse Helms, a blabbermouth from the extreme right with no interest in parapsychology. Ed's good connections with Senator Cohen have evaporated and D'Amato's job is hanging by a thread, since Senator Byrd won't chair Defense Appropriations in the new Congress.

A Colorado researcher has given me details of Bootsie Galbraith's trip to Europe, in the form of a letter from Daphne F. Wood, who works for the BSW Foundation (**38**). Their work naïvely aims at "collecting the best evidence from every nation."

"They were well aware of your extensive network, but you haven't been contacted," my friend said with a chuckle, "because you're too analytical about the Extraterrestrial Cause!" Just as well…

Hummingbird. Thursday 1 December 1994.

I've spoken to a man who knows all the personalities involved in the French trip: "Pamela Harriman was there; she is one of the *Grandes Dames* of the Democratic Party," he told me. "She has been named by Clinton as Ambassador to France. Her husband's father, the late Averell Harriman, was the son of a robber baron. As for Bootsie Galbraith, she's the wife of Heathen Galbraith, who is still alive. He is, among other things, the importer of *Moët & Chandon* champagne to the United States. A staunch conservative, he was Republican Party candidate as Governor of New York. Reagan named him Ambassador to France. Bootsie has been very active on the Board of the Children's Museum; she's turned it into a darling of millionnaires."

He paused, then resumed in a sterner voice: "You're talking about the Upper Crust here, Jacques, make no mistake about that. These people knew each other as children. Some may be voting Democratic, others Republican, but they go to the same parties."

He caught himself: "Actually this isn't quite right. Mrs. Harriman, as a young woman, was a nobody, a working-class girl. She went to England before the war and happened to marry Winston Churchill's son. She even became a confidante of Winston's in the darkest hours of the War. That was when Roosevelt sent Harriman to London. They fell in love and had a torrid affair that was the scandal of the British Isles. She divorced the Churchill son. When Harriman's wife died, he married her. Soon she was the rage of Washington and the Kingmaker of Democrats, although the Harriman children have always hated her."

The two ladies were accompanied by John L. Petersen, futurist and strong ET believer, who directs the Arlington Institute. He has written *The Road to 2015*, a book that mentions a "wild card scenario" in which the First Contact takes place when a team of volunteer researchers financed by a private Foundation meet extraterrestrials and produce videotapes of the encounter. Dan T. Smith, too, claims his family was always close to the Galbraiths.

Hummingbird. Sunday 4 December 1994.

Last night Diane Darling came over to see us at the ranch, bringing a bottle of Absinthe and her good spirit, although the pain of her recent break-up with Otter and Morning Glory was still obvious. We talked about Spring Hill and its moods and the Devas who might be reigning over the valley. Diane suggested they were the spirits of the giant Redwoods, feeling betrayed: the whole valley used to be covered with them. Now greedy humans are cutting down the finest of the remaining trees. Soon the tall redwoods we've preserved at Spring Hill will be the last grove standing in the area. "Tomki Road is very ancient," she added, "it's the old wagon trail, way before the highway was built. No wonder there are strange things around here."

Now I've just spoken to Hal Puthoff, one of the few stable points of reference. He'd heard about the BSW project through Ingo Swann, who knows the two ladies socially and "is mystified about the situation." I laughed. I've never known Ingo to be mystified about anything. Hal's other source is John Petersen, the futurist.

"John's a great guy, he's arranged for me to present my work to the Navy and to the Marine Corps at Quantico. Kit was there too, talking about the future of automotive technology. John has spent a week with Greer and wrote up the proposal to Rockefeller.

"Is he impressed with Greer?" I asked in some amazement.

"Well… He's still at the Gee-Whiz stage, if you see what I mean."

"That won't get him very far with the French Research Minister..."

I proceeded to tell Hal what I'd discovered about the way the two *Grandes Dames* had been received in Paris, and why I had been advised to stay out of it. Hal had a different opinion:

"One of these days we need to get together at some bar, you and I, so I can tell you what I've found out. It's scary stuff. There are serious people involved in this business, with observations on the scale of what you described about Brazil; animals were fried. This was all observed under official conditions..."

He gave me John's number. I will meet him in Washington on Friday at the Mayflower hotel, but the time hasn't come to talk about my experiments at Spring Hill: that might even negate the effects I'm seeking, if retro-causality actually works.

Hummingbird. Monday 5 December 1994.

Kit called this afternoon. We hadn't spoken in months: I couldn't understand why he'd urged me to meet Dan Smith, back in February. Kit said he'd come to consider two scenarios. The first one had to do with the fact that "You and I are just beginning to recognize to what extent many people are delusional. Five percent of the population is nearly psychotic by the time they reach age 50; many maintain their delusions and live normally. Occasionally they even become psychiatrists--or CIA analysts," he chuckled. Jolly West at UCLA thinks they're looking for a healthy outlet for their craziness!"

"Fine," I said, unconvinced, "What's the second scenario?"

"The second scenario is that the core story, the UFO story, is real in what you and I have called the 'coffee cup' sense. But it creates spinoff stories that infect people. In other words, it spreads a mental virus to which people fall victim. I'm really interested in this, because I think it's epidemiology pure and simple. Tests can be developed. 90% of the UFO soap opera is a mental illness."

I just had to counter: "You and I work every day with professional folks who believe that Mary remained a virgin even though Jesus had two brothers, and she flew up to Heaven in her earth body, and you don't call them crazy: you just call them Catholics. Catholics get promoted at GM like everybody else, don't they?"

"That's not the same thing at all," he replied testily. "Religion, as a belief system, is quite distinct from what I'm talking about."

"I'm not so sure," I said. "Look at the poor occult converts in Switzerland and Canada, those fake Templars who committed mass suicide. Look at the Peoples' Temple... The only difference between a crazy sect and an honorable religion is the number of followers."

Hummingbird. Tuesday 6 December 1994.

This afternoon I visited the HeartMath Institute in Boulder Creek. Ren Breck had introduced me to their staff. One of the researchers there, a Russian, claims the Soviets have a weapon that can stop the heartbeats of living people within a five-mile radius (**39**).

Now Fred reminds me of a statement by Robert Gates when he was interviewed as potential director of the CIA, pointing out that in the future "the study of mysteries will be far more important than the investigation of secrets" for the Intelligence Community.

Washington, Hotel Madison. Saturday 10 December 1994.

Yesterday morning, under a pale, cold sky, I took a cab to the French Embassy, a modern, white building on a hilltop on Reservoir Road. I was following up on Boudier's suggestion last May regarding possible sharing of UFO material. I was quickly ushered into the office of General Pouliquen, who pretended to have no idea why I wanted to see him, even after I mentioned the connection with General Letty, so I told him how I had become interested in this research.

The general asked me a few bland questions, but he didn't offer any follow-up, so I gave up. Another dead-end, trying to communicate with French authorities. It could be an effect of their regalian prerogatives, but it's more likely it hides pure and simple ignorance.

In the afternoon I met John Petersen at the elegant coffee shop of the Mayflower hotel. He's an intense, bright futurist, about 40. We ordered Ceylan tea and spoke of Rockefeller. I told him bluntly what I had heard from my friends in France after Mrs. Galbraith's trip.

I was surprised at how little Petersen knew of the field. He was not aware of the *Iron Mountain report* and didn't seem to understand why Bootsie had mentioned the Human Potential Foundation to the French. It turns out that there are two ongoing projects under Rockefeller's control. One is run by Bootsie, charged with obtaining "the best data." The second is under Greer, who claims direct ET communication.

"I've spent a whole week with Greer, I've been at his house. I'm convinced he's absolutely sincere," Petersen told me. He even wonders if the man isn't an extraterrestrial hybrid: "I helped him setup project Starlight, I did the PR for him, but he's a guy with a big ego, like most emergency doctors. It would be easy for the Aliens to have a number of human agents like him among us," he added. "There are amazing telepathic events around Greer. He's flown out at night, mentally, to remote locations... He's had UFOs come within 100 feet of where he was, signalling with light. Why would they do that if they were not seeking contact?"

To me, this is reminiscent of the Uri Geller days at SRI, when Hoova was about to reveal itself to the world. Like Andrija Puharich, Greer and Petersen are hoping for "The Big Disclosure" that will mark a discontinuity. They're sure it is just around the corner.

Hummingbird. Sunday 11 December 1994.

It rained all day yesterday while the SSE Council met at the Crystal City Holiday Inn, a gloomy place on the outskirts of the Pentagon. There were eleven of us, including Mike Epstein, Brenda Dunne, Bob Jahn, Peter Sturrock, Bob Wood, Roger Nelson, and the most cautiously reflective of us all, Ian Stevenson. I got up to urge the group to use the Internet for communication and visibility. Funding is in the hands of Bob Jahn, in touch with Rockefeller and Prince Hans-Adam, but I stressed that going through wealthy men would not necessarily open any doors among scientific institutions, it might have the opposite effect: political pressure is a double-edged sword.

Hummingbird. Saturday 31 December 1994.

An enjoyable interlude: my son and Janine's brother Alain joined us for Christmas. Yesterday, after kissing goodbye to Olivier and driving Alain back to the airport, I had a long lunch with Fred Beckman, eager to tell me about a phone conversation with Robert Durant, who spoke about Bootsie and her friend Sandy Houghton:

"They have big plans," he reported; "big but vague. No conspiracy there, mind you. They're simply bright, middle-aged people who need an answer to the mysteries of life and believe that Greer will explain everything. They have no idea how research is done. They think they've already met the Important People, of course."

Fred went on, after a sip of his wine: "they're completely absorbed in Petersen's ideology: The Aliens are here, real good guys, we must be prepared, a revolution is coming... Disclosure…"

"I see: The paradigm shifts, guess who the Facilitators are...?"

"Something like that," Fred concluded with a tired sigh.

Hummingbird. Sunday 8 January 1995.

The Russian River has reached flood stage. When we left the ranch our own little creek had grown into a torrent. It makes a series of foaming cascades as it rushes furiously among the redwoods.

A letter in *New Scientist* (**40**) comments on an article by Susan Blackmore entitled *Alien Abduction: The Inside Story*, in their 19 November issue. It centers on Michael Persinger, employed by the U.S. to develop behavior-modifying electromagnetic weapons under project *Sleeping Beauty*. Persinger published an article entitled "Possible cardiac driving by an external rotating magnetic field" as early as 1973. And Paul Tyler, director of the Armed Forces Radiobiology Research Institute, wrote in 1986 of a technique "to disrupt the electrical signal in cardiac muscle," producing "complete asystole with a resultant fatal outcome." That reminded me of the statement at the Heartmath Institute about Russian weapons that killed by stopping the heart. The next big war will be interesting.

Keith Harary remembers having tea with Susan Blackmore in Utrecht. A bright, sincere researcher, she became disillusioned with parapsychology and became an avid debunker. Her *New Scientist* article, along with Jim Schnabel's paper in *Dissociation*, is promoted as the high intellectual ground against paranormal research.

Hummingbird. Sunday 15 January 1995.

An intense week lies ahead. I must raise new financing for two of our companies, Accuray, and Ubique. The former is a project in which I believe intensely.

The product is a robotic device to attack inoperable brain tumors through hard X-rays, but the venture community won't finance it, arguing that reimbursement is uncertain and recalling the expensive failure of Resonex, an MRI company that came too early. At present, our Fund is Accuray's only hope of fighting another day.

Hummingbird. Tuesday 17 January 1995.

Dick Farley reminds me that a lot of behavior modification research has been done through the Bureau of Prisons and the VA: John Lilly, Timothy Leary, Stan Grof, and other New Age gurus have all worked as psychiatrists and MDs in the pay of the government, under the umbrella of research designed to "help" alcoholics and addicts.

Messages on the Internet propagate a new meme from England. It was initiated three days ago by Reg Presley, lead singer of the rock group *The Troggs*: he claims that a videotape has been discovered, showing the autopsy of an Alien at Roswell. He said there were fifteen such videotapes, totalling 150 minutes of footage, dated 1947. The media aren't buying it.

Videotapes had not been invented in 1947.

Hummingbird. Tuesday 24 January 1995.

The death of Dr. Andrija Puharich a couple of weeks ago (he fell down some stairs) has brought back some memories. Millionnaire Josh Reynolds had been Andrija's last protector, but his executors evicted the old man from the North Carolina estate.

Services were conducted by a partner of medium Phyllis Schlemmer, a psychic channel of the "Council of Nine." And now a real shock, as I just opened a letter from the second wife of Dr. X, raising doubts about his medical claims.

Hummingbird. Sunday 29 January 1995.

Is it time to sell Spring Hill? The notion of a spiritual retreat for quiet research in the woods fades away: it's too hard. In the redneck culture the loggers are only interested in beer and car races, while the hippies are only interested in pot and Star Trek reruns.

We did get indications that the phenomenon was alive around us, and our research has clarified the methodology and scrubbed the data, but the social context of Mendocino County has become too heavy for us, with the increasingly scary criminal gangs and the recent intrusion of international drug networks.

Yesterday we spent time with our new neighbors in San Francisco, Kevin and Sheila Starr. He's the State Librarian for California, and a wonderful historian. Then, for Janine's birthday, Catherine invited us for pastries on Union Street. I relish this time with her, her courage in a difficult world, with uncertain job prospects for her generation.

Hummingbird. Monday 30 January 1995.

Fred Beckman has mellowed out since his vascular brain incident. He looked a bit lost today in waterproof jacket and his old tan trousers. He reminisced about his friendship with composer Easley Blackwood, whom he had met in the 1950s. He also talked about his father, whom he hardly got to know because he was sent off to war in Indonesia while little Fred was struggling with puberty in Mattoon, Illinois. Fred's father was an athlete, a football player who was hoping his son would take up sports. Instead, Fred, small and not very strong, surrounded himself with piles of philosophy books.

We discussed Schnabel's recent article about abductions in *Dissociation*. The apparent logic of the argument is couched in a way proper to impress the Academy, whose members don't have the time or the inclination to look at real data, as they proved in 1969 when they lent their credibility to the phony Condon report. Even the smartest people keep falling for superficially clever explanations.

Astronaut Gordon Cooper has stated again that he'd seen flying disks in Germany at the end of World War Two. They had been recovered by the Germans, not by us, he claimed. He also suggested he'd flown a tethered flying saucer in Utah, a true Alien craft (**41**).

"Kit Green is a friend and a knowledgeable scientist, so why do you think he sends me all this stuff, brushing off abductions as dissociative mental phenomena?" I asked a well-connected friend.

"He's trying to confuse you," he answered without hesitation. "There are not more than five people who can get behind Vallee on this topic; Kit Green is one of them. So, he's throwing you a curve."

"Either that, or he's a bit confused himself, like Gordon Cooper…"

"Don't be ridiculous, he's one of the top experts in mind control!"

Hummingbird. Thursday 2 February 1995.

The America we see around us is gravely troubled. The new generation watches their parents' failing lives within the system: hard work, for what? "Downsizing," "restructuring," current euphemisms for abrupt layoffs, and often the unfair termination of pensions and benefits, sending middle-class Americans into poverty.

John Mack's assistant tells me that "Harvard is now taking an interest in John's work," which sounded hopeful until she added that he'd retained an attorney to help him answer charges that resulted from this "interest."

The attorney wants me to help explain why abductions should be studied. But this attorney is Sheehan, from the Christic Institute. I cannot get drawn into that fight.

Then I took the recent events (the scanning of my mail, the manuscripts stolen from Fred Beckman's car, the odd requests from people claiming ties to the CIA) to a high-level law firm in Manhattan. As a general partner in a venture fund charged with the responsibility for investing other people's money, I have a duty to disclose to my partners any unusual pressure put on me, or any attempt to compromise my decisions.

The attorney read my memo. He was incensed:

"What they're doing is blatantly illegal, and I don't care if they have support from the DCI," he said. "Which I doubt, by the way. You're simply dealing with weirdoes and crooks within CIA. This government is full of them. We trust your integrity, or you wouldn't be in my office." He added, "Don't worry if things get rough. Keep doing what you're doing."

Hummingbird. Saturday 11 February 1995.

Over lunch with a TV producer who is impressed with the Bootsie affair, she did acknowledge that the two great ladies swallow everything Greer tells them.

"What about Cooper's claims of having flown a saucer?" I asked.

"Cooper's craft wasn't Alien. It was a plain human reconnaissance machine," she stated. "The technology has been sold to the Saudis."

She went on to boast she'd been offered the Holloman film, which made me laugh: everybody in Hollywood has been "offered" the Holloman film, with worthless hints of UFO hardware to follow.

Hummingbird. Monday 13 February 1995.

Stan Friedman came over for dinner yesterday and stayed for five hours. It was a relaxed, friendly evening. He reported several things of interest: (i) It is for alledged "malpractice" that John Mack is being sued by Harvard. He is also accused of wrongful billing of his patients, whose files he won't release, (ii) Stan has done excellent research on Menzel's life. The man was highly regarded in Intelligence circles, advised several Presidents, and survived loyalty hearings, but does this prove that he was part of a UFO coverup? Maybe Menzel was only briefed on the tradecraft side? I suspect he wasn't allowed to reveal to his former student Allen Hynek that many of the reports had to do with government disinformation and fake craft.

Scott Jones called my office today. We discussed the Rockefeller Initiative in the context of Bootsie and Greer's actions. He did clarify what had happened in Jack Gibbons' office, adding useful touches to the scene: there were no less than three meetings with Gibbons. At the first meeting the President's advisor was extraordinarily nervous.

"I've known this man for ten years," Scott told me, "and I'd never seen him so uncomfortable. He wasn't ready for the meeting and couldn't imagine why anybody, let alone a distinguished insider like Laurance, would take that UFO stuff seriously."

At the second meeting he was waiting for the CIA's report on UFOs and hadn't received it, so he was mad at the Agency. It was a very irate Jack Gibbons who requested a classified briefing. Scott believes that Kit went up to deliver it, and he may have briefed Al Gore, too.

"Dick Farley took off in a huff, and he kicked up a lot of cow pies on the runway as he did. Laurance didn't write to the President but the matter went as high as the White House Chief of Staff."

This confirmed that Clinton's Chief of Staff had been briefed to make sure the President wouldn't be open to further manipulation.

Hummingbird. Thursday 16 February 1995.

We heard very sad news from Gerald Askevold last night: Thad Wilson, Janine's former colleague and my old assistant at the Institute for the Future, is dying of a brain tumor in Montana. We called one of the women who nursed him. She assured us that his wish to die at home was being respected. She will pass along our final message.

I went to see Peter Schwartz and Laurence Wilkinson at Global Business Network in their white, airy offices in a trendy section of Emeryville. Peter is skeptical of the Intelligence community's ability to seriously look into UFOs: "I gave them a scenario, years ago, about the collapse of the USSR. When it seemed that it was actually happening, two years before the Berlin Wall came down, I went over to talk to Robert Gates, then deputy director of the CIA. He told me, 'your scenario isn't going to happen within your lifetime!' He practically threw me out."

Hummingbird. Monday 20 February 1995.

Professor Eric Walker died three days ago. He was the former President of Penn State University who served as executive secretary of the Pentagon's R&D board along with physicist Sarbacher, who claimed to have attended a secret meeting at WPAFB to discuss crashed Aliens. Ufologist William Steinman reportedly had validation of the statements, but Walker wouldn't confirm or deny to Kit that four Aliens had been picked up and one had survived.

New York. Wednesday 1 March 1995.

For many years I have been warning about the cultist danger behind the fascination with UFOs. Now we learn that the Solar Temple cult in Switzerland had an inner circle that was initiated into contact with supposed extraterrestrial masters from Proxima (**42**). They used optical tricks to create images of their Unknown Superiors and holographs of mystical sights during the ceremonies. I feel both vindicated and depressed at the news.

Our life is quietly changing again: having passed her real estate examinations, Janine, who doesn't plan to retire, is valiantly embarking on a new career, license in hand. She will work at her own pace, working on the sale of properties on the Peninsula.

Now I'm back in New York, at a meeting devoted to the new online services that are sweeping the country. These new firms, growing on the model of my old InfoMedia but taking advantage of the cheaper, expanding networks, are creating new markets. They offer information sources that revolutionize the publishing and entertainment industry.

At the first panel this morning Russ Siegelman of Microsoft announced that the giant software company would launch its own network services, in competition with America Online, Prodigy, and Compuserve, which will have to struggle to retain their market share: The Internet continues to devour its own children.

New York. Thursday 2 March 1995.

This morning I met with Udi Shapiro and an AOL executive at the law offices of Fulbright Jaworski. AOL proposes an investment in Ubique and a product licence that would launch our technology throughout the Internet.

Afterwards we discussed the deal with Fred Adler, burdened by his reputation as a mercurial investor (**43**). I am hopeful, given our current successes, that we will be able to save Accuray Systems, still struggling to position itself in the medical market, shaking the skepticism of doctors and investors alike.

Hummingbird. Saturday 11 March 1995.

We have worked all day, speaking with colleagues on the phone, sorting out old papers. I am so happy, so happy... To be here with you, watching the rain hitting the great glass windows in fierce streams, the city white and gray with blurry swirls, while we huddle above mankind's madness. I have just received copies of *Dimensions* in Russian under the title *The Great Mysteries - The Parallel World*, so I sent one to Dick Haines, a man I admire, and who reads Russian.

Hummingbird. Monday 13 March 1995.

Fred Beckman called today, as he often does, in an urgent conspiratorial tone. “There's a new rumor,” he said, almost as if he was about to accuse me of some dreadful crime. “It's about you!”

I had to laugh: “What did I do this time?”

“My sources tell me that while you were in Brazil, the military down there showed you some films of alien autopsies.”

I laughed louder: “Where are these rumors coming from?”

“From Durant, surprisingly,” he confessed. “And Dan T. Smith.”

I must have given an audible sigh of disgust, because he went on:

“I know, it figures, doesn't it? Dan Smith got it from Ron Pandolfi at CIA. Pandolfi claims he got it from Kit Green.” (Note)

“What do you want me to do about it?” I asked drily. The question took him aback, because he had been expecting me to react with a flow of loud protest. I never put energy into silly rumors.

“I'm just relaying what they say,” he replied defensively, “I have all that on tape, you can listen to it; they think you saw the same film that surfaced in England...”

“Is that the same movie where you and Hynek are examining the little cadaver while eating a hamburger?”

This time he got the joke and laughed heartily.

“I couldn’t eat a hamburger, under the circumstances. I understand the men are shown pulling out the Alien's intestines, in a desperate attempt to save him…”

(Note) Planting such rumors, as I learned much later, is standard CIA practice. It serves to draw people into narratives the government wants to spread, either to make the yarn look more interesting, or to question the credibility of researchers who may be too close to the truth about a particular situation. But is it legal for the CIA to dupe the U.S. public in this way?

"Remind me: isn't the Alien's intestinal system connected to his brain?" I asked, laughing in turn.

"I remember something like that from Bill Moore's television special with Rick Doty, alias Falcon." He paused, realizing I was joking.

"Come to think of it, I know a lot of humans who function like that." Fred chuckled. I was glad I'd disclosed the earlier events on the record for my partners, but I'm getting a bit tired of these idiots making up such stories. Any response, of course, would feed the scam.

Hummingbird. Sunday 19 March 1995.

On Thursday night we drove up to Spring Hill, expecting to forget the tumultuous world of venture capital, but the first phone call we got came from Fred Adler. He had spoken to the French who were ready to launch the second Fund with me, he said in a collegial and complimentary--almost respectful--tone for once. We agreed that we should concentrate on American startups. Based on the situation in Europe, looking for high-tech investments in France would be a waste of time, as our previous experiences have shown.

Hummingbird. Wednesday 22 March 1995.

Psychotherapist Maralyn Teare has captured the fallacy of current ufology in professional terms: "Abduction research has gone astray," she said, "Too many egos, too much false analysis. Just look at Budd Hopkins' art, his sadistic paintings. Now he keeps 'discovering' the same features in his abductees' stories under hypnosis. (**44**)"

"Don't you think we're fortunate to have been cutoff from their circle of initiates, you and me?" I asked her. She exclaimed:

"Thank the higher planes! Do you know that I was excluded from their talks with the Dalai Lama? John Mack and his entourage pushed me aside when we all met in Toronto. They wanted to feed him 'scientific' facts…Jacques, the man is a Buddhist! He doesn't look at the world in that narrow way. It was ridiculous; they were all crowded around him in their Bermuda shorts, and the women in tank tops. There wasn't a real scientist in the whole bunch, and is that a way to dress when you meet a holy man?"

It's hard to turn on the TV without finding a program on abductions these days. Yesterday I saw Arthur C. Clarke himself peering through a cheap telescope and commenting on the abduction of Betty Hill, who was later seen caressing an Alien bust. John Mack followed on the screen, hypnotizing somebody. The whole thing looked very silly. A smart-looking astronomer from SETI followed, studiously adjusting a multichannel analyzer. The subtext spelled out the concept that Aliens were indeed out there, but very, very far away indeed, and completely harmless.

Benjamin Zuckerman of UCLA (**45**) has noted that the raw material needed to form a giant gas planet like Jupiter is not available among most young stars. Yet it is the gravitational pull of giant planets that protects smaller bodies such as the Earth from collisions with big asteroids, making civilization possible.

New York. Hotel Renaissance. Friday 24 March 1995.

Fred Adler was remarkably clear and focused this morning, as he often is in private, one-on-one sessions with me. We discussed Ubique's virtual collaboration software, our second venture Fund and the problems in the French business culture.

At the bottom of the French soul, along with the heroics, the loyalty to ideals and the occasional clear grasp of realities, there lurks an odd mixture of pettiness, jealousy, cowardice, vanity, and envy that defeats all attempts to turn France into a truly great power.

Tel Aviv Hilton. Saturday 25 March 1995.

The non-stop flight from New York landed at Ben Gurion airport in wind and rain. The sound of the surf kept me sleeping quietly all afternoon, although my brain was busy sorting out through the problems of half a dozen little companies. But there is a basket of fruits on a side table, and my balcony overlooks the Mediterranean.

My fiction work reads like a quest for the unknown wise man: it first surfaced in *The Blue Prism,* never published. I looked for him in the Xarius Chimero of *Dark Satellite*, and in *Fabricant d'Evénements Inéluctables*. I hoped to find him in real life too, in Anton, Kit, or Fred Adler, but none of them turned out to have valuable answers.

Tel Aviv Hilton. Sunday 26 March 1995.

As I study the life and style of Anaïs Nin, whose Journal I carry on this trip, it becomes obvious that any diarist is torn between raw art (the evanescent stream of emotions, anger, bliss, or terror that spills onto the page in real time) and the more polished reflection made understandable, smooth in its transitions, clear in direction. Nin scholars say that her edited diaries, captivating as they may be, were nothing like the insightful shimmer of her manuscripts. Anaïs Nin edited heavily, so she had to carry around a thick file labelled "lies."

Tel Aviv Hilton. Monday 27 March 1995.

This morning I joined Yadin Kaufman and Dan and Donny Tolkowsky at the new offices of Veritas Ventures in Herzliya. After a brief meeting with a French engineer who had a patent for a new type of smart keyboard we flew to a kibbutz at Kiryat Schmona, near the Lebanese border. A group of clever, rugged settlers in the area are busy developing *Logal*, fine science education software. The CEO took us to lunch at a trout farm on a plateau from which we could see Mount Harmon of Biblical fame while we debated the imminent changes the Internet would produce in the business world.

After lunch we drove up to the Golan Heights, passing a crusader fortress and some Druze villages all the way to the Syrian border, where a lonely UN outpost surveys the No Man's Land that separates ancient enemies.

On a nearby hilltop an array of Israeli radars, antennas, and microwave dishes monitor Syrian airspace all the way to Damascus. We came back through Tiberias and Capharnaüm, leaving the Sea of Galilee shrouded in the gray dusk.

TWA flight from Tel Aviv to Paris. Tuesday 28 March 1995.

At Ben Gurion airport grown men in black suits stand up in isolated spots where they sway back and forth, a book in their hands and a blanket over their heads. I got there before dawn to face close interrogation by the pretty girls of the security detail. Barely out of high school, they swing their loaded Galils like grizzled warriors.

Hummingbird. Friday 31 March 1995.

I had a puzzling lunch today with John Petersen at the Garden Court. One moment he told me that he was instrumental in obtaining funding of 2M$ for Dr. Greer, and that he setup project Starlight for him and Bootsie "to convince the leaders of the world of the reality of UFOs." The next moment he professed to be skeptical, claimed that Bootsie was uninformed and complained about big egos in the way. Petersen denied knowing anything about Greer's White House contacts, but he assured me that Clinton had signed an Executive Order giving immunity to Gordon Cooper and Ingo Swann to talk about "what they knew." When I pushed him, he no longer seemed certain the order actually existed, so I went away confused.

Tomorrow Janine and I will get away to explore the roots of the contactee movement in the Mojave Desert, with our friend Roger Brenner, a long overdue research trip. Also, *Omni Magazine* has just published my classification scheme for anomalies (**46**).

Indio. Tuesday 11 April 1995.

The population is still growing in this land of millionnaires. When the little commuter plane reached Palm Springs we landed in a wide array of lights. Roger met us in an open red truck and gave us a tour of the wealthy towns, all the way to Indio. As we sat down for dinner he told us about his scary experiences as a child molested by a couple of music teachers who implied they were from outer space.

The wife told him: "We're not from here; we're studying humans. Is there anything you can tell us about them?"

Indio. Wednesday 12 April 1995.

Walking to a coffee shop for breakfast, we began to realize how tired we were, exhausted by the grinding of our schedules back home.

Roger took us around the area, explaining its history, telling us about his old school and the possible abduction of one of his friends. This historic region encompasses Eisenhower's house and Patton's desert headquarters. Tomorrow we drive out deeper into the areas where the Contactees of the 1950s used to meet their Venusian friends.

Indio. Thursday 13 April 1995.

We joined Roger's regular Jeep tour this morning, driving into the hills above Palm Springs, visiting shaded canyons inhabited by the Cahuilla Indians for at least 3000 years. The landscape is spectacular, with its palm trees, waterfalls, colorful fields of flowers, and barrel cactus up the slopes.

Over lunch we pursued Roger's recollections. The music teacher and his wife may well have been nothing more than average neighborhood perverts, artistically gifted, but there was more: Roger recalls coming out of a trance once, his head between the legs of an older woman; another time they showed him a movie of a naked boy, but told him, "We didn't show you the good parts." Ominously, *they asked him if he had invisible friends as a child.*

It was odd to discuss such memories against the glorious background of the canyons, driving through fields of exotic flowers, wild primrose and Mojave Yucca. The hills are punctuated by the red ocotillo and the white, dangerous datura.

Roger showed us the house where he remembered seeing little people in his bedroom as a boy. We also reviewed his research about the schedule of President Eisenhower at the time in 1954 when he was rumored to have been shown the wreckage of a flying saucer and Alien bodies. That yarn is another famous UFO legend: Roger located relatives of Eisenhower's dentist, who confirmed that he'd indeed fixed the President's teeth, and that the episode was not a cover for any secret trip to a military base. Ike was preparing a major speech against McCarthy at the time. He'd broken a cap on a tooth, and had other things on his mind than hypothetical Alien contact.

Indio. Friday 14 April 1995.

We just went up to Idyllwild, a surprising Alpine village from which one can see the desert all the way to the Salton Sea. This is Alien Contact land: We drove back on the aptly named "Palm to Pines" highway to Anza, a high valley at the foot of Mt. San Jacinto, where a local ufologist serves as counselor and historian for the local folks.

She once saw a disk escorted by black helicopters: it shot straight up into space. March AFB is just beyond the hill: What did the military have to do with this device?

The peace-loving Cahuilla Indians who lived in the canyons above Palm Springs worked part of the day to gather and prepare their food in a complex world, mastering their environment over millennia.

Indio. Saturday 15 April 1995.

We drove out West of Indio through Windy Point with its rows of windmills, north to Yucca Valley, and then further north to Landers. On the way we saw the famous Integratron built by contactee George van Tassel in the Fifties, a well-maintained structure in the desert. New Age folks had rented it for an overnight retreat "featuring the unique fields, exploring the connection between the Integratron, prophets of Old Testament and Christ," as their brochure said.

We moved on to Giant Rock, another high point of contactee folklore, a few miles away, where a few dune buggy enthusiasts were thundering through the old dry bed. The rock has been heavily defaced. Little remains of the mysteries followers of Adamski and Truman Bethurum felt in its shadow when huge events attracted up to 50,000 people to hear their rambling revelations.

We went back to Joshua Tree for lunch, then headed south to the National Monument where flowers were in full bloom. If you take Route 177 towards Parker, Arizona, and if you proceed 10.2 miles from Desert Center you reach the foot of the Cox Comb mountain range, as dark red or purple as any volcanic hillside vomited by the earth. It is here, to the left (northwest) of Route 177, that George Adamski met his Venusian behind a rise that hid him conveniently from the view of other "witnesses," including George Hunt Williamson, as the latter told me when I met him twenty years ago. He nonetheless signed an affidavit about this momentous event.

We had coffee in Desert Center, a place that hasn't changed much since Patton used it as his headquarters to train the million-man army that was to land in North Africa. Most of the area is still occupied by military bases: the Twenty-Nine Palms Marine base to the north and the bombing range of the Chocolate Mountains to the south. At the George Patton Museum a dozen tanks squat in the rough landscape. Roger told us about the year-round agriculture techniques of the Indians who still live there, stories of the desert, and tales of Coyote.

From Adamski and van Tassel to Puharich and now to Dr. Greer, the contactee myth remains alive in America. At nearby Desert Center our young waitress had never heard of George Adamski and laughed heartily when she heard we were looking for a Venusian contact spot. She called it "far fetched."

"Yet there's something grandiose in this landscape, almost Biblical," Janine remarked. "It isn't surprising that simple souls were so powerfully touched. Desert Center is the poor man's Qumran."

Indio. Easter Sunday 16 April 1995.

Roger picked us up for the drive to the Salton Sea, the largest body of water in California, created by a mistake of man: About 1900, developers tried to boost agriculture, so the water company diverted part of the Colorado River into the desert east of Indio; unexpectedly foul weather opened the breach and changed the course of the river.

That accident poured water into the desert for years. Now the Salton Sea is fed by two Mexican streams and the polluted outflow from local farms. Early dreams of great resorts and rich marinas have floundered.

St. Francis Hospital. Friday 21 April 1995.

Early this morning I felt a hard leg cramp and jumped out of bed to relieve the pain. A second later I was dizzy as words deserted my brain. That brief void in my consciousness was the most horrible sensation I'd ever encountered. The doctors shrug it off as a simple *syncope,* but they kept me overnight. Catherine arrived with purple flowers, a cheerful card and a copy of *Newsweek.* All day I have watched the aftermath of the Oklahoma City explosion on television.

Hummingbird. Sunday 23 April 1995.

The doctors released me: my heart and brain were fine, they said.

There was a prayer service today in Oklahoma City. Clinton responded to interviewers about the bombing and its echoes of Waco, evading responsibility for the tragedy, blaming the Koresh cult for killing its members. But that first federal assault was absurd, the second one unnecessary. Why send tanks crashing into a house full of kids? I hate the cults, but there is shared responsibility here.

Hummingbird. Friday 28 April 1995.

At the invitation of Dr. Marilyn Schlitz I drove over to the Institute of Noetic Sciences to hear John Mack presenting his work to a select group: Willis Harman, as jovial as I remembered him, and SRI psychic Duane Elgin (now with the Institute of Integral Studies), Nick Herbert and Fred Alan Wolf whom I hadn't seen since our dinner at Francis Coppola's house, Keith Thompson, Peter Sturrock and Bernie Haisch, and Karen Wesolovski, a young woman who travels with Mack as research director. I counted 22 people.

John Mack appeared a bit more bent, walking unevenly. He played a videotape of "Kredo," a South African shaman raped by a demonic figure that smelled of rotten fish, and his investigation of a close encounter near a school where three girls related seeing strange beings who inspired them to "feel sadness" and to clean up the Earth.

Mabillon. Sunday 7 May 1995.

The coming of spring has brought out the Parisians along with tourists. After recounting Persinger's work, *Science-et-Vie* has explained UFOs one more time, as a "simple" combination of epileptic hallucinations and psychosomatic stigmata (!) I feel no compulsion to challenge them. Nor do I plan to vote in the second round of the elections today, having reluctantly cast my ballot for Chirac in the first round, *faute de mieux*: He has made pledges he cannot keep and carries unsavory characters in his suitcase. The problems of France have to do with her culture, more than with her policy. The latter will be similar whether Jospin or Chirac is the winner.

None of the candidates has the charisma or power to influence a French culture more concerned with the preservation of privilege than a vision of the future.

Mabillon. Monday 8 May 1995.

The heavy sun over Paris, unusual for May, combined pollution and celebration last night. The air became stagnant, sticky, grayish-yellow, eye-stinging. From a brasserie near *Le Chatelet* I saw cars speeding along, horns blaring, as rightist militants waved the tricolor to celebrate. The flags looked brand new, like Chirac as the president who will take France into the next Millennium.

The alternative would have been another seven years of tired socialism under Jospin.

This afternoon I went back to see my mother. Gabriel joined us. She greeted us with apple juice, coffee, and new cookies from Switzerland, all impeccably served. She is able to go on thinking, arguing, observing, even if the landscape around her becomes more disconcerting with the passage of time.

Paris is back to normal. Celebrations are over, flags furled. The flame burns bright under the *Arc de Triomphe*, yet the future hangs in a stale, smoggy air.

Mabillon. Sunday 14 May 1995.

A sudden storm cleaned up the sky and washed the trees, ready for summer in their full glory. A wonderful freshness fills the city. I walked over to the *Mutualité* where a show of old and rare books was taking place. I pulled a copy of Edouard Laboulaye's *Contes Bleus* from a shelf, only to discover I had in my hands the magical stories I loved as a child, legends admirably told and beautifully illustrated, so I went to see my mother again and showed her the rare book I had long searched for. Denis, my psychiatrist nephew, was with her. She was lively and funny. She said a series of new planetary satellites had been discovered in the solar system, which I'd missed.

Now I get ready for five hard days of negotiations and presentations with my partners, including the mercurial genius Fred Adler.

Mabillon. Tuesday 16 May 1995.

Patrick Corsi is a former IBM manager who later worked at Thomson-Syseca in France. He tracked me down and invited me as a consultant on the *Esprit* programme. He casually mentioned, almost as an afterthought, that about 1982, as he was working in *La Gaude* for IBM, he was asked by a man who lived in Nice to help translate a set of massive American documents about Roswell. They contained descriptions of hardware *and of bodies*; the texts were thick, detailed, highly technical, confidential, and hard to translate.

In the afternoon I met my old mother at a service in memory of my aunt Francine, who died recently. Afterwards I took her to a dinner of pancakes and cider. The weather has briefly cleared up, the sun came out. Fourteen years of socialism have come to a very tired end. A different France is arising, with a weary eye on the complexities of Europe. I fly home on Saturday morning.

Hummingbird. Tuesday 30 May 1995.

TV producer Jacki Dunne has invited me to join a hush-hush meeting at Asilomar. It will include astronauts and cosmonauts as well as ufologist Bob Dean (who claims four different races have bases on the moon), Steven Greer, and Ralph whose amorous adventures with *La Belle Hybride aux Yeux Noirs* haven't been forgotten. Dick D'Amato is supposed to be there, as well as Bootsie, Sandy Wright, Laurance Rockefeller's lawyer George Lamb… A few hours later Keith Harary called, urging me to stay away: there are leaks about this supposedly "discreet" gathering. He came over with Barbara Gallagher, a parapsychologist who brought a copy of a "secret" memo from Hal Puthoff reporting on his meeting with an alleged first-hand witness of the Roswell crash, Glen Belcker. Evidently the memo already circulates in the Bootsie group.

Hummingbird. Wednesday 31 May 1995.

Hal is upset at my news of the Belcker memo: He can't understand how it got out, because only two "trusted friends" had a copy; he had personally guaranteed anonymity to the witness.

"What are these people doing? It makes no sense at all," I said.

"I've been wondering about the same thing: Rockefeller, all that money... what's the point? They're in fantasyland," Hal agreed.

Hummingbird. Thursday 1 June 1995.

Today I hosted a small SSE meeting in my offices, providing sandwiches and refreshments to a group consisting of Peter Sturrock, Ed May, Bernie Haisch, Halton Arp (of quasar redshift fame), Dick Blasband, and his wife Kathleen. Dr. Ed May said he was close to being funded again, having received assurances of support for a retrospective study of remote viewing experiments of the last 20 years, including the classified "operational" studies at SRI.

Hummingbird. Thursday 22 June 1995.

Adler and I flew back to California together. He was tired after a rushed trip to Paris and only two hours of sleep and was torn apart by insecurities that seem inappropriate in a man worth a billion dollars. When I told him I'd recently met with eminent Stanford professor Pitch Johnson, who sent his regards, he mumbled something about the fact that this reassured him, that he was still one of the best minds in the business. Fred is a unique blend of genius and egotism. He is capable of profanity in the midst of the finest analysis of men and situations. The insight he delivered to the prospective investors we've met, about the western world's economic future and the role of smart finance, was invaluable, although spoken in rapid-fire, Brooklyn English few of them could follow. Yesterday Fred Adler and I had lunch with legendary lawyer Larry Sonsini and with investment banker Sandy Robertson, pillars of the high-tech community. Both spoke diplomatically but skeptically about the future of Europe.

My daughter delighted me in suggesting a Father's Day breakfast at *Les Croissants* on Polk Street. I told her about Paris, my fears for a France split apart by economic exclusion.

In the Brussels-Paris train. Monday 26 June 1995.

Patrick Corsi is a solid fellow, a bit shorter than me, with curly dark brown hair, and glasses suitable for the Eurocrat he's become. We made the 3-hour drive to Brussels through the fog of the Lille countryside and the dull plain of Waterloo. Thanks to the new European accords, we passed the Belgian border without seeing it.

Patrick told me he'd returned to France in June 1981. He lived in *Saint-Laurent du Var* and worked for IBM at *La Gaude*. He started a group there to discuss yoga, astrology, and related topics.

"It must have been early in 1982, in the winter, when the man who had the documents contacted me through the yoga group. I think his name was Sergès, or Serge Bernard ... He requested my help."

"How did he earn his living?" I asked.

"He ran a small factory that made clothes, sweaters."

"Did you ever visit him at work?"

"I went there once. He must have had 10 to 20 employees at the time. The factory was in Nice, near place Garibaldi. I could go there again, I would know the way: things haven't changed much. The files he wanted me to translate were in big binders, hundreds and hundreds of typed pages. They read like military reports. I orally translated while he took notes. He wouldn't let me keep them. I do remember something about a UFO seen on the ground in Arizona."

"What did the documents look like?"

"Photocopies of official American papers, with stamps all over them, *Secret* and all that, no margin."

"Where did he say he got them?"

"From the office of President Mitterrand, recently elected. They contained allegations there were bases on the moon; that humans were regularly taken there for two or three years at a time."

The documents seem to be "active measures" from the same hoaxers now spreading disinformation in America. Shrewdly, Mitterrand suspected a CIA setup, so he relied on that private, unofficial channel to get them translated and screened, and smelled the ruse (**47**).

Fribourg. Hotel La Rose. Friday 30 June 1995.

Janine made the trip to Switzerland with me for an art festival. Yesterday we had a splendid lunch, just the two of us, at a restaurant by the lakeside near Vevey, admiring the blue haze over the Alps.

The show takes place at the *Belluard*, a medieval bastion with wooden beams. Today Mr. Broillet, a local official who has read my books, invited us for lunch. He told us about a curious episode in which UFO witnesses became enveloped in a suspicious pink fog that reminded me of the Cergy-Pontoise abduction.

Fribourg. Hotel La Rose. Sunday 2 July 1995.

Hopkins has arrived with his charming wife Carol Rainey who videotapes his lectures. Budd was ranting against John Mack's recent deviation from his "Missing Time" dogma. Anything that doesn't fit Budd's scenario must be a screen to be eliminated by subjecting the witnesses to repeated hypnosis sessions until they finally "get it."

There is a steep climb to the Belluard, a ten-minute hike along the streets with their shops and local restaurants. Along the way I had a warm talk with Terence McKenna. Later we went to the Cistercian abbry at Hauterive with artist Homer Flynn. We made many new friends, like French researcher Yves Bosson. He'd driven over from Marseille with three buddies, displaying impressive mustaches.

Mabillon. Monday 3 July 1995.

It rained hard in Geneva when Janine and I arrived at financier Odier's house. He'd invited us for a review of some parapsychology results with Gabriel Veraldi, a former associate of Jacques Bergier and Aimé Michel at *Planète*. Tomorrow morning, we fly back to the States.

9

Hummingbird. Sunday 16 July 1995.

As soon as we got back we had two phone calls. The first one was from Peter Sturrock, who said he had been invited by Mike Swords of CUFOS to join a conference sponsored by the "Coalition" of the three major UFO groups who had secured research money from Mr. Bigelow. I was intrigued by Peter's academic way of saying he expected Dick Haines and me to "give him our ideas for research projects" so he could present them formally to the Coalition.

"Who's invited?" I asked.

"Oh, people like Dick Henry, Bernie Haisch, Ed Kahn, Kasten Hollings from Oak Ridge, Roy Craig whom you probably recall from the Condon study, Danny Schnick from Kansas, Frank Salisbury from Utah, David Pritchard from MIT, William Hartmann who also served with Condon, and some others."

"Will Mr. Bigelow be there?" I asked.

"I don't think so." There was a brief silence.

"Then it might be better if I didn't participate," I said.

"But … everybody knows you have ideas," Peter objected.

"Really? If they wanted my ideas they would have invited me," I pointed out. "My proposals might be too radical. Besides, the Condon study has taught me about cooperation in the absence of supervision. It limits one's ability to critique future results..."

"You may be right, Jacques," Peter said after a pause. "You wisely keep your head down. I should probably do the same."

I hung up and just as I was mulling over my awkward response to Peter, whom I deeply respect, the phone rang again, and Robert Bigelow was on the line.

"I'd like to bring you up-to-date on my activities," he began with his usual directness. "I've just done a one-year experiment with the Coalition, those guys from the three UFO groups, as I told you back in Texas. It turned out they had no horsepower."

"Well, these people are sincere, but they've never run large R&D projects," I said vaguely, in an attempt to be diplomatic.

"That's exactly what I found out," he replied. "I gave them $250,000 the first year, and they couldn't even spend that; we have a $60,000 surplus. They certainly couldn't handle the half-million I wanted to spend the second year. So, I've decided not to continue with them. I want to work directly with the people who do research. New blood is desperately needed, there's no scientific discipline among ufologists. I'm forming an institute, and I want to attract world-class scientists to study UFOs and the paranormal, including consciousness beyond death. I want you to think about it."

Hummingbird. Monday 17 July 1995.

Robert Bigelow has called again, confirming he had disbanded "the Coalition" after a meeting last Thursday during which he was grilled for hours by ufologists who refused to give him a vote.

"I've realized that by not having a vote I'd end up being cutoff from the information. That's not what I'm looking for. My intention is to stay involved, to sponsor good science, without any handcuffs. I need to attract the best. I'm hoping you can help me. I have a relationship to Dean Radin, as you know, and to Linda Howe, whose work I've supported. What do you think of John Alexander?"

I told him about my good discussions with John over the years. Bob went on: "John's looking for a new job. He's out of Los Alamos, where funding has been cut. I'm going to need advisers, board members..."

He speaks like a businessman who knows what he wants.

"Would the project be located in Nevada?"

"The core management would, as Dean Radin already is. I'm thinking of an endowed chair at the University. We'll call it something like 'Exo-human intelligence.' I need a director who's good at administration but also understands the phenomena, with a director of operations under him, and people to head up analysis, human encounters, crop symbols, PR and education, databases..."

He offered to fly over in his private jet to see me in San Francisco.

There was a time when I would have jumped at such a job: I certainly know what to do and I could handle any friction with Bigelow about research priorities. But the problem has proven more complex and messier than any of us anticipated ten years ago. It isn't the "exo-human" aspect that bothers me, but the human one.

Projects I would run? Yes, I know where to go. A follow-up to little-known cases with high value would yield insights. But they would need to be kept confidential in order to bring out long-term results.

Hummingbird. Sunday 23 July 1995.

On Tuesday I called Linda Howe, in anticipation of Bob Bigelow's visit next week. She explained how he'd broken off with the three groups: "Bob rightly insisted on knowing the details of cases, which they kept to themselves," she said. "Mind you, it's easier to be a consultant for his outfit than to work directly under him."

She laughed with her easy, throaty laugh: "The so-called Coalition wanted to put Walter Webb in charge of field investigations. He's not the man for the job, so Bob got frustrated. All their ideas had to do with rehashing old statistics. They wanted to go back over Blue Book. He wanted them to include cattle mutilations in their studies, but they chickened out. Bob kept arguing for hard physical traces."

"Is John Alexander a possible director?"

"At least for the UFO part, with Dean Radin for the psi part."

She paused: "Dianne Arcangel is on the Board, she's done good NDE work. The goal is admirable: Investigate the paranormal, build a bridge to the academic world... A big part of me wants to do it, but I have concerns I can't explain."

Next, I was able to reach Hal in Texas. He confirmed the three groups drowned in bickering: "They just couldn't get a research program together," he said; "no surprises there, they hate one another fiercely."

Later the same day.

I was working on the manuscript of *FastWalker*, my first priority this summer, when my mother called to say that my uncle Charles Passavant, her 92-year old brother, had died yesterday in the Bronx. She seems to have taken this new blow philosophically. We went on to talk about the heat wave sweeping both France and the U.S. "People are affected in their mental state, too," she said. "Lots of crime here. The kids often gain the upper hand over the police. A woman across the street went crazy last night; she set fire to her apartment. The fire engines woke me up. They were there for hours."

Hummingbird. Wednesday 26 July 1995.

Robert Bigelow arrived punctually last night, wearing a dark suit over a short-sleeve printed shirt. He admired the City view, declined a glass of wine and stated he was ready to answer any questions I might have about his motivations. My answer surprised him.

"I don't have any questions," I told him frankly, "You're a businessman, I understand what you're doing. I also understand why things didn't work out with the Coalition. When we had that dinner in

Princeton, and later in Austin, you were clear about your goals. But how far can a private institute go? How can we know what the real situation is within the government?"

He answered he didn't think the government knew very much. He gave me a copy of his proposed organization chart and went over his contacts, notably his talks with a man named O'Dean ("Dean") Judd who was at one time NIO for Science.

"Dean tells me he's never run into any significant UFO study during all his years in Intelligence," Bob said. "He should have known."

This confirms what I've heard from Kit, from John Alexander, and privately from top military men like General Johnny Johnson and Rear-Admiral Bill Hauser. But it could simply mean that the real stuff is at a different level. If the UFO problem is treated with the same covert methods as arms trafficking, cults or drugs, most official levels could be left in the dark. I left this contradiction hanging.

Over Janine's excellent dinner ("It must be nice to have a gourmet restaurant in the building!" Bob joked at one point, savoring the scallops, winking at her) he recounted how he'd tried to straighten out Rhine's institute at Duke. Bigelow is bitter at the arrogance of the ufologists, who told him he couldn't have a vote because he had only been studying the phenomenon for seven years! The only fellow who made any sense was John Schuessler.

"Why not bring him in, if you setup a new Board?" I asked, having always respected Schuessler's solid insight. I suggested assembling the core team in Las Vegas for a "blue sky" session. As a general partner in a venture Fund I have a 10-year commitment to my investors: I can't just leave and take another job in Nevada. But I could commit to serve on an outside, private board.

Yesterday an Islamist terror group blew up a bomb at Saint-Michel metro station in Paris, killing 8 people and injuring 117. The bomb was a gas bottle filled with nails. There were so many victims that a nearby restaurant, *Le Départ* (one of my favorite places), had to be turned into a field hospital to sort out the injuries.

Hummingbird. Sunday 30 July 1995.

Bigelow's assistants have set up a meeting for Hal and me in Las Vegas on August 19th. Bob called this afternoon. He began by urging me to bring over my foreign contacts: "Very few researchers in this country have any awareness of what goes on elsewhere," he said. I replied that foreign specialists were staying behind the scenes like me, leery of developments in America. I reminded him of Bootsie's pointless excursion to Europe, and of the Greer fiasco.

Next, I brought up the name of "Dean" Judd. Bob didn't remember mentioning him. "You've got a good memory," he said. Well, I have learned to pick up the important items, and this connection is a key. The man is John Alexander's close friend at Los Alamos. Alexander has been feeding him UFO information for the last three years.

"I took him along on a couple of trips," Bigelow said, "to see Dr. Levengood, and Dr. Altshuler. He's committed to the idea that something very strange is going on."

Spring Hill. Friday 11 August 1995.

This evening I circled back to John Alexander, disclosing that I'd spoken with Bigelow, that I had declined his nice offer to run the project, but I could be of more help as a board member. John plans to buy a house in Vegas after reaching agreement with Bigelow.

"I try to bring in senior scientists," he said. "I'll work part-time for Bob, but I'll continue to deal with my non-lethal issues as a consultant. What the Institute needs is some real science, with research protocols before the fieldwork gets done, not afterward. Bigelow keeps funding the same folks, but their findings get torn to shreds whenever I bring in experienced people to review the results."

"I have serious misgivings about the state of the field," I said. "Ufology as practiced today is headed for disaster, between bungled hypnosis and bogus autopsies. I don't want to be in the middle of that."

John was non-committal: "Bigelow needs to hear it," he said flatly. "He needs to bring in people like you and Hal— who know how to do science." All well and good, but how will the new Institute keep its data from the spooks and their puppets among ufologists?

Spring Hill. Saturday 12 August 1995.

Visitors have come and gone: Hans spent one night here, telling us about his continuing saga of itinerant work prospects. He has just married Anna. We took a picturesque drive along the unpaved back road to Willits, fording the seven creeks. My experiments here remain inconclusive. We've had many close friends at the ranch recently, including precious artist Eve Berni, Keith and Darlene Harary, Roger Brenner, George Kuchar. Elusiveness is the major factor in the rough spirit that hovers mysteriously over these, our savage hills.

Hummingbird. Sunday 13 August 1995.

Well, it had to happen. The Sunday paper carries an explicit item about Hopkins follower Richard Boylan under the headline *Space-alien shrink loses his license*: "The State Board of Psychology has revoked the license of a Sacramento psychologist who specialized in treating the survivors of alleged encounters with space aliens. Psychologist Richard Boylan was found guilty of seven counts of gross negligence involving three patients." Boylan "abused his role as a therapist when he imposed his personal views on the existence of extraterrestrials into the dreams and memories of two patients," the Board had concluded.

Las Vegas. Saturday 19 August 1995.

Hal Puthoff and I just spent the day with Robert Bigelow and the Board of his newly-created *National Institute for Discovery Science*. As I'd expected, initial members are Dean Radin, who directs the parapsychology side, and Dianne Arcangel who conducts survival research. Hal has received funding to explore UFO physics, and Dick D'Amato has been approached by John Alexander.

Hal had dinner with CIA director James Woolsey after he left office, so he asked him about his review of UFO documents at the Agency. Woolsey punted, telling him he'd asked his historian to give him an assessment of what CIA knew. Not true, according to Kit, who brought up the question of classified files with the historian: The man didn't want to touch it. This is either miscommunication or another instance of Agency double-talk. I'm starting to get used to it.

Hummingbird. Tuesday 22 August 1995.

Today I sent a memo to Dean, Dianne, Bob Bigelow and Hal, entitled "Assessing the UFO situation - a thinkpiece." It begins in simple business terms: If we think of ufology as a "turnaround" situation, as if we had to rebuild a bankrupt company, we must look for the reasons for past errors before injecting new resources.

I made four specific points: first, we must analyze the causes for 50 years of failure before defining any new approach. Failure could originate with (1) the wrong people, (2) the wrong timing, or (3) the wrong strategy. It is always easiest to blame the people. Ufology has indeed suffered because top-level scientists never became interested in it. However, this does not explain the poor state of the field today. Scientists like Hynek and McDonald, Salisbury, Haines, Sturrock, as well as Poher and Guérin in France were not lightweights in their fields of specialty. But sound management was missing.

"The phenomenon may not be mature enough for direct attack. Its appearance is misleading because it combines with our own cultural bias (Western, 20th-century) to suggest an extraterrestrial origin for the objects. This axiom ("UFOs, if real, must be some sort of spacecraft, hence the occupants must be some sort of Aliens") is seductive but incomplete. It has never been seriously questioned.

"My *second recommendation* is to surface our assumptions (especially the hidden ones, those that "go without saying") and to make a special effort to challenge them."

"My *third recommendation* is to begin a systematic effort at modelization. The model should not start from the assumption that UFOs are spacecraft. An alien origin is only one hypothesis among many. The best modelization that has been done so far was developed by Claude Poher at CNES. I am familiar with it, but it is 20 years old. It needs to be adapted and expanded."

Finally, there is the matter of personnel: "The *fourth recommendation* has to do with the choice of a director of operations. In a business turnaround you don't take the same people in the same roles and just give them more money..."

Hummingbird. Sunday 27 August 1995.

Bob Bigelow has called to tell me about a meeting he'd attended at John Alexander's house. Dean Judd gave him a long paper outlining his reasons for skepticism about UFOs. Bigelow wants me to answer it. He also told me my memo resonated with him because it was couched in terms of "turnaround," a business topic he understands very well. He's about to fly to Saskatchewan to investigate a case of multiple cattle mutilation.

Hummingbird. Thursday 31 August 1995.

The Golden Gate Church, which stands on a grassy hillside in San Francisco's Pacific Heights, holds regular services in the Spiritualist tradition. It's a fine white building with wide windows, a flat roof, a nice library. George Kuchar has a girlfriend who frequents the church and took us there. His twin brother Mike joined us, prophet-like with his long beard.

We sat in red armchairs while an organ played softly. Official documents in golden frames lent authenticity to the proceedings. The service was opened by a Chinese man in his forties who invited us to sing hymns. Music alternated with readings from the lectern by the ministers: Janine, who was smartly dressed, was treated by the Spirits to a short sermon about the evils of high-heel shoes. George was told he'd soon come into money. Mike heard he was not going to go on a trip and that "his late grandmother was taking care of him."

Most people heard from departed grandmothers. Since everybody has two of those, and chances are high that one of them has passed on, such readings are almost certain to hit their mark.

Nice "Spirit paintings" hung in the healing room. But the true richness was in the 50 people or so assembled for the service: Blacks, Asians and Whites, from the very young to the old, many bruised and lonely like this epoch full of abrasiveness and sorrow. No wonder the Departed Spirits are running out of sensible advice.

Montréal. Wednesday 6 September 1995.

My investment work has taken me back to Canada. It's a fine day in the *Belle Province*, with sunshine and a pleasant breeze. My French colleague and I spent the morning at a huge financial institution. It is an interesting time to be in Québec: a new referendum is being organized about independence. People argue and wave flags, white *fleur de lys* in a field of azure, or red maple leaves over white, fluttering in the warm wind.

Lambertheim, Germany. Wednesday 13 September 1995.

It rains all over Germany. There's a traffic jam under my windows: workers from Mannheim going home, trucks passing through, people driving to Frankfurt for the auto show. The fellow who greeted me at the airport is in charge of customs and exports for an electronics company where I have just joined the Board. In the distance, across the fat green fields, he pointed out the factories of ABB and Ciba-Geigy, the smokestacks of a German land that dominates Europe again, even if the economic outlook is as gloomy as the rain over the Main River.

This is hard industrial reality in the grayness of Europe, and a chance to break away from the myths that sweep America.

Mabillon. Sunday 24 September 1995.

In Mannheim, where our Board met in the luxurious Brown-Boveri conference room, all talk was of Daimler-Benz's unprecedented six-month loss of a whopping billion dollars.

The French are worried, too: they feel betrayed by Chirac. Rising taxes exacerbate their anger. The *patrons* are upset because the government doesn't dare take the unpopular measures that might revitalize an economy strangled by bureaucracy.

I had lunch with Pierre Lagrange. He told me that Guérin remained a firm believer in the Roswell crash, complete with *exquisite cadavers*. Paris alternates between tepid, heavy rain, and timid sunshine.

Because of the recent tragic bombings at Saint Michel there are fewer people in the streets, no singing.

Soldiers and riot police everywhere.

A week of arguments with Fred Adler has exhausted me. In typical fashion our negotiations took place as we ran down the Champs-Elysées together, dashing between cars, after an hour-long meeting with Laurent Dassault and his financial adviser.

Spring Hill. Saturday 30 September 1995.

This trip to the redwoods was perfect. Tonight, by fair seeing, I was able to observe Saturn's rings (on edge at the moment, only a thin line), the Pleiades, and the Andromeda nebula. I continue to make progress with database implementation and causality experiments, but we haven't caught any unexplained phenomenon.

Hummingbird. Sunday 1 October 1995.

We got back to the City and were watching an uninteresting 49ers game when Bob Bigelow called again from Nevada. He told me space had been rented for his institute: three thousand feet of prime office space—and no one to run the place. He's hired George Knapp on a part-time basis to keep alive his network of researchers, but he runs out of candidates for the $90,000 a year job of UFO chief: Bob Wood, primarily interested in government coverups, won't move to Las Vegas. Bigelow prefers an astronomer, but any astronomer knows that UFO research would be the kiss of death for his career.

Bob has just come back from Saskatchewan where a man, his wife, and their three sons had reported seeing a craft and short beings. It hovered for 20 minutes above the treeline.

"We took plant samples," he told me. "The grass had died. A cow's rectum and sex organs were removed; a one-foot diameter circle had been cut in the animal. The cut left a charred substance, almost no blood."

"What happened to the object? What did it look like?" I asked.

"It made the sound of an arc welder, 200 yards away, they said. They saw some silhouettes, small people; the witnesses called out, 'Whaddya want?' The beings reacted with excitement, they scurried around, and the craft took off.

The farmer had no insurance. The RCMP took pictures but they didn't bother to answer any questions."

Bob does have the impression that media coverage of the subject has made it popular again in the US.

That may be true, but the sensational "Alien Autopsy" film, coming after the empty promises of one Roswell "special" after another, has left the public confused.

Hummingbird. Wednesday 4 October 1995.

A week from today I will be packing my suitcase for another trip to Asia on behalf of our second venture Fund.

Hal Puthoff has sent me a copy of an article by Jim Schnabel (**48**) dealing with psychic espionage. Not only does he cite the *Scanate* project, but he gives the code names for those that followed: *Grill Flame, Center Lane, Sun Streak*... He also cites the names of remote viewers employed by DIA: Angela Dellafiora, Robin Dahlgren.

Other writers are injecting their own view of the field. In *Psychic Dictatorship in the USA*, Alex Constantine claims that parapsychology never worked but served as a cover for mind control, while he expands on the CIA's infiltration of cults. He also claims that some abductions are staged events hiding illegal experiments. I do have four or five such cases in my files where the victim was coerced into a cult that exploited – or provided – visions of Aliens, like the mass suicides of the *Order of the Solar Temple* in Switzerland and Canada. We've strayed far indeed from ufology as I once understood it, a clean exercise in scientific analysis. The loss of innocence has come with the murky role played by governments.

Hummingbird. Thursday 5 October 1995.

Today, as I joined my former associate Ruthie Smith for what I expected would be one of our occasional lunches on the San Francisco waterfront, I found myself mobbed by a bevy of laughing women, the reunited "Infomaniacs." They were buoyant, full of energy and good humor, busily engaged in new careers. Ruthie had brought two bottles of cider for my recent birthday: her husband is a wine expert branching off into the apple and pear business. It was a delight to see them all again, at a time when networks have caught up with the concepts and products our "InfoMedia" pioneered fifteen years ago.

North Haven Holiday Inn. Saturday 7 October 1995.

The Omega Communications conference is being held in Connecticut. John White is here, as well as John Timmerman who said Mimi was fine, busy with archaeology. I saw Linda Howe in the coffee shop, and Stanton Friedman sorting out slides in cigar boxes. He expounded on the alien autopsy "film," taking it at face value, although of course there's no film, only a video.

Today Bootsie Galbraith introduced herself and told the charming lie that she'd made the trip from New York just to hear my lecture.

We had lunch at the coffee shop where strangers were talking loudly. A baby was crying at the next table. When she could no longer stand the bawling, she stood up and firmly instructed the parents to keep their offspring quiet. We had been speaking French, so she addressed them in that language, adding to the stunning effect.

Bootsie confirmed she'd visited Poher, Guérin, and Velasco: "The CNES people denied any concern about UFOs, until they relaxed after a few good bottles." Predictably, she learned nothing in the end.

Also attending is Colin Andrews, who showed an interesting video of crop circle investigators being buzzed by British Army helicopters. Andrews mentioned they had a French researcher from CNES with them, "who went on to work for the American government," another indication of ongoing high-level contact between French and U.S. Intelligence about UFOs.

North Haven Holiday Inn. Sunday 8 October 1995.

I quietly left the room when Dick Hoagland started showing maps of five-sided pyramids forming cities on Mars, sphinxes in the plains of Cydonia and castles floating above the moon. He derived mathematical constants from their dimensions. It reminded me of Dr. de Vaucouleurs' classic joke about the size of his desk, whose length, width, and height could be combined in various arithmetic ways to yield every important constant in physics, including the latitude of Paris Observatory where his office and that desk were located!

North Haven Holiday Inn. Monday 9 October 1995.

Over private conversation this evening, John Timmerman told me he had gathered 1,000 cases as a result of his exhibit tours, and he didn't know how to preserve them. On behalf of CUFOS, he made it a point to apologize for the insults some of their members have heaped upon my work, shattering a potentially healthy relationship that went all the way back to Allen Hynek's legacy. In the lobby Leah Haley and Marc Davenport described to me the incidents in which ordinary humans were staging false "UFO abductions" that involved harassment and overt attempts at mind control.

United Airlines flight to Asia. Friday 13 October 1995.

Janine has shown me an obituary in the *New York Times* for Gérard de Vaucouleurs, who died last Saturday of a heart attack. He was 77 years old (**49**). Now I fly off to Asia for two weeks, sad not to take her with me. She is busy trying to locate the ideal house for our friend Brian Pinkerton, the author of the *Webcrawler* he recently sold to America Online. Yesterday, a friendly dinner with Hans and his wife Anna.

10

Singapore. Hotel Westin Plaza. Sunday 15 October 1995.

The flight to Hong Kong and Singapore follows the California coast to the North, overlooking Inverness, the calm beauty of Point Reyes, Timber Cove, and Fort Bragg, where we veer off into the North Pacific. It will take 14 hours to reach Hong Kong, and I won't be in Singapore until midnight tomorrow, having lost a day.

A hundred lighted ships became visible in the rain over Hong Kong harbor when we broke through the clouds. There was water all around the aircraft as we landed, water as we took off again, a planeful of businessmen tired and sweaty with stubble on their chins and blood in their eyes. Singapore airport, by comparison, was calm and easy. I reached Janine before she went to work, calm and happy: "Catherine suggested going out for pizza, ice cream, and laughter," she said. "She was so cheerful everything seemed to clear up."

Here in Singapore a thunderstorm was bursting in the hot, moist atmosphere. Suddenly I felt reconciled to the prospect of two weeks of hard meetings with Asian financiers.

Singapore. Monday 16 October 1995.

Some forty French managers and bankers on a marketing junket have quietly assembled here. "Too quietly," the Ambassador tells us: the group is not "vibrant" enough to impress the quick-witted Singaporeans. Now we argue about commerce with Chirac's unimpressive minister of Foreign Trade. The French spend all their time talking to each other about what goes on in Paris instead of mingling with their hosts, the industrious local Chinese. I skipped the formal dinner offered by the Ambassador to the French trade group, unable to face their predictable official speeches. Better stay focused.

Singapore authorities wonder why they have difficulty attracting high-technology developers, now that they have cleared their jungle and built a fine mini-replica of Silicon Valley. But their culture is so regimented that the atmosphere of rebellion and hedonism that comes with California creativity is simply lacking.

Singapore. Wednesday 18 October 1995.

At the official luncheon yesterday, I was seated next to Mr. Tang Guan Seng, political secretary to the Prime minister. After the usual speeches about technology and investment I leaned over to ask what he thought the impact on the region would be if China were to take over Taiwan. He showed no great trepidation at the thought.

"That has to happen eventually," he said, "but China isn't in a hurry. If things go well with Hong Kong's integration, the Taiwanese may not feel too much fear. Remember, China has an enormous population, immense needs, and her economy must be liberalized, one way or the other. Her leaders understand that it will take time and new skills. Taiwan is one of the largest investors in China..."

He quickly added that Singapore was confident it could help in the process of liberalizing China by creating technology parks where

Western companies could move in with the assurance of finding adequate services, security and freedom from corruption.

"Chinese officials are eager to show their bosses how efficient they are at bringing in new jobs. The days are gone, of a Chinese bureaucracy moving as slowly as the glaciers of the Himalayas."

Yesterday another bomb exploded in Paris, injuring 26 people. That was the eighth terrorist attack by the Algerian GIA (Armed Islamic Group) since the bloodshed at Saint-Michel on 25 July.

Taipei. Hotel Regent. Thursday 19 October 1995.

The discrepancies of Southeast Asia become obvious when one leaves the Singapore Airlines jet to go through customs in Taiwan, where shabbily dressed officials process long lines, all in Chinese.

Turning on CNN brings back the reality of the bomb in Paris. This time the culprits are obvious: Muslim fundamentalists want France to drop her support for the Algerian government and let them spread their insane version of Islam. Men and women are dying in dark tunnels under Paris. No one has anything to gain from such folly, except the neo-Nazis with their ugly racist hatreds.

My French colleague and I keep hearing conflicting opinions about the future of Taiwan in the context of ominous Chinese military maneuvers. One investor warned that the real estate bubble was about to blow up, as it did a few years ago in Japan. Yet investors keep raising new funds for Taiwan. They bet that the local stock market, something of a casino, will start climbing again.

We shared juicy gossip about the state of both Chinas with an astute young man, the scion of a powerful Taiwanese family. He presented a welcome contrast with the boring bureaucrat we'd just met at the French Institute (which serves as the unofficial French Embassy). A typical *énarque*, he had listened to himself for an hour, paying no attention to our inquiries.

Tonight, we went to Snake Alley with another local Frenchman from Suez Bank and his Chinese wife. Jean-Pierre Rampal, in town for a concert, sat at the next table. Cameras are forbidden there because of the crude way in which snakes are dissected alive and lobsters cut in half with a single skilful blow of a sharp blade.

Tokyo Prince Hotel. Saturday 21 October 1995.

In Taipei this morning we were held up by a grave accident on the way to Chang Kai Chek airport. When he tried an alternate road our Chinese driver lost his way. That gave us an opportunity to wander through green hills and dusty Chinese villages, passing soldiers on maneuvers and gray bulls loose on the road.

The flight from Taipei to Tokyo only took a couple of hours. The weather has been fine, affording views of Mount Fuji, Nagasaki, and the approach to Narita airport. But the bus that drove us into Tokyo was again held up by emergency trucks that clustered around an overturned van and bodies on stretchers, incongruous as only wounded strangers lying on a road can be.

Finally, the immensely boring, impeccable peace of the Tokyo Prince hotel.

Tokyo Prince Hotel. Sunday 22 October 1995.

Last night an interesting incident took place during our dinner with Yukio K., a financial executive. He took us to a wonderful crab and seafood restaurant named *Sereyna* (The Mermaid) with his wife and his demure daughter Kasuko, who is the age of my Catherine. When Philippe mentioned my UFO interests she suddenly perked up and volunteered that as a little girl of nine in Singapore she had once heard a strange loud sound and seen a disk with windows all around, flying up. This took place as she stood near her house, waiting for the school bus. The object left burning traces. It was oddly small, close to her, and disappeared in midair. When I asked how it looked she picked up an inverted soup bowl and held it up.

Her parents reacted with typical Japanese embarrassment at this breach of protocol:

"Kasuko, how come you never told us about that!" She was telling a stranger a personal story she had never revealed to them. I was delighted to see her freedom, typical of a new Japanese generation. Other witnesses have been disoriented by apparent violations of perspective and geometry produced by these objects.

Researchers who think of UFOs as machines operating in our ordinary spacetime have not listened carefully enough to those who have seen the phenomenon up close.

After the confusion and ruthlessness of Taipei, Tokyo is dignified, well paced, even easy, although our meetings of the last few days have taken place against a backdrop of economic crisis and monetary quagmire that astonishes even jaded Japanese businessmen.

Tokyo Prince Hotel. Monday 23 October 1995.

This was a splendid autumn day in Tokyo. We walked all over between appointments. We met with Nippon Investment and Finance (NIF) who confirmed their decision to participate in our new Fund.

We also spent several hours with Gérard Moré, a friendly manager of *Caisse des Dépôts*. When he tried to take us to see his boss, Maxime Roche, it turned out the man was "too busy." Then Roche recognized my name and his attitude suddenly changed. He told me he'd read my books, was deeply interested in the paranormal: could we have dinner, and a long talk? We promised to see him tomorrow night.

We spent the evening with Frank Caufield of Kleiner-Perkins, a director of America Online. Maxime Roche spoke of archaeology, Chinese politics, Tantra secrets, and the stresses of Japanese life. He pointed out that our modern knowledge sadly ignores everything that's important for our spiritual future.

Tokyo Prince Hotel. Tuesday 24 October 1995.

Going insane is not hard in this complicated city where even cab drivers can't find their way. This morning my driver dumped me in an alley with a helpless gesture. I walked over to the boulevard and found the place in time. Moré was late, out of breath, disheveled, his papers held in a funny square of purple silk embroidened with flowers. How typical of a French expatriate! The modern Japanese are not so romantic: they carry leather briefcases they bought in America; their wives fuss with over-priced Louis Vuitton handbags.

We attended the investment meeting of a major fund, which presented the astonishing spectacle of young Japanese managers asking pointed questions of their elders, no longer intimidated, even though they bow deeply to them at the end of the day—as we do.

Hong Kong. Ritz-Carlton. Thursday 26 October 1995.

Hong Kong is as fine as Rio or San Francisco. To look at this city from the top of the island is an experience out of a sci-fi film. I took a night trip on the harbor at Aberdeen on a sampan, like a tourist. But today, at the Paribas office the manager told us: "Expect poor prospects for Hong Kong. Prosperity was built on British law and western entrepreneurship. Poor management is certain to creep back in as soon as China takes over."

Hummingbird. Wednesday 1 November 1995.

I just got an excited phone call from Bob Bigelow: "We've made progress on our board of advisors," he began. "Keep it confidential, but it will be chaired by Kit Green. Hal Puthoff will join, also Marty Pilch, Dean Judd who was SDI chief scientist for two years, general Jim Whinnery, an Air Force MD doing consciousness research who had an out of body experience, and John Petersen, too."

Bob went on: "Among the others is Emily Cook, who studied with Ian Stevenson at Virginia, and we're trying to get Jessica Utts, and Bruce Grayson who does survival research, and also Senator Harrison Schmidt, and Richard Deckart, who has a company that does EEG work. I'm not saying this to flatter you, but we really do need you to join us."

"Where did those names come from? John Alexander?"

"Most of them did," he answered. "We've met them at his house."

"But nobody in the group has done any extensive field research, even within the U.S.," I pointed out. "They've got narrow filters."

"That's why we need you to join the Board."

I told him I would talk to Kit and Hal to hear their plans.

"Have you picked a director for the project?" I asked next.

"We haven't made much progress on that," he confessed. "Perhaps we ought to find an astronomer, a cosmologist."

This assumes that astronomy is of primary relevance to the problem, which isn't obvious to me.

Hummingbird. Thursday 2 November 1995.

Roger Rémy called me today from Albuquerque. He'd seen the Roswell autopsy video and was skeptical.

The stock market continues to build up a bubble. Estimates of the value of our portfolio now sound respectable, with two more companies (Synaptic Pharmaceuticals and IPAC) about to go public.

Janine met me for a romantic lunch on Market Street. The weather was turning cold but still lovely. We spoke about Russian artist Sergei Ponomarov who has agreed to sell me his painting for *FastWalker*. Any idiot with 90 million dollars can buy Van Gogh's *Blue Irises*... I'd rather own the modest cover of my little novel.

Spring Hill. Saturday 4 November 1995.

We spent the morning reading, and in late afternoon we drove up to Willits through the back road, crossing the seven creeks, to try out our new four-wheel drive Ford Explorer. On the way back, I told Janine the evening felt "lugubrious" to me. She smiled, "You can say that about people, but you can't say it when there's nobody around."

The sun had set, leaving only a narrow band of pink over the hills; the landscape was hazy, empty, oddly silent. I turned on the radio to dispell this heavy feeling and we heard the announcer say that Yitzhak Rabin had just been assassinated. I spent the evening filtering "lugubrious" thoughts about human stupidity.

Hummingbird. Sunday 5 November 1995.

Hal confirmed that Kit had agreed to chair Bigelow's Board. "If that much funding is available," he said, "it could be interesting, with good people involved." I voiced my reservations: there isn't anyone on that Board who is knowledgeable about UFOs. "Are we going to repeat the haphazard research done back in 1965? I was there..."

Our colleagues view the phenomenon through the lens of their convoluted Intelligence world. We know what mistakes it precipitates: the CIA missed the collapse of the Soviet Union, so what are the chances they'll understand UFOs? Hal was well aware of these problems; he didn't think Kit had much information either. We went on to discuss the Alcubierre warp drive (**50**).

Hummingbird. Wednesday 8 November 1995.

Kit has made it clear he welcomed a chance for us to work together. We cleared the air. When Bigelow suggested he head up the science board he put down a series of conditions: the board would have an independent policy, not dictated by Bob; Kit would have right of first refusal on any name proposed for membership; he would request "sensible confidentiality, not the silly kind." In addition, he would be free to pursue the psychological paradigm of dissociation that he felt was most useful to account for the abductees' belief system.

"They got me to Santa Fe by using the promise of rock-solid data as a hook," he added. "Alexander told me they had four very strong cases to show me. They turned out to be garbage. I even have trouble with Hal, when he trusts all the remote viewing claims."

"Who else will be on the board?" I went on.

"I think we can get Jack Schmidt," Kit answered, "and authorities in psychiatry, people I've long wanted to work with. We need to stand on established credibility."

I made it clear that I might take a point of view opposed to his, that I didn't believe his dissociation model accounted for the abductees' experiences any more than Hopkins' sado-masochistic obsessions. He accepted the debate.

Under those conditions, I called Bob Bigelow and told him I would join the board.

Hummingbird. Sunday 12 November 1995.

Over dinner with Keith and Darlene last night we spoke of the poor state of parapsychology, and of an upcoming high-level meeting at Noetics. Keith was nervous, even looking over his shoulder at the next table as if he expected other diners to spy on what we said.

The forthcoming Noetics seminar list includes a number of people I know: Jeffrey Mishlove, Mike Murphy of Esalen, astronaut Ed Mitchell, Ken Pelletier, and Willis Harman.

Marilyn Schlitz told me that my presence at the meeting had attracted a number of Noetics Board members who rarely came, and she liked the fact that Bigelow would be there:

"This way, if we agree on new research directions having to do with UFOs, the work could be picked up by his new Institute rather than Noetics, because we can't touch it."

Hummingbird. Sunday 19 November 1995.

Bob Bigelow didn't make it to the Noetics meeting in Tiburon because the fog was so deep his jet had to return to Vegas, but the psychic elite of the Bay Area was there, in corduroy pants, soft fabrics and expensive sweaters. I was happy to find Dan Drasin there, in charge of recording.

Once everyone was settled there was an announcement that a parked Mercedes had its headlights on, then the day's work began. Sandy Wright set the tone by bringing us more greetings than we deserved from Laurance Rockefeller, and regrets from Mrs. Butros-Ghali, the wife of the U.N. Secretary General.

Keith Thompson introduced the speakers. Brian O'Leary spoke on free energy, mixing metaphors, from Sai Baba's materializations to meditation to the Casimir force, which was supposed to help us save mankind. He provided comic moments by pulling out a blue pig puppet that imitated Carl Sagan, but the humor seemed forced.

Greer presented himself in a dignified way, as an emergency doctor who had become interested in the phenomenon after a personal encounter: at age 18, in 1973, he saw an object close to him and a strange being blocking his path.

As the day went on, however, it became clear that Greer's plans, supported by Mrs. Wright, followed a political agenda, hinting at high-level contacts, discussions with White House officials and plans to turn the human race into a peace-loving, space-faring species…

New York. Tuesday 21 November 1995.

Janine and I stopped over in New York on the way to Paris for dinner with industrialist Pierre Simon and his wife Jackie in their splendid

Fifth Avenue apartment. This morning we visited my publisher John Weber at Marlowe; then lunch *à deux* in the Village.

Mabillon. Friday 24 November 1995.

We landed in a country on strike against the policies of Chirac's technocrats. No trains are running, buses are rare, government offices are closed. Yet my mother remained enthusiastic about the future, in contrast with my brother who now turns his back on a France that has disappointed him. I cannot blame him.

In the gloomy dawn Janine and I reflected on the meeting at Noetics. Janine remarked that all the psychic exploration of the last 20 years hadn't taught us much about the human condition, or even about "consciousness." I argued weakly that we kept making slow progress in defining the problem, but the hard fact is that she's right.

Mabillon. Saturday 25 November1995.

French Defense consultant Gilbert Payan, with whom I had lunch at *Punjab* yesterday, continues to believe that an Alien spaceship crashed in Roswell. He is only interested in classic physical models. Anything that doesn't fit he ascribes to "magical tricks."

Mabillon. Sunday 26 November 1995.

Paris is still idle this morning. The rain and the strikes linger on. Janine and I had lunch with Pierre Lagrange, who seemed quite frail. He told us that Payan had inspired most of Velasco's latest book, which hypothesized that UFOs were antimatter spacecraft flying from a base within the asteroid belt, a bizarre idea with no basis.

In the afternoon Janine found out that a medieval music group was performing at the Cluny Museum, in the ancient Roman Therms, which gave us the opportunity to admire the *Pilier des Nautes* once more while listening to ballads by Guillaume de Machaut.

Paris. My partners' offices. Monday 27 November 1995.

The strike is getting tougher. The so-called "social fracture" recognized by government and economic pundits turns out to be a chasm, with a majority of French workers rightly feeling they have no "democratic" access to the levels where their lives are controlled.

Europe remains a work in progress, a mirage of pompous bureaucratic dimension. People's imagination could have been captured by the goal of achieving political and economic unity by the year 2000, opening the third Millennium with a new vision. That opportunity is being missed.

No wonder French workers cling to their few hard-won privileges and their tiny margin of security.

Mabillon. Tuesday 28 November 1995.

The Algerian cleaning lady unlocked the door for me when I arrived at the office early this morning. She worried about her return home: the trains are still on strike and the subway is unpredictable. Poor workers like her are the first victims. People are edgy and scared. Even Janine has her tense face of the days of uncertainty; she dresses in a rough gray coat, zippered up to her chin. I walked home, a 50-minute hike in the cold night air, passing a long line of buses from *Force Ouvrière* that brought demonstrators.

My publisher Simone Gallimard recently died of breast cancer.

Mabillon. Wednesday 29 November 1995.

We had our major meeting of the second Fund today, before the formal presentation to our investors that has become a yearly ritual. Twelve of our shareholders managed to come, some of them from faraway provinces, with stories of traffic jams reminiscent of past crises.

The situation is simply rotting away, day after day. In this gloomy landscape our team appears as a beacon of hope, since we report upbeat results from our first portfolio.

As we start this new project I can look forward to eight or ten years of stable professional activity, with opportunities for technical innovation. In today's world such a development amounts to a special privilege: the ability to influence, in some small but definite way, the path of technology.

"Look at all these people walking along," said a cab driver I was lucky enough to grab on my way home tonight. "They've lost hope; they don't know what's going to happen. Stores are deserted, just before Christmas... A lot of people are going to get hurt."

Mabillon. Friday 1 December 1995.

Over lunch one of our investors, a top executive of Peugeot, railed—not against the striking workers but against the Juppé government: "Those ministers of his are theoreticians, a bunch of bureaucrats, their noses in their *dossiers*. They've never spent any time on a factory floor; never stuck their fingers in a can of engine grease."

The rail and subway strikes are spreading to postal services and the Utility Company, whose employees fear privatization. Paris is paralyzed. Early yesterday morning I walked across the Seine, through the great courtyard of the Louvre and down the Tuileries gardens to a meeting with a financier who was late. His view of the strike also put the blame on bureaucrats rather than the Unions.

Yesterday the *International Herald Tribune* published patent lies about remote viewing, running on the front page. It reported that the CIA "was told by Congress to take over the secret program from the Pentagon last summer." They concluded that "no more public funds should be spent on it." Such is the way history gets written.

Mabillon. Saturday 2 December 1995.

The sunshine of the last few days had made long walks through Paris bearable, but it has given way to the squishy dampness of winter.

I had another lunch at *Jardins du Bac* with Payan. I gave him the manuscript of *Enjeux* and I mentioned Renaud Marhic's latest book (**51**), hinting at connections between the belief in Aliens and the extreme right. Later I spoke to Marhic, who recommended that I read *Les Meurtres de l'Occulte* by Facon.

He said Raymond Bernard, former head of Amorc in France, had formed an *Ordre Souverain du Temple Initiatique* that sounds similar to the *Ordre du Temple Solaire*. "The Templar temptation keeps coming back," he said, "forming a pattern behind the extreme Right movements."

Hummingbird. Thursday 7 December 1995.

We flew back on Sunday. In our overflowing mailbox was a letter from Bob Bigelow apprising me of the first meeting of the Scientific Advisory Board ("SAB") of his new National Institute for Discovery Science. He sent along the slides presented by Kit Green.

My Noetics article is published (**52**).

Also in the mail was Ann Druffel's manuscript about Jim McDonald. It brings to light some facts of which I had not been aware: Jim's briefcase was regularly searched or "borrowed" by unknown parties, his slides disappeared, his suitcases were riffled through and cars with no license plates often followed him around.

Yesterday evening I attended the yearly Christmas party of Sutter Hill Ventures, a tradition among Silicon Valley insiders, and I visited Com21, Paul Baran's latest startup, where my friend Steve Millard is now vice-president. Share prices of networking companies are booming. The Dow-Jones average flirts with the 5200 level.

Spring Hill. Sunday 10 December 1995.

We spent Friday night at a screening of avant-garde films (including George Kuchar's *Things Never Get Better*) among a public of pierced girls with short purple hair and boys with rings in their lips. After that we were ready for the peace of the remote forest. Yet Spring Hill caught us off-guard again with the anguish of its mystery and its majestic loneliness, the sky obscured by high mist.

The review of newspapers reveals a continuing pattern of disinformation about remote viewing, originating within the CIA. Beyond the *Herald Tribune* article, similar pieces have appeared in the *Washington Post* and the *Baltimore Sun* of the same day:

"After functioning 17 years under the Defense Intelligence Agency, the program was transferred in July to the CIA, which now wants to kill it." The *Post* emphasizes that the CIA study has concluded that "the line drawings and other descriptive material produced by the psychics" never aided US national security agencies, a plain lie (**53**).

Hummingbird. Thursday 21 December 1995.

Fred Beckman called today "to try to check up on some hearsay." He'd learned that a new group had been formed to study UFOs under Bigelow funding; that it included Kit Green, Hal Puthoff, Dean Judd, Major McDuff, John Petersen, and me; that it had links to (CIA Director) Woolsey and to E-Systems; that Bob Lazar was working with it through a project involving Hal, Bob Wood, and his son Ryan, that John Alexander and Ron Pandolfi were once considered to run the group but had been "excused," that the goal was propulsion technology, and that it was all a front financed by the government.

I gave an evasive response, then called Hal, angrily pointing out that given so many leaks we could never protect my witnesses.

Spring Hill. Saturday 23 December 1995.

John Alexander confirms: "Pandolfi turns out to be the source of the leaks. Ron was at one meeting I setup. He's violated our confidentiality agreement. He knew all the names. Schnabel, too."

Evidently the non-disclosure agreement we signed with Bob Bigelow has already been violated and is worthless. (**54**)

"Why are they spreading all this?" I asked.

"I don't understand it. Pandolfi is on sabbatical from the Agency, on a GM program. Schnabel couldn't have put all that together alone."

"That'll make it difficult to recruit good people," I observed. "Personally, I'm proud of my association with Mr. Bigelow and you guys; others may not feel that way. Careers are at stake."

In my dismay I was glad to hear that Blackburn had commented, "With Vallee in there, it may come to something good," but the fact remains that I can't trust the new Institute to do the needed research.

Hummingbird. Christmas Day, 1995.

The radio mentions another series of assassinations among members of the *Order of the Solar Temple* in France. My mother, when I called for Christmas, said she saved the newspapers for me. We're reading a book by a survivor of the massacre in Switzerland last year (**55**).

What strikes me about the Templar disciples is that they were grossly manipulated, *yet their basic ideas were not wrong*. Their founders said that Man had access to a higher level of consciousness, that the body held undiscovered powers of healing. These statements retain a noble, uplifting value. Yet the Solar Temple leaders built a hideous cult on that basis, turning dozens of well-intentioned people into mindless automata, fooling them with carnival tricks about Aliens, and eventually butchering them, to what end?

Spring Hill. Thursday 28 December 1995.

Winter night: New thoughts swell from swirling depths, and rain pounds this roof. In far away Willits we dined on steamed rice and spicy soup. Diane Darling told me that a new monastery, run by Thai monks, would soon move to upper Tomki road: The *City of Ten Thousand Buddhas* has given them some land.

We are of the fortunate generation that came after the invention of the Pill and before the outbreak of AIDS. What comes after us? Diane had a dream, of a curious English girl who kept coming into her bedroom, asking about our conversations.

Hummingbird. Sunday 31 December 1995.

Over dinner with Keith and Darlene we discussed remote viewing again. In the days of Jimmy Carter, Keith was asked to produce a psychic assessment of a hostage in Iran (**56**). The target was American diplomat Richard Queen, who was ill: "They called me one morning. I stopped at an isolated spot to clear my head on the way to SRI. After the session I was exhausted. They've never understood the process!"

"What happened to the hostage?" I asked.

"Based on the data we gave the White House a military plane was sent to pick him up. I didn't even know the target was a hostage, yet I accurately described his physical and mental condition."

He went on: "When they asked, 'where will the target be in 48 hours?' I saw him aboard a plane. Our data was so precise they went to pick him up. The fellow was never told what we'd done. Today he's still sure the CIA had a spy there, all the time he was a captive. He couldn't begin to guess we knew this by psychic means."

"That work was excellent, so why such contradictions at the CIA?" I asked, "Admiral Turner and General Stubblebine rave about the accomplishments. Why muddy the waters? Why kill the program?"

"You're on to something," Keith responded somberly, adding, "There are factions. The managers didn't foresee they would be overruled by higher-level people."

We left it at that. At midnight we drank Champagne. We toasted one another and especially Hamlet, their neurotic cat.

Part Fifteen

WILD CARDS

11

Hummingbird. Monday 1 January 1996.

A new year is here and technology rages on. Anyone returning to Silicon Valley after a two-year absence would be astonished at the rapid changes, first among them the new cultural attitudes and escalated prices. Confusion about psychic research is a case in point. Our friend Dr. Keith Harary was on television today, interviewed by a former San Francisco mayor about his role as "a psychic for the CIA." The man kept asking if psychics could win the lottery! Similar confusion is rampant whenever aerial phenomena are discussed, occasionally creating mental collisions that fascinate me.

In one recent case an abductee reports seeing human arms and legs piled up like firewood in a corner of a dark room, lit by a blue glow. Ufologists take it at face value. To me the scene has a stunning mytho-poetic connection to Germanic fairy tales where a hero spends the night in a haunted castle; *little men* force him to play bowling games as they knock down bones using human heads that keep dropping down the chimney. In the tale *a horrible being reassembles itself* out of members that have appeared chaotically. Is that clear enough?

Hummingbird. Friday 5 January 1996.

John Petersen just called me about the strategic plans of Bigelow's new National Institute for Discovery Science ("NIDS.") He outlined ten ambitious tasks followed by a thinkpiece in the style of management consultants, with words like "broad assessment of plausible futures… **(1)**"

Hummingbird. Saturday 6 January 1996.

Skeptical of Petersen's approach, when we have not even listed basic facts, or researchable issues, I drafted a two-page letter to NIDS asking Bob Bigelow what was actually funded and what results were sought.

I also recommended the appointment of a public information officer as a focal point for the media. Within an hour John Petersen was calling me: planning had started out well, he said but Kit, like me, had reacted negatively. "This strategy business is a waste of time," he'd said, rather upset. "Why do you want to plot future scenarios?" Petersen flew back to Washington in a foul mood:

"Bigelow is working on four real estate deals, each worth 100 million dollars, so he doesn't pay much attention to the Institute. His assistant McDuff has been putting together a security plan and a computer plan. When he took it to Bigelow his proposal was shot down, so he's just sitting there with nothing to do.

Hummingbird. Sunday 7 January 1996.

Bob Bigelow called this afternoon, answering my queries. Petersen wanted $40,000 to orchestrate a strategic plan for the Institute. Bob stopped him: "We'd have become bogged down. I've applied the brakes because we don't have the right management in place yet."

Leading parapsychologist Dean Radin has moved over to the consciousness research lab funded by Bigelow at the University of Nevada: "He'll do the daily research, concentrating on the psychomentum work, which implies a scrying environment. As you know we have three open positions, two for consciousness and one for aerial phenomena. The hardest thing is to convince people, after all these years that a genuine effort is under way, with real University connections. I've also spoken to a fellow named Ron Blackburn, whose resumé came through John Alexander, d'you know Blackburn? He's a technician, not a manager."

Here, I could only agree. Bob went on: "I've interviewed De Angelo, Ed May's boss at SAIC. He's a nice man, motivated, with a nuclear physics background, but he only wants to look at strategy. Our best candidate is Larry Lemke from Ames, who has an avid interest in UFOs, a guy in his early 40s. He's coming over. We spoke to his boss Scott Hubbard, but Larry's wife doesn't want to move to Vegas."

"I'll help interview Larry if you want me to," I said. "But what about the consciousness work?"

"John has spoken to parapsychologist Dr. Robert Morris; that went nowhere, then Ken Ring's name was suggested, but he's too busy."

"What about ongoing research?" I asked.

"We've only had a one-time exploratory trip to see Colin Andrews. He claimed to have photos and all kinds of data about crop circles, but it was disappointing, 13 years of stuff kept in a hodge-podge way, not segregated. What's odd is that Colin himself said 90% of all circles after 1989 were fakes. Well, most of what he's collected came in the last six years, so why should we be interested?"

"Who went there with you?"

"There was John Alexander, George Knapp, Dean Judd, and Pete McDuff. The contract would have been through the Bigelow Foundation." So, the Foundation continues to finance independent work on paranormal subjects, outside of NIDS.

Next, we discussed the past activities of the Coalition.

"I want to follow up on the discussion you and I had in Austin," Bigelow said. "You ought to come over and spend a few hours here, going through the files. In 12 months, I provided $192,000 for the projects they voted on, out of $250,000 I had committed, with no strings attached. I didn't have a vote the first year. The only thing that was accomplished was the purchase of the Ruppelt papers. We tried to get the APRO papers, but that went nowhere."

So, Tina Choate is still holding out, I thought. "The whole Coalition effort exploded for two reasons. First, Richard Hall left the room in a huff, never to return when I asked for a vote. I felt I should have been trusted by then. Hall had gotten $20,000 to research a book, and CUFOS got $15,000 for a rapid-response team."

He laughed: "That rapid-response fiasco led to our second blow-out. Mike Swords and Mark Rodeghier asked how I would vote on Webb's assignment. I said I would vote against him. He hadn't even written a report. The CUFOS folks were indignant. They had committed to an 18-month contract extension without my authorization. You're welcome to review that."

"Bob, I'm not talking about an audit," I said, "the point of my memo was only that we ought to know what was done, so we don't reinvent the wheel." Bigelow laughed:

"You don't have to fear that, Jacques, we gained nothing from the ufologists, after one year and $250,000. All we learned was about their egos and territoriality, and lack of protocol. Schuessler was the only one who made sense; the others were all at each other's throats."

"What happened when Webb was called out to investigate?"

"There was only one case that seemed interesting, a crash-retrieval event in Santa Rosa, New Mexico, that had taken place in 1963. There were credible eyewitnesses, transcripts from police radio. Walter Webb just went there and started filming, without trying to gain the confidence of the witnesses, a real disaster."

Spring Hill. Saturday 13 January 1996.

This is the dark of the moon. We watch Orion rising at the center of a vast circle of diamonds: Sirius, Procyon, Capella, Castor and Pollux making a magnificent crown over the tower.

Under the dining room lamp Janine is sewing large drapes for the bedroom. When we called up our son in Paris he told us that Mitterrand had died on Wednesday. Olivier was reading my library catalogue; it made him want to spend time here, he said.

Our developer neighbor has called a bit sheepishly to request a meeting. After my recomputation of the foresters' maps it's obvious that his logging road cuts into our property in three places, and even his main driveway intersects our land. I suggested he come up to the ranch for some old-fashioned, Western-style horse trading.

Mission Street office. Wednesday 17 January 1996.

My moods always depend on the way Janine feels: from pits of sadness if she treats me indifferently to a great equanimity of the soul if she smiles. Only then am I able to do real work, rather than executing the automated tasks of the brain. Today Janine behaves as if she thought it a foregone conclusion that we will be apart some day, that I will go my own way, seeking my own pleasure. I don't know how to convince her otherwise. The weather doesn't help: I have been waking up early with allergy flare-ups. When I try to rest I fall into a dreary, false sleep. Last evening was very sweet, however. We went to a concert of the Saint Petersburg Philharmonic, conducted by Yuri Temirkanov. We heard the first American performance of

Slominsky's *Saint Petersburg Visions*, which entranced us both. They also played Bruch's first violin concerto, and Mahler's First Symphony. The effect Mahler produces on me is like watching a toddler having a temper tantrum, not the awesome deployment of transcending forces, as in Berlioz or Wagner.

Dan Tolkowsky has called to comment warmly about my *Noetic Review* article. "This is a problem that isn't going to be solved for a long, long time," he told me.

Hummingbird. Saturday 20 January 1996.

This afternoon I flew to Hollywood for a Board meeting at Isocor, which gave me a chance to see Bob Weiss at home. He gave me a tour of the amusing robot museum in his basement. We reminisced about the old days when we were doing online conferences on the Internet with Timothy Leary, Barbara Marx Hubbard, and the artists of the Future Presentations agency, years ahead of everybody.

Whitley Strieber is said to be scared of the reported "implants" recently removed from abductees in Houston. The doctor, Roger Leir, is a podiatrist who is convinced that the items are Alien devices. He claims he found a metallic core, and growth within the encapsulation, allegedly "integrated with the nervous system."

Hummingbird. Sunday 28 January 1996.

As always, Dr. Richard Niemtzow was warm and friendly when I called him on Wednesday. He said he'd been picked for a promotion to full Colonel, to be effective in June.

"Any sightings in your neck of the woods?" I went on.

"Not much, although we did have an unidentified object right here at McGuire Air Force Base, at the end of our runway."

I have four manuscripts to study at the moment: Ann Druffel's edited Journals of Jim McDonald; Whitley Strieber's *Secret School*, for which he'd requested a quote; Douglass Price-Williams' book about Carlos Castañeda and his own psychic experiments; and Bob Pratt's work on Brazil, for which I have written a foreword (**2**).

In a statement on the Internet, Ingo Swann gives me credit for using "addresses" (in the sense of automata theory) to trigger remote viewing in the early days of his SRI work. This became the methodology basis for Scanate, although Hal and Russell could never pursue it: their sponsors never explored the implications (**3**).

On Friday afternoon we celebrated Janine's birthday at the Sheraton Palace. Catherine helped organize it, calling our Greek friends from Palo Alto and Rhea with Brian Pinkerton, and Darlene Harary who works nearby in the financial district.

Hummingbird. Friday 2 February 1996.

Whitley Strieber came over for dinner with Ann last night, wearing a broad-rim hat and a beige suit. We spent a warm evening together, talking about life in Texas and his forthcoming *Secret School.* They now spend most of their time in San Antonio, while their son Andrew studies English and archaeology.

Whitley's anecdotes are peppered with unverifiable references to friends who can make themselves invisible, to his own travels through time to the Roman Empire, and to enigmatic contacts with Secret Orders. He mentioned his family's connections with the Intelligence community, and an uncle's link to General Exon (**4**).

Las Vegas. Later the same day.

The NIDS Board is assembling here for the second time (I missed the organizational meeting in December.) Some members arrived late, and a few are still away because of extreme weather conditions across the country: snow and ice all the way to Texas, many airports closed. Our group at the Sun Harbor Budget Suites climbed aboard two vans for the evening proceedings at the new Institute facilities on Tropicana—a suite of offices, comfortably furnished.

We met in the spacious library, which Diane Arcangel has started to fill. Most members were people I hadn't met before. First was Pete McDuff, an Air Force Lt- Colonel who served most recently as head of security for Nellis Air Force Base. A friendly fellow with a tall lean frame and a grayish beard, Pete seemed eager to get into the field to interview witnesses. Next to Hal sat a potential new recruit for the position of director of research for the parapsychology department, Dr. Kenneth Klivington. A solid fellow in a suit and tie, mid-forties, he hardly said ten words. He didn't strike me as especially interested. He serves as vice-president for science at the Fetzer Institute in Kalamazoo, Michigan.

To his right was Marty Pilch, physicist at Los Alamos, and Diane Arcangel, a dynamic lady. John Petersen, a bit tense, sat next to Harrison "Jack" Schmidt, the geologist-astronaut and former Senator from New Mexico; I also met Johndale Solem, a mathematician and theoretical physicist from Los Alamos, and Dean Judd, an oval-shaped man in a blue suit, with an oval-shaped face, the most senior member at the gathering. Next to him was a man from the UNLV finance department who serves on the NIDS corporate board.

Across the table were Jessica Utts, a sharp statistician from UC Davis who has just completed a formal study of remote viewing data, Air Force Brigadier General Jim Whinnery who holds both a PhD in physics and an MD and specializes in aircraft accident investigations, and also a woman in her early forties, a smart researcher of near-death experiences named Emily Williams Cook.

The evening discussion began with Kit's summary of the first Board meeting. He asked me to comment on my letter where I'd requested that the Board be brought up-to-date on earlier research funded by Bigelow. This triggered some lively comments on our goals, vision, and mission. Jack Schmidt was most vocal in defense of strict scientific standards: "Frankly, the first sign I saw that something was wrong was when I received a UFO book in the mail from you guys," he told Bob Bigelow with a tone of reproach. "We shouldn't jump into this without a strategy; there's much to be done. Remember that NASA has never done a good job in life science research, when so many topics demand attention, even the possibility of fossils on Mars."

When my turn came I pointed out that independent researchers could benefit from the assistance of a larger group equipped for research. But this required assurance that the privacy of witnesses would be protected.

As I suspected, however, secrecy was already compromised: Steven Greer's coterie knew all about our meeting and "wanted to join forces in planning for the Alien landing in 1997!" They're certain we're preparing it in secret, as a channel for Disclosure, the release of official information. That would be nice…

Las Vegas. Saturday 3 February 1996.

I am sad to be away from Janine today, a mere 37 years after our first meeting. I called to hear her voice and to say how much I loved her.

Last night, after an informal buffet dinner at NIDS, John Petersen, Hal and I gathered in Kit's room for a late-evening chat. Kit introduced us to a young woman with long auburn hair named Kristin Zimmerman who is sharing his life. Kristin, who works at GM, is in her early 30s and holds a degree in materials science. An accomplished pilot, she has a quiet sense of humor and a great smile.

I hadn't seen Kit in a couple of years. He was leaner, more subdued, yet tougher than I remembered him, more of an enigma too. His new position at GM research sends him to China frequently with new responsibilities for materials research. In the evening he wore a pair of small round spectacles that actually made him look almost innocent, in combination with his graying mustache and beard.

Once seated on the cheap furniture—a brown sofa and two plastic chairs supported by aluminum tubes are all the amenities provided to Bob's tenants—we plunged into our favorite topics. Hal told us Ed Mitchell had just attended a Rockefeller-sponsored meeting where individuals with first-hand experience with UFOs in the government or the military were invited to tell their stories. One man is said to have flown "higher-ups" to Holloman Air Force Base in time to watch three UFOs approach. Two hovered, one landed, and Aliens came out to confer with the officers. Another story, which is gaining credibility in that crowd, is that of a demonstration at Edwards Air Force Base. After an air show attended by dignitaries, this group was taken into a hangar where they saw several disks that flew around. They went to a test area where they watched one of them take off. Hal couldn't say if there was anyone inside the disk, or who the "higher-ups" were.

"Why couldn't it be a reconnaissance device based on Dr. Moller's technology?" I asked. "I've seen his flying disk do all those things, over 15 years ago in Sacramento. He sells them to the military **(5).**"

Hal wants to believe all this is part of a super-secret Alien technology, but I remembered the exact same discussion in Princeton, in June of 1992. We are making no progress.

"I'm told one of the dignitaries was Senator Cranston," he said. "He's come to visit my lab, UFOs were mentioned."

Hal showed us a piece of metal he had just received from Pratt & Whitney, a sample of titanium aluminide. The story that circulates is that the Air Force turned over such material to industrial firms for duplication. They took 30 years to manufacture it in any quantity--hence the speculation that the original came from a crashed saucer.

I brought up the puzzling leaks again.

"Pandolfi's office has antagonized people in Washington," was the answer, "Dan T. Smith continues to spread rumors and confusion."

"Why did you ever push me to meet with that crowd?" I asked Kit.

"I was really impressed with them at the time," he answered.

Las Vegas. Later the same day.

We had another full day of meetings with people whose relationships and talents are coming into focus. Ted Rockwell, a late arrival, introduced himself modestly as a "nuclear engineer." Marty Pilch explained that his background was in laser physics at Los Alamos and the Max Planck Institute, while Johndale Solem said his interest was in "the relationship between existence, time, and consciousness."

A man who joined as an observer—one of two young scientists I hadn't identified the day before—was Warren Burggren, interim Dean of the College of Science at the University, a friendly bearded fellow. John Alexander arrived with his new wife Victoria, a woman with long dark hair and a jaded view of reality.

I found it strange, given the informality around Bob Bigelow, that most of the members who had been wearing suits and ties when they arrived still had them on today, keeping their official look.

The meeting came to order, and Kit began talking about Vision, Mission, Strategy ("competency before creativity") and Initiatives ("creativity followed by accountability").

The group picked up on the previous evening's debate: Do we really need to have UFOs and survival of death as a double focus, or should we begin with more legitimate subjects?

"We're a resource, not an advocacy group," someone else said.

"Yet our founder has outlined a giant reach," Kit pointed out.

"True, but we must conduct it through science," was the verdict.

Ted Rockwell spoke up: “Tell me again how these two topics were picked? Why UFOs and survival, rather than ESP and Bigfoot?”

“It harmonizes with the interests of the public,” answered Bigelow. “By studying survival there’s a greater likelihood we’ll know more about our ultimate destiny. As for UFOs, they provide an example of performance on a scale where quality investigation is possible.”

The group debated this and decided the Institute would be “a leader emphasizing investigation and scientific rigor, a tool for legitimation, an unbiased source of information.”

“It's hard to disagree with that list,” I said. “It's apple pie. But what do we do when Uri Geller reveals he's in touch with Hoova, and ‘proves it’ by bending your spoon?”

Once the laughter died we redefined the problem by stating that the Institute would be “proactive, not reactive.” In other words, we only work on what we choose to work on; we don't drop everything just because someone shows up with a film of extraterrestrial autopsies. I insisted the word “impact” had to be in the statement: “If nothing changes in the field in two years as a result of our work, I'm not going to be in this room,” I said. That was the general feeling.

TV journalist George Knapp, dynamic as ever, brought a videotape of UFO events in Russia. He related his contacts with Nicolai Kapranov, a high-level advisor to the Soviet Navy and expert on national security, which led him to identify a Soviet UFO program under Boris Sokholov that had gathered tens of thousands of reports (about 90% explained, however, like ours.)

George Knapp, who is in touch with a general manager at EG&G, has gone on a follow-up trip to see General Maltsev of the Soviet Air Defense Staff. He’d investigated the case of a hovering UFO interfering with the launch sequence of a nuclear missile.

The most recent Soviet effort began as a result of spectacular incidents in 1977 over the Finnish border. According to George the Soviet Air Force had experienced three plane crashes after attempts to intercept UFOs. He said the most interesting case took place in 1982 and involved a missile base in Ukraine, when a silent UFO hovered over the base, which lost control of its nuclear weapon codes for 15 seconds. In 1989 the Soviets had approached the U.S. about the possibility of an exchange of data on the question, because they were concerned over the implications.

This ongoing Russian effort is known as "Thread Three." George also mentioned Yuri Platov and General Maitsev as possible contacts. From my own meeting with him I recall that Platov was a plasma expert, the Russian equivalent of debunker Philip Klass (**6**).

John Alexander and George Knapp advocated inviting the Russians for a private meeting, but Jack Schmidt strongly objected: "The Russians will do anything and promise anything to get a few dollars," he said. "None of that is reliable."

George circulated a list of sightings in Russian and in English and a binder with photographs. Unfortunately, the pictures were extremely poor—worse than those Martine and I had rejected in Moscow. Several were obvious lens flares, a fact that convinced me not to raise my voice against Jack in defense of a special meeting.

Bigelow and Alexander see the Santa Fe Institute as our model: they would like NIDS to have its own campus. They even consider leasing offices from the old nuclear test site. In spite of notes of caution from Dean Judd, the temptation to acquire a lot of fancy hardware before they know what to do with it may prove irresistible.

"The facilities should not drive the research program," said John-dale Solem, echoing my own thoughts, but we were not heard.

We had dinner at the Liberace Museum where the Board sat at a big long table. Kit offered a toast. Victoria arrived in a true Vegas outfit, a very short dress and black stockings. I learned that McDuff, who is something of a wine expert, had been employed by EG&G and knew Nellis very well, but he'd never entered Area 51.

Bob became fascinated with survival research after his 22-year-old son died a few years ago in the desert. He became interested in UFOs because he'd experienced unusual phenomena as a child, with his grandparents. His generous gifts to the University are well-known.

After dinner we went to Bigelow headquarters on South Eastern. The mansion is Nevada classic, yet quite elegant. We returned to the motel for another late-night chat with Kit, Hal, John, Kristin, and Victoria about crop circles and abductions.

I mentioned recent French research I'd been shown, suggesting that UFO abductions might be mediated by transmethylation triggering hallucinogens, but I got no reaction.

I continue to worry about confidentiality of cases and witnesses: Hal talks to Ron Blackburn, expecting his confidence but Blackburn brags freely to Beckman and McCampbell, who try to impress Dan Smith, so everything apparently goes to Langley. Victoria is a former friend of Rima Laibow... this isn't a group that can keep secrets.

Hummingbird. Monday 12 February 1996.

Spring has arrived early, bringing a dizzy feeling. The first phone call today was from Pete McDuff, who spoke urgently of his new assignment: in spite of the science board's recommendation to proceed slowly, Bob Bigelow has "tasked" him to immediately research UFOs in Mexico. He prepared a trip and wanted to know about my contacts. I recommended starting from the recent videotapes and checking them carefully. He'd already done that, he said, and now works through Bootsie and Greer. So, I didn't recommend anyone in Mexico City, because my friends there would never work that way.

Hummingbird. Tuesday 20 February 1996.

One of our portfolio companies, IPAC (Integrated Product Assembly Corp.), is about to go public while I try to save Accuray again. Our second Fund is finally raised and will "close" in ten days.

At last we are entering a new phase, where I can safely look out ten years or more.

Fort Bragg. Sunday 25 February 1996.

I just allowed myself a two-day sabbatical on the North Coast. Periodically I need to see that magical land: high above Willits, out of the cold ground, pure water bubbles up, hot and steamy, forming pools among the tall trees. I drove on to an inn near Mendocino for the night. Fort Bragg had mysterious antique stores and cavernous bookshops Diane Darling had recommended, as well as good restaurants and coffee houses filled with music.

Up the street a man named Larry Spring displays his weird inventions in his store, so I went in and was rewarded by a lecture on physics principles filled with references to Nikola Tesla, balls of light energy, and demonstrations of motors and parabolas supposed to "expose the errors of modern science." The old man was happy, full of humor. A former real estate agent, he proudly turned on the lights that illuminated his mineral collections and his treasured "found art." His wife Louise, in her sixties, blushed as she confessed how she had fallen in love with the blue-eyed dreamer.

The magic of "Mendonesia" is taught by the wind: tempestuous weather sprayed mist from the high tide into a fine cloud that engulfed the coastline. From the rocks at the foot of the cliffs, all the way to the horizon, it formed a swelling of gray-blue mounds broken by cascading white foam in fury. The whole mass rushed at the shore, filling crevices, storming up the black walls into caves, gurgling through tunnels and blowholes, disgorging into vast funnels.

Hummingbird. Thursday 29 February 1996 (Leap Day).

My novel *FastWalker* has returned from the printer. I wrote dedications to friends. Also arriving today were the extracts of *Enjeux* just released by a French economic magazine **(7)** — twelve pages that give me hopes of renewing some publisher's interest in doing the book itself. It might inject some new ideas into French venture capital and help a few struggling entrepreneurs.

Tomorrow Olivier starts in his dream job on the young staff of a dynamic investment firm in Paris. I am proud of his determination.

In San Francisco it's cold, rainy. On Tuesday night, when Janine and I came out of the Palace of the Legion of Honor after the annual Robertson-Stephens conference reception **(8)** the wide steps were glistening, and the Golden Gate was blurry. I envied Rodin's sculptures in the courtyard: they knew how to let the liquid darkness of winter roll off their strong shoulders.

Hummingbird. Monday 4 March 1996.

Saturday was spent in the forest. We climbed up to the top landing and explored the canyon. Later I traced out part of a route over the ridge through pines and madrones, and pesky manzanita brush where thousands of butterflies flutter around the rocks and the creeks.

Bob Bigelow called: they haven't found a leader for the Institute yet.

They've contacted older profs who just wanted to retire comfortably. “We've had to go through a strategy change,” Bob said. “I've interviewed senior people for the position, but they're not prepared to do real work, they don't have the energy.”

I have been invited to join the “Band of Angels,” a group of senior executives who get together once a month in Palo Alto to hear startup entrepreneurs present their plans. This invitation follows recognition in the *Venture Capital Journal* (**9**).

Spring Hill. Saturday 23 March 1996.

On Thursday night novelist Chris Curry came over for dinner at Hummingbird. A gifted producer of horror novels (*Thunder Road, Panic, Haunted, Moonfall*) she follows channeling groups, notably the “Michael Teachings.” She has tracked down many ghost reports.

We drove up here on Thursday to meet with a forester and count the stumps left on our land by the loggers, and a water expert (who turned out to be a gifted dowser) to restructure the lines along the creek. All day we scrambled up and down from the canyon to the top of the ridge. I love this weather, cool with only a passing threat of rain. Springs were oozing out of every bank, every ravine full of life. But the Mendocino paradise has been marred again by a kidnapping in Potter Valley. A 14-year-old girl who went looking for “drugs and a good time” was last seen naked at a popular bathing spot on the Eel River, along with a local drug dealer who has now vanished (**10**).

“She wasn't a bad kid; her mother teaches Spanish to my own children,” the forester told me as we scrambled down the canyon. “She just ended up with the wrong crowd.”

Hummingbird. Sunday 24 March 1996.

Yesterday I resumed my experiments at the observatory. It was a magnificent night, clear and bright. Venus was resplendent, near maximum elongation from the sun, magnificent on the video display. Comet Hyakutake rose over the eastern horizon, hanging from the handle of the Big Dipper. Turning the Celestron on it, we could clearly analyze details in the nucleus and the tail.

Self-appointeded "skeptics" and assorted Guardians of Rationalism keep pouring scorn on psychical research. Keith Harary tells me, "When I think of all the time, and all the sacrifices along the way in the name of science for the SRI project, and now Jim Schnabel ruins the whole effort on national television, it makes me sick..."

Las Vegas (Sun Harbor.) Sunday 31 March 1996.

Perhaps I'm simply exhausted, but last night at dinner with my friends from NIDS I had a scary experience. We had just sat down, Janine and I, Diane Arcangel, and a few others, when my right eye became slightly blurred as if by a shimmering curtain. Worse, I partially lost the meaning of words—a terrifying episode.

I was relating French sightings when I found myself searching for appropriate terms. My speech suffered long pauses, of which I was painfully aware, as I looked for words like *pond*, or *wire*, and even for common city names like Bordeaux.

I expected at any moment to become physically sick, or to black out. Neither happened; Janine helped me with my faltering vocabulary, and I went on to regain fairly normal speech, although the rest of the meal was a private ordeal. Janine later told me that my face had suddenly looked extremely tired.

Later the same day.

We've made progress during this third meeting, the second one for me. I took Janine to visit the NIDS offices on Tropicana, where we met Kit and Hal, Jim Whinnery, and Pete McDuff. It is to John Alexander's credit that he's assembled a stellar group of researchers.

The evening session began with two new members including Dr. Ian Stevenson, and one notable absence, that of Dean Judd. In the magnificent meeting room of Bigelow headquarters Kit polled us for a new statement of purpose and ran quickly through a preliminary agenda that included a review of recruiting efforts.

Jack Schmidt insisted again that NIDS should abandon esoteric topics and turn to research acceptable to the mainstream: "Nobel prizes will be won in areas that lie slightly outside current research," he said, giving Hal's zero-point energy as an example. "That's what we should be funding, not some dubious medical research."

John Alexander reported mysteriously on various contacts he'd developed within NATO through his non-lethal weapon work. He is in touch with the chief of staff of the Belgian Air Force, now retired.

The Institute has also connected with Illebrand von Ludwiger, who investigates abductions in Germany and Austria, and Bigelow has an interest in Puerto Rico where he has sent a scout, Chad Deetken, researching crop circles and mutilations. He's also gotten veterinarians to report cases gathered by the American Association of Bovine Practitioners, who will poll their members. He has agreements with the U.S. Department of Agriculture pathology lab and the College of Animal pathologists in Irvine.

The Institute also pursues its project in Mexico, where numerous sightings have been alleged in the last four years, resulting in hundreds of dubious videotapes. Pete McDuff has arranged for his trip through a company that runs commercial UFO tours. They are in touch with Jaime Maussan, a television celebrity. ("Good luck," I thought.)

Nothing was reported on a new communication device project, described as a "Pandora's box." Hal, Kit, and John seemed to know what that was about, but I wasn't taken into their confidence. Finally, the staff reported they had paid a visit to SARA (Scientific Applied Research Association), a TRW spinoff that did work in acoustics, low-frequency sensors, and DSP systems (16Hz to several gigahertz). They had picked up UFOs in their work for unnamed agencies.

Las Vegas. Hotel Excalibur. Monday 1 April 1996.

During the main meeting of the Institute on Saturday we first heard about a visit by Knapp, Hal and Alexander to a Florida retiree named Colonel Philip Corso. I recalled Bob Emenegger's comments after meeting the man early in 1994 (p.199.) At age 80 this former soldier, who lives in a mobile home, has decided that "the time had come for his information to come out." So, he's talking about what he saw when he was at White Sands, and later when he worked for Lt. Gen. Arthur Trudeau, Director of Army Research and Development. His revelations, which come in the middle of sensational stories about the "ferret flights" of the 1950s and the capture of Americans by the

Soviets in the Korean War, have to do with UFO hardware.

Corso claims that he was given bits of a craft from a crash on the plains of San Augustin, and that he was charged with replicating the material. He gave it to Rockwell and other labs, telling them as a cover that it came from the USSR. They also had a charred chip, which went to Bell Labs, and strong lightweight metal with "aligned atoms" (?) that went to Lawrence Livermore, as well as "a piece of a flight suit" and various autopsy reports from Walter Reed Hospital.

We saw a videotape of the man, who claimed that he once saw a saucer materialize before his eyes on the White Sands range. An Alien who came out supposedly told him to turn off the radars for ten minutes, so the UFO could take off in peace. Corso complied but one radar didn't get the order and stayed on. I don't know what to think of that tape. The man's son is deeply involved in ufology, so Corso and son have hired an agent, who advised to include the UFO stories in the biography. Kit is scheduled to meet the man. Hal is excited about the possibility that he's telling the truth, while John Alexander suggests "this fellow has been watching the X-Files too much. Some of his statements about historical events he's supposed to have attended don't make sense. He told us the atom bomb had been reverse-engineered from mathematics..."

In the afternoon Dr. Roger Leir came over. He had operated on the foot of a woman who had two implants and on the hand of a man who had one. Derrel Sims and Leir had brought us the samples in question—tiny, wire-like objects—as well as half a dozen other samples removed from abductees. Our Board found it hard to believe that the implants were anything but accidental bits of metal that had entered the victims' bodies. Amusingly, Leir and Sims were spooked by a green light on the floor of our meeting room, marking an electrical outlet. They seemed to think a laser was zapping them.

The main implants removed from the woman's foot turned out to be made of boron nitrite, a common industrial material.

Finally, we were introduced to hypnotherapist John Carpenter, a friendly fellow based in Springfield, Missouri, who was supposed to speak about six abduction cases. Instead he launched into a long dissertation about Budd Hopkins' theories, flashing slides of reptilian Aliens, lurid descriptions of abductee ordeal, and speculations about Alien activities. Surprised to see everyone swallowing this, I elicited a confession that none of these claims had been confirmed: the key witnesses in Hopkins' notorious Linda Napolitano/Cortile case, for instance, were never found. Do they even exist?

He went on to present a drawing of an Alien body, "by the nurse who saw it at Roswell." That was new to me, so I asked: "You did find her, then?" "Well, no, she's still missing," he had to admit.

"Then whose drawing is this?" I sensed Senator Schmidt, next to me, getting hot under the collar while Kit and Hal seemed hypnotized by the breathless, undocumented anecdotes.

"It was drawn up by the undertaker, based on his recollections."

"His recollections of what?"

"Of the drawing made by the nurse."

"Did he make that drawing in 1947, then?"

"Oh no, he drew it for Len Stringfield just a few years ago."

The rest of the presentation was similar. Carpenter even stated that "There's a 90% correlation between abductions and mutilations of cattle," prompting Jack Schmidt to jump up and challenge him.

I was upset by what I saw and even more by the fact that no one intervened to bring us back to the topic we'd been assigned. The Board is getting very loose, I thought, chasing wild tales.

Later the same day.

When we took time to visit the NIDS office again this afternoon, Janine and I found Pete McDuff upset because his plans of a research trip to Mexico were complicated by unforeseen schedule changes. He'd been led to contact a notorious hoaxer to firm up his plans. What does it say about our ability to conduct real research?

Over a cup of coffee with Victoria at the Excalibur she told me of her life-long passion for mysticism and church history. A sharp, vivacious woman, she has an idea to promote "the next level after abductions and implants" as a step to new beliefs: "Medieval nuns developed a psychosomatic impression of an 'espousal ring' on their finger," she said, "received from Jesus in person. Will abductees begin to report something like that?"

Tomorrow I dive back into technical reality, spending the day at the

Interop trade show, updating my knowledge about Internet networking hardware, connection standards and interface equipment.

The scary episode of Saturday night has not recurred, so I remain puzzled, at only 57, about my passing cerebral episode. I am enormously grateful for Janine's presence. We drove out happily in the sunlight to visit mighty Hoover Dam, an impressive site.

Spring Hill. Sunday 7 April 1996.

Easter at the ranch, a chance to put events in perspective before another trip to Europe. Foliage colors are violent purple, the mauve of lilac, tender yellow, and the white blossoms of apple trees that bring sweet tears to Janine's eyes, recalling her Norman childhood.

We had a quiet dinner with our sci-fi writer friends Gary Shockley and Lori at the *City of Ten Thousand Buddhas*.

Mabillon. Saturday 13 April 1996.

On the plane I've read Ted Rockwell's fascinating book on his former boss Admiral Rickover and the Nuclear Navy (**11**).

My mother now complains about changes in familiar objects in her apartment. Some items are simply not recognizable to her because her muscles have become weak, so she assumes bronze statuettes and crystal vases have been replaced by coarser, cheaper imitations. She is lucid and up-to-date on other subjects, however: we debated recent discoveries of planets in far-away solar systems.

Mabillon. Sunday 14 April 1996.

Tonight, Janine and I will drive to Belgium with Patrick Corsi, with whom I'll screen research proposals to the European *Projet Esprit*. In anticipation of the trip I called the folks at SOBEPS, the best-organized UFO research group in Europe: "We have over 20,000 pages of interviews and reports," Lucien Clérebaut told me. "We made much progress since your last visit!"

The bleak weather only lifts occasionally.

The first leaves are barely visible atop twisted black twigs along the banks of the Seine.

Brussels. Thursday 18 April 1996.

Hotel Bristol-Stéphanie. We spent last evening with SOBEPS physicist Léon Brenig along with Patrick Ferryn and Lucien Clérebaut. The lengthy investigation of the Belgian wave involving flying triangles (possibly US prototypes of a battlefield drone designed to detect electromagnetic sources) has left serious scars. Clérebaut suffered a heart attack and had to sell his Breughel paintings to survive financially. After all that work they reached no firm conclusions, but their group continues bravely.

Nanterre. Wednesday 24 April 1996.

Industrialist Gilbert Payan just explained to me with some humor why the French General Staff disliked non-lethal weapons: "You can't walk proudly down the *Champs-Elysées* brandishing a pot of glue," he observed wrily. "Besides, the Americans aren't sharing their microwave secrets with us, and they also keep secret the use of magneto-hydrodynamics in their missiles." He blames Jean-Pierre Petit for the disrepute into which MHD research has fallen in France.

I wish I could fly home early instead of visiting startups on the edge of one dreary industrial park after another, in the blight of a suburb where the last few acres of countryside are being plowed under.

Paris. Saturday 27 April 1996.

A memorable lunch today with Thérèse de Saint-Phalle *Chez Georges*, near Place Notre-Dame des Victoires: she had an appointment next door with Mr. Trichet, governor of the *Banque de France*. Our conversation ranged from Mitterrand (Plon tried to publish a book by his doctor, now banned) to De Grossouvre: she knows the circumstances of his death.

"He wrote to me several times," I told her, "and I saw him in that same office where he killed himself. I'm left with the feeling of an unfinished conversation." She reacted immediately:

"De Grossouvre didn't commit suicide, *mon ami*, even if he was found with a gun in his hand. My cousin Alexandre de Marenches told me the gun weighed a kilogram: it would have jumped out of a dying man's hand. De Grossouvre had recently written the first 200 pages of a manuscript that told the truth about matters that horrified him, ugly French politics. Someone didn't want that exposed."

We spoke of Umberto Eco. I told her that his *Foucault's Pendulum* danced around the occult domain, but he completely missed the door that led inside. She shrugged: "He's only an academic, an ethnologist," she said. "You can't expect him to understand the paranormal."

Our waitress came over. Apropos of something on the menu, Thérèse asked where she came from. The girl's family was from the center of France, like herself. "Here's someone who must understand the paranormal better than Umberto and all those professors," she said, asking the girl, "Did your grandmother know how to read the future?"

"Ah Madame, if you only knew..." she answered, blushing. "The future, and many other things."

Sorcery is alive here, even in the middle of Paris, a few yards away from the *Banque de France*, although the Sorbonnards will deny it.

"The greatest gift you gave your children was to stay with Janine," Thérèse said as we commented on the disintegration of families. I humbly confessed it was the other way around: Janine had stayed with me in spite of my faults, not an easy achievement.

It is sad that the French—even the best-informed intellectuals like Payan or Thérèse—know nothing about Scanate, still classified. Yet they pretend to be fully informed about what goes on in America.

On the flight to San Francisco. Monday 29 April 1996.

We went back to see my mother, who complained of her weak legs, but in the next sentence she said she had just walked all the way to *Place du Luxembourg* because they sold the best pastries in Paris: a half-mile trek, uphill all the way. My clever son is optimistic about France. He expects people to understand the pressing need for economic reform and budgetary restraint. Having lived through more French upheavals than he did, I have serious doubts about that. This society with its entrenched privileges will defeat any restructuring.

Ten years ago, every country was expanding; European unity looked like a logical merger of happy partners. Today the German economy is overloaded, and the French suffocate in unemployment.

Hummingbird. Thursday 2 May 1996.

The neurologist tells me that my brain scans and EEGs are clean. He ascribes my Las Vegas incident to stress and a random spasm in an artery. This reassures me as I prepare to fly back to NIDS tomorrow afternoon to meet Lieutenant Colonel Corso.

The clarity of California always startles me after the intricacies of France. I contemplate life from a 7th-floor corner office over Market Street, Kearny and Geary. Nothing fancy, but I have a nice view of Lotta's Fountain, a most charming monument (**12**).

Las Vegas. Friday 3 May 1996.

The Sun Harbor Motel has become familiar. John Alexander kindly met my plane. He'd been in Rome for a meeting on non-lethal weapons, so he'd stopped over in Washington to check up on Lt. Colonel Phil Corso at the National Archives. He found that most of what we had been told was true. Corso is prominently mentioned in the oral history of Trudeau's tenure as head of Army R&D.

"This guy is who he says he is," Alexander told me. "He had responsibility for counter-intelligence in Rome after the war, when he was only 27. He went on to work on the NSC staff under Ike, and then held a major command at White Sands. He never trusted CIA and hated James Angleton who got Trudeau fired because of his disagreement with his own assessments of the Russian situation."

We went over to the gate where the flight from West Palm Beach was expected. The old man walked out, slim and determined. Balding, rather short, his eyes calm and his pace steady, he greeted me warmly, saying he'd wanted to meet me for a long time, "to discuss time dimensionality in private." We launched into a review of his experiences. He assured us that the SDI missile project was a cover to defend Earth from Aliens, not the USSR. Yet in the same breath he said that NSC was so concerned with world events that nobody had any interest in tracking the material at Roswell.

"We did a study; MIT told us the atoms were aligned. The metal was very light, incredibly strong. It could've been used to make an invincible spacecraft. By the way, I'm not talking about the metal they describe in those Roswell books, that gets crumpled and straightens out. I've never seen that."

"What did 'your' metal do?" I asked. "It could block off radiation, or let it go through; it could even become transparent," he said.

He turned to me: "How did the being know, at White Sands, that I was the commander, the only one who could turn off all the radars? That's what I want to ask you, Dr. Vallee. I've read your books; you're the only one who's looked at this rationally. But you're wrong to put such emphasis on the Robertson Panel. We never paid any attention to those scientists, Nobel Prize or not; that meeting was just a cover. Their report had been written up long before they met."

"Did you ever meet Hynek? Or the French? Or Battelle?" I asked.

"No, we just kept to our own very small group."

"What about Art Lundahl?"

"Doesn't ring a bell."

"Did Ike know about the UFO situation?"

"Yes, but he never told me so, although I spoke to him often."

"So, there's nothing to the tale of his seeing Alien bodies?"

"I don't think so." That answer reassured me. It checked with my friend Roger Brenner's quiet findings in Southern California.

"What artifacts did you actually handle?"

"We had the chip, and optical fibers, and a device that I first thought was a flashlight, and autopsy reports from Walter Reed."

"What did those say?"

"The beings had scaly skin. Their brains had two frontal lobes. By the way, on the autopsy movie the brains do have these extra lobes. And the double eyelids. Those are light intensifiers. Some animals have double eyelids. The camel, for instance."

"Anything else?" John asked.

"They had atrophied sex organs."

"Were any of the beings still alive?" I enquired.

"That's questionable. I don't know the answer."

"Did anything go to Los Alamos?"

"No, the debris picked up at San Augustin went to Wright-Patterson. A few years later they had an explosion, I believe it was a flying saucer that disintegrated. The EBEs picked up at Corona transited through Fort Riley, Kansas."

"Were you already calling them EBEs at that time?"

"Yes, the term dates from the Eisenhower White House, at least."

In describing physical effects Corso displayed superficial knowledge of basic science. He kept mixing up gravitation with magnetism. When I later pointed out these discrepancies to John Alexander he replied that Corso had never been in charge of R&D but was strictly a manager under Trudeau, who relied on him for his integrity in managing operations, never for science.

Las Vegas. Saturday 4 May 1996.

Our group has spent a second day with Colonel Corso, probing into his reminiscences, which include a remarkable case of Alien contact in the desert. At 81 Colonel Corso is a likeable man with a sense of humor, intense and vibrant, well-balanced, with a remarkable memory; but he has little technical data to give us. When Hal and I took him to breakfast at the Stardust casino much of the discussion had to do with the ferret flights and what the White House knew of Soviet missile capabilities. I had woken up at six in the morning and gone for a pleasant swim, so I felt relaxed and had facile contact with our guest.

We moved to the NIDS office and ran many names through that surprising memory of his. He mentioned a briefer at the White House by the name of Frank Hand, who knew about UFOs, and an officer he worked with, General George Sammet. He had known Hermann Oberth, whom he considered more brilliant than Von Braun. When John pulled out a list of Paperclip scientists Corso recognized two of them who worked in Army R&D. The topic of ex-Nazis in America was a sore point between Corso and the CIA: he felt that many were criminals who should have been shot, never allowed into the country.

One name with which Corso was very familiar was that of Wilbert Smith, from Canada. Smith had come to the Pentagon to meet General Trudeau, who had introduced Corso.

"When did Trudeau retire?" asked Bob Bigelow.

"In June of '62," was the answer.

John Alexander winked at us: the date checked.

"What happened to him?"

"He became president of Rockwell Research. In 1961 we'd turned over a chip from a saucer to two men from Rockwell. I think Mrs. Trudeau has a replica of it on a plaque at her house."

Hal leaned towards me: "It's a type of phototransistor," he whispered. "I've seen a description of it."

Corso claims two direct experiences with the phenomenon. At Fort Riley (Kansas) in 1947 he gained the friendship of a group of sergeants who showed him several boxes, five or six feet long, where bodies were immersed in a preserving liquid. They were supposed to be in transit from New Mexico. And at White Sands, in the Red Canyon area, he once went into a cool mine for a siesta, waking up to see a short being with a helmet at the cave's entrance. He felt a telepathic message to turn off the radars for ten minutes.

"What do you offer?" he asked.

"*A new world, if you can take it*," was the answer. One site, E. Battery, didn't get the order. It supposedly recorded an object moving at 3,000 miles an hour.

"What did the creature look like?" asked Hal.

Corso pulled out a drawing of a classic dwarf. Its hands wore gloves with suction cups and it left footprints like Indian moccasins. The next day he saw a saucer in the desert, which played disappearing games with him. It crushed a big rock when it rematerialized before his eyes. He touched it but got scared and got away, gunning his command car, driving it in reverse. He wasn't tempted to go inside, he said: "I wanted to control my own destiny."

"What was the date of that incident?" I asked the Colonel.

"October 13, 1957," he answered without hesitation. "And three years later I was in the Pentagon, and I was put in charge of the material. Was that what the being meant, when he said, 'A new world, if you can take it'? It almost sounds like a threat, doesn't it?"

It also sounds like what they told abductee Herbert Schirmer: *"Watchman, some day you will see the Universe,"* I thought. So I went over to the library shelf and pulled down *Passport to Magonia*. There was an entry for White Sands just two weeks after Corso's sighting; two officers in an Army Jeep saw a very bright object at ground level at 3 am. My source was Aimé Michel's book, 1958. My friends were stunned at the coincidence. Corso didn't seem to know about it.

"That's why you need an information scientist," I joked. "It helps to have a good database."

"Did you report your sighting?" Mr. Bigelow asked.

"I didn't dare. I had orders on my desk to take command of a combat battalion in Germany; I didn't want to screw that up."

I pointed out the parallels between his story and what General Glenn E. Miller had told me when I met him as the Deputy Director of the Defense Audio-Visual agency at Norton Air Force Base. Miller, too, said he'd seen a saucer in the Mojave. He had gone inside. I told Corso perhaps the being's request to him had nothing to do with radar, but was a symbolic test. When we asked Corso what he thought of the coverup idea, he shrugged: "There may not be any coverup," he said, "I've never met a group like yours."

"Do you want to see your ideas made public?" asked Bigelow.

"I don't want my life to be upset; I don't want dozens of crazy ufologists knocking on my door. On the other hand, I did write this book, twelve publishers have it."

He is clearly flattered by the sudden attention to his place in history, yet scared of the consequences. We concluded that the most important first step was to find George Sammet who is now with Martin-Marietta in Orlando, and any other members of their group of eight or nine who may still be alive.

During the day I also had a chance to take George Knapp aside to discuss the Russian situation. He confirmed that things were closing down. His last trip to Russia was a failure: his contacts were suddenly "sick"--or "away from Moscow."

Hummingbird. Sunday 5 May 1996.

My mother called this morning: the headquarters of *Crédit Lyonnais* were ablaze in the heart of Paris. The bank fire, which started in the trading room and was probably due to arson, is symptomatic of the malaise that underlies French business and its troubled mood.

Reviewing my notes, I make a list of the contradictions in Corso's statements. *First*, he talks as if there was no government group looking into UFOs, yet in the same sentence he speaks of major projects to build bases on the moon for extraterrestrial warfare and of the SDI effort being a cover. *Second*, he speaks of the Roswell material as the basis for invincible platforms, yet he claims that spacecraft made out of this same material were shot out of the sky by primitive radar or simple thunderstorms. *Third*, he claims that fiberoptics came out of the material recovered at the crash site, but what he described was only a bundle of glass "light guides" of a type known before World War Two, and unrelated to communication. *Fourth*, he never alludes to precautions against contamination in any of the instances when they handled devices that were to be reverse-engineered, or even cadavers. *Fifth*, he claims that he held a position actually filled by a man named Spangler, from Pentagon records. *Sixth*, it is highly improbable that as a Lieutenant Colonel he would have served as Inspector General of the Seventh Army.

Spring Hill. Sunday 12 May 1996.

As soon as we drove up, nature embraced us with a lush greenness that felt almost scary. Grass came up to our waist, vines cascaded into our hair, roses burst in blood-colored surprise in places where we didn't recall planting roses, and the apple trees in majesty extended their canopy over the pool. There were new noises: strange birds, a lone bullfrog and thousands of crickets.

There are so many television shows on UFOs now that one can't keep up, all wallowing in the wake of the X-Files. The most recent one features Gordon Cooper describing an incident in which his military camera crew filmed an object landing nearby while they monitored a flight test at Edwards Air Force Base. The report didn't have much impact: believers are already convinced, while skeptics will brush it off as just another simulation.

New York. Tuesday 21 May 1996.

Fred Adler greeted us with a twinkle of greed in his wrinkled eye as he hung up the phone on another sweet deal he'd just made on cheap warrants. He was in turn nasty, venomous, seductive, and brilliant, snapping at people, yelling at secretaries, cajoling associates. The stock market has just broken another record, so the rich would be getting richer even if they didn't make any sweet deals.

New York. Kennedy airport. Wednesday 22 May 1996.

Waiting outside Adler's office for an hour, I spoke with a financial associate until it was our turn to get chewed up and spit out. The quarrel this time was about my efforts to obtain a raise for my faithful assistant. Adler's idea was to fire her and to replace her with an answering machine. I won the battle for Julie but the whole exercise was funny, crude, colorful, and as abrasive as the rest of New York City, like all the rusty junk we could see from that office window high above 55th street. In the afternoon, in happy contrast, I met with John Weber at Marlowe, in the Village.

John's assistant told me in confidence about the time when she saw three angels. This happened three years ago, at 6:20 am: she had looked at her clock. Their fluttering in mid-air had awakened her—a man and a woman of beautiful, radiant appearance. She recalls the weight of the white baby they put in her lap. They told her she had to do three things, which she doesn't remember. In the following weeks she changed apartments and took the job at Marlowe, but she still wonders if those were the things they meant.

Spring Hill. Sunday 26 May 1996.

Sunny Memorial Day. I've removed our Jolly Roger flag, instead flying the *Stars and Stripes* for the occasion. There are fresh claw marks on the retaining wall, a clear signal from our bear. We swim, sleep, and read between two excursions up towards the Monarch ridge, still in dispute with our neighbor.

Keith Harary has given me a tape of an X-file episode borrowed from *FastWalker*. One of the characters is a "Major Vallee," hommage in passing (**13**). He sent copies of an interview where Army remote viewer Dave Morehouse makes statements about Hal's program "ruining his life and career," even hinting that the CIA tried to assassinate his wife.

The crickets have fallen silent. At the foot of the tower the pond is brimming with mysterious life. Sunset arrives. The bullfrog looks over his kingdom and bellows his content.

Flying back from Las Vegas. Saturday 1 June 1996.

I landed in Vegas in time to take a swim and discuss the *Lives of the Saints* with Victoria, after which we were all driven over to Bigelow headquarters and ate dinner while discussing the business of NIDS.

This fourth meeting (not counting our private sessions with Corso) was excellent, thanks to three separate presentations led by General Jim Whinnery. He showed videos of pilots losing consciousness in centrifuges and in actual cockpits, heads falling into their laps as they pulled 9g. Most interesting was how they went from consciousness to unconsciousness to sub-consciousness and sometimes death, in various sequences. Many pilots have "dreamlets" inserted into their memory as they recover from extreme maneuvers, Jim told us: one patient, a fighter pilot, recalled opening a package his sister had given him for Christmas when he was a toddler, while his F-16 was out of control in a dangerous dive. Jim described troubles with vision and the sequential way the brain shuts down, which helped me understand my recent episodes of near fainting. The other presentations (one by Edgar Mitchell) also touched on the near-death experience.

The implants from the last session have now been analyzed at Los Alamos. All five turned out to be made of common elements: aluminum and iron with calcium, copper and other components of the soil. "Dirty metal wires" is the best way to characterize them, with nothing more than accidental transition through the body.

Mr. Bigelow has interviewed a group of people in a small town some 200 miles North of Vegas, in the Alamo-Caliente area. One man swore that while at Wright-Patterson he'd seen a large disk with portholes being unloaded from a HET (Heavy Equipment Transport) vehicle. When he asked about it a German scientist supposedly told him they could see inside the object but hadn't been able to open it.

Hal and Martin are designing communication systems for the Utah ranch, with a 20-mile range in one case and only one mile in the second. But Johndale thinks the communications scenario is unlikely to lead anywhere and "sounds silly."

Hummingbird. Wednesday 5 June 1996.

A professor of communications from Montréal came to interview me today, to my surprise. He made me feel very old by asking me about the early history of personal computing, notably my involvement in Engelbart's project. He had tracked me down after reading *Network Revolution*, which he said was now in most University libraries. "People are very surprised, even technical folks, when I tell them the mouse was invented twenty years before the Apple Macintosh!"

Spring Hill, Sunday 9 June 1996.

This was a special pleasure, to hike all over the land with Janine and our daughter, climbing my new road over the ridge through the thick brush, and sitting on the log pile at the landing to lunch on apricots and oranges, the valley at our feet. We feel like true "Ridge Walkers" now, like the old Indians. A blue column of smoke rises in the still air miles away; turkey vultures circle the canyon.

For the first time in weeks I slept deeply on both nights. My migraine headaches, undoubtedly caused by work stress, are fading away: when asked if they would agree to be among my personal references as a high-tech investor, several senior executives I contacted said they would be offended if they were *not* on that list.

Hummingbird. Saturday 22 June 1996.

My trip to Brunei was postponed at the last minute. Checking our mail yesterday I found a box of the beautiful Marlowe edition of *Forbidden Science*. My spirits lifted with the twin pleasures of lunch with my wife and daughter at a Polk street coffee shop, and the unexpected arrival of this book, the work I care most about. I told Janine that if there was an eternity, she is the only one with whom I could spend it.

"I hope there isn't an eternity," she countered soberly, bringing me to tears. "I hope we go on to something else—or it all stops. If people haven't figured out this thing called 'life' by the time they're in their eighties, is there any hope they'll do it later?"

Gary Shockley has seen our elusive bear behind the cottage. Local authorities have erected a fence around the town dump in Willits, keeping the animals away from the smelly trash they love, so the big brown rascals are now foraging far and wide into people's yards.

Hummingbird. Saturday 29 June 1996.

My planned trip to Brunei has been postponed again, so yesterday I found myself with free time and had lunch with Fred. He gave me somber warnings about Puthoff, Bigelow, and John Alexander: “You're dealing with dangerous people, Jacques,” he kept assuring me: didn't Gordon Novel call up Jim McCampbell to ask him to join a mysterious project “to build flying saucers in the desert with Hal Puthoff?” Didn't the invitation include a threat of death if he ever talked about it?”

Silly rumors solely based on bluster and deceit.

Spring Hill. Friday 5 July 1996.

Last Sunday Janine and I visited our friend Roger Brenner in Half Moon Bay. We had lunch with him on the harbor. He lives on a boat and seems happy. The weather was warm, the sun filtered by the ocean mist. Kids were fishing off the pier.

Whenever I’m in Half Moon Bay I recall the pleasurable shock of seeing it for the first time in 1969, a profound invitation to spend our lives in California. Now I find the same feeling, better expressed, in the *Journals* of Edward Abbey (**14**):

“On the shore of the ultimate sea. Here the bulging Pacific glitters and sparkles, surges and roars, crashing on the sand, green waves translucent with sunlight, creamy foam, salt to the taste, the seminal smell of the sea, pregnant as ever, powerful with its sound of eternity, its smell of birth and death, its tireless cycles, its calamitous sense of doom.”

Abbey, in contrast, hated France. Like many Americans he found it affected and arrogant. I would agree if I hadn't experienced the other France, the realm of the poor and generous, the forgotten poetry of the back streets.

Yesterday I called my cousin Francis Passavant in Massachusetts. We laughed: it's been nearly 50 years since we played together in Pontoise. He is retired, with three grown kids. He had a good career as a management consultant.

A peak of happiness here, Janine at my side. We keep our life simple and free. When I grow older I won't seek the company of rich folks. It's to the bookworms that I feel close.

Spring Hill. Saturday 6 July 1996.

A funny guy, Edward Abbey. I just put down his *Journals*. All the irony of human life stares at us from the bottom of his contradictions. He curses mysticism but much of his writing is a mystical glorification of the desert, the beauty of the savage West where he lives a hermit's life. He's consumed by desire for women, but he insists on spending his time alone in forest service towers and rock ayries. He despises the eastern literary establishment but remains glued to the *New York Times Book Reviews*, even while fighting off scorpions and coyotes in the mountains of Taos. He's bitter, unfair, egocentric and narrow-minded. But his description of what he calls our "syphilization" is sharp and accurate: We are ravaging the Earth, spreading our absurd techno-military subculture over every bit of goodness.

And the crazy women! They're attracted to him because he's such a wild, self-reliant character who strolls across deserts and runs rapids, a larger-than-life man who sleeps under the stars with wild beasts. So they insist on marrying him but as soon as they stumble on some Journal entry where he alludes to another girl or just an old affair, they get all upset, make a scene, tear his life to shreds and take the kids away. Abbey would have delighted in the observation of our system breaking down and our stuttering productivity machine. He would have reviled the greedy media as they take over the new digital networks and turn them into a mean tool of manipulation.

Later the same day.

I often think of my father these days. I want to ask him about World War One, to hear the real story of Verdun and the *Chemin des Dames*. He might not want to revisit those memories, however. I recall his low-voice conversations with my uncle Maurice on Sunday afternoons in Pontoise: this regiment had gone there; this company had moved into this position. They pored over detailed ordnance maps. It was all factual, clinical, and terribly sad.

When I grew up and realized the immensity of the disaster that war represented I had the only sane reaction possible, rejecting the whole mess as idiocy, especially since it was repeated a generation later by the same generals, the same régimes. He could not understand this rejection. What makes me think we could talk about it now? I simply realize that, pointless and insane as it was, Verdun was not any more idiotic than half a dozen episodes of wide-scale butchery that have happened in my own lifetime: Bosnia and Africa, Jerusalem, Tibet, and that my father, with millions of soldiers on both sides, mired in the mud, dying in the barbed wire, must have touched a depth of horror that contained precious lessons we've lost.

Perhaps men simply agree to go to war because it's the most interesting thing they've ever done. Where else would you find the thrill, the comradeship and the heroic tenderness — yes, the tenderness! — of collective tragedy? Look at Bosnia, the orgasmic ecstasy of the Serbs? The only two avenues of solution for such conflicts are transcendence (create an even bigger threat to jolt people's minds away) or attrition (wait until most of the valid men are dead before trying to impose a solution to exhausted leaders).

Hummingbird. Sunday 7 July 1996.

The release of the UFO disaster movie *Independence Day* (after the more complex and subdued *The Arrival*) triggers new interest. Alien abductions are a central theme in comedies, thrillers, and cartoons. Delusion intrudes upon reality to a greater degree than ever.

We are not simply dealing with passing fashion or the aura of a powerful book like *Communion*, because witnesses are certainly not lying: Maurice Masse, Renato Nicolai, Herb Schirmer, Barney Hill, all of whom I've met, did experience a sudden confrontation with another form or facet of reality.

"True enough," says a skeptical voice, "but look at Doctor X—our friendly, convincing teaser. And look at Whitley, who transcends his own universe, and ours."

Hummingbird. Tuesday 9 July 1996.

The line of people waiting to see *Independence Day* was so long that Janine and I gave up. The Alien theme is now mixed with anti-establishment paranoia. On Long Island a leader of the local UFO Network, John Ford, has been arrested for plotting to kill a prominent politician, using radioactive material. He believed that a UFO had crashed in a county park in Brookhaven and that men in black jumpsuits had taken Alien bodies away (**15**).

Now novelist Tamara Thorne eloquently sums up her visit to Rachel, Nevada: "Fundamentalist right-wing UFO nuts with guns. The *Little A'le'Inn* was marvellously creepy, from the picture of Clinton pulling off his mask to reveal Hitler, to the waitress with glitter in her cheek blush who channels an Alien named Jérome... The motel consisted of mobile homes, subdivided rooms with shared baths. There was a bigfish self-proclaimed UFO expert-astronomer, ex-military type who held court and led everyone nightly to the Black Mailbox where UFO watching takes place."

Chicago. Palmer House. Thursday 11 July 1996.

A business meeting in Good Ole Chicago: the Sears Tower, where I will go tomorrow with Dr. Peter Banks, rises above the smog. It's all coming back to me, flooding my memory of 30 years ago, when we lived here: those cracked sidewalks along Clark Street, greasy papers caught in the wind, the Elevated train screeching along its tracks. The smells, too: Stale beer and the acrid odor of fast food cooked in bad oil; yet Lincoln Park is resplendent, people smile, children play, joggers run along the lake. I find no beauty along the "Magnificent Mile" but the Loop has the solid credibility of its massive American architecture. The fever of discovery died here long ago, yet Chicago's personality feels like a strong old friend. What lingers? The charm and the courage and the smile of Janine in those places along Lake Michigan where we loved, laughed and occasionally despaired. I am glad our son was born here.

Hummingbird. Sunday 14 July 1996.

Last night Oberon (Otter Zell) came over to Spring Hill with his new love. I gave him *FastWalker* and *Forbidden Science*. He gave us his sculpture of Venus.

We spoke of Bob Lazar and of the growing paranoia in the field: No longer amusing or pleasantly weird, ufology has turned downright scary. But my experiments at Spring Hill have not revealed anything new either, lost as we are in layers of infinity.

Spring Hill. Saturday 20 July 1996.

TWA flight 800 blew up after take-off on Wednesday. How many times had I taken that flight, with Janine and my children? I remember Catherine sleeping with her head on my shoulder on her way to France when she was little. We may have flown that very aircraft. It now rests, shredded into pieces at the bottom of the Atlantic.

Now Fred swears that Gordon Novel and Puthoff are actually building a flying saucer in the desert with Bob Wood.

Hummingbird. Sunday 21 July 1996.

Last night Dan Stewart came over to the ranch with local poet Dan Roberts, who read to us his funny and disquieting "patriot poetry." Diane Darling came along too, and an astonishing coincidence took place. She asked our help with a play where she was going to read something in French. She wanted to retrain herself in the language by studying some dialogue, so Janine picked up a book from the shelf and passed it on to me, a novel by Barjavel entitled *La Peau de César*. I turned to a random page and read this passage: "I was in the Boeing that blew up after take-off at Kennedy Airport, a bomb in the hold, 132 dead, you remember?"

Then I stopped, stunned. Only three days since TWA 800 blew up. Such coincidences can be so chilling it's impossible not to see them as a wink from another side of reality, an *intersign*, a small tear in the fabric of existence. Yet it wasn't precognition, and none of it is explained by quantum mechanics. Is it possible that my experiments have started to work, facilitating connections in information space?

Hummingbird. Monday 22 July 1996.

I am increasingly concerned about my mother's health. Unable to get an answer at her apartment I called my brother: she was in the hospital for a series of tests, and would go home "in a day or two," he said. She comes from a German Protestant family where one must not bother one's relatives with petty medical annoyances.

Spring Hill. Sunday 28 July 1996.

With backhoes and a bulldozer, workers are reshaping our pond and deepening the ditches around the tower, smoothing the slopes ahead of next winter's storms and summer fires. There's hardly a breeze.

My brother finally confessed that our mother had undergone an operation — "a superficial thing," he said. I had to force him to use the word "tumor," small but malignant. It hadn't spread, he said. It was a simple procedure. She wouldn't need radiotherapy.

Can we ever trust what doctors say?

An explosion at the Atlanta Olympics has killed one person and wounded many others: A change for the worse is happening in American life. Then Bob Bigelow called. He said that Harry Reid, the leader of the Senate, would attend my next presentation.

Las Vegas. Saturday 3 August 1996.

Janine and I landed here on Thursday night with much anticipation, given the scientific caliber of the group. We had come early to see George Knapp. We had a pleasant dinner with him but Mr. Bigelow was upset because his security guards had been forced to shoot at construction workers who started a brawl on a development site: one man was wounded in the leg.

"Let's talk about what we're going to present to the Senator," I said, "what does he expect to hear?"

"Harry Reid is a friend of mine; I've had many discussions with him on the subject. He doesn't want his staff to know he's coming. He'll just be here with his wife; he wants to be one of the crowd."

"How long has he served in Congress?"

"He was in the House for two terms, and this is his second term as a Senator. By the way, he's close to Dick D'Amato."

Bob said he'd just hired three staff scientists: a biochemist, a molecular biologist, and a physicist, to support his field teams. NIDS will employ eleven people as of September, six full-time. Always eager to move ahead on several fronts, Bob is also funding a chair in consciousness research at UNLV, to be setup by Jim Whinnery, and he's completing the purchase of a Nevada ranch near Mount Wilson where UFOs have been seen, along with an elusive ghost. He plans to have the head of SARA come over to discuss instrumentation.

Later the same day.

On Friday we were driven over to Park House for a leisurely talk with Bob, who agreed to preview my slides. Kit, Ian Stevenson and Bruce Grayson arrived about noon. We were soon joined by John Mack and two women: Karen Wesolowski from *Atlantic Monthly*, and Roberta, a psychiatric social worker described as a clinician with knowledge of hypnosis. She screens requests for John's attention: some 20 phone calls a week from abductees and five from clinicians. Evidently Pam, who was with him in the early days of PEER, left a year ago. Barbara McLeod of UCLA works closely with them.

John was very tense. I tried to put him at ease by greeting him warmly, since I was the person in the room who knew him best; I introduced Janine. We were immediately impressed with his staff while Mack gradually took control of the meeting. Kit asked each of us why we felt abductions were an important issue. I thought Janine gave the best statement when she pointed out that the answer would lead to a major re-assessment, no matter what it was: if it turns out that abductions are real, then science has to revise its definitions of reality, but if they aren't real there are equally drastic consequences.

The discussion turned to partnerships between PEER and NIDS, perhaps with the Noetics and Fetzer institutes as facilitators. Eager to secure funding, John picked up on Janine's comment, stressing that abductions were "a potential game-changer." He said it was important to go beyond distinctions between the physical and the non-physical; to focus instead on the elusiveness of the experience.

Kit spoke of pragmatic issues: what kind of joint program could we setup? Who would be involved? John and his staff indicated I would be welcome to come over to Boston with my own unpublished abduction files, but that offer wasn't confirmed. Instead, the meeting turned to legal questions of control and publicity. Well, they know where I am if they want me. I am happy to stay on the sideline.

Dinner was served in the grand boardroom when the rest of the SAB assembled, with the addition of GianCarlo Rota, Italian-born mathematician and philosopher (he specializes in phenomenology), leading thinker in combinatorial mathematics, consultant to NSA and member of the National Academy of Sciences. Kit returned the floor to Dr. Mack, who spoke of his troubles with Harvard.

John made a poor presentation in that setting. Hunched forward, one shoulder higher than the other, his eyes staring over the top of his glasses, he fumbled with his notes and made a series of disconnected statements, culminating in the same video I'd seen at Noetics, featuring the shaman who'd been raped by a foul-smelling corpse as well as the two girls from South Africa who saw flying saucers in the courtyard of their school and were then led by Mack to state that a strange being spoke of the need to "save the Earth."

While the group regarded this as a novel challenge to modern science I tried to broaden the debate by pointing out that there were ancient documents about the kind of experience the African shaman had described. John countered testily that the features that distinguished modern events from folklore were "obvious." So I pulled out a second-hand copy of his own earlier book about *Nightmares* (**16**) and cited his striking observation that children faced with terrible visions often reframed them as a series of stories involving monsters. After the initial shock (he seemed astounded that I had researched his prior work) he brushed it all aside. To reinforce my point, I placed the book in front of him, saying it was enjoyable reading. He said "Oh, that's a true collector's item!" to which I responded it would be even more valuable if he inscribed it, which he did good-naturedly.

Hummingbird. Sunday 4 August 1996.

On Saturday morning we held a closed session of the Board with eighteen members present. Administrative issues threatened to bog down the discussion, starting with the changing definition of the Institute, no longer a granting agency. Bob wants to turn it into a working body that performs its own research and builds relationships with centers of expertise, never delegating the analysis. Thus, the SAB is elevated as a working group rather than merely a review and strategy board. We struggled with issues of publications and publicity. Rota stressed that we underestimated the hostility of the academic world. Legal issues also involved the custody of samples submitted to us. The next point was the definition of Bob's endowed chair at UNLV, to study the survival of death.

Staffing was considered next. Additions include Dr. Eric Davis, an aerospace engineer with a PhD from the University of Arizona, Jim McDonald's old campus. He worked on Voyager 1 and 2, was at NASA for ten years, after which he taught in Korea under a DoD Intelligence program. Dr. Colm Kelleher, a biochemist from Ireland, has already spent time in England for Bigelow, studying crop circles. Finally, microbiologist and veterinarian George Onet, a PhD from Romania who has spent the last ten years in the U.S., brings field and laboratory experience. He has published five books, eight textbooks, and hundreds of articles in his field.

In addition to this permanent staff, which still includes John Alexander, an executive secretary and a receptionist, NIDS employs a part-time editor as well as George Knapp, Diane Arcangel who builds up the library, a person in Canada studying cattle mutilations, and Shelly Wadsworth who does field work in Northern Nevada. Bob is also talking to John Schuessler about a position.

Another notion introduced at this meeting was that of *The Day After*: "What would happen if the government was to announce Alien intrusions? Has there been a 50-year program of indoctrination of earthlings?" asked Bob. "Are we just along for the ride? Is this knowledge digestible? Would the country freeze at a sudden revelation? Would people bother to go to work the next day?"

In my view, they would first go to church, and the issues would quickly be reframed into religious terms, at least in the U.S.

The group turned to a discussion of the "implant" samples. Four items are being analyzed and several others are in process of recovery under NIDS control, not to mention a piece of alleged metal from Roswell. But are we giving too much dignity to the topic, asked some of our members? On the opposite side, will we be viewed as unresponsive if we don't publish our results? I argued in vain for issuing a series of sober, regular technical bulletins.

A small group of us (Kit, Bob, John Alexander, George, Hal, Martin Pilch, and I) lunched in private with Senator Harry Reid and his wife. A very nervous staffer equipped with a clipboard and a portable phone accompanied them. Reid made some nice remarks about his old friend

George Knapp and mentioned his own work as a member and possibly future chairman of the Water and Energy committee that controls the money for all the National Labs, after which we went back into the big room for my presentation.

During the question-and-answer session Kit asked what I thought of the alleged evidence from Roswell. This led to a discussion about biological samples. I'd made the point that we might not be able to understand the hardware, even after 50 years, but biological evidence should have resulted in a discontinuity in science. Kit countered that the situation in biology might be the same dead-end as in physics.

The lecture was followed by another executive session and a debriefing after Mack's talk. I pointed out the abductionists had only been able to get away with their claims because Hopkins and Jacobs censored any data that didn't fit their promotional efforts—witness the prevalence of "Short Gray" stories.

Later I cornered Hal to ask if he did work with Gordon Novel. He said Novel "was busy with legal work on the Waco massacre, but still talked about building a flying device." Hal didn't like the fact that Novel associated his name with the project, and insisted he'd never actually worked with the man. He was distressed with the fact that we hadn't gotten around to the topic of communications: "In a few weeks NIDS will have staffers running around the countryside with laptops sending messages to the supposed Aliens. What are they gonna do if they get a reply?" We had an open dinner, including Kristin and Victoria. Janine and I had a chance to ask Ed Mitchell about details of his experiences on the moon (Figure 11.) Then Victoria and Kristin engaged in savage gossip about the women around John Mack.

As soon as we came home I felt homesick for France, so I called Olivier in Paris. He was a bit sick, worried, unsure of his next step in life. Then I spoke to my mother, about to leave the clinic for a month at a home near Fontainebleau, on recovery from cancer surgery.

Los Angeles. Wednesday 7 August 1996.

On a brief excursion to visit Isocor and a startup with an ambitious technology for power production using MHD (**17**), I heard the important announcement from NASA of organic evidence in an ejected Martian rock found in Antarctica (**18**). This comes after the discovery, in very fast succession, of eight large planets found through the perturbations of the radial velocity of nearby stars like 51 Pegasi, 70 Virginis, and 47 Ursae Majoris in the Big Dipper.

Hummingbird. Tuesday 13 August 1996.

On Thursday we had distinguished dinner guests, our neighbors Kevin and Sheila Starr. Educated by the Dominican fathers and widely read in history and literature, Kevin is the Head Librarian and State Historian of California. Janine had prepared an exquisite feast, conducive to long discussions that included our paranormal interests.

Letters are piling up from readers of *Revelations*. I try to answer all. Poor Ann Druffel is distressed: the leaders of CUFOS would only publish her book about McDonald if his references to a government coverup were edited out, a blatant bias since this idea was indeed central for Jim. What did he really know? The continuing alignment of CUFOS to every Pentagon whitewash is increasingly suspect.

Caliente, Nevada. Thursday 15 August 1996.

A special trip, at Bob Bigelow's request. At Park House this morning I had a chance to talk to physicist Eric Davis, more briefly to Colm Kelleher. John Alexander was there as well. I learned that we wouldn't be driving up to the Nevada property until tomorrow because another, even more interesting situation had popped up - a ranch in Utah where cattle mutilations, strange lights and bizarre objects were being reported "almost daily." So, Hal and I soon found ourselves in Bigelow's sleek private jet, climbing in the desert sky en route for Vernal. The jet is named "Cosmos," a dual reference to Bob's metaphysical interests and to his real estate dealings: the lettering stands for "Can Our Savings Match Our Spending?"

We ate sandwiches on board while listening to Bob's recorded conversation with the ranch's owner, Terry Sherman. They have found several sets of circles where vegetation was removed, and have had three animals mutilated, one of which had been seen fifteen minutes before. Indian lore in the area includes songs about this accursed place.

One of them is poetically titled "Path of the Skinwalker," and another title is "Fire in the sky brings death."

As soon as we arrived Hal was seized with an intense reaction, sneezing miserably, but he felt better after taking one of my allergy pills. With us was Dr. George Onet, the Romanian veterinarian recruited by NIDS to study mutilations. I liked him immediately.

Terry Sherman and his wife Glenn greeted us: we followed them to the property, located 18 miles away at an altitude of 5,200 feet; nearly 500 acres of beautiful pasture broken by poplars and cottonwood at the edge of a sandstone cliff strewn with boulders. Two creeks run along gaily, but the atmosphere is tense after the disappearance of eleven cows, three of which were later found mutilated, with holes punched into an eye and the rectum cleanly cored out. We walked over to one of the cows still lying among the bushes with no sign of putrefaction. The Shermans had noted a "dank, musty, medicinal smell" for two days after the event, and found a gelatinous substance on the side of the animal, none of which they preserved, however.

The most surprising item was the discovery by Terry's two children of graphite cylinders, one inch thick, next to the animals. Another, smaller cylinder was of the right diameter to have made the hole in the eye. As in other mutilation reports I have studied, predators stayed away, there were no agonal movements, and other cattle also avoided the carcass. Only last night the Shermans reported a craft flying over their land, emitting a blue beam with speckles, and a headlight that went down into the cottonwoods. In a recent episode, which scared him even more, Terry heard the voices of two men seemingly hovering above him, speaking in an unknown language.

Bigelow advanced negotiations with the Shermans for the purchase of the property, asking them to continue to manage it. He would have specialists from SARA instrument the place and would buy more cattle of the type that tends to disappear. In vain I proposed instrumenting the cows themselves with biological recorders.

"You haven't told us about your dreams," I reminded Terry.

"Everybody'd think I'm crazy," he replied. "I find myself up in the air, looking down on my body. Two men are with me; they wonder if I'm going to understand what's happening."

Fig.11. With Dr. Ed Mitchell and Victoria Alexander: Vegas, Aug. 1996.

Fig.12. On our field survey at Bigelow's Mount Wilson ranch, Nevada, with Dr. Hal Puthoff and Dr. Tim Rynne from SARA. August 1996.

"What do they look like?"

"One is short; the other's a big fellow with a beard."

Tonight, we are all staying in Caliente, a long drive north of Vegas. We checked into the Shady Motel, a surprisingly modern establishment next to the highway and the railroad, where passing trains regularly break the silence of the night with that dreadful, "lonesome whistle" familiar to lovers of cowboy songs everywhere.

Las Vegas. Friday 16 August 1996.

We spent the day exploring the Mount Wilson ranch (**19**). Dr. Tim Rynne of SARA brought along a positioning device. We drove through Pioche where we met Shelly Wadsworth, a blonde grandmother who is one of Bob's local contacts, and three men from his construction company to measure and inspect the property.

We reached the place mid-morning. The first thing we saw was a row of wooden Western buildings that reminded me of Dodge City in the movies, with peeling paint on their tall fronts. The balusters along the porch-like sidewalk seemed to await the arrival of tired cowboys on their tall horses. The back panel of the bar had been brought around the Horn all the way from Boston: its sculpted board was well worth the visit. There was a piano and an electric organ, and a row of fine tables where plates and glasses were set, as if awaiting the rough-and-ready miners who had given Pioche and Caliente their intriguing European names. The ghost of a tall Native American is rumored to show up in one of the rooms.

On the way we learned that blue lights and an X-shaped white glow were seen back in 1993, but I wasn't convinced by Shelly's stories of craft following cars at night, of the UFO that shot intense beams, of hovering black delta craft, and tinfoil-like squares that folded on themselves in the sky and vanished. All this is reported "in the neighborhood," a Nevada term that can embrace hundreds of miles of brush and rugged stone. A local man has sworn to Shelly that an accident happened at Area 51 about 1972 in which "Aliens who were building a craft for the U.S. were killed, as well as our scientists:" He claimed he had to transfer the bodies to the morgue.

While we pondered these stories a storm came, slowly rumbling over the ridge of Mount Wilson. The wind kicked the dust in front of the saloon. I challenged Hal: “This town ain't big enough for the both of us,” I said as we laughed and hugged in friendship.

“Back at SRI, when you were doing your Arpanet computer stuff and I was busy with Geller, did you ever think that we’d end up climbing over mountains, looking for flying saucers?” he asked. While the others were scrambling over boulders, taking GPS readings, he told me about a case when a UFO had been reported shooting dart-like beams in all directions. “The witness was none other than Ingo,” Hal said. “Our protector in the Senate told him he’d be contacted by someone. The man took Ingo to an underground facility to remote view mining operations at two sites on the moon.”

“Could he have been looking at the future?” I asked.

“He was never told,” Hal answered. “But some ten years later, in the eighties, he was contacted again at SRI and taken to a site in the Far North where a military team was watching a lake. A triangular object emerged and darted intense beams while the team scattered. Ingo's contact broke his arm as he fell during the ensuing confusion. Nobody could find out what the object was (**20**).”

While we waited for Bob to complete some negotiations, Hal and I discussed various theories of propulsion, sitting on the tailgate of the Chevy van in front of the Old West saloon (Fig. 12). Hal mentioned that he’d reconstructed the experiments of T. Townsend Brown, without success. He now thinks Brown's theory is wrong, and he’s considering my idea that one has to change the spacetime matrix to build an effective drive. He’s been invited by a NASA group to present his plans. A man named Frank Meade, of the Air Force's Phillips lab at Edwards AFB, is interested in this work.

Spring Hill. Sunday 18 August 1996.

We woke up to the soft pinkish orange glow of a sun filtered by the gray smoke of the Forks fire, out of control near Clear Lake. Last night, as we drove back from a poetry reading in Willits, we could already see its bloody light on the horizon. Here our creek flows gaily into the resculpted pond. Wild turkeys are staring at us with reproach in the bright red bend of their goitery neck.

The art gallery where the reading took place was filled with hippies in various states of deferred maintenance, still wearing the jeans they owned in college, shocked at finding themselves approaching 60. They spoke about life in the nourishing forest where mushrooms and pot grow, sustaining the illusion. Poetess Robin Rule described herself as a "tough old chick with tattoos." Gary Shockley read two funny stories about his life at our Spring Hill Ranch. Later someone wrote on an online bulletin board, capturing the mood of Willits:

"The whole time the poetry reading was going on, the backdrop was the huge front window of the store, through which was the fascinating tableau of a parking lot full of horribly pregnant little girls pushing baby carriages between pickup trucks full of laughing idiot boys (...) A drunken Vietnam vet, stripped to the waist, periodically wandered by the front door and shouted in."

Hummingbird. Tuesday 20 August 1996.

In a big huff since I gently challenged him in Vegas, John Mack has mailed all his books, papers, and patient files about nightmares to Victoria, puzzled by this sudden flood. She told him of the dreams she experienced earlier in her life. Now she is busy rebuilding his files but he says he "no longer needs all that" because abductions are real and his earlier work was only preparation for that true challenge.

Hummingbird. Wednesday 21 August 1996.

Over lunch Fred and I covered our usual subjects: classical music, the philosophy of consciousness, political events. We even argued about Free Will and agreed it was an unresolvable issue since we have no choice but to behave as if we did have free will. We agreed that defining consciousness remains a blind alley: philosophers are at a loss, wondering if the mind can come to any conclusion about itself. Recent books speak of the "End of Science" just as new, exciting astronomical discoveries are being made. This week biologists unveiled a methane-producing microbe living in extreme conditions, a third branch of Earth life: organisms called *archea*.

Hummingbird. Friday 30 August 1996.

Victoria Alexander has sent me a draft of an original analysis of abductees' experiences, comparing them to those of the early Catholic Saints, with two important differences, she says: the abductees have no message and give nothing back.

They don't minister to the poor, heal the sick, "or even drive out demons," she observed drily.

I reminded her that credit for the "Save the Earth" notion rightly should go to the old contactees of Adamski's generation, not to John Mack's abductees. And that Koestler once wrote to me that he found contact stories vaguely embarrassing, "like a poorly-told dirty joke."

Spring Hill. Monday 2 September 1996.

Early this morning we walked all the way up the ridge with the cat skinner. We spent time at the log pile, contemplating the valley, talking about wine and land.

The wind rose in the afternoon.

My greatest frustration is my inability to explain clearly how and why I love you, and how deeply. It can only be measured by the sorrow I would feel if I were without your presence, unable to listen to your voice, or to touch you when I extend my hand in the night.

This evening I went up the canyon to the place where Gary had discovered a "garden," an illegal pot-growing operation enclosed in chicken wire with a hose that came down from the ridge. I climbed up the ravine clinging to trees, listening for any sign that someone might be keeping watch.

Since authorities now seize the land of pot growers, illegal groups plant marijuana on other people's property: ranches like ours can be summarily confiscated by the Feds. The unforeseen result is that both lawful landowners and illegal drug gangs are threatened and hate the government with equal mistrust.

Nights get colder now; our canyon remains swathed in fog. We can taste time here, exuding from the thyme and the peeling bark of madrones, indifferent as the neighbor's cat, quick as a dreaming lizard, watchful as the circling vulture that follows our every move as if to warn us, Caesar-like, "Remember you are mortals."

Spring Hill. Tuesday 3 September 1996.

The work piled up in the library discouraged me so I turned to another job long neglected, cutting down wild bushes. In the process I killed a young lilac plant that Janine had been nurturing. I felt stupid. In the afternoon my mood improved. The files found the right drawers, but what a mass of data! My wonderful readers save things for me. An anonymous fellow sent me a 1962 tale by Pierre Versins entitled *La Ville du Ciel*, with a note: "Founding text for the hoax of which Jean-Pierre Petit and others have fallen victim... (**21**)." The tale describes a world like Ummo, a twin "enantimorphic" universe.

Spring Hill. Thursday 5 September 1996.

Our friend Hans came to see us yesterday morning; Janine will drive back to San Francisco with him. The three of us spoke about life's challenges: he told us he was still unable to find stability in people or places. Sadly, he's about to separate from Anna.

When I called Paris, my mother was back home in her sunny apartment, optimistic about her ability to go on living and walking. Now I'm alone at Spring Hill. Full-shaped white clouds seemed to announce autumn: A call to renewal, to faraway travels.

12

Anchorage. Saturday 7 September 1996.

Leaving work behind we flew north from San Francisco with nothing more in mind than a week of rest. A slow bus took us to Seward harbor along a road lined with red fireweed and dark pine, crossing mountain streams. In the peculiar light of Alaska, the weather was mild, colors vibrant. We're amused by sea otters playing in the harbor like kids in a schoolyard. The *Regal Princess* sails tonight.

We've brought books and magazines we hadn't had time to open for weeks, and research material on UFOs I'd set aside. It strikes me, once again, that if I hadn't seen an unexplained object myself, with two witnesses, and if Paul Muller, back in 1961, hadn't thrown away a letter by Aimé Michel in my presence, I would never have become so involved in such an apparently pointless endeavor.

Gulf of Alaska. Sunday 8 September 1996.

First day at sea. Slowly, gradually, the mind empties itself of inconsequential worries. The ship sails up College Fjord: Glaciers reach the water line: An eerie landscape of prehistory, an ice age sea, still and dirty with melted dust, the mud of centuries. Sleep again, release of stress. We've left Prince William Sound. Nothing to see but light-blue ocean, the sky vaguely brushed with elongated clouds.

Just before we left an interesting letter arrived from one of my readers, Marshall Tate of San Jose. He wrote that in 1976 and 1977 he was in charge of a military detecting installation, the U.S. Naval Space Surveillance Station at Elephant Butte, New Mexico.

"The facility was run by the Naval Weapons Command in Dahlgren, Virginia; its data was also linked to Norad HQ. The system operates like this: at Lake Kickapoo, Texas, a 10-million-watt RF signal is generated and transmitted, in an extremely narrow east-west pattern termed "the fence," covering the entire U.S. Objects that fly through this "fence" of RF energy reflect a portion of it back to the ground. Equipment determines speed by the Doppler Effect and altitude by the phase differences of the signal received at antennas separated by a known distance. Computers predict when the target will pass again if it's in orbit and looks for it. Subsequent passes permit the prediction of apogee and perigee, as well as the time of reentry. The equipment is sensitive enough to log mere pieces of wire from exploded rockets; the range extends tens of thousands of miles."

Marshall Tate goes on to write: "Several times per week I was noting very fast objects going through the fence. Recorded speeds of 6,000 to 20,000 miles per hour were common; one object was recorded at 55,000 miles per hour. Tests of the equipment revealed nothing unusual. Curious, I called headquarters at Dahlgren. They advised me to forget it; nothing could go that fast, it was just an anomaly of the system, yet… as I said, the equipment was working perfectly."

Glacier Bay. Monday 9 September 1996.

Second day at sea. The ship prowls along walls of tidewater glaciers. From our balcony of the 10th deck we watch entire slabs, many stories high, collapsing into the sea as they continue to melt. This is the ideal setting for me to read *Wedge*, the long history of the secret war between the FBI and CIA from the days of "Wild Bill" Donovan to 1994, written by Mark Riebling (**22**). The book unveils a litany of bureaucratic bungling of such proportion that no serious effort could have been mounted to conduct multi-year, advanced international research such as the UFO phenomenon required. Instead, the mess described in Riebling's exposé of political idiocies and turf wars can be extrapolated into exactly what we've seen over years of paranormal research: individual enthusiasm among a few sharp analysts and a handful of semi-clandestine "studies" among serious professionals like John Alexander or Marshall Tate, intrigued by the strange behavior of the sensors they monitored.

None of this could lead to a scientific re-appraisal. It would have demanded international cooperation of the type Allen Hynek and I had pleaded for at the UN in 1978, summarily denied. As I recall, the British delegate rose against our proposal. And no wonder: any effort to operate a collection network for UFO sightings would have dredged up a number of hush-hush military projects that used bizarre platforms or advanced energy systems that nobody wanted exposed.

My Journals, when I review them, hint at secret weapon projects, from Skyhook (no one wanted to tell Mrs. Mantell her husband died pointlessly, chasing a secret Navy balloon) to Ren Breck's curious disks in Pine Gap, to the Belgian triangles, crop circles...

After nightfall I went up on the open deck with my shortwave radio. On a frequency used by the Militia, survivalist Bill Cooper was ranting about coming world crises, advising everyone to buy gold.

Skagway. Tuesday 10 September 1996.

We went ashore today, for fish and chips and obligatory shopping in this Alaskan settlement nestled among the mountains that separate it from the Yukon gold fields. Janine and I already feel relaxed to the point of ineptitude. Decisions—even minor ones, such as where to go for coffee—seem as cloudy as the massive peaks that hide us from the Klondike. Janine enjoys *The Man in the High Castle* and I continue to plow with astonishment through *Wedge*, a lucid account of the cratered landscape of the Intelligence community.

Juneau. Wednesday 11 September 1996.

Time is suspended around this great white vessel shrouded in fog. The water broods in silver tones while a lazy band of clouds is draped around the hills of Juneau like a shawl on the shoulders of an old dowager. It rains in the damp obscurity of the town center, government buildings lacking in charm, unlike the rough weirdness of Skagway.

From the gondola that grips its cable above the gold mines the majesty of the site becomes obvious, a blend of water and sky constrained by the hills, a flood plain to catch the melting ice.

If I were ever tempted by a career in Intelligence (I flatter myself that I would have made a good analyst) or if I was hungry for access to secrets, Riebling's book would put to rest any regrets. It depicts an atmosphere of mutual suspicion, perpetual treason, and petty greed. I have to keep reminding myself that these people, in spite of all their failures, have managed to maintain the planet in a reasonably safe state. Perhaps their very failures helped, thanks to the interpenetration of services on both sides that revealed their weaknesses and reassured their leaders. That a nuclear war was averted, first at the time of the Cuban crisis, then after JFK's assassination, testifies to a level of sanity underneath the mess.

In the Inside Passage. Thursday 12 September 1996.

Fifth day at sea: we sail beyond Decision Point towards Ketchikan. Yesterday's fog has lifted, yielding a more romantic mood. We make new plans, discuss what turns we would want life to take; we watch the islands drift by. The people of Ketchikan, whose debates I hear on my little radio, worry over a change in logging rules in the Tongass forest. When pulp mills close, a massive cleanup job will be needed. Indeed, we can see thousands of stray logs along the shores.

The sky is gray, the peaks truncated by clouds. Even Dolly's House, a charming little brothel closed in the early 1950s when American puritanism overwhelmed the spirit of independent ladies, brings only a brief sense of faded thrill. Today the babbling river carries as many dead fish as live ones, and *Married Men's Trail* is deserted.

On the way back to Vancouver. Friday 13 September 1996.

Sixth day at sea. Janine finishes reading John Alexander's *Warrior Edge* while I reach the end of *Wedge* in astonishment over so many policy errors and the bungling of essential government decisions. (But what wonderful codewords these guys dreamed up: *Baggy Pants* and *High Holy*, *Pigeon Paradise!*) The bureaucratic squabbles, scary as they are to those who risk their lives, are only part of the story.

Now we sail down the lower Inside Passage, hugging Vancouver Island on our right. Dolphins rush towards the ship, playing with us. They jump out of the sea in unison like well-trained ballerinas, then glide under the hull. On forested shores we see increasing evidence of ugly clear-cutting: great gashes of dirt lie open among the pines, the water is strewn with rotting logs, tangled branches and vines. In places the loose earth has given way to naked swaths, rocky gaps or crumbling hillsides amidst groves colored by the brush of a Canadian sunset over the pines and the hemlocks, the flutter of the white, red-legged puffins that congregate on every rock to watch us pass, and the patience that comes with the slow drifting of the ship towards the Lion Gate. We will be home this weekend.

Hummingbird. Monday 16 September 1996.

Back in business: a letter from former Prime Minister Edith Cresson invites me to meet her in Brussels to discuss new government plans for the financing of innovation.

Several developments have taken place at NIDS. According to John Alexander the carbon cylinders we brought back from the Sherman ranch belong to soil inspectors testing for conductivity: they routinely drop them off after use. Bigelow sent a team to watch over the area ... and nothing happened. Terry Sherman and his wife spent their best couple of quiet nights in a long time while the Institute team camped on the ridge. Hal's engineer failed to find evidence. New cattle have been bought: will things take a different turn?

John Alexander tells me he's met with General Sammet to check up on Phil Corso. He heard that Corso "was genuine but tended to exaggerate." On the topic of the alleged Alien technology Sammet would only say "he had heard the same stories."

John Petersen, who called me later, claims to know someone at Livermore who handled a material sample of Alien origin that couldn't be cut with the finest diamond saws. Petersen was seeking my concurrence for a project to "expose the UFO truth" to the world. Funded by a surgeon in Baltimore, it is inspired by Steve Trevino, who claims occult connections. But we have heard that before.

Hummingbird. Friday 20 September 1996.

Israel experiences a wave of UFOs, writes my venture capital colleague Gideon Tolkowsky. One witness who reported being abducted ended up with an unknown powder in his hair.

I had lunch with Ed May, who is looking for a new job. His termination with SAIC after three years was messy. Dean Radin, too, is out of work: one morning, Bob Bigelow just told him to drop parapsychology, to work only on survival issues. Dean said "fine, get the SAB to give me some guidance."

"No, don't get the SAB involved," Bob answered.

"Perhaps I should resign," Dean said, offended by the response.

"Don't let the door kick you in the ass on the way out," was Bigelow's terse answer.

Ed May remains skeptical of Hal's theories: conservation of energy but not of mass doesn't make sense, he says: "Remember Hiroshima? Hal's theory of inertia and mass doesn't seem right." D'Amato tells me that 26 boxes of remote viewing data have never been opened by the analysts, even though the CIA was supposed to "scientifically review the entire project" before issuing its conclusions to Congress.

Spring Hill. Sunday 22 September 1996.

Janine and I hiked up the new road again, with its smell of freshly moved dirt and dead leaves. Up on the ridge the view was splendid, the canyon all dressed up in rich greens, birds peering at us from the top of bushes, blue jays loudly complaining against some invisible threat. I spent the morning at the top of the hill, flagging a new trail.

Bob Bigelow was kind enough to call with news of the Utah ranch. The staff of NIDS had gone there twice, with greater precautions and stealth this time, and the three men saw some unusual things. On 17 September Dr. Eric Davis, the physicist in the group, noticed a bright object about 1:20 am. All three watched it descending slowly, changing colors and going through erratic movements.

The same night Terry and his wife woke up with bloody cuts on their thumbs; the horses stampeded, enhancing the atmosphere of primeval terror around the place. The previous owners have expressed dismay at the fact that the phenomenon, which was noticed as early as 1928, was going to be studied by scientists: they seem to regard it as something spiritual and sacred that shouldn't be disturbed.

When I ran my own sky calculations for the night in question I had to raise the possibility of a confusion with Altair, which was setting and would have been scintillating wildly at the exact position where the team saw the "slowly descending" object, so I sent a memo to Bigelow to suggest improvements in field procedures.

Hummingbird. Sunday 29 September 1996.

Cheerful news from our Pagan neighbors: Morning Glory and both of her future husbands, Oberon and Wolf, invited me to their wedding, so I drove to the thresome ceremony at the Isis Oasis, which houses two ostriches, a llama and a unicorn, an Egyptian theater and a chapel of Nuit. The plywood pyramid left me unimpressed but there's a swimming pool and a pond with swans, and cages for white birds and parrots. Circular yurts and a teepee complete the grounds. A painted Buddha meditates at the dining room's entrance.

California is a land of anachronisms, so these incongruities in the shade of the Oasis' 500-year-old pine tree don't require an apology.

About fifty people came to the ceremony, some in black costumes with pentacles, some in green dresses, others in medieval garb. The wedding started late but the atmosphere of joyful anticipation rose to a healthy pitch when Morning Glory arrived in a red velvet dress. Standing at her side Oberon was in purple, Wolf in blue. Candles were lit. A priest and a priestess ran theatrically around the circle with drawn swords, inviting the Elements: "Hail and Welcome!" A parade of gods and goddesses were invoked in a way that would have been confusing to a medieval wizard; among the plywood obelisks of the Oasis it all seemed logical, somehow.

I had not imagined what a complex affair a triple wedding could be: Vows need to be exchanged among husband A and wife, husband B and wife, and more delicately among husband A and husband B: "You are the brother of my heart..." they each said. Bread, water, and wine were blessed and passed around the circle: "May you never hunger," Oberon told me as he offered the bread. When I took the water, I thought of Robert Heinlein's *Stranger in a Strange Land*: "May you never thirst." I hope their brave experiment succeeds, but I also thought of those who were not there, like Diane who told me of her anger when the first triangle had blown up. She had taken me to the vertiginous cliffs of the Mendocino coast to show me how the foam of the breakers answered the turmoil in her heart.

Hummingbird. Friday 4 October 1996.

More news now filters from Israel about the UFO flap that happened just before the recent explosion of political violence. About 14 September a Russian immigrant from Nazareth named Uri Iskov claimed he was abducted from his house by short bald humanoids with three-fingered hands. They pulled him by the hair, he claimed.

Last night I joined Steve Millard, Paul Baran, and Stewart Alsop at the board meeting of electronic startup COM21, which began with a frugal dinner inside the factory cafeteria. The passion of the venture was summed up in those oddly poetic terms that are the special dialect of our Valley: tape-out, first silicon, first customer shipment.

Some 40 people were there, many white-haired like me. Their idea of an entertaining after-dinner presentation was a series of slides by the chief engineer describing the intricacies of a cable modem. Work continues around the clock, the obsession of technology tearing up the world. Historians have missed the upheaval, so they will just have to ponder its consequences for decades, trying to make sense of the breakthroughs by reading old marketing brochures.

Paris, Mabillon. Sunday 6 October 1996.

We took the old lift, now so familiar. The bells of Saint Sulpice rang in welcome but nothing else in France seems to work. Sporadic train strikes, teacher protests, social malaise, grumbling doctors, all of it rehearsal for a major strike in ten days, the time my French partners have picked for our semi-annual meeting with our investors.

Commenting on all this, my mother is clear-headed. We spoke of her recent operation, from which her amazing vitality has allowed her to bounce back, and of the recent death of her last remaining brother, Benjamin "Eddie" in Saint-Maur at age 89 (**23**).

A bistro on the boulevard. Tuesday 8 October 1996.

I am early for a visit to Jean-Jacques Chaban-Delmas at Matra. Lagardère's company has proposed to buy Thomson, in competition with Alcatel. There is considerable suspense about the deal, which will be decided by the Government in a few days.

We hope the fair weather will hold as we travel to Germany, where we'll join Dr. Peter Sturrock and the SSE for their annual meeting.

Freiburg, Germany. Saturday 12 October 1996.

Manly Hall has died, and an associate is suspected of hastening his demise. Hall's alchemy collection went to the Getty museum. What about the other books? Maurice Chatelain, too, has died, and his wife six hours later. He was a man of wit, curious about everything. At our SSE meeting relativist Costa de Beauregard read a brief paper. He seemed tired and distracted. Janine and I re-introduced ourselves, but he hardly recalled his visit to our Chicago home many years ago.

Mabillon. Sunday 13 October 1996.

We flew back from Strasbourg to reach Paris in time to catch esoteric scholar Serge Hutin's lecture about the P2 Lodge and the *Order of the Solar Temple*, a rare event. Tree colors were wonderful along the Basel-Karlshruhe expressway. We arrived at the lecture room to find a fat bald man with beady eyes, thick glasses and a frog-like frozen smile, handling some papers: time has been unkind to my old Rosicrucian friend, who never found the recipe for the potion of eternal life. He now lives in the Pyrenées, he told us, in a retirement home. After his lecture, over a drink in the lobby bar, he told us that former Imperator Gary Stewart, replaced two years ago by Christian Bernard, was suing Amorc and claimed to be the rightful leader, in the spirit of endless squabbles among occultists.

Jean-Luc Chaumeil, a gutsy investigator, attended the lecture and asked pointed questions. He was clearly the best-informed person there. Others were converts of various occult groups who could only trade dark hints about vague traditions and odd rumors.

TGV to Lyon. Monday 14 October 1996.

The day began (cool, light, overcast turning to drizzle) with breakfast at Club Leonardo. Jim Barksdale, the CEO of Netscape, spoke about strategy before some 200 financial and business executives. Later I went to Edith Cresson's office in a well-appointed old building across the street from the National Assembly. Her staff introduced me to the former Prime Minister (**24**) in a stylish office with a curved white desk. The windows showed a tree-shaded courtyard as we discussed her plans to re-awaken flagging innovation in France.

Now the train punches its way through the fat land of Burgundy. Mist rises from the hollows. The rain has stopped. There are white cows in every pasture. Janine has fallen under the spell again: “Why can't we just stay here?” she asks. We could, but to do what, my darling? So far from the vibrant Pacific, so far from the starry sky? You were so unhappy and frustrated, when we lived here…

Continental flight. Sunday 20 October 1996.

We return through Houston, a perfect flight, a chance to catch up on reading: Jimmy Goldsmith's analysis of European economic follies in *Le Piège* (co-authored with Yves Messarovitch, who gave me the book this week at *Le Figaro*) and Captain Barril's exposé of Elysée secrets. Like de Marenches, he accuses the antiterrorist cell in Mitterrand's entourage to have assassinated De Grossouvre, who was about to reveal the corrupt deals around the socialist government.

Janine doesn't trust America any more. I can't blame her: America's creative chaos turns to sordid apology for crime, its technology an excuse for sloppy information, virtual worlds of noxious drugs and rotten greed. But Europe is getting just as evil. Patrick Corsi, when we saw him yesterday, described a continent where governments are incapable of new vision; in France entrepreneurs regularly fall into the grip of industrial predators, so early investors get discouraged.

As we left Paris Paul Hynek left a message on our recorder and we heard the very sad news that Mimi had died alone in Scottsdale, of a heart attack: Barry Greenwood, a UFO researcher, had gone to her house and found it oddly silent. We hadn't seen Mimi in years, although she still responded to enquiries. Her passing closes an era: Northwestern has folded its astronomy department within the engineering school and razed Lindheimer Observatory in Evanston.

Spring Hill. Saturday 26 October 1996.

The second rainstorm of the season has passed over the Mendocino woods, renewing our creek and the pond, putting an autumn mood everywhere. To the north a logging road climbs towards Willits, "quiet dimlit cowboy and Indian town, full of vague twilight streets, winter six o'clock dinner smells, woodstove fires gravy newspapers, raw leaves kicked into October gutters by schoolchildren let out..." in the poem by Robin Rule I read out to Janine this morning.

Robin wrote me she was halfway through *Forbidden Science*, "comfortable to read some and put down to attend to other things and pick up again, and be in Paris, or the French countryside. As a poet I am struck with the simple but sonorous depths of your descriptions, in particular the joy of your meeting Janine."

Kit called yesterday. "I need to talk to someone sane," he began, adding he loved the ending of *FastWalker*. We discussed the NIDS meeting I'd missed: "We'd invited the family from the Utah ranch," he said. "They were treated with consideration, but what they told us was out of a bad movie: huge ships of football field length over their house with 150 lights—yes they had counted them! — but nothing ever happens now that we have our people at the site. I'm beginning to think we're dealing with collective hallucinations. I'm reading everything I can find about *folie à deux*."

Hummingbird. Sunday 27 October 1996.

The amount of money flowing into Silicon Valley has reached heady proportions. Entrepreneurs whose only claim to fame is a vague knowledge of Internet buzzwords are walking off with tens of millions without creating any value.

In Paris, to the surprise of many, Thomson-CSF has fallen to Lagardère. I was amused when a spokesman explained the deal: "Thomson is worth nothing," he said, "14 billion francs in debt..."

Twenty years ago I recall standing before a Thomson treasurer, discussing their dangled investment in my fledgling company: "Infomedia is worth nothing," he'd told me as an introduction to an offer to grab the technology from me if I agreed to return to the fold as an obedient engineer in their employ. In retrospect their refusal to acquire InfoMedia was a blessing, and I was right to walk away.

Spring Hill. Saturday 2 November 1996.

Alone in the tower, thinking of ufology, its vertiginous follies and stubborn enigmas, I picked up Hynek's *UFO Experience*, with his dedication in wide, well-formed letters: "To Jacques and Janine, without your pioneering this book would hardly have been possible..."

I thought of Mimi's recent death, and suddenly felt poignantly sad and alone with my memories of a time when one could grapple with the genuine mystery, not yet exploited by the media. Let's hear it for neglected topics, abandoned by academe, held in contempt by crowds: from such pursuits light will come.

Albuquerque. Sunday 3 November 1996.

The Wyndham hotel. For dinner, an omelet at the Village Inn with physicist Roger Rémy. Screaming patrol cars search for somebody: Roger tells me that the gang situation is getting worse. Our waitress, who came here to study, is scared and will soon return to Colorado.

Roger is skeptical of Roswell and claims of technology derivatives. We spoke of space exploration, of the Russian *Red Star Three* (Roger knows Stephanov Pomarev, the project head), and of Topaz, which the Russians are developing with Japanese money.

Light spheres have been seen between Kirtland and Socorro, and there were radar interferences in connection with the orbs.

Hummingbird. Thursday 14 November 1996.

I spent the day planning my next trip. A scholarly paper from Brussels points out that Europe, which used to be three years behind America, is only two years behind now. What they don't see is that, in industries like semiconductors, three years used to represent one product cycle, while two years today covers four product cycles: therefore Europe has, in reality, suffered a big setback.

Hal's "communicators" are ready: two people can sit miles away with the devices on tripods pointed at each other, and type messages. His engineer designed these gadgets for $36,000. Both devices are now in Utah, ready for any encounter with the unknown but there's nothing there, except for unmarked crane helicopters that carry suspended devices, possibly ordinary magnetometers? Terry says that one of them landed and a man came out, claiming he was checking for…fire hazards! There was a foot of snow on the ground.

Life is simpler here: Janine and I went to see *Picasso at the Lapin Agile*, after which we walked happily home in the mild evening.

United flight to Paris. Thursday 21 November 1996.

Fast dawn: a fine pink streak appears far ahead; soon it encircles the leading edge of the jet engines. Down there the landscape is frozen. Town lights are still on. It must be Scotland. The trip will be short: a visit to Brussels with another invitation by Edith Cresson to a conference on information technology. In Paris I'll bring gifts for my son's birthday. Olivier is 33, with a good career, his own apartment. "How fast this has happened!" said Janine the other night, squeezing my hand, moving me to tears. I don't care how life passes. I am not bitter about getting older, somewhat to my surprise. Our love is a treasure that grows in time, more precious every day.

Mabillon. Saturday 23 November 1996.

The drive to Lausanne was magnificent. The first snow had fallen over the Alps, creating a landscape of lofty pines and glistening ice high above the road. By contrast it was a cold, dreary day in Paris. I walked all over the Latin Quarter, meeting my son for lunch and my old mother for evening coffee. There were cops all along *Rue Monge*. They encircled the Sorbonne area, blocking all vehicle access to the square where Chirac, in a fine cosmetic move, was lecturing the crowd while enthroning the ashes of Malraux in the pompous Panthéon, the ugliest pile of stone in all of Paris, even more pompous than the *Arc-de-Triomphe*, of dubious fame.

Our neighbor at Mabillon is a teacher of classics. There are some 4,000 books in his studio. When his generation dies "nobody will bother to teach all that stuff anymore," he says. Who needs Plato?

Mabillon. Sunday 24 November 1996.

The sun came out this morning, touching up the banks of the Seine with pink and blue, putting tiny flames on the golden grillwork of the *Palais de Justice*, but the gray and the bitter cold returned. I gave up on my plan to walk along the river, looking for books. Tonight, I meet Patrick Corsi for the trip aboard Thalys, the TGV to Brussels.

Brussels. Tuesday 26 November 1996.

This city is dark, friendly, greasy, muddy, decrepit along the edges and equal to its boring self. The financial conference is attended by my old investment colleagues: Dag Tellefsen, Philippe Claude from Atlas, and Annie Brooking from Cambridge. There is a faint sense of new hope for independent companies, even as striking truckdrivers block French roads. Physicist Léon Brenig, brave Lucien Clérebaut and photographer Patrick Ferryn, my colleagues in ufology, took me to an old brasserie on the *Grande Place*, of alchemical inspiration.

Brussels. Wednesday 27 November 1996.

Parting the blue curtains of my Novotel room reveals a square with an incongruous statue of Don Quijote and Sancho, two Spaniards who must have lost their way in the hopeless fog that drowns Belgium. I know how they must feel, wandering in the cold like me.

Little happens at this conference. People still adhere to the principle that all good will come from governments. When they need new industries, they turn to the government to finance them, creating super-governments to manage the process.

Brussels. Thursday 28 November 1996.

This damp cold in a polluted city triggers asthma again. I could never live comfortably through Europe's winter. It makes my lungs feel like frozen asparagus. Across the border the truckers' strike has entered its 12th day, the economy rotting away along with antiquated social stratifications. Several invited French speakers are missing from the conference, delayed along the blocked highways.

Spring Hill. Sunday 8 December 1996.

Back to California. Our blue bird, the great wild heron has returned to our pond. When I closed the door of the observatory this morning I heard his big wings flapping and caught sight of his graceful shape, a blue-gray blur flying away like some prehistoric pterodactyl, long legs dragging behind as he cleared the manzanitas. We've had two days of rain; clusters of red bays sparkle with hanging diamonds.

Hummingbird. Sunday 15 December 1996.

This is a proper time for re-assessment: Christmas lists, quiet reminders of old friendships. My home office is in shape, with a second computer (a Toshiba Infinia) for fast online work. I have attempted to place a few new ideas on record in *Le Figaro* (**25**).

Our Christmas party at the Garden Court gathered Keith Harary, Bob Johansen, and astronaut Rusty Schweikart who mocked rumors about the UFO sightings attributed to his NASA colleagues.

A man named Robert Joe Moody, who claimed space Aliens made him kill two women in November 1993, has been sentenced to death in Tucson but he smiles: the ETs will surely resurrect him.

Hummingbird. Friday 20 December 1996.

Carl Sagan died today. Towards the end he must have felt angry at meeting with such resistance when he offered imaginative theories such as the presence of water on the moon (once "impossible," now a near-certainty) and the probability of planetary life. Later his skeptical pronouncements about paranormal phenomena failed to earn him the official accolades he craved from fellow "rationalists."

Hummingbird. Thursday 26 December 1996.

Christmas was happily spent at home with Annick and Michel. Weakened by the flu, in less feverish moments I pick up Deveney's wonderful biography of Paschal Beverly Randolph (**26**). Poor Randolph! His lofty knowledge of esoterica did not help him much in the mundane world. He was a genuine seeker in a chaotic crowd of *faux* mystics, spiritualist believers and occult pretenders reminiscent of today's phantasies.

Now rain lingers, the San Francisco skyline buried in gossamer, a picture of satisfying melancholy. I work from home, sending faxes, rehashing Internet web sites. Janine has driven off to get some hot soup to Catherine, hit in turn by the flu virus. I look over the rooftops of this fine City, where Pascal Beverly Randolph founded two Rosicrucian centers: First in 1861 (with ophthalmologist Dr. John B. Pilkington), and again in December of 1874, creating his grandiose *Triplicate Order* "with authority over the entire continent of North America and the Islands of the Sea."

He took pains to point out that those who searched must travel straight towards the setting sun, "and at the end of the journey the Light will be seen."

There's a similar longing in our minds. A passion remains, a vision that transcends the limitations of a specific epoch, even one as frothy and juicy as this.

13

Hummingbird. Monday 6 January 1997.

The sunshine of a San Francisco winter has come at last, the sky all pastel, the big ships on the Bay lazily drifting at anchor. I'm attending a medical investment conference where two of my portfolio companies are featured. Everything feels new and bright.

Las Vegas. Sun Harbor. Friday 10 January 1997.

Our sixth meeting of NIDS. Over dinner at the blue marble table in the boardroom at Park House, John Petersen presented alternative futures, using the tools of futurology: complexity theory, game changers, "day after" scenarios, wild cards. Bob Bigelow handed out a chronology of NIDS, founded in October 1995. A study of electronic voices from the Beyond yielded little result, like my own experiments at Spring Hill. As a man of action Bob emphasized expeditions, acquisition of the Utah ranch, and instrumentation, but I think we neglected methodology.

Senator Schmidt, sitting next to me, urged us sanely "to work with one foot in hard science, and one foot in the unknown." About Roswell he asked, "Is there a community that cares?" In contrast, Hal is sure that Corso's book, to be released on the 50th anniversary of Roswell, is about to create a huge surprise, a watershed.

Las Vegas. Sun Harbor. Saturday 11 January 1997.

The weather is staying cold, in the low 50s. GianCarlo Rota and Martin Pilch have arrived, so the only missing members are Ian Stevenson and Ed Mitchell. The morning began with an excellent summary of the NIDS budget (27). Bob clarified our focus: he doesn't want NIDS to hire guest investigators, but he'll sponsor John Mack, who has a staff and a clear scope of work. "Let's be careful not to organize ourselves out of the right answers," he said wisely. "Let's not become enamored with our own echoes in the ductwork."

The latter was in reference to a building where a local developer had a persistent problem losing tenants, complaining of loud noises. An exterminator discovered a family of mice settled in the air conditioning ducts: they liked their own music so much they had developed a habit of reverberating drum rolls throughout the structure for entertainment. While we all laughed at this true story, so characteristic of Bob's pragmatic wisdom, Jack Schmidt brought us back to our goals: "What fundamental areas should we tackle?" he asked, offering evolutionary biology as a candidate, "Does consciousness have another source than evolution?" The idea fell flat, unfortunately. Instead, Bob outlined a new plan with two parts:

Division-I is devoted to "Survival of Human Consciousness," with three objectives, support the UNLV chair, specific projects (but still no grants to outside investigators), and aggressive interaction with Fetzer and Noetics. Division-II, "Aerial Phenomena" continues surveillance at both properties, networking with ranchers, veterinarians, and the police on mutilations and sample analyses.

Ted Rockwell suggested that we should become the "definitive source" on specific subjects, as his former boss Admiral Rickover had done for nuclear topics within the Navy. And Jack Schmidt patiently returned to the study of the background physical data at the Utah ranch. He pointed out the area was geologically special, a well-known site of hydrocarbon deposits and a focus of exploration by oil companies, which explains the helicopters. Hal also mentioned that at least one survivalist group was using the Uintah Basin as a training site, which further complicates the situation.

Johndale Solem critiqued what we had done with the implants submitted to NIDS and he said we'd rushed too fast into Utah without thinking about how we were going to perturb the system.

"The effect has disappeared; we no longer have science there," he said, voicing my own thoughts. In fact, Bigelow has pulled out his observers, leaving only Terry Sherman, because NIDS activities attracted unwanted attention. A group of men have shown up, dressed in fatigues, and (in one case) carrying a rifle. They drove up in a car with Michigan license plates. They told Terry he was "working for bad people" and that the Institute was a cover for the government, in cahoots with extraterrestrial Aliens! As proof they showed him a videotape of the staff with Hal's two devices, with an unidentified light that the staff had never seen, a probable fabrication.

John Petersen aptly said we shouldn't be "a job shop for anything that comes along." I stressed that in some activities we'd been hampered by our own assumptions, which we failed to question. After lunch Kit noted the Board was split between transcendentalists and classical scientists but GianCarlo observed that the key disciplines were still missing: law, philosophy, structured thought.

Jack Schmidt was asked to give a presentation on the lessons learned during the State Hearings he'd organized in the 1970s about mutilations. His statement was sketchy and surprisingly short on data. He spoke of things we already knew, like Gabe Valdez' investigations and the high frequency of reports, but there was no fieldwork, no analysis. So how could they come up with negative conclusions?

Schmidt said reports had dropped after his Hearings, but this shouldn't be surprising. He didn't even mention Ken Rommel. When I corrected this, Kit confessed he'd sponsored the man. But Rommel did no necropsy, no serious fieldwork either. It was all a whitewash.

George Onet reported on his questionnaires to ranchers. Dozens came back, with five mutilation incidents but in no case had a veterinarian been called. George estimates about 2,000 cases are reported every year in the U.S., so he will try to involve bovine practitioners in his study. I pointed out things had changed with the higher attention finally paid to BSE (bovine encephalopathy).

Terry Sherman claims that 14 cows are missing out of his herd of 300 head. Within those 14 were 8 of the 12 special animals he had bought, which had the same genetic make-up but were visually indistinguishable from their companions. Jessica Utts computed that the probability for this situation was infinitesimal (about 6 times 10 to the minus 26.) The abducted animals must have been selected.

Seated to my right, General Whinnery kept drawing elaborate labyrinths in silence.

GianCarlo then made the cryptic statement that the discussion showed "how limited our imagination was." He went on to say that "preconceived thinking is hard to shake" and that *statistics were only helpful in excluding certain hypotheses, but not in leading to a solution.* GianCarlo reminds me of Fred Beckman: he is capable of very fundamental ideas but would much rather stay silent and keep them to himself. I decided I would try to draw out his thoughts.

The afternoon went on with a "brainshop" on sensors and detection, in which Hal Puthoff and Jack Schmidt participated. I stressed that nothing could be better than a well-equipped, well-trained human observer in the field, augmented by simple instruments, but I also insisted on the crying need for unobtrusive remote monitoring.

Once again Hal, John, Victoria, and I gathered after dinner in Kit and Kristin's room at the motel. We learned that the team had seen an unidentified light on 13 November at 1:08 am. There was good visibility under the clouds. The object made no sound; it was bright orange, turned to blue, flashed once a second for a while.

Much of the ensuing conversation had to do with the NIDS budget. Kit noted that the spending didn't include the cost of the jet, or Bigelow Foundation grants to researchers, or the $3M endowment for the Chair of Consciousness Studies at UNLV. Dr. Roll, who was going to fill it, has declined a drug test, so that position is vacant.

Other facts are coming to light. Bob once created a company with Bob Lazar, the *Zeta Reticuli Corporation*, to exploit the wondrous supposed properties of Element 115. Lazar exhibited a substance that was light, foam-like, and almost weightless, hinting it would revolutionize energy and propulsion. The cooperation only lasted until the day when Bob noticed a container of Lazar's secret sauce in a corner and recognized it as a commercial emulsive product!

Going over the afternoon discussion, I stressed again a matter that had bothered Emily Cook and me: it's clear the Board will not be consulted or even kept informed about grants funded by NIDS, such as John Mack's work.

This creates a problem: when I lend my name to a Board I regard it as my duty to remain fully informed.

On the flight back to San Francisco. Sunday 12 January 1997.

Today a private briefing introduced by John Petersen centered on Steve Trevino, an intense, neatly dressed man of about 35, with jet-black hair and black eyes, with the odd intensity of the true believer. Flashing a low-level Rosicrucian initiation ring, he began with slides about Aliens and took a long time to come around to esoteric groups, which he claimed to have infiltrated. I failed to see the point.

Still certain that a major announcement is imminent, John Petersen keeps worrying about "the Day After." My advice for the Day After is simply to kneel in the dust and pray, just in case.

The three NIDS staffers picked me up afterwards. We went to the Strip for a late lunch and they grilled me on everything from the Gulf Breeze and photo analysis to cattle mutilations. "Expectations of frequent sightings of UFOs at the Utah ranch have not materialized," they said, "so what are we supposed to work on?"

Hummingbird. Monday 13 January 1997.

Colonel Corso called me at home this morning. He believes that the bodies allegedly recovered at Roswell must have been artificial beings "given" to us by the visitors, since there was no water and no food on board the craft.

He appears troubled by the fact that the analyses he saw, reportedly coming from Walter Reed Hospital, were very superficial and "just didn't seem right."

Austin, Texas. Tuesday 14 January 1997.

Hal and Adrienne have kindly invited me to stay at their house, where I will happily sleep in the guest room, the only sound the rustling of the trees. Hal shares my assessment that no one on the Board has knowledge of the secret stuff. John Alexander has met a DIA man who follows the subject, but he simply has a desk in some corner and collects what everybody else collects.

After dinner we drove over to the Institute's lab, where I saw the remains of seven purported free-energy systems that EarthTech had tested with negative results, and a more promising test of cold fusion in a special calorimeter. Hal gave me copies of some official papers from 1943, notably correspondance between Vannevar Bush and Einstein about the latter's wartime assignments. There are alleged reports about a crash in 1947, purportedly from General Twining, but the style is all wrong, like something from the fake Aliens of Ummo.

Hummingbird. Sunday 19 January 1997.

From Austin I drove to San Antonio where I was greeted by Sony Semiconductors personnel, donned a white plastic suit and went into the clean room to interview the users of a new monitoring device invented by an Israeli company in which we're investing. Later I drove over to the Alamo and took a tour of the structure, inspiring in its simplicity. The Alamo is quiet and tragic, very eloquent. It is characteristic of the spirit of the people of Texas that they would commemorate a heroic defeat rather than a lucky victory, as more pompous governments do: no "Arch of Triumph" in Texas.

Gerald Askevold tells me that Willis Harman, recently operated for a brain tumor, is at the hospital and isn't expected to live.

Hummingbird. Sunday 26 January 1997.

Occam's Razor: The skeptics cite it, but I have always thought the quotes were inappropriate. Now *The Economist* agrees: "Occam's Principle did say that superfluous things should not exist; but it was devised only to cut through the metaphysical mess. The *Principle of Economy* is traced by philosophers back to Aristotle... Long before Occam, it was used for excising unnecessary entities from the theory of perception. The belief that Occam's Razor is a scientific principle stems from a subtle confusion between *parsimony* (the denial of unnecessary entities) and *simplicity*. Parsimony—ie., not believing in unseen entities, be they tiny particles, intelligent life on other planets, or God—is merely a philosophical principle, not a scientific one. You don't have scientific evidence that Aliens don't exist, simply because you've never seen an Alien. There's no logical reason why a parsimonious theory, rather than an extravagant one, should be true."

Spring Hill. Saturday 1 February 1997.

Still sick with a stubborn form of the flu, I drove up to the ranch with Janine this morning. The idea of selling it is a source of conflicts. So, I went up to the top of the tower and looked at the landscape swept clean, sensing the early end of winter. I walked along the creek that dances around the feet of giant redwoods. I don't mind leaving the trees. They have nothing to complain about: we've saved them from the logger's saw. What I mind is losing that special sense of transcendent beauty.

"Listen, I'm just one small woman," Janine says. "All I see at the ranch now is a waste of time and money. We come all the way here; I keep the place clean while you do your own work, I cut the vines every year, I help you tear out the weeds, I sweep the pool, there's not much more I can do. And then it's always time to drive back."

"And I'm a Knight of the Rosy Cross, on special assignment from the Cosmic Forces," I reply to tease her, "I need a sacred space on Earth as a base for my important mission to save the Galaxy."

"Ask your psychic guide, then," she says, sending me an evil look, "maybe he'll tell you who's right."

"It's a *She*," I interject viciously. She burst out laughing:

"Fine. Let *Her* do the cooking."

I'm not going to win that argument. And what about the friends we were supposed to assemble? The best minds in the region, Diane and her Pagan hedonists, Robin Rule in Willits, all revolve in a world that is getting rapidly overwhelmed by the new drug gangs.

Those are somber thoughts, as we begin the year with a lingering weakness, sleeping badly, wondering when spring will come, and where my work will take me.

Spring Hill. Saturday 8 February 1997.

Two books just arrived. One came from Pierre Lagrange, his *Rumeur de Roswell,* a critique of the claims about crashes (**28**). Pierre had inscribed a warm dedication to both of us. The other was Jim Schnabel's *Remote Viewers*, a well-documented paperback retracing the history of Grill Flame and the SRI remote viewing program.

Last night we had dinner (at *Les Joulins*) with Darlene and Keith, whose birthday we were celebrating along with the 37th anniversary of my first meeting Janine. They enjoyed the music and the food, but Keith felt depressed by Jim Schnabel's book. I had to reassure him that he came out positively. In fact, the book is elegant. The conversation turned to what should be done to properly research remote viewing.

I have long felt that the analogy between psychic functioning and software "addressing" in automata theory (note) was a fertile avenue for research: that idea launched Ingo Swann into coordinate remote viewing when I had that initial conversation with him at SRI in the early 70s, but it was never pursued by the research team, because Hal's sponsors in Washington never grasped the concept.

Keith gave me an impassioned description of the physiological impact of the sessions. He insisted this should be studied from a biochemical angle, by analyzing brain processes, not just statistics. He kept coming back to the essential point that there are multiple physiological correlates to psychic work that extend to neuro-transmitter release and that influence body states and behavior.

The lack of research into these aspects is sad, while so much hoopla surrounds the more sensational (and flaky) laboratory work with Gansfeld theory, telepathy with plants, and psychokinesis. Not to mention the bending of spoons.

On a cold and clear day, driving between Spring Hill and the Valley of the Moon, we finally agreed to sell the ranch. Janine had seen that it was the right course, but I had trouble letting go.

Hummingbird. Sunday 9 February 1997.

At NIDS Bigelow has hired Gabe Valdez, a retired New Mexico State Police officer who has researched cattle mutilations for years. The Utah ranch was found to be in a clean area from a geomagnetic standpoint, with no fault lines and no seismic activity worth noting.

(Note) Ingo Swann mentioned our conversation in *Report on Project SCANATE* (published 29 Dec. 1995):

"I consulted a number of scientists outside of the SRI orbit, but not far away, in Silicon Valley. No one could recommend anything. But Dr. Jacques Vallee recognized the problem as one of 'addresses.' He said that you need an address that gets the perceptual channel to the right place, exactly as one needs a street address to find a house, or an address menu code in a computer to find and call up the desired information."

This notion led him to use coordinates and became a basis of the SRI remote viewing program.

So, Harrison Schmidt's expectation of physical anomalies has not been verified. Now I fly off to Paris again, on venture business.

Mabillon. Sunday 16 February 1997.

The sun has just cleared the rooftops, a pale and gallant sun in near-freezing air. Guérin, older but not wiser, keeps writing insulting letters to Lagrange. He lumps me together with Bertrand Méheust in a conspiracy to hide the Horrible Alien Truth.

French technology keeps lagging behind, with one of the lowest penetration rates of the Internet in Europe, but in the heart of Paris the flames of history are kept burning, a city so steeped in the emotions of its own past that it embraces you at once in a subtle distress of the heart. Yet there's something drastically wrong with a country where even archaeologists have to go on strike (**29**)!

Mabillon. Tuesday 18 February 1997.

Between two business meetings I met Pierre Lagrange at his apartment, a picturesque lodge in a dark building behind Saint Sulpice. The place is filled with books, piles of magazines, and report drafts. We had lunch at *L'Enfance de Lard* where he hardly ate anything. I told him about remote viewing.

Later, over dinner at Thérèse's apartment, I met Serge July, chief editor of *Libération*, debating investment politics.

Mabillon. Friday 21 February 1997.

Slow dawn, dark skies. France is in an uproar about immigration reform. A stupid law that would require French citizens to rat on illegal aliens has been proposed, reminiscent of Nazi edicts to report the Jews. White buses of riot police kept moving down the Boulevard Saint Michel. Violence is in the air between the *Front National* and students, but there are sharp differences with the situation of 1968 when the protesters were in search of a vision, in quest of hope. Today the Left is paralyzed – and afraid.

Hummingbird. Friday 28 February 1997.

Robert Temple came to see me this morning. He was in town for a Board meeting of Vitacom, a satellite communications company he represents in China. He gave me two books: his new translation of the Gilgamesh Epic, and *Open to Suggestion*, a work he published in England (**30**). He suspects the CIA is preventing its distribution in the U.S. because it exposes classified research into hypnosis. He is certain that abductions are the result of a covert government project that has nothing to do with flying saucers. The Franck Fontaine case at Cergy-Pontoise would fall into that pattern. Temple likened UFO waves to a rash, an eruption through a membrane.

Now Yves Messarovitch, chief editor of *Le Figaro Economie*, asks me to write a regular column from a Silicon Valley perspective (**31**).

Hummingbird. Sunday 2 March 1997.

We spent Friday night at Spring Hill and signed a thick pile of papers to put the ranch on the market. Another busy week ahead, with a conference on privately-financed startups in Monterey.

John Mack has become a zealot for a new spiritual current, while Strieber publicizes claims of implants (which he doesn't dare to have removed and analyzed, for fear of death…) and subtle contact with unspecified forces. I have little to contribute to either cause.

Monterey. Tuesday 4 March 1997.

The ranks of the more rational advocates of paranormal research are becoming thin: Willis Harman died two weeks ago.

After a long day of meetings, I drove, almost fled, along the ocean last night. The excuse for my escape is the American Electronic Association's financial conference but the fact is I need time alone.

I feel the distress of leaving Spring Hill. I thought I had built something permanent there, planted a stake, established a base: the ideal home for research into states of meditation, for the study of life in space and life from space. Janine insists that nothing is permanent. I am torn between that realisation and my need for a spiritual center, reflecting an inner vision I am not willing to betray.

Churches and opulent temples have little meaning to me, but the forest has become my spiritual *locus*, the hillside my altar in infinite time. Plaster divinities come and go but the trees, the magnificent cathedral of the redwoods of Spring Hill, will always evoke for me the forces of terrestrial creatures reaching for the sky.

Hummingbird. Sunday 9 March 1997.

The financing of Accuray Systems is an endless ordeal. I still hope to save the company. Setting aside the financing papers I sent my first "Silicon Valley Chronicle" for *Le Figaro* before flying to Vegas.

Two items stand out with respect to this seventh NIDS meeting: Jessica Utts' masterly presentation on statistics in parapsychology, and George Onet's report on his first necropsy of a mutilated cow in New Mexico, supported by a videotape. Bob Bigelow also showed us an excellent television documentary on near-death experiences. It featured two NIDS members, Dr. Melvin Morse and Jim Whinnery. Kit, fresh from China, ran the main sessions.

In the evening we had a party at John's house. Victoria showed me her library and the framed print of a medieval green devil Janine had given her. She also displayed the documents sent by John Mack, his research on nightmares. I was disturbed by Jack Schmidt's absence. Ian Stevenson wasn't there either, and Dean Judd has long ago dropped out, so the Board is now down to 14 members, with the only addition of Joe Kaufman.

I remain concerned about the restrictions on dissent. I spoke out about the responsibility of the Board not to fall into groupthink and about the need for open-minded skeptics. I showed them Sue Blackmore's latest book *Searching for the Light*. Intelligent skeptics like her are valuable: we need something against which to push.

Through the Institute, Bob Bigelow is channeling money to: (1) a European book by von Ludwiger, (2) John Mack's exploration of multiple witness abduction cases, (3) immunology related to NDEs by Kelleher and Melvin Morse, (4) communications devices built by Hal, (5) John Petersen's "Day After" scenarios, (6) an evaluation of mediums by Stevenson and Emily Cook, (7) the cattle mutilation survey conducted by George Onet, (8) a seminar series on survival of consciousness led by John Alexander, (9) a crop circle study run by Kit and Kristin with Kelleher and Deetken, and (10) a new Roper poll.

I am among the rare ones who are not exploiting the Bigelow purse, even though several of those ideas came from me.

The hard truth is that the NIDS board is too busy trying to invent gadgets and feed their own projects to stop and think seriously about science fundamentals and the deeper nature of the phenomenon.

Kit made it clear the Mack project was strictly a psychiatric evaluation of experiencers *in which outsiders observed the experience itself.* They'll test them for dissociation tendencies and will try to assess their state of mind. "We're not trying to find out if abductions actually occur," he said. But then, why do it?

Progress has been made in the mutilation study. George has followed up on a case reported by Gabe Valdez, a cow mutilated near Taos on February 22nd. He was on the scene three days later, performing a necropsy and taking samples. For the first couple of days a strong smell of battery acid came from the carcass. An animal control officer at the scene suffered from coughing and loss of sensation in the lower jaw. This points to a terrestrial agent, not E.T.

Later the same day.

On the ride to Park House I sat next to GianCarlo Rota, who hardly says anything during our meetings and with whom I had wanted to speak for a long time. When I asked him what he thought of what he'd heard in earlier sessions he seemed surprised anybody cared about his opinion. Dr. Rota answered calmly that there was a major flaw in our attempts to describe the phenomena with the terms of current physics, or even of science in general. Many fields of human endeavor, he said, simply didn't fit into the current scientific vocabulary, and the so-called "paranormal" was one of them.

Novel terms must be invented, he went on, to describe new phenomena. He supported this view with scholarly citations of various philosophers, and thereby lost me, but I went away from the discussion with the realization that at least one person within our group shared my impression that we were simply not bold enough, or creative enough. He wanted us to analyze the phenomena in their own terms--yet to be discovered--rather than trying to fit them into conventional schemes: a lesson to remember.

Hummingbird. Monday 10 March 1997.

Dick Haines, whom I hadn't seen in years, met me for lunch today in Palo Alto. He hasn't changed: calm and focused, he told me about his work at NASA on airport design and his trips to Russia and Ukraine.

Another day, and Accuray Systems is dying, out of cash again. I could put the blame on Fred Adler (who waited until the last minute to tell us he didn't want to co-invest with a Los Angeles group that proposed a financing) but the deal had become so twisted that Fred was probably right to decline. It is hard to believe that we may lose such a fine company for reasons that have nothing to do with its product or its market, simply the poor timing of its financing (**32**).

Hummingbird. Wednesday 19 March 1997.

Janine and I love the amusing scenes this City offers, its micro-cultures. On Monday, middle-aged Chinese women who lined up to catch the bus on Kearny Street were all wearing green in honor of St. Patrick. I am packing my suitcase again. *Le Figaro* has published my first *Letter from Silicon Valley*, to the dismay of my French partners, envious of my access to one of their favorite newspapers.

Tomorrow I'll be in Washington, on a visit to the French scientific attaché who wants to understand why French innovation fails.

Washington, D.C. Ritz-Carlton. Thursday 20 March 1997.

It snowed in Washington yesterday. I had dinner with Connie McLindon and a writer friend of hers. She gave me a book about the Internet that painted a distorted picture, from the single point of view of Bob Taylor. Connie now works for Bob Kahn at CNRI, developing a universal identifier for publishers, and with Neil Brownstein who funded my networking research at NSF ages ago.

United flight to Paris. Friday 21 March 1997.

Three hours away from Washington over the Atlantic, my first flight in a Boeing 777. This morning I did meet with the science attaché at the French Embassy, tasked with writing a report about venture capital: why it works so well in the United States and so badly in France. Wasted time for both of us, as is often the case with French officials. His office displays the elegant impotence of diplomacy.

Back in my room, long phone conferences to support Accuray and Ixys while watching Israeli emergency teams on CNN, cleaning up yet another suicide bombing. The issue, once again, is Jerusalem. When will the world get rid of the supposedly "holy" men of every stripe, who keep driving us to collective disaster?

Mabillon. Sunday 23 March 1997.

At 8 in the morning, alone in *rue Saint-André des Arts*. This early, on a weekend, everyone is still asleep, except for the cleaners in bright green coveralls who have already swept away from the sidewalks the evidence of last night's excesses. At Saint-Michel where I have breakfast a dozen young men and women wearing white smocks and carrying placards were getting ready for today's demonstration of hospital personnel angered by government reforms.

Yesterday I found my mother increasingly frail, but her eye was clear, her spirit intact. Conversation becomes difficult, however, as if she were ready for another realm where logic has no part.

Brussels. Hotel Leopold. Monday 24 March 1997.

Belgium again, the Thalys train speeding through northern grime, skies the gray hue of dust. A two-hour trip, long enough to read Viviane Forrester's bestseller, *L'Horreur Economique* (**33**). She reviews the nightmare of unemployment with a pedantic assessment of its roots. Contrasting the "good but helpless" masses (!) with a global plot woven by "the rich" makes little sense when ownership of major firms is in the hands of enormously powerful workers' retirement funds. She lives in the days of Dickens and Victor Hugo.

On Saturday, timed to the equinox, the cult of the Solar Temple triggered five more deaths. Like Amazonian tribes that try to turn back time itself, denying in collective suicide the advent of the new world, some modern men and women join cults that pretend to take them back to the simple discipline of medieval knighthood and ultimately to live on Sirius, on the other side of death.

Patrick Corsi, a romantic soul who drives his old white Citroën at unsafe speeds through cobblestone streets of Belgium, has shown me an ugly yellow coin: the prototype for the Euro, the future currency.

Lille. Hotel Mercure. Later the same day.

My presentation to the Science and Industry Directorate of the European Commission in Brussels was well-received. Later I took the train to Ghent, where I changed trains for Lille.

The ramshackle hotel where Janine and I lived so passionately nearly 40 years ago is for sale. I wrote *Dark Satellite* there. This area, upbeat if not elegant in the sixties, has become dilapidated, with a shabby hairdresser at the corner and a fast-food hole in the wall. For old time's sake I went to *Place de la Gare* for dinner, in a suitably lugubrious bistro. The radio played a silly, vaporous tune. I thought back to our days here, our eager young love, our favorite dish, Frankfurters with French fries, Edith Piaf belting out *Milord.*

This old city is a museum from which energy seems drained. Forlorn patrons in cocktail bars wonder where their life has been spent. The train station is surrounded with new buildings of glass and steel but the streets I walked at night, looking for my way back to the hotel, were silent and dull, as if expecting the bulldozer. A few blocks away one falls into disquieting ruins, boarded-up houses. Cars drive fast along sad boulevards, no one stands on the sidewalk except for the occasional frail girl, a *fille sans joie* in search of a few francs.

Lille. Wednesday 26 March 1997.

During our financial conference this afternoon, advocates of Easdaq and *Nouveau Marché* fought one another on our panel. Afterwards Edith Cresson gave an overview of the European programmes for innovation (**34**). She lamented the fact that European committees demand unanimity among the 12, soon to be 15-member nations.

This makes decisions impossible, of course, unless the group gives in to every country's blackmail.

She enquired about the progress of my book.

Mabillon. Friday 28 March 1997.

A nasty bug hit me in Lille, building up into a full-force cold with sneezes and aches. Back in Paris I dragged myself through a few bookstores, only to collapse in bed. The French media report on the suicide of 39 adepts of a San Diego cybersect, "Higher Source," who expected to make a spirit transition to a spacecraft hidden behind the Hale-Bopp comet. Also known as *Heaven's Gate*, they are the disciples of "The Two," the sect of extraterrestrial believers against which I published a strong warning in *Messengers of Deception*.

On *Rue de Buci* the sun is shining. France is getting ready for the long Easter weekend. There are fruits, pastries, and victuals everywhere. At *Le Figaro*, Messarovitch's office on the seventh floor sports a full-length balcony with flower boxes where beautiful tulips bloom. As I expressed surprise, he laughed: "When our president instituted drastic cuts throughout the company he got rid of typists and editors but he kept the gardener. He was always fond of plants, so the paper maintains a full-time expert who goes around the empty building, watering and pruning all day long..."

Janine just called with more news of *Heaven's Gate*: the dead leader was none other than our old acquaintance Marshall Applewhite, the same one Gerald Askevold and I went to hear at Stanford in 1975 (**35**). Some alert journalist has dug up my warnings about that group, so Janine's phone has been ringing in San Francisco. This sent me back to the book, and I felt a chill when I read my notes again, after Applewhite's presentation of his group: "*It only costs your life*," he had told the audience.

"Your book was prophetic," commented Lagrange.

"That doesn't help," I replied, "I should've been more direct in exposing these cults. But the book alienated most ufologists..."

"That's always the problem," sighed Pierre, "publicly denouncing abuses can actually amplify them."

I went over to the window, pulled open the drapes. Comet Hale-Bopp was there, hovering above the steeple of *Saint-Germain-des-Prés*, all bluish and fuzzy like the flame of a gas stove, very alien indeed. The disciples of *Heaven's Gate* thought they were going to be transferred to a spaceship. This stupid notion began with an amateur astronomer whose photograph showed an anomalous light next to the comet, undoubtedly an optical artifact of his cheap telescope. Then a self-proclaimed remote viewer named Courtney Brown psychically "saw" a spaceship there. That "discovery" was picked up by Stanton Friedman and Whitley Strieber on the Internet, complete with rehashed accusations of government cover-up…

Spring Hill. Saturday 5 April 1997.

Mood swings. We still go through emotional extremes when we come here. All evening I felt disoriented, alienated. "What was the point of all this work?" We ask ourselves, looking down at the new pond from the top of the tower. Then the perfumes of spring drift up from the meadow, we see the apple trees in bloom, the pool covered with white petals, the bushes purple with delicate clusters of flowers, and we feel delight again until we realize that this gorgeous region is also home to drunken cowboys, drug dealers, pregnant dopey girls on welfare and irascible "cat skinners," bulldozer operators who spread gearboxes and oil all over the landscape. There are too few trustworthy friends.

Janine turned away from me and cried, saying the tower made her incredibly sad. She wished to go back to France, she said, rather than die in this country.

Hummingbird. Sunday 6 April 1997.

The point that irks me most in the ufology dogma is the absurd idea that the Aliens gave us modern technology: the often-heard notion that the transistor derived from Roswell is met with ridicule in Silicon Valley. Not only did the work of Bell Labs begin well before July 1947, but German inventor Oskar Heil had demonstrated a field-effect transistor on a lab bench in Germany in the early thirties. Heil is listed as owner of British patent 439-457, filed in 1934. "The document neatly described the working principles of a modern FET," says *New Scientist* (**36**). As early as June 1904 a device called the "Telemobiloskop" had been demonstrated.

Now Fred Beckman amazes me by telling me that he knew Oskar Heil: the man was his neighbor in San Mateo! He did invent the transistor in the thirties but never made much of it; his main interest was in sound reproduction and speakers. He used to ask Fred to test his latest gadgets, relying on his fine musical ear.

Hummingbird. Wednesday 9 April 1997.

Bright sun sneaks in between the shutters. I stay home this morning, returning phone calls. Yesterday I met with the new French Consul, André Parant, and with Alain Dupas of CNES, who works in their Prospective group. Alain, who knows Poher well, says Claude's career was shattered by his research on UFOs: he expected too much too soon. The CNES dispatched him to Cannes, where little is going on. They exiled him to work with Aérospatiale in a dead-end job.

Hummingbird. Friday 11 April 1997.

The French Consulate invited me tonight to meet René Monory, President of the French Senate, second in line behind Chirac for the Presidency. He is a cheerful, dynamic gentleman who spoke with effusion of meeting Bill Gates and the luminaries of Sun and Silicon Graphics. The French Senate has just passed a law that makes stock option plans even more difficult to set up, however, so there is little likelihood that the California miracle will be repeated in France.

Hummingbird. Sunday 13 April 1997.

We spent Saturday morning driving to the coast through the apple orchards of Sebastopol and Occidental, reaching Irish Hill over Bodega Bay to look at a new property.

This evening Mr. Bigelow called, thanking me for my work on Illobrand von Ludwiger's manuscript on European UFOs. We went on to talk about recent events at the Utah ranch. They began with the mutilation of a newborn calf and continued with Terry Sherman firing at a strange animal hanging in a tree, with eyes that glowered at him. The animal vanished on the spot, and so did an object they had seen at ground level. A track was found, ten inches long, a trace with three fingers. There are reports of Terry's compass spinning and four bulls impossibly lifted into a trailer from a closed corral with latched gates: a bizarre force is lurking at the ranch.

Hummingbird. Sunday 20 April 1997.

In his lively autobiography (**37**) George Kuchar writes in his quirky style: “Another fun couple to eat out with is Dr. Jacques Vallee and his wife, Janine. To hell with French restaurants. They love stopping off at Denny's and getting a big breakfast at any hour of the day. They also treat me to wonderful gourmet food joints and are the only married people I know who have breakfast in bed together. You'd think that after all those married years one or the other would get a grapefruit in the face but no, these are genuine love birds.”

Hummingbird. Sunday 27 April 1997.

Bob Bigelow called me after my latest memo, alerting him to the fact that the phenomena at the Utah ranch might feed on violent emotions and that we must not leave the staff in harm's way. I urged him again to speak to Dr. Douglass Price-Williams about joining us.

From Spring Hill to Fort Bragg, I spent the weekend in the lovely paradise of Mendocino in full springtime succulence. We attended an old George Bernard Shaw play. Diane, who follows the Pagan scene, gave me the shocking news of our friend Adam Rostoker's violent death. He’d separated from his wife, moved to Orange County to stay with a friendly couple, and was assassinated in their house in February. The police have not found the killer. Adam got embroiled in drug scenes as well as occult practices, a risky combination.

Las Vegas. Friday 2 May 1997.

Las Vegas had mild weather today, and a welcome breeze. Again, I had time for a swim before the group assembled for our eighth meeting. Steve Trevino, who had just made a presentation to Kit and Bob, was there as well as Tommy Blann, an investigator from Texas who now lives in Florida. He seemed astonished to see me there.

The evening session was devoted to cattle mutilations. Bob had invited Lou Gerardo, Sheriff of Los Alamos County in New Mexico, who has studied cases since 1973 in Trinidad County, the largest county in Colorado; Edmund Gomez, of the New Mexico Agriculture

Department, who holds a degree in animal science, has suffered 23 cattle mutilations and lost one horse; Gabe Valdez is stationed in Dulce; and Henry Valdez, no relation to Gabe, serves as District Attorney for Rio Arriba County in Los Alamos.

Gabe was the most verbose of the group, describing case after case of well-documented mutilations. Lou Gerardo was the most impressive, concise and clear. Gabe Valdez appeared convinced that the objects responsible for the incidents flew in and out of Dulce.

We heard a clear statement of how predators of every conceivable species operate (mountain lions and bears grab at the neck, dogs go for the back legs) and the major characteristics of mutilations as opposed to death by illness and other natural causes. Another aspect of the phenomenon that has become clear is its human origin. Carcasses have suffered injections and traction by clamps or other devices. It is common for the animals to be dropped, sometimes from considerable height. Also common is the sight of helicopters. I asked about the earliest cases they could recall: unanimously, they said it went back to the early 40s.

On the way back to San Francisco. Saturday 3 May 1997.

In the van I had a chance to discuss various theories with Edgar Mitchell. He thought there was a change in the UFO phenomenon between the early and the late 40s. He believes there is a secret group, a spinoff from the U.S. Government, with access to captured technology. It has reverse-engineered the craft and is busy creating a false threat, to be attributed to "bad Aliens," he said, or to satanic forces. But I recall that Ed has been influenced by Steven Greer.

The science board spent most of the day discussing the Utah ranch in closed session. Three members were missing: Ian Stevenson, Melvin Morse, and GianCarlo. So, there were thirteen of us with Bob, plus John Alexander and Diane Arcangel. Victoria and Kristin joined us for some of the sessions. Amusingly, Kit and Kristin were wearing identical denim jackets from the *Hard Rock Café* in Beijing.

There are currently 120 head of cattle on the Utah ranch. The sequence of recent incidents was as follows: the calf mutilation on 10 March at 10 am, then the encounter with a dark "animal" that resulted in two shootings on 12 March at 23:45; the transfer of the bulls to the trailer on 2 April at 16:00, and a scattering of the herd as if in response to an apparent magnetic anomaly on 3 April at 11:00.

The calf incident isn't a classic mutilation. The bones show both teeth marks and two cutting instruments, according to the forensic pathologists who examined the remains. There was chewing on the hide, but the ribs were gone, the entrails were gone, all the blood was gone, the whole thing in 45 minutes. The staff has finally been instructed to install monitoring instruments, but no remote access will be implemented—a mistake in my opinion.

Edgar Mitchell (who, to my surprise, smokes heavily) gave an interesting summary of the Greer briefings on April 8, 9, and 10. Six witnesses spoke before 60 to 70 press people, and representatives from the White House, Congress, the military, and the intelligence community. An unnamed Congressman offered to be the lead for future Hearings. Several government officials stated in private that "something (a project) was going on, but they didn't have access."

Much of the afternoon was spent discussing candidates for the position on consciousness at UNLV. One of them is Charles Tart, controversial among stodgy scientists. This started another series of debates. Tired of the arguments I went out for a walk, sought refuge from the heat in the men's room and met Kit there.

"I'm not used to these academic discussions any more," I said. "If Charlie's candidacy is unacceptable to the engineering faculty, maybe UNLV should fire its engineering faculty..."

When I went back inside the room Bruce Grayson was describing his proposed study of mediums. The afternoon ended with another round of hypotheses for the Utah ranch incidents: (1) We could be the victims of a hoax by ranchers or the militia, (2) We could be the victims of a hoax setup by some skeptics group, equally unlikely, or (3) There is indeed an unknown agency at work. It must also be noted that no UFO is being seen at the ranch, in contrast with earlier claims.

Hummingbird. Friday 9 May 1997.

Illobrand von Ludwiger came here on Sunday with his daughter Corina, followed by Alain Dupas from Paris. Illobrand is a German physicist. A remote noble ancestor of his was an alchemist, so his family crest shows the bright sun of the Great Work.

Alain Dupas expressed an interesting idea, that one shouldn't read current books about the latest technology but the works of ten or twenty years ago, because they contained the germs, the pure form of the important concepts, as opposed to all the hype one finds in *Wired* magazine about the Internet. In that regard he learned more from my *Network Revolution* published in 1979, he said.

Hummingbird. Sunday 18 May 1997.

Yesterday nine black buzzards were circling the ranch as I removed the painted glass windows at Spring Hill. They might as well have been flying inside my brain, because I felt a sense of desolation and doom: it took me all day to get over it. Turning away from the beautiful ranch and all it represented is a passing that has to be mourned. At noon we went to the Celtic Faire in Willits where young couples in jeans pushed baby carriages next to knights in armor and duchesses in ancient embroidery drinking Coca-Cola out of sculpted cups. There were jugglers and banners, jesters and merchants: a fine day for the Society for Creative Anachronism.

Hummingbird. Monday 26 May 1997.

Colonel Corso's attribution of the invention of the transistor to Aliens is contradicted by real data: Julius Lilienfeld had developed a field-effect transistor device as early as 1925 (**38**).

Memorial Day. We have been following the first round of the French elections, a victory for the Left due to Chirac's betrayal of his campaign promises, the rising unemployment figures and the absurd policies of his Prime Minister Alain Juppé who raised taxes without liberalizing the economy. Yet the socialists under Jospin appear as an equally sorry lot. I am sending Dupas the text of *Enjeux* while Janine and I plan quiet dinners with Olivier, soon to be a father.

Hummingbird. Sunday 1 June 1997.

French Socialists have indeed captured the high ground. Jospin is the new prime minister. My mother is delighted: “I had bet on this!” she said. "People were sick and tired of the scandals, the fat cats filling their pockets while so many people were out of work..."

As if the Socialists were not filling their pockets too, from hidden commission fees on international industrial and military contracts... But crowds are dancing in the streets, so everything is fine, for now.

Las Vegas. Monte Carlo Resort. Thursday 5 June 1997.

Dean Radin, who now runs the Consciousness Research Lab at UNLV, hosts this conference for the small gathering of SSE members who come together once a year. He's left Bigelow's organization, returning to general parapsychology research. I was the first speaker, but we left at noon to talk with Bob Bigelow who starts a project to send Americans back to the Moon and build a permanent base there. It occurred to me that if anybody was going to do it, it would not be a politician or a scientist but a real estate developer from the Nevada desert, where there is no usable land, no breathable air, and little available water – not unlike the moon.

My SSE presentation reported on my statistics from Larry Hatch's catalogue. Peter Sturrock followed with his investigations of sighting frequency. He claims that it increases at the rise or setting of Neptune and correlates with local sidereal time, with more cases when the local zenith points to an area of the sky about 21 hours in right ascension. This left me skeptical, because he doesn't start from the latest dataset. He'd have benefited from inviting comments before publishing (**39**).

Jean-Jacques Velasco also spoke, in his broken English, aided by a blonde woman who ran his transparencies. She seemed as confused by his instructions as the audience was confused by his slides.

Jean-Jacques attributed the Belgian triangles to US experimental platforms. There's only one case in France, he said, in a pocket of the border that one craft ignored, flying in a straight line at low speed and low altitude, so the witness saw it clearly. The devices are rigid dirigibles with electric engines. They come from Germany, maneuver over Belgium and always turn around at the French border, Velasco said. The sightings stopped at the beginning of the Gulf War, another indication that the Belgian wave was rehearsal for military action.

Were the maneuvers used to calibrate civilian reports, with the ufologists in the role of opportunistic intermediaries? The exercise is reminiscent of the *Pentacle Memorandum's* recommendations in the 1950s: a secret, large-scale military maneuver exploiting known stimuli – and useful idiots.

Later the same day.

Janine and I had dinner with John Petersen at *New York New York*, the latest casino in Vegas, an architectural wonder. Today's *New York Times* carries Senator Strom Thurmond's repudiation of Corso's claims about Roswell. Petersen told us he'd spoken with an Army general who told him he'd actually seen a captured saucer and knew of a reverse engineering effort going on at four locations in Western States, in private companies. He added the technology was so weird he couldn't locate any scientist interested in spending time on it.

George Onet, Colm Kelleher, and Eric Davis are at the conference, back from their latest trip to the ranch where strange events continue. Bob Bigelow had given us a private briefing on the happenings, which include peculiar lights at night. These events began at 11:30 pm on Monday (June 2nd) as Colm and Eric went to the old homestead to take infrared photographs: an unusual light had appeared in one of the windows of the abandoned cabin. It was a moonless night, the starry sky clear.

They saw a globe of white light, slightly larger than a baseball, about 100 yards away, 20 feet off the ground, in front of a large tree. It blinked four times. Two dogs who had been cavorting became silent and still: "Each dog took up a position behind us, so close they touched us," Colm and Eric wrote.

Five minutes later Eric saw a large black shadow, about 60 feet by 60 feet through the branches of the tree. It obliterated the sky and the stars. It had definite boundaries but no shape. He felt it was watching them. The object faded slowly, and the dogs resumed their playing. No evidence of any traces or intruders was found in the ensuing investigation.

In recent days a mosquito infestation at the ranch, "worse than the plagues of Egypt," has driven the observers away. "They bite us even through our gloves," Colm told me.

Las Vegas. Monte Carlo Resort. Friday 6 June 1997.

John Petersen is angry because I pretend to check up the statements of his mysterious general, but I am tired of hints and rumors. If there's a crashed saucer somewhere, let's find it; but if it's just another disinformation yarn, let's ground it once and for all. I won't be another soft target for silly tales. Plenty of others play that role willingly.

Over a long talk with Velasco I learned that the French Institute for Advanced Defense Studies (IHEDN) was doing a new study. He twice testified before them. In the meantime, his son Manuel, a graduate of a biotech school with full qualifications, cannot find any work in Europe. "I never imagined that my own son would be on welfare," Jean-Jacques said sadly. I suggested that Manuel meet us in Amsterdam at the biotech congress where I give a talk later this month: many potential employers will be there.

My friend Dick Shoup, from Interval Research, left the SSE audience puzzled today, describing the "Roots of Not" that lead to his multi-dimensional logics. Later, Dean Radin spoke of meta-analyses of parapsychology statistics, promoting his book with thunder and lightning from the magic theater's special effects.

Janine and I concluded that if the results were so meager it didn't follow that parapsychology was wrong, simply that for the last 50 years psychical researches had not been re-stated radically enough.

Hummingbird. Tuesday 17 June 1997.

Bob Bigelow just called to discuss recent events at the Utah ranch. "The phenomenon allows itself to be photographed, it observes us," he told me over the phone. Contact has been achieved, he believes, in the form of the message to Eric. But where are those pictures?

I worked all day on the financing of a new startup, Class Data Systems. I will setup their headquarters in the U.S. (**40**).

The French police have caught Ira Einhorn, Catherine told us this morning. He was arrested near Bordeaux in a converted windmill where he lived since 1992 with his Swedish wife under the name "Eugène Mallon."

14

Mabillon. Saturday 21 June 1997.

The Solstice finds us in Paris again, waking up in socialist bliss. Last night we had dinner with Olivier and his wife (at *Mandarin*) as he gets ready for a conference in New York. In a happy mood we sought names for the baby boy, expected in August.

Le Figaro has paid for my first article, a piece about the Band of Angels. I had to laugh when I saw the details of my stipend. They owed me 1700 francs, out of which came insurance, social security for illness and retirement, "widowhood dues" of 1.70FF (do I have a widow?), "supplemental" insurance, and "generalized social contributions," a newly-invented tax from the fertile mind of bureaucrats.

Thus, I get 1287.06 francs, some $200, a sum on which I am naturally expected to pay French income tax! The paper itself contributes to all these plans so my little piece ends up costing them 2536.70 francs. Government bureaucratic parasites get 1249.64 FF off the top, a whopping 49.3%. How does this help the poor French worker?

Mabillon. Sunday 22 June 1997.

My mother, more emaciated than at my last visit, remains well aware of the world. On a lively tone she spoke of meeting writer Roland Villeneuve down the street and recalled drinking our fine spring water in Belmont: "I can still taste it," she told us with delight.

Amsterdam. Thursday 26 June 1997.

The Golden Tulip hotel, also known as Barbizon Palace, is near the central station where the dark red *Thalys* makes its final stop. The "high speed" train takes over five hours to come from Paris because it still uses the old tracks in Belgium and Holland. It rained all day long, with chilly drops over muddy fields and the hazy horizon. We walked through the narrow streets after lunch, admired the Old Church and its carillon, elbowed our way over canal bridges busy with the crowds of the red-light district, and then slept through the rest of the afternoon, nestled in the fluffy luxury of a warm Dutch down comforter. We can afford to rest a bit: The last few days have been marked by constructive meetings with my partners. Tomorrow I speak about the financing of startups at the biotech workshop.

Mabillon. Sunday 29 June 1997.

The French government talks of support for innovation while suppressing stock options, blocking pension funds and imposing a wealth tax. It will save money by increasing the ranks of bureaucrats to stimulate the economy (!) while reducing the work week to 35 hours and will "create jobs" by forcing managers to retire at 60…

Defense consultant Gilbert Payan believes the Roswell crash was a setup on the part of extraterrestrials who influence our destiny. He did provide valuable background on Bernard Veyret and François Louange, whom I plan to invite to a new workshop planned by Peter Sturrock under Laurance Rockefeller's sponsorship. I already knew Louange, who digitized the Costa Rica photograph for me. Veyret, from Bordeaux, is an expert on biological effects of radiation.

"Few Frenchmen have understood that the State was dead; the State is a parasite, like the Mafia, extracting payment in the form of taxes," said Dupas over dinner at *Chien qui Fume*. "The State won't really die, of course; it'll simply linger on as a huge, obsolete skeleton while creative activity moves elsewhere." The marginal tax rate for middle-class French folks now reaches 61%, an absurd level.

Mabillon. Monday 30 June 1997.

There's a sense of luxury to the rain. It makes everything shine. Time becomes even more irrelevant as the visible horizon narrows down to a few shops, the bus stop, and the shelter of a storefront.

French shares are at record levels, an artificial phenomenon: Jean-Jacques Chaban-Delmas, when I saw him at Matra, told me the de-nationalization program had unleashed vast amounts of money.

Hummingbird. Sunday 6 July 1997.

Along with its roving robot, NASA's Pathfinder probe has landed on Mars and is alive, the first ground-level exploration of any planet in over 20 years. This afternoon we spent three pleasant hours with Paul Hynek reminiscing about Mimi and Allen. He now works with Bandai, a Japanese multimedia firm. Mimi, who had never lived alone, had adapted to Scottsdale, busy with archaeology.

Douglass Price-Williams tells me he met with Bob Bigelow at my suggestion, with mixed results. Bob was frank in explaining the situation at the Utah ranch but he wouln't tolerate any interference with "his" phenomenon. He wants to deepen this relationship without any help. He only perked up when Douglass spoke of his own psychic experiments, but he ignored the plea for deeper research.

Hummingbird. Wednesday 9 July 1997.

A typical day in the life of a California venture capitalist: up at seven, on the computer for quick updates, then at the office to review business plans, meet with my French assistant and run off to finalize documents. In the early afternoon, brain aflame with impractical research schemes, I drive to Cupertino to the new offices of Class Data Systems, the latest Internet start-up we incubate.

Hummingbird. Thursday 17 July 1997.

Stephen Greer and an acolyte are spreading the story that they've developed cancer as a result of harmful beams from government coverup agents in the desert aiming instruments at them (**41**).

Michael Corbin, in Denver, has made some important notes from Ruppelt's files, of which his group had custody until they were bought up by CUFOS, using Bigelow's $5,000 check. He writes:

"In Ruppelt's secret file marked 'not for publication under any circumstances' he notes that at a crucial, secret, explosive conference, furious that he had not been told the whole truth about UFO cases within his command, (General Charles) Cabell demanded a new Air Force UFO investigation. He screamed to his subordinates: "I've been lied to, and lied to, and lied to!" Ruppelt also notes that, unknown to Cabell, a wire recorder under his chair documented every word.

Shortly after this, Cabell was picked to become the number 2 man at the CIA." Evidently, a lot of people including scientists and Presidents have been "lied to."

Las Vegas. Saturday 19 July 1997.

John Alexander, who picked me up at the Vegas airport for the board's ninth meeting, is concerned about a botched palace revolution on the part of the "consciousness group" on the NIDS Board: Ian Stevenson, Emily Cooke, Diane Arcangel, and Bruce Grayson have sent abrasive letters criticizing the lack of research.

Bigelow didn't take this well: the group had made only minimal contributions and failed to fill the open research positions on the staff. John wanted my help in patching things up. Oddly, the meeting that followed was one of the most constructive I'd attended. Bob chaired it genially, and the absence of the 'consciousness' group actually lifted a black cloud from our discussions.

After sending out 1131 questionnaires George Onet had obtained 160 responses from Utah ranchers, including sixteen mutilation reports, all bovine. Most occurred on ranches of over 100 acres with more than 20 animals. All the incidents took place in the warmer months.

Hal told us about a terrifying encounter his 20-year-old son Devin had while driving near Phoenix on 17 June. The object was boomerang-shaped, had four huge lights and dived out of the sky in a vertical position. It was as big as a Boeing 747. This led us to discuss coincidences in our lives. Hal recalls the day when, as a very studious boy, he left his engineering studies in a fit of atypical behavior to wander downtown, got into a bookstore and mechanically picked up Adamski's book, "and it changed my life," he said, "even after I recognized his story was bullshit!"

For me it was the disk in Pontoise in 1955, then the coincidence of being in Paul Muller's office in Meudon when he opened, and threw away, the letter from Aimé Michel offering to turn over all his files to Paris observatory; then the meeting with Peter Sturrock at Stanford, and my move to SRI that "happened" to coincide with Hal's project.

We heard good staff reports about the Utah ranch. In previous sessions I had advocated to deploy a spectroscope. Hal has built such a system, combined with his LED communication device. Eric demonstrated it for us: a Fresnel lens in front of a simple system focuses the light onto an optical fiber that takes it to an off-the-shelf spectral analyzer and displays the resulting curve on a laptop computer. All we need now is for an Alien craft to come and pose…

San Francisco. Sunday 20 July 1997.

I flew back to San Francisco with John Petersen. We discussed his new book *Out of the Blue*. He told me of having lunch recently at the Pentagon with a high-ranking officer to whom he showed Jim Schnabel's *Remote Viewers*. In walks another distinguished man, greeted warmly by his friend. Seeing the book, the man comments, "Yeah, this is real stuff. I've got eight people doing remote viewing for me." Thereupon his friend told John, "I should introduce you guys, this is the new director of the Defense Intelligence Agency." So much for the story that work on military remote viewing is dead.

I felt lazy today, had lunch in Chinatown, and I enjoyed the spectacle of the fog rolling in around Telegraph Hill and the flames in the eyes of the kids who dance at Union Square.

Now I come across this wise comment by physicist Paul Dirac: "The hardest part of scientific progress is getting over prejudice."

Spring Hill. Saturday 26 July 1997.

Around our tower the air is pure nectar. There are apples in the trees and tall flowers everywhere, bowing like Geishas as we pass. I can't shake the feeling of an undeciphered secret here, and that we're missing it. The night sky was so powerful, swirling close over the trees, that Janine herself had sudden doubts about selling the ranch.

Yesterday I had a frank discussion with a producer for the Discovery Channel. "What would it take to get you on the show we're preparing about abductions?" she asked. "We can't imagine doing it without you." I said thanks, but anything I'd say about the new research would be overwhelmed by the outlandish Hopkins trivia. I was stunned when she asked, "Would you reconsider if we postponed our program?" But I see no reason to jump into this; or interfere with it.

Half-Moon Bay. Monday 4 August 1997.

I am recovering from surgery, the removal of nasal polyps that blocked my breathing. We're leaving for a week on the road, along the coast with a visit to Roger Brenner who takes care of a small yellow house with a flower garden next to the ocean. The surf pulses in the salty air. Roger writes poems and physics theories.

A reader sends me "Greetings from the Exterior Circle of the New Flesh Palladium," in the tradition of Randolph, Crowley, and Maria de Nagloska. The convergence of abduction stories with sex magic is obvious in the sado-masochistic stories told by Hopkins and Jacobs.

Timber Cove. Tuesday 5 August 1997.

Frank Drake, founder of SETI, was on the radio today. He made sure his listeners knew he didn't believe in UFOs. "So, *perfesser*, you've been looking for these signals for what, 37 years? And you haven't found anything?" asked the host with heavy irony. To Drake's dismay most of the calls from the public asked about UFOs.

Fort Bragg. Noyo River Inn. Wednesday 6 August 1997.

We left Timber Cove late after lingering in a hot bath and wondering how the rascally raccoons had sneaked into our room and stolen the bananas Janine had brought. The charming burglars even opened her handbag, ignored the money but dug out her tasty lipstick.

We stopped for lunch in Elk, the weather a hint of the eternal spring that surely awaits us in Paradise. At the Little River cemetery, the path leads to a sinkhole and a terrifying view of the crumbling cliffs. Further north, just before Point Cabrillo, a State Park preserves a uniquely fantastic landscape of blowholes and caverns where the ocean foams and tumbles, lifting seaweeds, kelp, and rotten timber.

Spring Hill. Thursday 7 August 1997.

While Fort Bragg was sunny, Glass Beach looked like the setting for a saucer crash with its rows of rusted metal and acres of rounded pearls, left over from a city dump that burned so hot and fierce all the bottles exploded and melted while a metal river spilled over the sand. As we walked back from Larry Spring's quaint shop a stranger recognized me: he asked about our research, and my trip to Russia!

We drove north to the Lost Coast and through the redwoods to Leggett. Back at the ranch the pool is very tempting; a carpet of fallen apples fills the air with the smell of cider.

Hummingbird. Friday 22 August 1997.

Maxime was born this morning in Paris. Olivier tells us there were some tense moments: the baby didn't cry at first and had to be reanimated. He will be under observation and antibiotic treatment for several days: both mother and son remain in the hospital.

The latest issue of *New Scientist* (**42**) seems to deal a blow to Miguel Alcubierre's concept of a space drive: two physicists from Tufts University have computed it would take an inconceivably large amount of energy to sustain the spacetime warp he proposed.

Hummingbird. Sunday 31 August 1997.

On the way back, we heard the news of the horrible death of the Princess of Wales and her lover in a car crash.

Tabloid photographers hounded Diana; her Mercedes ended up shattered in a Paris tunnel. Such a tragic symbol: A reminder of the fallacy of celebrity; but people sense a warning about an uglier world to come.

Boston. The Eliot Hotel. Tuesday 9 September 1997.

Another trip, negotiations with financial power brokers: weariness, short sleep in this gray, greedy city I detest. Meeting at Oppenheimer.

Last week we received very sad news from Jean-Jacques Velasco: his younger son Nicolas had committed suicide, disgusted with the state of the world. Jean-Jacques and Danièle are devastated.

Here Janine is my great support. Her venture into real estate is an obvious success; she just sold a beautiful house to an executive from WebTV.

Hummingbird. Sunday 14 September 1997.

John Alexander has produced a scathing analysis of Corso's book, highlighting its many contradictions. I urged him to publish it, but the last thing he wants is to be thrown into the swamp of ufological controversies, accused by the believers of being part of some coverup while being trashed by science reviewers. Yet, if John and I don't come forward with the information we do have, how could these lies ever be stopped? John said he'd only sent his list to Hal, Kit, and me.

We went to Peter Beren's 50th birthday party in Berkeley yesterday afternoon, and to a get-together at the home of a Robertson-Stephens executive in Menlo Park, both crowds interesting in different ways.

Spring Hill. Friday 19 September 1997.

Guérin, who is reading *Science Interdite*, has sent me two letters, warm and friendly now, with a passing reproach for devoting too many pages to my private life. Yet other readers find those pages valuable because they show how research acquires meaning among concerns with job and kids, bursts of joy, and occasional depression in defeat, all those items that classical books try to hide. After all, my record begins as the simple diary of a confused teen-ager.

Guérin is struck by my very first description of him as a tall fellow: "You make me laugh," he writes. "Is that the impression I made on you? That's surrealistic, you're taller than I am... On the psychological side you describe me as choleric, which I take issue with, and disliking contradiction, which I concede…." My turn to giggle.

Hummingbird. Monday 22 September 1997.

The Internet group around theoretician Jack Sarfatti reminds me of Ira's network by its wide-ranging set of skills and its political overtones. Alluding to NIDS, Jack writes: "You chaps are obviously part of the Others predicted to me in 1952 by a sort of conscious computer and spacecraft from the future that we will now attempt to build. Even if that is simply my creative imagination at play, it would be a fun thing to try. Let's test Vallee's hypothesis!"

Meandering through Jack's group led me to Nick Herbert, who seeks "a new pathway for science incorporating previously discarded and marginal ways of thinking into a new synthesis." He would start with alchemy and tantra: "Alchemy is based on the notion of a partially psychic chemistry in which the mind of the alchemist merges with the material cooking in his alembic. Tantra teaches that the universe is not mere motion of dead matter but the sexual play of two divine beings and seeks techniques to directly participate in that holy play. Tantra begins with the surprising claim that sex is not only holy, but that it is a direct participation in the creation of the world."

Hummingbird. Saturday 27 September 1997.

Today is my mother's 97th birthday in radiant Paris, where she says fall has begun with splendid weather. Olivier plans to go see her with his baby son and my gift of *Forbidden Science*.

Alain Dupas called with the good news that Hachette would publish *Enjeux*. I continue to look at France with a mixture of idealistic love and gut-wrenching suspicion. The bureaucracy keeps expanding while elegant ministers make empty speeches about the need to create productive jobs and to trim government. Unfortunately, they have no skill to do the former and no intention to do the latter.

Yesterday one of our French visitors unfolded a financial paper from Paris with large headlines about a new round of tax increases. "How are we going to stimulate innovation in this climate?" he asked with a sigh. "Anyone with smarts will either leave the country, as you did, or keep a cushy job in some government office." But I didn't leave because of taxes, I told him: I was much too poor to be taxed.

I turned 58 on Wednesday, so we gathered some friends for a party. Handwriting expert Ted Widmer came over with Diana Hall (ex-Diane LaVey) in a stunning dress and frosty blond hair. Catherine joined us, and Gary Shockley. Ted returned the six pages of Jim McDonald's manuscript that I had selected from his diary. The assessment he gave was insightful: "The most striking feature is the small size and the high speed. This is an obvious contradiction: you can't write fast and tiny. He does have large capitals, a sign of strong ego, like a man who needs to be at center stage. This is a highly emotional script, characteristic of someone who is logical but impaired by emotions that cloud his personality. Irregularities in pressure could relate to infantile trauma. He concentrates well and is bright, but I'm struck by the emotionalism that gets in his way. There is no spontaneity; he is compulsive, probably had a strict mother. He has a short fuse; he is impatient and tries to control himself. The last entry shows amazing changes of pressure, as if he was under tremendous inner stress."

I told Ted the writer had tried to kill himself the next day.

On the way to New York. Sunday 28 September 1997.

Peter Sturrock has contacted a small group to conduct the first scientific assessment of the UFO problem since the Robertson Panel. It will assemble at the Rockefeller estate in Pocantico Hills.

Forbidden Science is starting to have some impact in France. Writer Michel Picard says he found himself both "irritated and fascinated: you have published intimate truths deliberately, in full awareness, measuring the risks that implied, from *mièvrerie* to grotesque through indecency, the whole thing on a background of auto-analysis, candy for the psychology sect! You emerge with little harm from this assessment which concerns a particular epoch, a past era pre-eminent in any life, when hair refuses to turn gray, when the mind ignores its own limits and aspires to sublime conquests."

He goes on with an essay in personality analysis: "I find a chaotic soul in you, always under tension, not a balanced state. Tension between that image of the humanist you carefully cultivate and your fear you will be taken for something else; tension between your disdain for false glory and your desire to be recognized as an avant-garde mind; tension between science and conscience, aspiration to a form of mysticism (you mention "ecstasy") and that powerful opposite, pragmatism, even rigor; tension between pessimism and exaltation, thirst for intimacy if not solitude (retreat) and the glow of notoriety; tension between occasional sadness and fugitive happiness, between disgust and determination, between desire to understand—therefore to invest yourself by grabbing the enigma and challenging it—and desire to exist, to go down inside yourself.

"This gets translated, in your case, into ambivalent introspection (in your image?) wandering between sorrow and appeasement, exaltation and ponderation; tension between the secret hope to reach the very top of your intellectual and spiritual faculties, and the vanity of things and people, of all existential quest..."

So much for his "irritation." He goes on to describe what "fascinates" him: "The historical interest of your book is considerable. From that viewpoint it is captivating. For two reasons. We are witnessing here, from the inside, the birth of two Copernican revolutions (and a paradigmatic collapse). The concept of "non-human/superhuman consciousness" is introduced both through ufology and through informatics. You are at the heart of the action; your testimony is crucial. I note, as we go along, that ufology is an inexhaustible source of frustration since all pioneers, you included, once hoped to solve the enigma..."

Yes, revealing so much makes me open to misinterpretation but that is the price one pays to achieve change. Past feelings and old traumas, those biased gyroscopes of personality, lose their power as intimate baggage once they are in the public arena.

New York. Sheraton Manhattan. Monday 29 September 1997.

The sun came out when I walked over to see Shel Gordon, and the streets were dry by the time we went out to lunch at Castellano's. Shel looks a bit older and mellower, but he remains a prince of finance with no trace of bragging or arrogance, no ostentation: his Amex card is plain ordinary green. He's come out of retirement for the second time, to serve as non-executive chairman of *Union Bancaire Privée*, an institution of which I'd never heard. It turns out to be Europe's largest private bank. As I noted the simple elegance of his fifth-floor suite, he joked that it was the first time he had an office low enough in a skyscraper to allow him to see the faces of people walking on the sidewalk. We spoke of Ira with little doubt that his uncontrolled rage, not some complex government plot, killed Holly.

A Rockefeller limo took me to Tarrytown in less than 45 minutes of sunbathed countryside and Hudson vistas. Mark Rodeghier, John Schuessler, and Erling Strand were already in the sitting room of the mansion. Later I met Hal as well as Jean-Jacques Velasco, courageously keeping his commitment in spite of his son's suicide, and François Louange, eager to discuss Corso. Other investigators arrived: Dick Haines, Illobrand von Ludwiger among them.

Kykuit ("lookout" in Dutch) was the Rockefeller family home for four generations before it was turned over to a Trust. It is a sensational location for Sturrock's conference, and far more beautiful than our group of tired, middle-aged academics deserves.

15

Kykuit. Tuesday 30 September 1997.

Twenty-two participants gathered this morning in the efficiently-furnished conference room of the Rockefeller retreat. Peter hopes the data will be compelling enough to wake up the science community to the reality of a truly novel problem. The science panelists he'd handpicked were introduced: Gunther Reitz, a German aerospace expert specialized in microgravity and ionizing radiation biophysics; Jay Melosh of the planetary laboratory at the University of Arizona, an expert in impact cratering and meteorites; Jim Papike of the University of New Mexico, a geologist and geochemist specialized in lunar evolution and Mars missions; Randy Jokipii of the University of Arizona, expert on space plasmas and cosmic rays; Tom Holzer of NCAR in Boulder, space plasma and interplanetary physics; von Eshelmann of Stanford, concerned with planetary exploration through radio techniques; and my guests Bernard Veyret, of Bordeaux, who studies the bioeffects of microwaves, non-ionizing radiation and plant biology, and François Louange, an expert in signal processing, photo-analysis, and detection networks from the european space agency and Fleximage. David Pritchard, MIT physics professor and student of abductions, completes the panel.

We began with high hopes that a group of this level of sophistication would generate new insights. None of that happened.

Erling Strand's presentation about the Hessdalen lights left the impression that the phenomenon was only a geophysical effect that had little to do with our main problem: the panel had naïvely expected to see the most convincing evidence on the first day. Pritchard reminded them that the objective was only to provide a perspective to explore the question, "What additional research is warranted?" but not to decide if the material "proved" the existence of UFOs. But Peter noted a mismatch between the presenters and the panel: the scientists shouldn't have to do the summing up.

Pritchard took me aside: since our meeting with John Mack in Cambridge he'd "gone to shaman school" with Michael Harner, the author of *The Way of the Shaman* who had roamed South America in search of wisdom. David went down into his own spiritual underworld, but he confessed that lingering scientific hangups interfered with the guidance into another realm.

David remains committed to the abduction concept while others on the panel roll their eyes whenever that is mentioned. He told me that 90% of ordinary reports turned out to be false UFOs while abduction reports, in contrast, were 90% genuine. It was my turn to roll my eyes: my own experience with the 70-odd abductions I have studied indicates that many (but not all) details are by-products of botched retrospective hypnosis or horribly biased reconstructions.

Over dinner I spoke to Veyret, an urbane and friendly fellow. He's intrigued by the Prioré machine and by the work of Benveniste. I also had a rare chance to talk to Mark Rodeghier, knowledgeable and lucid when he speaks of technical topics like datamining.

I do hope this workshop can bring us closer together, leading to constructive teamwork. Yet palpable fear hangs over the science panel. They are terrified of what their colleagues might say if their presence here was revealed.

They seem especially afraid that UFOs might turn out to be real.

When I asked Jim Papike why the Mars robots hadn't been sent to any of the dark areas that had a better chance of showing signs of life, or at least significant seasonal changes than the yellow-orange deserts, I learned that such a probe was indeed scheduled to reach the south pole next year.

Kykuit. Wednesday 1 October 1997.

On this hilltop overlooking a bend of the majestic Hudson the weather alternates between sunshine and beatific rain over trees and pastures. Both are the work of man: the pastures were bulldozed by the Rockefellers' landscape architects and the giant trees were brought over, fully-grown, from many parts of the world, and planted by helicopter. In a few places the leaves are spotted with yellow but the view from the terrace is of idyllic green lawns.

We were given a tour of the art galleries and the mansion itself. The modern statues that frame sublime views of the valley show slender bodies in aerial dances, in contrast with our group of professors, all beer bellies and bushy beards, talking of their plans to hit Phaeton, a dead comet, with a projectile that will throw off material for study.

Peter Sturrock redefined the challenge: "When Condon wrote his report he said two things: There wasn't enough evidence of a threat, and there wasn't any evidence that science would be advanced by a study of the phenomenon. Well, thirty years later there's ample unexplained data, so science would be advanced by studying it."

Jay Melosh disagreed: he hadn't seen convincing evidence; he wasn't ready to sign. Even Von Eshelmann said he couldn't state that science would be advanced.

Later the same day.

Over a private lunch in the old hayloft with Mr. Rockefeller, Peter Sturrock, and Counselor Henry Diamond, Dick Haines introduced the mathematical precision of English crop circles, in which he deciphers an alphabet of symbols on a large scroll. When I pointed out that those circles that aren't hoaxes were probably caused by British beam weapon tests Henry Diamond thanked me for clarifying the issue. Earlier Dick had given a balanced presentation on pilot sightings, so his change of focus was puzzling when he speculated about crop circles as a communication system with undisclosed "higher worlds."

Yesterday, when he gave an analysis of the Vancouver Island photograph of 8 October 1981, both Jokipii and Melosh commented the disk seen in the picture could be an artefact of the film or a hoax by the processing lab. Others found it incredible that the witness wouldn't have seen the object. Later Mark Rodeghier took the floor and spoke of some 500 cases of vehicle interference, and John Schuessler impressed the panel with the Cash-Landrum vehicle. But wasn't that a human prototype? Opinions are starting to change; the critics are shaken as the talks go on. I have turned over my file of the Council Bluffs material analysis case to Melosh.

Even later.

The reception and dinner at the Playhouse were interesting to the point of spookiness. The august structure includes a bowling alley, two swimming pools and tennis courts, a croquet field. The dark wood-panelled walls of the grand dining room bore portraits of the family in the early days of World War Two, the Rockefeller sons in uniform. Henry Diamond asked me to sit with Laurance Rockefeller and Maurice Strong (under-secretary of the UN), Bob Jahn (who arrived yesterday), Hal, Jean-Jacques, Veyret, and Gunther Reitz.

Laurance at 86 is urbane, curious about everything, an inquisitive spirit with a global vision. He explained with some humor how he had forced Princeton to accept his funding for Jahn's research: two engineering grants from McDonnell were going to be withdrawn…

I gathered that it was Henry Diamond who recruited Sturrock to head up the workshop when Laurance inquired who had the credibility to produce a report that could influence scientific opinion. Such a report is essential before one can go before political entities such as Unesco, the essential step in approaching the U.N. again.

Maurice Strong recalled with a dry smile it had been done before, in the 70s, under the not-so-credible auspices of tiny Grenada (**43**). Later, as he was concerned about getting back to U.N. headquarters, Laurance asked graciously: "At what time do you want the helicopter tomorrow, Maurice? Is 9 o'clock all right?"

Kykuit. Thursday 2 October 1997.

Dave Pritchard, who sat next to me, is a clear thinker capable of lightning calculations whenever physics is discussed. Mike Swords is rougher. He keeps drawing shapes in three colors of ink. They become increasingly elaborate as the day goes on. When he heard of my research on physical specimens Mike told me there were cases of slag-like residue in the NICAP files, but he didn't offer to share them.

While we walked from the conference center to the great mansion, Dick Haines told me in confidence he'd been training teams of night observers, hoping for human-initiated contact *à la* Greer, with no success. Hal told me that, like me, he'd gone to the edge of Area 51. He saw extraordinary lights he couldn't explain.

Most of the panelists are formal, except for Melosh, wearing the same sweater since the first day. In another era he would have smoked a pipe. He keeps grumbling that most of the sightings are probably hoaxes; he plans to leave early.

Mr. Rockefeller attended my lecture on luminosity estimates (**44**) with Henry Diamond by his side. We heard of some good French data. None of the investigators knew of the Council Bluffs case that was the focus of my second presentation (**45**).

Jay Melosh took the sample in his hands and said he had no explanation for the case. He'd read my material, including the police photos, analysis reports, and the Air Force study, and was re-considering his negative position.

Seattle. Sorrento Hotel. Tuesday 7 October 1997.

The workshop is over; the group of eminent scientists has disbanded, and I have the feeling this ambitious project is simply going to fizzle out. It won't re-open the debates that the Condon report had closed. The academic community has no interest in new investigations, contrary to what Prof. Sturrock and Mr. Rockefeller were hoping for.

Getting back to the real world, I landed in Seattle in a rainstorm. Before flying home, I will visit a new medical device company with products to treat tendons and ligaments, pain and inflammation.

I hear from France that Maurice Papon, the most obvious symbol of the police state in the hypocritical French Establishment, finally goes on trial in Bordeaux this week. He was the man who allowed the 1962 police riot and the Charonne killings (**46**) and covered it all up as he had covered up deportation of the Jews during the war.

Spring Hill. Sunday 12 October 1997.

Yesterday Olivier visited my mother in Paris. She was moved at seeing Maxime, marvelling at the baby's composure. She reads *Science Interdite*, she said, with intense emotion. I feel a sense of fulfilment, knowing that both of these events have brought her happiness, and that I can go on to my next self-imposed missions: setting the foundation for another ten years of professional and research work; none of which would be possible without Janine's energy, weaving together the strands of a busy life.

Hummingbird. Thursday 16 October 1997.

When I met him for lunch yesterday Fred Beckman was incisive, inquisitive and hopelessly self-pitying. I'd brought him my two Pocantico papers as a gesture of comradeship, but he quickly set them aside to start on a list of questions. "Someone" had given him a roster of the workshop participants; would I confirm who was there? "Someone" had said Corso's agent William J. Birnes (who is also Sturrock's agent) was close to Pandolfi at CIA. I tired of his nagging interrogations. If he weren't one of my few remaining links to Allen's memory I wouldn't see him again.

Las Vegas. Friday 17 October 1997.

One of the most interesting topics we must study is that of synchronicity, after Carl Jung and Arthur Koestler. What was the probability, for instance, that another Jacques Vallée might exist, who (1) was an astrophysicist and (2) was interested in the study of extraterrestrial intelligence? Sending him some articles yesterday, I looked up his address, *Chemin des Mésanges* in Gloucester, Ontario, and shuddered: when I invented a fictional street name to hide my mother's address in my early Journal I named it *Rue de la Mésange!*

Las Vegas. Later the same day.

This is the tenth Science Board meeting at NIDS. We assembled early in Bob Bigelow's office as a small task force composed of John

Petersen, Kit, Hal, John Alexander, Edgar Michell, and me. The staff has now recorded 38 paranormal events at the ranch.

"What if two-way communication does happen?" Bob asked. He is convinced that one-way exchanges (from "them" to Eric) have already taken place, in the form of telepathic messages and dreams. Yet the staff is fearful of the property; they sense an evil presence, some even call it demonic. Chad Deetken always prays to protect himself when he keeps watch at night. I emphasized the need for a medical and psychological screen, and informed consents from everyone.

In the ensuing debate I was surprised to find that Hal was the only one who knew of the 1972 Philip Group experiments in Toronto, where an imaginary ghost with physical effects was created (**47**).

We assembled in the boardroom, the group now stripped of its "consciousness" cadre. Kit set the tone smartly: "Let's begin the analysis of the body of data, let's avoid telling ghost stories."

Las Vegas. Saturday 18 October 1997.

There was an incident at the ranch on 28 August about 2 am when Chad Deetken and Terry Sherman saw a light from the ridge. Chad saw a glow and his photos show nothing, but Terry observed a ring of light opening up above ground and a black creature emerging from it. Going to the site later they found no tracks: ghost stories, after all.

During the observation Terry, a big tall strapping cowboy, was reportedly trembling with intense fright. Chad, who had looked through the same night-vision system, saw nothing. This triggered a technical discussion among the physicists, and it caused Bob Bigelow to make an emotional speech to suggest that "They" might be using means beyond our physics. He went further: what if there were undetectable presences there, even during the day? (Note next page)

Ed Mitchell said an image might be created nonlocally in the vision center of an observers' brain, so the phenomenon might be observer-dependent. The next evening, on 29 August, there was an even more dramatic incident when the cattle left the ranch *en masse*, crossing a shallow creek. Terry had much trouble herding the cows back towards the property. They were in two groups that seemed highly stressed, as if confined by invisible entities, while a small red light darted around the herd. (Note). When it came to the head of his horse the animal bolted and threw him off. It jumped into a ravine, hurting itself, while the cows climbed all over one another. One animal subsequently died.

In the ensuing session Colm listed the 38 incidents he had graphed. Johndale Solem partially reassured us when he described a private flight to Utah, during which his plane triggered our surveillance cameras at the ranch, proving that some reported "low-flying lights" actually came from ordinary aircraft landing at Roosevelt.

Chad Deetken gave an impassioned, but unscientific description of the English crop circles around Alton Barn and Silberry Hill. He discounted the hoax hypothesis.

In the afternoon I said it was time to reinvent the Institute. We had lost sight of our constituency, I emphasized: do we work for the public good? The science community? Paranormal researchers? There was an urgent need to tighten up our procedures and to better protect our people in the field. I suggested using the Nevada (Wilson) ranch as a control site against the Utah property.

Hummingbird. Monday 20 October 1997.

My mother says again how delighted she is at reading *Science Interdite*: "It reminds me so much of all the discussions we had," she told me, "on so many topics." On the way back from the ranch Janine and I suddenly realized this was our 37th wedding anniversary, so the Champagne bottle came out as soon as we reached home, and we gave no further thought to serious work.

(Note): In 2015 a young English professor named Robert Guffey sent me his book entitled *Chameleo* about government experiments with invisibility. Although presented as a work of fiction, the book was based on a series of strange events in the San Diego area, involving encounters with agents who controlled invisibility devices and were harassing various researchers. Therefore Mr. Bigelow's assumption may have been prescient.

After I published *Revelations* I received a phone call in the middle of the night from a man who didn't give his name but made it clear he was involved in government experiments in optical control, including actual military maneuvers involving nearly-invisible vehicles.

Reverend Pat Robertson, founder and chairman of the Christian Coalition, recently launched a diatribe against those who believe in Aliens (**48**). He said if UFO occupants exist, they can only be demons trying to lead people away from Christ. People who believe in space Aliens should be put to death by stoning, he concluded.

Spring Hill. Saturday 8 November 1997.

Speaking of demonology, Anton LaVey has just left the planet. San Francisco feels oddly empty, although we hadn't seen him for over a decade and were repelled by his recent behavior. Janine says that more than a page has been turned, rather a long, colorful chapter.

"The Black Pope died on Halloween," a journalist said, the kind of rumor Anton and his entourage would plant. Anton actually died of pulmonary edema. His daughter Zeena called the registrar to verify the date: it didn't happen on Halloween. He died at 9 am on October 29. Diane told us she only felt an empty space. No progress on her book: she has reviewed what she wrote recently, hated it. "Now that the story is complete, at least I know Anton won't be reading it."

"Don't be too sure," I said, "He may be in heaven looking down. Wouldn't that be ironic? He did die at Saint Mary's Hospital."

She laughed and replied, "If so he must be angry! Anton wanted to appear immortal. The time, place, and manner of his death were supposed to be a grand mystery."

His grandson Stanton heard of the death from a girlfriend, so he went to the black house on California Street with a toy for Anton's baby boy Xerxes. He also brought flowers for Blanche Barton: a thoughtful gesture.

Hummingbird. Sunday 16 November 1997.

We drove away from the ranch late last night in another rainstorm, leaving Catherine by the fire, happily wrapped in a blanket. In the tower half-filled shelves remind us of all the moving left to do. Yet Spring Hill has enabled us to make tangible progress. Here we've assembled a body of data that challenges extant theories about the phenomenon, new software codes to study it and an epistemology inspired by information physics and retro-causality.

Back in Utah the latest devices have failed to document any hard data. Kit is increasingly weary of all this. He reverts to psychological explanations that leave me cold.

In the middle of all this General Hollanda Lima is said to have committed suicide in Brazil.

Circumstances are murky. He'd appeared on a television show on July 20th, confirming his participation in Operation "Prato" in September 1977 and the filming of numerous UFOs. Apparently healthy, the 56-year old colonel was lecturing and planning a book. He died on October 2nd.

Seattle. Bellevue Doubletree hotel. Friday 21 November 1997.

Storms have come a month early this year because of an El Niño condition in the Pacific, so the season's first snows newly cover the mighty volcanoes.

The scenery is so beautiful (not to mention memories of Bill Murphy and the elusive Lemurians) that I am thrilled to fly north along the range of the Cascades.

This meeting, hurriedly arranged by an executive recruiter, is with the founder of an investment fund who looks for a CEO.

Hummingbird. Tuesday 25 November 1997.

The broadband company COM21 is filing to go public in February. This IPO should please my partners since I spearheaded this investment, yet innovation is still a threatening concept to European business leaders, not an opportunity for social and economic change. So, it is without much optimism that I fly to France in two days for a venture capital summit at Sophia Antipolis, near Nice.

Mabillon. Saturday 29 November 1997.

Two in the morning, awake since midnight. We went straight to work when we landed yesterday, meeting briefly with Alain Dupas at *Mandarin* to give him the manuscript of *Enjeux*.

Now I can spend time with my son and grandson. We saw the baby for the first time yesterday. He was relaxed, losing his newborn hair, smiling in Janine's arms. Her happiness brings a special glow to her beauty, a loving woman with a new child to cherish.

Paris is subdued, busy as ever, closing down under damp fog. The problem of French industry is that every institution here is designed to exploit the labor of others rather than releasing their creativity.

Nice. Hotel Beau Rivage. Sunday 30 November 1997.

Little Maxime put a welcome touch of joy in my mother's apartment when we visited her yesterday. We spoke of people we had known and thoughts we'd shared. One of the accomplishments for which I am proudest, is to have been able to give *Forbidden Science* to her, and also to Aimé Michel, repaying some of his spiritual gifts to me.

A warm afternoon in Nice. The sun is setting on the *Promenade des Anglais*. I called Claude Poher. We agreed to meet after my panel.

Nice. Tuesday 2 December 1997.

Claude met me at Sophia Antipolis, wearing a black sweater under a gray jacket. He was jovial and healthy, happy to see me. We drove to Antibes under the rain, chatting about my mother whom he remembered well. Over lunch near the harbor fortifications he spoke of his retirement research. He has gone back to astrophysics, using an electronic camera to study galaxies from a home observatory under the clear skies of Provence. Claude thinks he's found a relationship between the width of spectral lines and the distance of galaxies that doesn't agree with the expansion model. His theory involves graviton-like particles he calls "universons."

We also spoke of zero-point energy: he doubts Puthoff's theory because "the energy release would have to be extremely short in order not to violate thermodynamics." Yet if he were resuming research today he'd follow a propulsion model, like Hal, he said.

The sun came out again, so we walked along the piers of Antibes among multimillion-dollar yachts owned by wealthy Arabs and Britons: "Heavy gas guzzlers, hardly able to leave the harbor," he called them in disgust. Claude reminded me he'd travelled 26,000 miles with his wife on a real sailboat, "not some floating saloon…"

While at CNES they thought they'd discovered the mechanism that explained both muscle paralysis from UFO exposure (large nerve cells are depolarized by the appropriate field) and motor interference in cars, but they were unable to prove their theory.

High above the Ionian Sea. Saturday 6 December 1997.

We drink bad airline coffee, yet nobody is complaining, too glad to fly towards Tel Aviv at last, the first such liaison in three days because Israel is in the grips of a tough strike. Now we're over Crete.

Tel Aviv. Sunday 7 December 1997.

The sun is up, people at the beach. Last night I had dinner with Dan Tolkowsky and Miriam. They told me I'd been lucky to get into the country: the airport is closed again, thousands are stranded. Dan is keenly interested in psychical research, so we spoke of Uri Geller and Rockefeller.

Dan seemed tired, but his book-filled apartment was vibrant and his current life very busy: he's a member of a three-man Israeli government commission conducting an audit of Mossad.

Tel Aviv. Thursday 11 December 1997.

Furious Mediterranean waves are hitting the shore. Curtains billow out in my room. Yesterday I reviewed the legal structure for the proposed new investment company and was offered the top position, but I find the structure far too complex.

Today Gideon Tolkowsky and I drove out to Nazareth to visit two startups amidst rains that sent mud sliding along the banks. On the way back from Tadin, where we held our Board meeting, we stopped in Netanya to meet ufologist David Kornitz at his apartment, a clean place filled with watercolors of flying ducks and seashore scenes.

Kornitz has had an interest in UFOs since 1942, when he was helping build field hospitals for the British army in North Africa: He'd met a

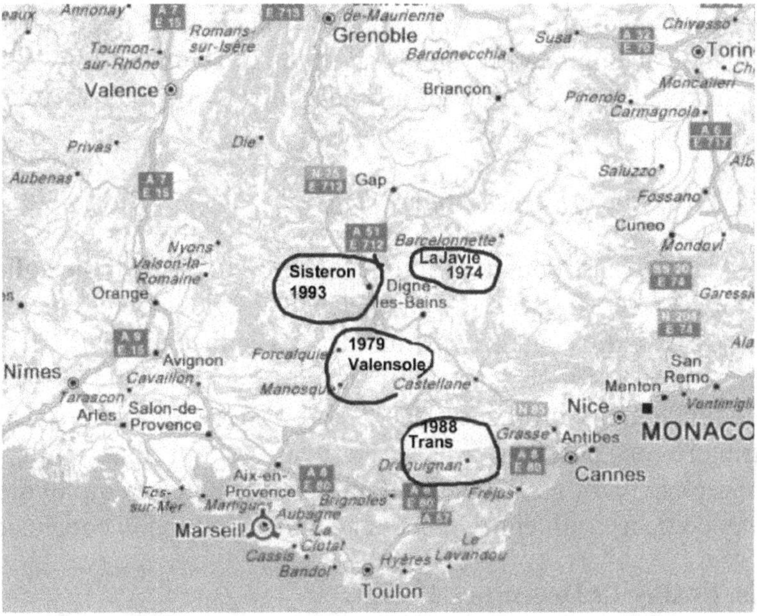

Fig. 13: Map of our primary field investigations in Provence, 1974-93.

Fig. 14: Private meeting with Laurance Rockefeller, Kykuit Oct.1997
Left to right: Sturrock, Diamond, Vallee, Rockefeller, Haines.

wounded Canadian pilot who had seen foo fighters over Germany. The man is an engineer, former head of the Israeli hydrology service. He confirmed that a sample of a fluid allegedly poured on a witness during an encounter had been recovered.

Paris. Thursday 18 December 1997.

Little Maxime has brought everyone together, in time for the holidays. He smiles when he sees my mother and giggles over dinner at *Le Suffren.* He smiles again when his parents gather up their friends, a dynamic group of high-tech and finance managers. Yesterday we had a long lunch at my brother's place. Gabriel was witty and relaxed, but doctrinaire on political issues. He was certain that cutting the workweek to 35 hours, as the Left proposes, will save employment. All my contacts with entrepreneurs lead to the opposite conclusion.

Paris. Friday 19 December 1997.

This morning I dived into the first Métro that came along and heard someone call out my name. Jean-Jacques Velasco was there, on the way to a meeting at CNES: a chance in thousands that we would meet this way. He was upset because a trashy ufology magazine had accused him of incompetence. He plans to sue, even if his bosses don't support him. I told him that it will only give his detractors the publicity they seek. He didn't see it that way: "My son who died a few months ago would never have accepted to see his father treated this way."

Of course, there was no possible answer to that argument.

Bayeux. Tuesday 23 December 1997.

I've left all business behind. The Christmas tree sparkles in the darkness. For the first time this year I really have no worry.

Now the entire clan is assembled, including Alain who just sold his Charleston restaurant. The annoying thing in France is that so many of the folks we know, even those in their early fifties who still have 30 years to live, are only thinking of retirement as if that represented life's goal. I suppose that in the French landscape of blatant exploitation, being paid to do nothing is a considerable achievement.

Part Sixteen

FOUR ELEMENTS

16

Spring Hill. Saturday 3 January 1998.

The rain hangs on over the forest, steady and cold, occasionally intense. I wonder why this place still excites such an affinity in my soul, an echo of faraway knowledge. There is a level of the spirit that hosts our higher faculties, engaged by the class of precognitive insight that occasionally flies us to a glimpse of the future.

The mistake of occult groups isn't to affirm this knowledge but to institutionalize it. They try to use it operationally on the wrong level.

In a recent interview Rosicrucian imperator Raymond Bernard finally confessed his extraterrestrial contacts (similar to the rumors that inspired the murder-suicides of the Solar Temple) were fictional.

His experiences with an Unknown Superior called Maha, as I had suggested in *Messengers of Deception* (Note) were imaginary as well: proof again that spiritual principles should not be exploited on the mundane level.

Hummingbird. Sunday 4 January 1998.

Peter Sturrock called me to request a review of the report produced by the scientists after Pocantico. I was disappointed when they dismissed all the hard work done by the private groups, even as they stated that the phenomenon was "worthy of scientific studies." He suggested an additional paragraph to redress this impression.

We went on to discuss follow-up at NSF or NASA. I reminded him of the failure of NASA to act twenty years ago under Press and Frosch, when Carter pushed for the same thing. Peter is hoping that Laurance

---

(Note) At the time the Amorc Rosicrucian Order had threatened me with legal action. Believers have continued to spread the Maha story.

Rockefeller can influence Clinton's chief scientist, which I doubt.

In the mail is a warm letter from Guérin and his sober commentary about Corso. I was glad to see Pierre wasn't swallowing the whole story. Also in the mail were press articles about Ira Einhorn, released from jail after a French court denied U.S. extradition requests.

Hummingbird. Sunday 11 January 1998.

This weekend, attendance at the eleventh Science Board of NIDS was the best in a long time. Jessica Utts was back, everyone was happy. I had to leave after the last session, unfortunately, without attending Victoria's dinner party honoring Kit and Kristin's wedding.

In spite of the good spirits the sessions were a bit tense over the two days, and we didn't accomplish much. Colm gave excellent reports on work at the ranch, then discussions centered on Bob's plans to raise the visibility of "aerial phenomena" to the national level. Against Kit's protestations he led us through elaborate exercises designed to align us to his scheme. I stressed that the aspect of NIDS I most admired was precisely that we hadn't tried to grab headlines.

Kit confirmed there was an agency covering up evidence, so I took him aside and asked what he meant. Unconvincingly, he said he still thought there was no physical proof, just hard data that indicated the problem was real. (So where is it?)

The sociological effects continue to spread: A few days ago, Spanish police announced they had foiled a plan by 31 members of a sect known as the *Isis Holistic Center* to commit suicide on the slopes of Mount Teide, in the Canary Islands. This group, mainly composed of British and German members, believed that a flying saucer was going to pick up their souls as soon as they died.

The Utah ranch is quiet, with no new incidents. There hasn't been a single new case of a physical UFO there. The team is busy pursuing various hypotheses to explain previous cases that I've summarized in a small catalog. I suggested systematic use of our spectrographic instruments to establish a baseline of gases on site. Far from me to resurrect the infamous "swamp gas" theory, but we wouldn't be diligent if we didn't confront ordinary factors. As for Corso, he doesn't get much mention any more, although Hal told me the old soldier called him almost every day, an elderly man who embellishes his life.

The Robertson-Stephens dinner in honor of the 50th anniversary of the transistor, which Janine and I recently attended in San Jose, made it obvious that the silicon revolution came from bumbling humans, not smart Aliens in a crashed spaceship.

On the positive side, Hal's work on zero-point energy is featured in *Scientific American* but a critic wrote that all the ZPE on Earth "wouldn't boil an egg." At least it's no longer ignored as a theory.

Later the same day.

Bob Bigelow just called, intent on briefing me about the part of the meeting that I'd missed. He proposes to sponsor two new studies on the subject of the social effect of an announcement of (1) a major asteroid fall and (2) the reality of UFOs as extraterrestrial craft.

"What would be the consciousness aspects in both cases?" he asks, reasonably enough. But he has a deeper agenda, an inner certainty that a dramatic development (spectacular display by the phenomenon or striking announcement by the government) will happen "soon."

When I pointed out research at the ranch could lead to a statement about the reality of UFOs, however, he said he'd practically given up on this; the evidence would never be good enough. Even photographs would be discounted. He said, "The value of the scientific method has been overblown. We're in an area that's not friendly to it."

He may well be right: we are dealing with a meta-reality. Besides, we learned long ago that scientists were not getting the purest data. Yet Bob believes that there is an MJ-12 and that the phenomenon "has done things that could have had a large impact, but the public was appraised as not being ready. Things are kept under wraps. And I can't blame them!" he added. "That may have been the wisest course."

He also mentioned that Kit had expressed the desire not to be our chairman any more, but to remain as a simple participant.

Hummingbird. Tuesday 13 January 1998.

The Tenerife cult episode, in which Spanish police foiled a suicide plan by members of the *Isis Holistic Center*, continues to unfold. Keith Harary sends me a Reuters report that the group may be linked to a

Hindu apocalyptic sect, not to the Solar Temple as first reported. Today another attempt at suicide happened at the site, involving 19 members said to belong to a splinter group of Brahma Kumaris.

Spring Hill. Sunday 18 January 1998.

Rugged weather, thunder and rain, low fog in the valley: the tower looks down on the world from mossy walls and gurgling pipes. Catherine got here before us. She made the house feel hospitable, richly draped in mystery behind drawn curtains, colorful cushions, wood smells, a welcome break from arguments about bandwidth allocation and high-end server clusters for the Internet. Janine is here...Together there's nothing we cannot do. Soon we'll be in Paris.

Mabillon. Tuesday 27 January 1998.

Ice in the gutters, strike on the tracks: Paris is as cold as the ranch. It's also out of work. The only comic relief comes from Washington where Bill Clinton keeps denying his intimacy with a pretty intern: the French are puzzled at the puritanical, hypocritical reaction of America, whose media crucify their hedonistic President while inundating the world with torrid images of sex to sell everything from cars to toothpaste.

I spent the day with my potential Israeli partners, arguing about their chances of raising a bond issue for their new global fund. In their suite at the Méridien I finally decided their project was flawed.

Mabillon. Wednesday 28 January 1998.

My first meeting with Dick Haines' friend Dominique Weinstein, a private researcher: we had lunch at *Le Suffren* and he gave me copies of his most recent catalogues of pilot and radar sightings.

Dominique, about 40, works for the DST (the French FBI) in the anti-terrorist section. He'd hoped to get into science research as a student but was discouraged by the "New Math" imposed in French schools. He now does counter-intelligence work, an equally valuable form of research. He says it was the reading of the French version of *Passport to Magonia*, especially my landings catalogue that got him interested in UFOs.

Dominique drove me to my next appointment in a Peugeot from the *Préfecture de Police*. He comes to the U.S. in May, so we'll have more chance to talk about his research, which parallels that of Larry Hatch, Loren Gross, Ed Stewart, Jan Aldrich, Barry Greenwood, all people who now work by themselves, outside the ufology groups.

The best work is always done by lonely researchers with no money.

Paris. A café on the boulevards. Thursday 29 January 1998.

Pierre Lagrange has moved to a fourth-floor apartment on *Rue de Buci*, filled with so many books and papers that he had to sit on the edge of an armchair as he told me about his Kenneth Arnold doctoral study, ten years of hard work. He complained of pains, of feeling old.

I suggested walking over to a café at Odéon, where we enjoyed the hot onion soup while we talked about Corso and cults. He didn't understand why I had turned down the "opportunity" to have a portrait interview in *L'Express*; why I didn't want to be a celebrity.

Annick and Janine are happily playing with Maxime, who spent the night with us at Mabillon.

Mabillon. Saturday 31 January 1998.

"Westerners call sylphs or elves those beings that Moslems call Djinns," says Aziz Biazzane, my North-African reader. "These creatures existed long before Islam. Their effects are similar to those in Western folklore. The Djinn phenomenon still exists: lights in the sky, whirlwinds, paralysis of witnesses, abductions... "

We had lunch on Place Saint-Michel. Aziz kept his raincoat with the collar turned up, ordered poached eggs and hardly touched his food, seemingly intimidated. Janine discussed Morocco with him and found out he didn't speak Arabic, a disappointment. Aziz says the Djinns watch everything we do from a higher, subtler plane, like guardian angels. Perhaps they will give us a push in our research?

Paris sparkles, cold and cloudless. The streets and the stores are filled with busy people. Janine and I went out to buy carpets for the apartment, and of course more books. My U.S. partners arrive tonight. We will spend the next three days plotting our investment strategy.

Mabillon. Tuesday 3 February 1998.

At the new offices of Siparex, formally aligned on either side of a long narrow corridor, Fred Adler gave another masterful presentation. All investment papers are signed; peace reigns again. So, we will proceed with a second Euro-America Fund and my own future is a bit clearer, even if the envy of my French partners remains obvious: their boss loses sleep every time he reads *Le Figaro*, where my modest column now appears on a monthly schedule. Why are the French so damn envious, since I'm on their team?

We went out for pancakes with hard cider and *Grand Marnier*. Janine has gone off to see Maxime while I write at the green desk. Before me a vase full of colorful stones from the Mad River and a feather from the wing of a Spring Hill bird remind me that tomorrow night we'll be back in California.

Hummingbird. Wednesday 11 February 1998.

Weariness, bad sleep. The investment work is going well, however, I am completing a medical device investment in Florida (**1**) and considering a new round of financing at Class Data Systems with Sequoia Partners. It promises to be one of our more exciting endeavors. But I have travelled too much and lost sight of my own life work.

I am waiting for something else, and I don't know what it is.

Hummingbird. Saturday 14 February 1998.

Now it's a three-day weekend so we went to hear Luisa Teish's lecture at a local convention. The Ravenheart family was there, Oberon and Wolf and the witches, getting ready for their own Pagan show.

The Bay area is pelted by storms. As I write the windows vibrate, thunder rolls, hail falls so thick and hard it triggers car alarms on Van Ness Avenue.

Janine has found a fine condo for our friend Diana Hall, surrounded with flowers and early-blooming trees.

Hummingbird. Sunday 15 March 1998.

The storms have passed. When we drove over to Laytonville, spring was with us, gorgeous sudden spring in yellow blossoms and rows of pink fruit trees, tender shoots in all the bushes. We had a quiet evening with the Ravenheart family on the land they rent from a retired physicist, a home on a knoll overlooking a pretty lake. Morning Glory spoke of her trip to Greece as a priestess of Aphrodite. Oberon showed us his latest sculptures.

As I do every Sunday, I called my mother. She was lucid, aware of the elections in France and of events in the world. But she said she was not well, that she had intestinal problems and had seen a new doctor, after which she cut the conversation short.

Spring Hill. Saturday 4 April 1998.

It's never the right time to take a break, so we simply left the city and drove to Healdsburg to visit expert bookseller Todd Pratum. An accomplished scholar of bibliography, he rents a suite on the second floor of a sturdy, airy building overlooking the fine plaza. Over lunch at a nearby restaurant I asked him about Manly Hall and the magnificent library in Los Angeles, which I once visited with Allen Hynek. Persistent rumors hint that Hall was murdered. The library goes on, managed unevenly, but some precious books are missing.

Now time has slowed down. We'll spend one more day here, and then we'll drive where our fantasy takes us, towards the volcanic lands of Lassen, Shasta, and beyond.

Red Bluff. Monday 6 April 1998.

The compelling call from the wilderness pulled us from the City. It was an old dream of ours: on to Covelo for an exploration of Yolla Bolly along the precipitous course of the Eel River, as beautiful as it was 25 years ago when we made the trip with our children.

Yolla Bolly… The words mean "snow-covered peaks" in the Wintun language; a million acres of remote wilderness, almost as big as the State of Delaware, roughly square. The rangers told us that the dirt road that provides the only cut through the mountains from west to east was still closed by snow and ice, so we decided to drive north on another dirt road that climbs up to Mina and Zenia through a splendid pine forest, light enough to provide magical views of the snow-capped ridges shrouded in mist. We skirted the western boundary, only meeting three cars in 100 miles.

Beyond Zenia we got directions from a mailman, a middle-aged fellow with frazzled gray hair and a T-shirt that read, "I love my Dad." We drove on, reaching the snow about 5,000 feet, eating sandwiches by the deserted shore of a green mountain lake, then higher again through Trinity County on a paved road. Beyond Six Rivers, Route 36 brought us to Red Bluff: romance over everything.

Mount Shasta. Tuesday 7 April 1998.

Red Bluff has a mean business bypass, busy Interstate Five and fast food Chinese restaurants. We found a motel by the river. Next, we went on to Susanville through the Christmas card landscape of Lassen, up to 6,000 feet in the pine forest. At the edge of the northeast plain Susanville is like any other American town, a dull alignment: McDonalds, Burger King, Safeway, JC Penney... We drove on through an alternance of rain, snow, bursts of sunshine.

We had stopped for coffee in McCloud when my secretary caught up with us for an emergency conference call: Fred Adler from Florida, Veritas Ventures from Tel Aviv, trying to close the acquisition deal between Class and Cisco, a financial maze. Janine had her own business to unravel: a complicated loan for a client.

It was intriguing to solve these problems from the mysterious forested slopes of Mount Shasta.

Those issues behind us, we drove up the mountain and suddenly, at the 7,000-foot level, the sky cleared up above us for a rare view of the summit, the snow deep along the curves, the rough edges of rock sloping against blue afternoon sky: Master Shasta in shimmering robes, Lord of the horizon, rose above the storm.

Spring Hill. Thursday 9 April 1998.

While in Mount Shasta City we watched a TV program on abductions that was, as Janine put it, a mere juxtaposition of images and statements, zero research. Skeptic Susan Blackmore, her hair dyed green and red, dismissed abductions as nonsense simply because "She knows one individual who draws imaginary beings!" I had declined to be interviewed, Thank Heavens, but themes from my books were distorted to fit a slanted view of the problem's history: because medieval society experienced encounters with devils and elves, who naturally "cannot exist," modern encounters with ETs can be safely thrown out, as the skeptics argue with impeccable false logic, missing the main point.

Spring Hill. Friday 10 April 1998.

Over dinner Diane Darling and I spoke of our differing views of the future. She believes that mankind evolved from the (one-to-mother) relationship of the baby to the (one-to-other) mode of the adult. Monotheism has frozen it: one country, one God, one race, one husband, one tribe. She sees the Pagan movement as a chance to transcend this and move on to the next step: true relationship of the individual to all mankind, all of creation.

I take a different view. As social complexity increases there is more travel, more business and trade, intermarriage, immigration. Eventually it becomes difficult to hate people. Not because Mankind improves, but there are simply too many potential enemies for the limited human brain to handle. If paganism was the best answer it should have pushed mankind to evolve long before monotheism came along.

Diane answers that prehistoric paganism was tribal, hence limited. But isn't modern paganism tribal as well? She concedes that in Ireland the Pagans from Catholic towns will not "circle" with Pagans from Protestant towns. "The only thing those Irish factions have in common is their terribly bad food," she says, laughing.

Hummingbird. Wednesday 15 April 1998.

Formal breakfast with René Monory, president of the French Senate. We lamented the rise of a bloated bureaucracy. Laughing, he told us about an island where the French government has been trying to save a few dozen monkeys in the name of biodiversity. It turned out that 22 agencies and three ministers had to become involved!

Las Vegas. Saturday 25 April 1998.

The twelth meeting at NIDS: is our Institute becoming "just another Shirley MacLaine with lasers?" someone asked with humor.

After the last session Bigelow spoke to Kit on the phone for a long time, trying to convince him that events at the ranch were real and couldn't be explained on psychological grounds. Bob pushes hard for contacts with Indian leaders: Utes and Apaches, and tribes from Mount Archuleta. My thinking is on Bob's side.

Kit told us of his meeting with Sagan when he went to see him on the set of *Cosmos*. Sagan took him to his trailer, abruptly kicked out a blonde bimbo, and told him he would agree to be on his science board on two conditions: that he be told all about the SRI parapsychology work, and all about the government knowledge on UFOs. Kit answered that on the first point he was just getting involved and knew little. On the second point he said the government had no ongoing study of UFOs. Sagan said he was lying and under those conditions wouldn't work with him.

During the meetings I sat between Jim Whinnery and Kit. The former kept drawing labyrinths on white sheets of paper. Kit came equipped with thick drawing paper and a grease pencil that he sharpened periodically with a pocketknife; while he listened to the proceedings he made beautiful drawings of various people and objects in the room.

I think all of us continue to come to Vegas in part for the good cheer and companionship (how else would I see Hal or John Petersen regularly?) and in part on the fragile chance that the phenomenon might manifest fully at the ranch.

Hummingbird. Sunday 3 May 1998.

COM21, in which I'd invested, has filed to go public later this month, and we just signed an agreement to sell Class Data Systems to Cisco for ten times our valuation of two years ago. The next step for me is to negotiate a long-term framework, so I am going to Paris this afternoon with a strong wind in my sails.

Dominique Weinstein, on a visit to America, came over for lunch yesterday. He said he felt some sadness when he read *Forbidden Science*, because he realized the field was at the same point today that Aimé Michel, Guérin, and I had reached 30 years ago…

In the evening Dick Haines had invited a small group to his house: Peter Sturrock in great shape, Fred Beckman looking tired, Larry Hatch, Ed Stewart, Loren Gross who is the best historian of the field, and a psychology professor from Stanford. Jim McCampbell hinted at high-level Washington contacts, then confessed nothing came from them. Dick Haines, who sent an impractical $11 million research proposal to Bill Clinton, has reached the same impasse.

Lyon. Wednesday 6 May 1998.

On this trip I take time to see more of Lyon, first at lunchtime with Philippe Lambert, and again this morning as I walked over to *Place des Jacobins* to buy a flag of the city. The sky is gray, but the air is pleasant, and the mighty Rhône flows evenly. I had breakfast with Michel Faucheux, a Humanities professor, scholar of mythology, who views UFO sightings as an opportunity to delve into a powerfully constructed hidden world, physical as well as spiritual.

Paris. Thursday 7 May 1998.

After breakfast in Neuilly at Finovelec, an investment group, I went to see the ancient statue of the Alexandria Colossus, temporarily erected in front of the *Petit Palais* (**2**). Paris is busy and smart. The business climate is improving. Olivier, with whom I had a pleasant dinner last night, sees opportunities in the emerging world of European underwriting. Although I'd love to have him close to us in California, it seems clear that a new wind of investment is blowing over Europe. Last week saw the historic decision to launch the single currency, the Euro. Soon this old world will have new structures, obsolete cultures will crumble to dust. People at every level seem to recognize that the change is irreversible.

As for my partners, they are amazed at the realization that our little Class Data Systems (a team of 20 young engineers) was worth tons of money to Cisco. The French seem to have no concept of the value of Internet software.

Hummingbird. Saturday 16 May 1998.

Another breakfast with the Israelis. They're beginning to understand that their new project could not get off the ground in its present form. I urged them to restructure it as a global fund, but I don't want to run it. In a couple of hours, I leave again, this time to Tokyo.

Tokyo. Prince Hotel. Monday 18 May 1998.

Yesterday, after our board meeting of the Holontech startup at NEC headquarters, Graham Burnette and I spent the afternoon in panel presentations about American-style venture capital over the private NEC television network, broadcast to their offices all over Japan. We had rain, gray skies, a feeling of peace everywhere in spite of the current economic crisis; then an exquisite dinner with NEC executives at their guesthouse, *Sand Castle.*

This is my third trip here. Tokyo is closer to San Francisco than Paris, the trip far less tiring and the business atmosphere a lot nicer. I especially enjoy working here with Graham.

An added pleasure: Olivier's wife and her sister came over for a quick lunch. They brought Max, happy as ever, a bit confused about seeing me in Tokyo, trying to recall who I was and why I didn't speak Japanese like everybody else.

Hummingbird. Friday 22 May 1998.

About 11:30 pm yesterday, before I got home there was a poltergeist here. Janine was working on her computer; she heard a loud noise near the front door, which was locked. A heavy credenza where we place the outgoing mail seemed to be the site of the sound. A letter I had left there was thrown three feet away to the floor.

Hummingbird. Friday 29 May 1998.

Socialism isn't what it used to be. At a Chamber of Commerce dinner honoring Dominique Strauss-Kahn today we were 150 guests, the men in black tie, eating *asperges aux morilles* and *macarons à la mousseline de pistache* while discussing the future of finance.

My colleagues are licking their chops as they expect to see a wave of new funds freed up by the liberal laws enacted by the leftist government of Lionel Jospin and flowing into their coffers for future investment. Janine and I sat at Anne Sinclair's table where Jean-Louis Gassée kept explaining ADSL communications while DSK's chief of staff pointed out that the roots of socialism were in the creation of wealth, not simply its redistribution. "After all, Karl Marx wrote *Capital*," he said, "not *Social Security*!"

Spring Hill. Sunday 31 May 1998.

This morning I called *Rue de la Clef*. The phone was busy. I called again and was surprised to hear my brother's voice. He was waiting for an ambulance to take our mother to the hospital for tests: she had been taken ill after lunch and felt sharp pains again.

Spring Hill. Sunday 7 June 1998.

We held our annual medieval feast of Saint Agobard today, a splendid affair. Janine had surpassed herself with an ambitious menu of tender pork with lentils and wine-cooked poultry with swedes and apples to which I added venison sausages (bought over the Internet, from a ranch in Texas!) and *Père Patriarche* bottles from the convent of the Visitandines in Meursanges, "an order of nuns who come and visit you when you're in bed," as I explained to the guests. The men donned monk's robes, except for Robin Rule's husband who had draped a potato sack over his shirt to play a medieval shepherd.

To set the tone I passed around extracts from *Comte de Gabalis* and the works of Agobard, notably his great book against the superstitions of sorcery, *De Grandine et Tonitruis* ("About Hail and Thunder") where he explains that the loosening of storms in the atmosphere is the sole prerogative of God and relates the belief in Magonia among his contemporaries. It is an example of honest observation combined with healthy skepticism. As I read this, rare claps of thunder rolled approvingly across the canyon.

Everyone quickly got into spirit: Ted Widmer was positively ecclesiastical. Diane Darling stole the show in a rainbow cape, blue make-up and a starry headdress.

After dinner we sat by the fireplace to hear Daniel and Robin read some of their poetry.

Later the same day.

Gabriel just called: our mother is resting, uncomfortable but alive, in intensive care for a few days. The surgeon removed "a small tumor" and repaired an intestinal perforation that had caused her pains, but those French doctors are loath to provide details.

Hummingbird. Wednesday 24 June 1998.

Janine called from Paris on Friday after seeing my mother in her hospital room. She found her lucid but very weak, unable to get up and walk, yet fully confident she would regain her strength. Now my darling wife is on the way to Greece with Tia Helena, who will show her the village where she was born. I wish I were with her. I try to slow down my pace but there are a hundred interruptions every day.

Opportunities beckon as French funds burst onto the landscape of the venture business, wide open under Dominique Strauss-Kahn. An ambitious new team has contacted me to join a new trans-Atlantic organization run by Vivendi tycoons.

The streets are drizzly, grayish, shrouded in the misty curtains I so love, but this alternance of hot and cold and bright and dark takes a toll on the soul. I drove to Oakland for lunch with Catherine, went shopping for bread, a sweater, simple things.

Hummingbird. Friday 26 June 1998.

Feelings of imminence. I had a Crowleyan dream of ritual night moves last night, stealthy circling of a sarcophagus at the foot of the Pyramids, hieroglyphic keys to the unfathomed mind. I walked on, invoking the Queens of the Night: Nuit, Hadit, Lilith flying through their dark mystical moods, mere shadows in the velvety net of faint embers, flashes of hair and thigh, dancing with me.

This afternoon I will drive to Spring Hill alone. Our tenants tell us the bear circles the house, unhappy with forest food, stealing garbage, longing for the companionship of folks like us, who are good providers of rotten salmon.

Hummingbird. Monday 29 June 1998.

The Sturrock report about the Pocantico meeting is being received with polite interest. It doesn't say anything new about the phenomenon, only expressing a virtuous wish that it be studied. Journalists are jaded when they see scientists issuing generalities.

Today I said good-bye to the French colleague who has shared my office for two years. Some professional changes may be coming: tired of my French partners and weary of Fred Adler's caprices I have responded to a direct approach by executives from Vivendi (the former *Générale des Eaux* of Ambroise Roux) who are serious about starting a new venture fund. I finished reading *The Aryan Christ* (**3**).

Spring Hill. Saturday 4 July 1998.

Eternal skeptic Phil Klass just called me, sniffing around the edges of the Sturrock-Rockefeller panel. He wanted to know how extensive my participation had been at Kykuit, what I thought of the other presenters, and sneakily tried to make me say that Peter Sturrock was "leaning towards an ET interpretation."

I handled him politely because I don't despise his way of analyzing the phenomenon, only his aggressive behavior towards witnesses.

Klass said he'd undergone spinal surgery and was left with a walking disability and permanent laryngitis but kept an active life. His mind was as incisive as ever.

Las Vegas. Saturday 11 July 1998.

Last Tuesday we had a security breach of our office computers, while I was having dinner in Sacramento. Should I suspect government spooks? More likely, Vivendi goons checking up on me.

Kit, on an Alaskan cruise with Kristin, missed the 13th Science Board meeting at NIDS. Johndale Solem wasn't there either but all others showed up in good spirits. Marty Pilch chaired the sessions. Hal was just back from London where he'd met a mysterious VIP, possibly Prince Hans-Adam. Hal is increasingly involved in ufology research,

Fig. 15: French venture capitalists in Silicon Valley, February 1998:
Pierre Lamont (Sequoia), Vincent Worms (Partech), Jean Deléage (Alta), Philippe Bouissou (Milestone), Jacques Vallée, Alix Marduel (Alta). (Photo *Le Figaro*)

Fig.16: The main witness at the site of the 1998 Haravilliers encounter.

even paying an investigator to look through old files to verify reports of an alleged crash in 1941, but he keeps all results to himself and his sponsor(s). Sadly, this makes it increasingly hard for me to be frank about what I know. That is the problem with research institutes and organized groups: once you set them up you need cash to keep them running. Getting that cash is often a waste of time, resources and independence, because one can only work on theories that are aligned with a particular framework, that of your sponsor.

I am fortunate to be able to conduct my own research without reporting to anyone. But that too, has limitations: I can only work on small-scale projects that are focused, with a few dedicated friends. Nonetheless I do end up covering much ground and getting new knowledge, both in the U.S. and internationally. The databases have become a reliable resource and the peace of Spring Hill has opened my mind to a range of potentialities I hadn't suspected. My view of the phenomenon has evolved here, beyond classic physical and biological parameters, to a reality in multiple layers: it melds the pre-existing grid of its logic with the consciousness of the observer, manifesting a "display" of arbitrary complexity.

The NIDS sessions started out well, with a review of the Sturrock-Rockefeller report followed by a presentation by Al Holt who heads up NASA's advanced propulsion project. The high point was a presentation by Colm Kelleher of new events at the Utah ranch where a prize bull disappeared for two weeks, only to reappear near the main trailer, impeccably clean but thirsty and starved, on the edge of a muddy field that showed no tracks.

It is an ever-renewed pleasure to meet the group, yet I remain concerned at the direction we've taken. In spite of our financial and intellectual firepower we have not made concrete progress in framing the phenomenon. Even my suggestions to highlight "what needs to be explained" and to list researchable issues have been set aside. Yet such practical actions should be the logical starting point of any serious research. Simply sitting here and waiting for the phenomenon to present us with an opportunity to react is not serious methodology.

Bob Bigelow has made it clear he didn't intend to act on my advice to bring in a cultural anthropologist and a magistrate to the Board. Instead, he pushes for the Institute to become visible in the media.

Ufological politics leave me cold. Instead, I continue to push for "reframing," in the sense originated by the Palo Alto school of psychology. The urge to gain media attention ignores the fact that the communities we seek to impress, those of the New Age and ufology, are too often guilty of misrepresentation, witness the Gulf Breeze fiasco (**4**) and the mishandling of abduction victims.

Hummingbird. Tuesday 21 July 1998.

A strange character calls me every day. He claims to have resided in the US some 28 years, working at *Société Générale* in New York. He offered to invest money for our Fund, placing it at surpringly advantageous rates. He said he was acquainted with Bob Lazar "through a company run by a mutual friend named Bob Nichols." He went on to tell me that he knew a government agent ("in the military, higher than the Navy Seals") who told him in confidence that "all that stuff was real," meaning Lazar's claims about captured saucers.

Naturally this raised all kinds of red flags.

More rumors: he assured me he was an expert in "currency stabilization," exploiting schemes through which the U.S. "creates money by issuing securities below value and flipping them to leverage international intervention into currencies." He claims a few investors get into the deals at huge profit: up to 50% per year!

I suspect an attempt at entrapment. If he knows all those important financial secrets, why does he need to dangle such barely legal schemes to me? I told him I wasn't sophisticated enough to benefit from such systems, and anyway our investors were not looking to me to hedge their risks, only to achieve a fair return from straightforward technology investments; which is true.

Hummingbird. Wednesday 22 July 1998.

The *Diving Pelican* is a quiet restaurant with an outdoor terrace near the Marina in Redwood City. Over lunch with Fred Beckman we came around to discussing my calculations on the light energy output of UFOs. As I lamented the fact that Hynek had lost two of the slides he once took of a bright oval object, Fred corrected me:

"He didn't actually lose them. He'd taken two stereo pairs of pictures, and only one slide came back in each pair, the left one in the first pair and the right one in the second. The other two were holes, as if someone had simply removed them. He always had his UFO pictures developed at the same Kodak place in Evanston."

"What happened to the two pictures he got back?"

"I was sure he'd lose them, so I took them from him, placed them in a sealed envelope and locked it away at my lab, at the University of Chicago. When I moved I found the envelope, still sealed, but the slides were gone. Yet nobody should have known I had them…"

Obviously, "someone" is extremely interested in such material.

This reminds me of Dr. Jack Sarfatti's notes stolen from his car. And the time when recordings disappeared from the home of a French journalist. Or the recent intrusion into my computer at work. Or the weird fellow who offers me to invest at a 50% annual interest rate…

Spring Hill. Saturday 25 July 1998.

First day of vacation. Sadly, Janine and I quarrelled about Spring Hill. I am still reluctant to sell. A forester who came with me along our two canyons to write up a conservancy agreement almost fell to his knees when he saw the tall redwoods near the cabins, several of them over 180 feet tall, a living cathedral. Spring Hill has enriched my understanding of the spiritual world: the forest speaks to me of forms of consciousness in realms we haven't bothered to visit.

This morning I spoke to my mother. She was pinned to her hospital bed, surrounded by nurses. Her voice was weak and slow, but the message remained clear, a savage will to go on living — even if her wounds are slow to heal, even if her legs don't carry her any more. I don't feel such a will. I am at peace with the idea of gracious Death taking me by the hand when She comes.

Spring Hill. Monday 27 July 1998.

According to Colm Kelleher another curious incident has taken place at the Utah ranch on July 19: a power cord feeding three of our surveillance cameras at the top of a pole was ripped out, all the duct tape gone, recordings stopped at 8:38 pm. As I had recommended, one of the cameras at the top of another pole pointed to the first installation, so it should have caught whatever intrusion took place. Yet it only showed cattle moving around with no sign of disturbance.

Hummingbird. Thursday 6 August 1998.

Intruders: the security consultant I've hired is puzzled by the incident of July 7th. He first assumed a bored janitor has simply turned on our computers to play videogames, but that wouldn't explain why the audit logs had holes in them. There might be missing records if our machines were improperly turned off, so we ran experiments: the records were intact. He concludes we were subjected to the kind of snooping a big company could run against a prospective executive. And what about the fellow with his get-rich scheme? Was that an attempt by Vivendi to test my integrity?

John Alexander has given me the results of the forensic analysis of the cable at the ranch: it was cut by a rusty knife, with a single pulling motion of the blade. The perpetrator should be visible on our tapes: Tests run under similar conditions with someone climbing the pole clearly show that person on the intact camera on the other pole.

Hummingbird. Monday 10 August 1998.

Federico Faggin wants to discuss ufology and the paranormal. A physicist from Padua, he invented the integrated circuit at Fairchild, then joined Intel in 1970 and led the design of the first microprocessor, the 4004. In 1974 he conceived and built the 8080, first high performance 8-bit microprocessor, then founded Zilog where he built the Z80. Now he is deeply engaged in consciousness research. New projects have to wait, however, because we're getting ready for a short trip to France--and vacation in the Highlands.

Mabillon. Saturday 22 August 1998.

At the end of the Ivry metro line the buildings are new and ugly, made of cheap gray concrete. Beyond city limits a slow bus lumbers on to the hospital where my mother is huddled within a nightmare.

Occasionally she emerges from it, conversing in normal tones for a while, aware of us and events in her life. At other times she complains of ill treatments. She says she doesn't see well and can't read any more, which deprived her of a profound pleasure.

Paris is moist, the air dirty with car fumes. Janine and I had lunch with my brother and his wife near the Bastille, after which we visited a brand-new convalescent home where our mother could live the rest of her days in physical comfort. In her condition any return to her apartment is out of the question.

Maxime is one year old today. His little arms around my neck and his happy babble mean more than all the high-tech startups in France. We also celebrated Olivier's success in passing the second and toughest level of the international finance certificate, the CFA.

Bill Clinton is in trouble over his infidelities, exploited by opponents. It isn't the dirtiness of the politics that bothers me here, but the sad realization that, as the incarnation of an American generation that was supposed to transcend the obsolete moral codes of puritans, Clinton and his cohort failed to usher in a more mature culture, freer but saner.

Hardline Bible-thumpers are ready to take control. The French can only watch all this in stunned amazement.

Nairn, Scotland. Monday 24 August 1998.

Janine and I just went out for a long walk on the shore of Moray Firth. Night falls slowly in summer at this latitude, the Highlands being as far north as Moscow. It was still light when we returned after dinner on the harbour. The inn is a Victorian full of angles and flowered wallpaper, over-decorated without artistic restraint, having won an award for "perfectly respectable mild excentricity."

The windows open on the sea and a flower garden. We hear the waves crashing into tidal pools and the cries of seagulls. There is no phone or television. This afternoon we walked up to Cawdor castle, up on a hill with a splendid view.

Nairn. Wednesday 26 August 1998.

Flowers everywhere, tumbling over stonewalls and fences, overhanging balustrades and sloping lawns. We don't miss news of the tumbles of Monica Lewinsky and those of Wall Street. Instead we took the bus to Brodie and enjoyed the castle, its huge fireplaces, the dark carved wood.

At Cawdor the dowager countess Angelika, a tall clever redhead in her forties, a member of Peter Sturrock's SSE, greeted us in the sitting room of her exquisite castle and invited us to lunch at the house she occupies on the estate during the tourist season, across a grove of ancient oak and pine. We spoke of fairies and elves, Aliens and crop circles, and her favorite entities, the angels. She said the opening and closing of angels' wings might be a symbol of the human soul being freed up from its physical envelope.

After an exceptional lunch of succulent local products (shrimp from Moray Firth, *groseilles* and peas from the garden, *blettes fourrées*) she pointed out the nature walk along the river, a 40-minute trail that led us back around the castle walls. In Nairn the sun had come out as we walked along the "burn," as the Scots call a creek or a brook, casting blood-red tints on the tannin-laden waters.

Nairn. Thursday 27 August 1998.

Today we were content to follow a busload of tourists all the way around Loch Ness. Nessie jokes aside, the Highlands are splendid, the heather-covered hills in purple bloom this time of year, and the weather an exceptionally clear combination of filtered sunlight and silvery overcast, lifting to blue skies in the afternoon. A boat excursion on the water provided charming close-up views of the hills that have been formed by the collison of two tectonic plates. We stopped at Urquhart castle, beautiful Saint Augustus Abbey and the Boleskine house of Crowley fame, recently owned by Jimmy Page of Led Zeppelin. We hadn't realized that Crowley lived at Boleskin for 19 years. The house isn't a castle at all: contemporary occult books feature the wrong photograph to further the hype of his O.T.O. sect.

Nairn. Friday 28 August 1998.

It rained today, for the first time this week, an excuse to stay in bed till early afternoon, and then we walked to the town center for coffee and pastries. When we came out the rough weather had gone with the tide, leaving a silver sky, the sea the color of pewter, a diaphanous glow over the shore. We walked against the wind for six or seven miles along the sea. Black birds were digging into the wet sands in search of tasty worms and brittle shells.

We have been reading and discussing *The Last Years of Jesus* by Charles Potter. It brought memories of our trip to Qumran and the realization that biblical scholars are no more honest or conscientious than scientists whenever cherished dogmas are torn to shreds by facts.

The book also makes me want to preserve what we've assembled, possibly one of the nicest paranormal libraries in private hands on the West Coast, if not the most expensive.

The discoveries at Qumran show how important it is for depositories of raw texts to exist, away from zealots who would burn them and experts who would bury or censor them in the name of political expediency or divine revelation. Potter writes of an Essene center at Lake Mareotis near Alexandria, cousin to the Jewish mystical community at Qumran that gave birth to Christianity: "The Alexandrian branch was called the *Therapeutae*, but they were not physicians or attendants or healers, as the name might imply; it was a heavenly therapy they sought for themselves... They differed from the Essenes of the Dead Sea, for they were known to include women, they fasted, they did not prophesy, they were strict vegetarians, and they were not communitarian, each one having his own."

Potter praises their combination of plain living and high thinking, and "their sunrise worship, their repudiation of animal sacrifices, their connection with eastern (Persian or Hindu) mystic contemplation, and their studious love of books, especially the Enochian literature and similar "secret" writings having to do with the calendar, sacred numbers, apocalypses, and wisdom books."

This sounds like the kind of community where I would gladly apply, but there is no such group anywhere today.

Nairn. Sunday 30 August 1998.

Yesterday Lady Cawdor came to fetch us in her Range Rover for an initiatory tour to the Highlands. We went to the Cloutie Well, a site dedicated to the Fairies since ancient times. According to the rite we made our wishes there, tying bits of a flower handkerchief to an overhanging branch. We visited a cluster of Pictish Cairns, not shown

Fig.17: With Janine at the Spring Hill ranch, June 1998.

Fig.18: The reference library at Spring Hill observatory, August 1998.

on maps or tourist brochures for fear of vandalism. We walked through the ruins of the ancient church of Cawdor with its romantic medieval cemetery, and the hill where Macbeth is said to have met the Three Witches. We visited various Pictish standing stones in the area, adorned with suspiciously modern crosses.

Finally, Angelika took us to Findhorn, where the old hippie community survives thanks to the energy and drive of Peter Caddy's wife, who kept the group going when he dropped out and moved to Mount Shasta. Some of the buildings are beautifully constructed, but the rest is one vast trailer camp full of junk, where it would seem difficult to find enlightenment in spite of the environmental principles so highly trumpeted by idealists in the group. As for the giant vegetables of yore, they grew on nourishing sands full of seaweed, but rumor hints of chemical fertilizing when no one was looking.

We spent the evening at Angelika's house, with an intimate dinner that included heather-fed white hare, vegetables, berries from the castle gardens and French wines. We spoke of consciousness (that word again!) and the paranormal, of Dr. Greer's stupendous adventures that didn't fool our hostess, and of Jacques Benveniste's experiments in "water memory," which left her unconvinced as well.

Mabillon. Friday 4 September 1998.

We're back in Paris on a clammy, rainy Friday, our souls still loaded with Scottish history. This city is over-crowded and smoggier than ever. Holidays are over and financial markets are in free fall.

My mother is doing better. I found her moving around with the only assistance of a walker, her strength and morale clearly improved. A bright private room is ready for her at the convalescent facility.

Two days of work at the French Genopole have plunged me back into the reality of French medical research: so much scientific talent wedged between bureaucratic structures and feudal politics…

Mabillon. Saturday 5 September 1998.

Maman was surprised to see both of her sons at the door of her hospital room today. She was seated, staring at the floor, apparently indifferent to everything. She perked up quickly when she saw us. We told her she could leave in a few days; we showed her pictures and a brochure of a possible residence. Over the next hour we went over details with her. She is still able to make decisions for herself. We left with the feeling we had done all we could to provide the best environment, given her vulnerable medical condition.

Hummingbird. Monday 7 September 1998.

Labor Day: we stay home sorting the mail, pondering the latest financial shenanigans on Wall Street, and reviewing messages. When I told him I was sick of the ufology trash I read on Internet, Hal Puthoff said his own method was to "lurk and delete." But when I heard friends had been approached by yet another "secret" Pentagon source and that a new television program would soon describe in detail the "Alien autopsies of the KGB," I did feel like throwing up.

Hummingbird. Sunday 13 September 1998.

Attracted by the rise of the Internet economy, powerful groups are entering the venture investment field. After the Israelis and Vivendi, a Canadian group is proposing a deal with me after verifying my reputation as an ethical high-tech investor. Now Colm Kelleher sends me a database of Junior Hicks' cases in Utah. Reuters reports that Jean-Jacques Velasco has a videotape showing a disk-shaped UFO in the French Alps over Voreppe but the fanfare about a supposed renewal of scientific interest sounds very fragile to me.

Tonight, TNT will air the documentary about fake KGB files on Aliens: the material Martine and I rejected when we were in Russia.

Euro-America office, Market Street. Friday 25 September 1998.

The equinox came with a soft silver haze that enhanced the busy hills of the City. Janine and Catherine made my birthday a happy feast, including dinner at *Chalet Basque* with our neighbor Carlo Bartalini who shook the place when he sang with his opera voice, and a beautiful gift of his bronze statue of Pan, the finest thing anyone has ever given me. Days now pass in negotiations with Vivendi and Adler, preparing my next move.

Spring Hill. Saturday 26 September 1998.

I am slowly rebuilding the blue files and cataloging the library. We are happy: profoundly, quietly. I am worried about Fred Beckman, however. When I called him the other night he slurred his words, mumbling something about his car being totalled. Fred is one of the most intelligent men I've ever met, blessed with an extraordinary memory. But he is another researcher losing contact with reality.

Hummingbird. Tuesday 6 October 1998.

A supposedly secret document about a new research project called *Kairos* arrived from Joe Firmage, former CEO of USWeb.

This is a strange, suspended time of transition for me. Vivendi is checking my references, polishing up a letter of engagement. Fred Adler called as I was at a little restaurant on Second Street. After discussing my appraisal of Efi Arazi's new company (Imedia), I told him that I was ready to resign from Euro-America. He took it well; he was friendly and supportive, full of good advice.

Las Vegas. Saturday 10 October 1998.

Very tired: my brain wants to shut down. I have only slept four hours after intense talks with General Whinnery. The group reviewed the first three years of NIDS and I had a long conversation with John Petersen and Hal. Kit wasn't here, neither was Ed Mitchell.

Today the Board (our 14th meeting) tackled the challenge posed by Bob Bigelow, of engaging the scientific community. I said it didn't make sense to speak in the same sentence of getting visibility with the public AND with science (two radically different things,) impressing the media while gaining the confidence of secret sources (an obvious contradiction), taking an advocacy position while research is incomplete and crusading for the extraterrestrial visitation hypothesis while testing theories that may not involve ETH at all.

"Look at the data from the Utah ranch," I said, "where we have every paranormal phenomenon—except for flying saucers!"

The negative consequences of visibility were two, in my opinion: *first* we would create a market for unscrupulous media exploiting the issue, as we recently saw with the fake Alien autopsy and the hoaxed

KGB files; *second,* in a serious confrontation with scientific colleagues we wouldn't have conclusive data to present, as evident from our failure at Pocantico. We should ask all the hard questions ourselves, in the privacy of our labs, before raising our visibility.

17

Mabillon. Friday 16 October 1998.

The decision has been made and I have left the Euro-America partnership to join the Vivendi corporate fund. Janine helped me move boxes and framed photographs out of my office on Market Street, and it was done. She's a marvel of equanimity through all this. I flew to Paris with the files for our new fund in my briefcase, and the biographies of a few handpicked people eager to join me.

Mabillon. Saturday 17 October 1998.

Faraway rumors rise from the direction of the Seine: a demonstration for gay rights has brought out colorful crowds and buses of cops, on edge after several days of student rallies that ended in brawls. This morning's rain has given way to sunshine, a warm autumn day fit for walking around and for that subtle impregnation of the soul achieved through random impacts with familiar scenes: wet streets, church bells, cigarette smoke wafting over the brasserie.

Evening. A page turns. I should feel relief, but some bitterness lingers when I think of what could have been accomplished. The only limits are those we invent for ourselves. What I now need is a bit of solitude. It is late. Crowds have dispersed. Lonely drunks start yelling vulgar songs they never finish. Why do I worry? A kind soul has left a couple of chocolate bars in the refrigerator.

Mabillon. Sunday 18 October 1998.

My mother's room at the rest home overlooks a pleasant courtyard with trees and a lawn. When I visited her the sun was shining through the window. She sat in an armchair by her bed, clearly improved since she left the hospital, although she isn't able to make more than a few steps without support. I brought her a book of photographs from the old Paris, handsome pictures of *Les Halles*.

Mabillon. Friday 23 October 1998.

Dinner alone at *Le Lutèce*. I treated myself to duck confit, profiterolles for dessert. A black pianist in a tuxedo sings *Ne dansez pas le boogie-woogie avant de faire vos prières du soir*. (Note)

This afternoon I went to see Yves Messarovitch in his new offices at *L'Expansion* on the Boulevards. He was taking his new functions after leaving *Le Figaro* to join the publishing arm of Vivendi.

My brother and I went around our mother's apartment today. For the first time in our lives we worked together, however briefly. We opened drawers and cupboards, recognizing objects from our childhood and from our own children's life. Gabriel told me about Christmas nights on *rue de l'Abbaye*, at the home of grand-parents I never knew, when a copper dragon with a fine little bell was used to announce that Santa Claus had completed his delivery. The children would rush in when they heard that bell, but never got a glimpse of his red coat.

That was in the 30s, before the war, before my time, he tells me.

All this nostalgia is relieved by the fact that my mother is feeling better. We had a long conversation with her, sparkling in a royal blue blouse and scarf, frail but able to walk by herself to the elevators when lunchtime came. An alternance of sunshine and silver gray played on her window as she castigated her feather-brained sons for failing to bring some tools to hang her paintings. Sorting out the papers I find letters from my kids to their grandmother, my own letters too, silly scribblings on postcards. How deep these little words can carry when a presence is lost, a parent ill or a child far away...

(Note): "Do not dance the boogie-woogie before saying your evening prayers!"

Spring Hill. Saturday 31 October 1998.

Last night Carlo Bartalini had a show of his sculptures in his second-floor apartment in our San Francisco building, some 70 people came. His place resembles a museum crowded with photographs, paintings and the occasional sword, gaudy tapestries hung over red wallpaper, red carpets, red drapes. Chinese dragons and a statuette of Isis rival with Samson and busts of Persian kings.

His bedroom is a screaming display of every object that ever struck his mind: One marvels at entering a jungle where tiger rugs and exotic birds clash in happy violation of every rule of proper *décor*. A wooden goddess flies over the bed; paintings of a café in Provence hang on either side while the grimaces of African and Asian masks sneer with all the intensity of which paper-mâché is capable.

They are supposed to bring good luck and I hope they do, because Carlo is a wonderful friend, a huge athlete with a booming voice, a stream of stories and that appreciation of human nature gained through a lifetime of operatic tragedies, on and off the stage.

Hummingbird. Sunday 1 November 1998.

This morning I called Hal Puthoff to catch up with projects we'd explored together, like Joe Firmage's *Kairos* project. Firmage is the 28-year-old CEO of USWeb, an Internet company that experienced rapid success on Nasdaq, although it never earned any money. With John Petersen and Mike Lindemann, he organized yet another series of "Day After" UFO scenarios. I declined to participate.

Interestingly, most of the scenarios ended with the destruction of human society either because it couldn't physically resist, or because it disintegrated spiritually. All that is feeble science fiction and re-inventing of wheels. Firmage's *Project Kairos* is redundant with every dubious theory from von Daniken to Vorilhon.

We went on to talk about NIDS. Hal thought that my speech at the last meeting had brought balance to the discussion, even if Bob kept to his own ideas. We should be doing better research at the Utah ranch,

I said: “If we can't even detect human intrusions, what are the chances of going after paranormal phenomena?”

Hummingbird. Friday 20 November 1998.

My friend Ren Breck collapsed ten days ago in San Rafael. He was diagnosed with a brain tumor that was surgically removed but the doctors only give him a year. The area of Oakland where he lives is dilapidated and palpably dangerous: one drives between high fences topped by razor-sharp wire, walls made of corrugated boards and ancient warehouses replete with grime and malady. My old friend is going to die there, in a small wooden home where he lives with Barbara, an episcopalian minister kept on edge by neighborhood problems and the crack house next door.

When I visited him this morning he was eager to talk about the old days of InfoMedia, the high point of his life: “Your Notepad software enabled us to raise millions of dollars in two weeks for the victims of the terrible earthquake in Armenia, Jacques,” he said. “Remember that? We saved those poor devils over there.”

Ren talks with a slur, but his memory is sharp. He speaks of going back to school and getting a PhD in computer science, so I agreed to be on his thesis committee. He asked me to bring him a flag from France. I inscribed his copy of *Computer Message Systems*; he cried when he saw what I had written about our old friendship.

Hummingbird. Monday 23 November 1998.

We saw Ira Einhorn on television last week: he was being interviewed in France along with his Swedish bride, playing the indignant leftist intellectual genius falsely accused by the forces of fascism(!) He neatly eluded all the pointed questions, but his game was obvious, his callousness unmistakeable.

Ren has gone through what he describes as a brilliantly disturbing series of psychedelic experiences as a result of his tumor. He tried to write: his pen extended to the entire page while the walls dissolved. He kept control by praying, by setting up mental “battle stations,” by concentrating on a few cherished memories. In that last category were our times together when we used to talk about networking or discussed psychic phenomena and space exploration.

Our new Fund has started to invest but a manager from Mannesmann warns me to remain skeptical of Vivendi and European deals, an opinion I will test in Paris, Vienna, and the South of France.

Mabillon. Saturday 28 November 1998.

My brother met us yesterday on *Rue de la Clef* to begin packing our mother's possessions, an emotional project he might not be able to tackle alone. Every drawer, every book, every painting carries a memory. We keep finding little notes with personal resonance: *Baptême de Jacques - le 29 Octobre 1943 à Saint-Maclou de Pontoise. Parrain: Maurice;* in my father's hand, about my baptism.

There are decisions to be made about countless boxes, files, and letters. We set aside what she might want to see again: photographs, children's naïve drawings.

Vienna. Sunday 29 November 1998.

Hotel Forum on Wagrammestrasse. Austria is frozen and gloomy. Night fell early over this zone of highrises, no charm. Between buildings are vacant lots, construction areas and towering cranes. A slight drizzle in the greasy darkness is slowly turning to snow. Delegates from 15 countries are assembling for three days of discussions on the information future of Europe.

Before leaving Paris, Janine and I set aside a few more items from my mother's place: the dining room table from Pontoise with its carved lion heads, my father's red armchair and the books by Molière he valued: preserved, cherished memories to remain with us.

Vienna. Monday 30 November 1998.

Our vision of a retreat at Spring Hill has been drained of meaning. The California drug culture is too pervasive now, encroaching viciously all around us, the social infrastructure too rough for anyone to build anything of lasting value. Far more meaningful would be to spend more time in Europe, visiting those villages and secret sites we love, discovering new places, enjoying Paris and our friends, only to return periodically to our base in San Francisco, our eagle's nest.

Sorting through my mother's accumulated possessions, modest as they are, has convinced me to streamline our life as Janine has long urged me to do. A new understanding of the futility of ufology (even if the genuine underlying mystery continues to glow mysteriously through the haze) has freed up my energy.

Vienna. Tuesday 1 December 1998.

The banks of the Danube were beginning to freeze, and a mean wind greeted us when we walked over to the Rathaus for the Mayor's reception last night in a magnificent hall draped with flags, the adorned ceiling reflecting the sound of a chamber orchestra. Meeting with friends, we continued our discussions late into the evening, walking across the illuminated square and passing cheerful Christmas shops on the way to Café Einstein. My own presentation was about the future of AI and robotics (*The Rise of the Replicants.*)

Mabillon. Friday 4 December 1998.

Working hard with our new French team: revising budgets, raising funds, interviewing executives, all at a racing pace.

I had dinner with Dominique Weinstein at a restaurant on *Rue de Buci* to which he had been introduced, he said, by one of his North-African "sources." He is smart and precise. He deplores the absence of research into UFOs, given the abundance of good data. While he concentrates on pilot and radar cases, he is aware of other reports throughout France that are not followed up, simply because Velasco has no resources at CNES and private ufologists are only interested in debating Roswell and phantasizing about the CIA. A few retired generals from the Institute for Advanced Studies in National Defense ("IHEDN") continue their review of the UFO problem under the name *Cometa* but they are stuck in pedestrian physical models.

Cannes. Tuesday 8 December 1998.

Janine and I watched the sun rise over Cannes harbor today. It put fringes of golden lace over purple clouds, washing out Venus and turning sailboat masts into glorious candelabra all over the landscape. At such times Shelley comes to mind: "The sun sprang forth, rejoicing in its splendour."

Sophia Antipolis, the French technopole, hope of generations of local politicians, stumbles on. France Telecom and several foreign firms have subsidiaries here but there is no center, no thriving development and no sense of urgency. It is, quite simply, a nice place to work away from stress and risk, not exactly the next Silicon Valley. The conference center is almost inaccessible, hidden in a maze of curving roads, 40 minutes away from the hotels.

Mabillon. Wednesday 9 December 1998.

We're leaving for California in a couple of hours. Yesterday we went to Nice for a radio interview, after which we drove at random, following our fancy along the Var River. We missed a turn on a road we intended to take, climbed up the steepest peak we found and ended up in Levens, a high-perched village, for a quiet lunch at an old inn that seemed to be excavated out of the rock.

We drove down through Tourette-Levens and back to Nice in time for the flight to Paris, in a glorious landscape.

Hummingbird. Thursday 17 December 1998.

A year ago, Joe Firmage awoke shortly after 6 am to see a being clothed in brilliant white light. It hovered over his bed as an electric blue sphere emerged, floated down, and entered him. Shortly afterwards he founded the International Space Sciences Organization with $3 million of his own money to manage the new *Kairos* project.

Firmage was born in Utah and raised in the Mormon religion, which he long neglected but now rediscovers, with praises of Jesus mixed up in his prose among the heady revelations of *Majestic 12*.

At a formal party at Steve and Linda Millard's house in the foothills we chatted with Paul Baran and Carl Jerassi among a hundred scientific and business luminaries from Silicon Valley. Federico Faggin was there too, with his wife.

We had a warm conversation and it occurred to me that nowhere else in the world could you have the originator of the Internet (Baran), the inventor of the birth control pill (Jerassi) and the builder of the first microprocessor (Faggin) at the same informal Christmas party.

Hummingbird. Friday 18 December 1998.

Filled with apprehension, I drove off to Oakland to see Ren, but I found him speaking and walking around, dressed in a red T-shirt, busy among three computers, developing a multimedia presentation that began with the finest poem about death: "Rage, rage at the dying of the light! Do not go gentle into that long night..."

I couldn't get it out of my mind for the rest of the day.

Spring Hill. Saturday 19 December 1998.

I continue to be intrigued and upset by the security breach of July 7th. The intrusion into our two office computers came just one week after my French partner left California, which offered our empty offices as an easy target. It also coincided with the first serious contacts I had with Vivendi, where the team has a strong emphasis on computer security. It came only five weeks after meetings when I had emphasized to him the looming dangers of Internet hacking in financial networks.

Although there was no damage the incident left me bruised. It will be a long time before I entrust another laptop with personal data. The intruders may think they were clever, but their work has created a dark cloud over my relationship with my new partners. The year ends on a surreal note, with bitter acrimony tearing up Washington, missiles uselessly screaming in Middle-eastern skies, and Wall Street riding into new summits of absurd valuation on the waves of the Web.

Hummingbird. Monday 21 December 1998.

The cold wave continues today. Kit called, back from Shanghai. He told me John Alexander had been moved aside by Bob as scientific liaison, as well as Marty Pilch as Chairman, to be replaced by Al Harrison. I said I would stay on the Board for the opportunity to see Bob, Hal and the other members and the chance to follow the work at the ranch: although the opportunity was partially botched, I would not have known how to do anything better.

The Institute now studies a classic case 8 miles away from the ranch. A cow was mutilated, a fetus removed, with blue smelly liquid oozing out. Kit thought it was embalming fluid and analysis proved him right, so he now suspects Special Forces rogues. Bob insisted the team should spend "no more than a thousand bucks" on the tests, so we'll never find out the truth. He seems convinced that interdimensional beings have done the deed as part of a complex game.

This evening I spoke to Tina, still in Sedona with the APRO files. She and Brian are wisely staying away from ufological quarrels. Janine and I will visit, since we are among the few remaining links with the Lorenzens' work and could help assess the records.

Spring Hill. Wednesday 23 December 1998.

Fringes of snow on the roof and the brick steps, ice on the pond. Jupiter and the Moon sparkle. There is a new realization that water must be abundant on Mars, at least in the form of underground ice, and even on our Moon.

We plan a quiet holiday at the ranch, a series of new experiments. Retro-causality obviously works. It is a factor in the phenomenon. There are books to read and walks into the forest.

Spring Hill. Friday 25 December 1998.

We've caught the few days of rest that eluded us since the setting up of the new Fund, the rapid start of an investment program in the chaotic context of Internet. In the glorious peace of the country, sitting by the fireplace, dark night and silence around the house, we watched several movies (*The 5000 Fingers of Dr. T, Wag the Dog, Mars Attacks*) and videotapes of Wagner's *Twilight of the Gods*.

Spring Hill. Saturday 26 December 1998.

We drove into town today, finding Ukiah more forlorn and uninspiring than ever. A local Indian tribe has started a casino that has blown away what was left of the fragile local economy. Even the local pawnshop was forced to close: people were no longer able to retrieve their possessions after losing their pay at the gaming tables.

I've been reading *The Magicians of the Golden Dawn*, by Ellic Howe, an exceptionally objective, well-documented analysis of that occult order founded by London coroner Wynn Westcott in 1887-88, which fell apart 15 years later. As British occultist Miss Stoddart wrote in 1922, "The history of the Order consists of a long series of mystifications."

They began with a cypher manuscript allegedly discovered by Westcott, but evidently forged by him, and continued with fake correspondence from a non-existing Fraulein Sprengel in Germany and instructions from "Hidden and Secret Chiefs" that eventually ignited the Aleister Crowley mythology. Similarities with the current unfolding of ufology are obvious.

To my surprise, even educated people and business minds are now ready to believe that the ultimate truth consigned to the deeper recesses of the Intelligence Community "will soon be released" on the appropriate schedule through well-chosen intermediaries. From my own viewpoint, sitting on a steep hill of unidentified cases (which no current theory begins to explain) the only reasonable attitude is that of *Frater in Vino Veritas*, as I now call Fred Beckman, who advises me to sit back and enjoy the show while conducting my investigations in the background. So, I am testing UV and EM radiation detectors to improve my instrumentation for high-value UFO sites.

Later the same day.

The above thoughts bring me back to the Rosicrucian tradition. I have always felt — as did Allen Hynek — that the objective of most esoteric groups such as the Golden Dawn, Amorc and Masonry, was intellectually and spiritually valuable. It is the execution that is flawed because human and social structures prove incompatible with the ideals. Factors of greed and hunger for power precipitate these groups into a mode of operation diametrically opposed to their high goals.

Instead of helping their members shed human constraints, they get them embroiled in technicalities and controversies; where they should free the mind to higher forms of reality they bother it with rules and insist on meetings and dues, postures and silly medals.

Traditionally, the candidate for initiation must pass between two monsters represented as lions, sphinxes or dragons. Pity the New Age adept who has forgotten that the monsters stand for a basic fact of spiritual life: on one side the candidate is in danger of being devoured by credulity and pride, on the other side by skepticism and self-doubt.

Those who squeeze through, as I hope to do, cannot be motivated either by blind faith, curiosity or peer pressure. They need no occult catechism; they have left behind academic pretension and prestige. They do need help on the path, but it is help of a different kind: assistance in deciphering the great book of nature, which is not locked in some tabernacle or basement "SCIF" but open in full view of everybody--if only they took the trouble to read it.

This is the place I've reached in my own spiritual understanding. As Allen did, I am guided by the certainty that there is another level of consciousness and undiscovered structures of reality, or rather "meta-reality." It is that higher level I have been seeking, and occasionally finding in meditation at Spring Hill under the night sky.

The Rosicrucian tradition with which I feel a connection has little in common with the corrupted hermeticism derived from the Kabala as taught by the Golden Dawn, the O.T.O., and the modern Amorc. Nor do I respond well to the tedious Judeo-christian rehashings of most Masonic groups. Reframing the God of the Old Testament as the Great Architect does little to light up the spiritual path. Throughout history there were exceptional researchers and gifted adepts who broke through primitive formulas to investigate the underlying structure of destiny and reality without compromise. One byproduct of their work was the birth of science and medicine.

Among the names I recognize (and pledge allegiance to, in spite of their flaws) are those of Paracelsus, Flamel, Nostradamus, and Paschal Beverly Randolph. If gathered in the same room they would not agree on every subject, but they exhibit the same gifts, the same passionate drive to understanding, the same clarity, the same ability to function even in a society blinded by false beliefs.

They were occultists because their innermost thoughts had to be kept hidden from those who would have persecuted them; but their work was the opposite of an "occult" endeavor: it aimed at greater light, openness and freedom. It is this work—the only Great Work worthy of the name—which inspires me here as the sun rises over the meadow and the rare majesty of the redwoods: pages from the *Liber Mundi* I yearn to read.

Hummingbird. Wednesday 30 December 1998.

We came back to the City for a few meetings. Janine and I attended a reception on board the Navy ship *Jeanne d'Arc*, always an amusing affair among local French. On my reading table is a short but well-researched book on Heaven's Gate entitled *Cosmic Suicide* (**5**). It highlights the tragic role of self-proclaimed "remote viewers" who claimed they'd perceived a UFO behind the Hale-Bopp comet, an irresponsible statement amplified by New Age luminaries who should know better.

We're beginning to see the negative effects of the modernized Web. Keith Harary, tracking dangerous cults on the Internet with Steve Leibholz, is worried about the potential for renewed violence.

Spring Hill. Friday 1 January 1999.

Already there are young shoots on bushes, birds congregating in busy community meetings on tall trees, to the delight of Janine who loves to watch them and feed them at the kitchen window. Back in European capitals, 50,000 financial workers, programmers and traders work day and night to implement the conversion of securities into the Euro currency. Olivier is among them, hard at work on his own computers.

Hal has agreed to meet with me privately in Las Vegas next weekend. Bigelow was angry when he heard Hal attended the *Kairos* meetings: "Why didn't I know about this? My own Board members don't tell me anything!" Bob got even angrier when he realized that Bob Wood was analyzing the MJ-12 documents, but Wood had suggested that NIDS sponsor his effort, only to be rebuffed. (Note). Actually, Hal had hired

---

(Note) Ten years later the existence of a real Intelligence committee called MJtwelve was revealed when a previously-classified "Special Estimate of the Situation" surfaced. Dated 5 November 1961, it mainly dealt with the threat from nuclear-powered Russian space devices, but it also mentioned the possibility of nuclear material aboard crashed unidentified devices.

James Westwood, former CIA expert on fake soviet documents who had created similar fakes for disinformation. He paid him to bring his services to Bob Wood's project. Jim's verdict was that the "Eisenhower briefing document," cornerstone of the UFO coverup argument, had all the earmarks of a fake, an American disinformation document once meant to fool the KGB.

Las Vegas. Friday 8 January 1999.

Hal tells me he's met with a high-level government official (a Kissinger type) who told him there was indeed a hidden UFO project, but he'd never have access. This is reminiscent of Barry Goldwater demanding to know about the hangars at Wright-Pat and Curtis LeMay, his old friend, getting mad: "I will assume that you did not ask this question and we will never mention this conversation again."

A mental note: what Frank Pace had told me a few years ago (**6**).

Las Vegas. Saturday 9 January 1999.

Bob Bigelow is still fascinated with "Day After" scenarios. Standing before the full Board (Kit the only missing member) he went over the history of our efforts, from the initial intent to appeal to the military to the more recent idea of having our own contingency plan if it turned out, as he put it, that "we were cohabiting on the Earth with non-human entities that controlled our destiny."

With that introduction he gave the floor to Michael Lindemann, our guest as an evening lecturer. Michael, whom I hadn't seen in years, is a 49-year old former antiwar activist, turned futurist, and speaker on New Age subjects. He is convinced that the Star Wars arsenal was not developed against Russia but against an extraterrestrial enemy. Hal put him in contact with Petersen, which led them to the idea of running "First Contact" scenarios under the sponsorship of Firmage. For silly reasons we're not supposed to know that Joe is involved.

We ended up discussing *Kairos*. Al Harrison pointed out that "After spending $2 million Firmage has failed to have any impact. The idea of going to the public is fundamentally flawed."

This took some wind out of Bob Bigelow's sails. Yet he remains convinced we are confronted with a "scenario-selecting agent," which implies that "our state of acceptance will determine when and how confirmation occurs." John Alexander, who knows the world, disagrees: he aptly observes that all our scenario discussions start from a First World context, yet "there are some cultures that accept contact already, as something that has happened."

Edgar Mitchell pitched in: "At the time when we went to the Moon, the consensus was that we were alone in the universe. Look how much things have changed!"

Hummingbird. Sunday 10 January 1999.

Much of the time yesterday was spent discussing cattle mutilations. There have been many incidents in the Uintah Basin over the years. They continue: 16 carcasses have been found, all pointing north. I also enjoyed a side discussion of terawatt lasers with Eric Davis, who makes progress in wormhole physics, working with Hal's theory of vacuum polarization. There are lasers at Livermore that produce conditions similar to those inside a star, for a brief period.

Bob got up to dictate our new role: to provide information on sightings and other events. Bob and Colm will contact us twice and each member will be expected to call with current information. With a group as busy as this, I don't think that's realistic. Bob's strength as a visionary business manager (high demand for on-time results, quantifiable budgets with tight schedules) are not the best tools in fundamental research: one needs to pick extraordinary staff members and trust them; to give them the opportunity to fail.

In the meantime, interesting events did happen on the ranch, where humanoid shapes have been reported at night by several Bureau of Indian Affairs officers and Pete Pickup, and five cows have been missing for two weeks. I had repeatedly recommended that the animals be badged with radio locators: Keeping track of a cow in 3D isn't technically difficult. Unfortunately, this was never considered.

The main incident is a mutilation involving a three-year old Hereford that was alive on 15 October. It was dead the next day and the local vet did a necropsy on the 17th. The left eye was missing, the left ear cut. Again, a blue gel substance was found smeared on the eye area and the anus. The cow was a valuable animal, uninsured. Pete Pickup and Terry Sherman were on site three hours after the call, approximately 15 hours after death. They found a standard 2 mm hole in the brisket area over the sternum going only through the hide, and internal hemorrhage at the neck (7).

Consulted by phone, Kit said some new embalming fluids or gels met the description and he suggested element analysis, which was done. Tests revealed killing by potassium chloride. Dr. Whinnery said it was standard procedure at his lab for putting pigs to death, an injection in the ear. Perhaps that was why the ear was removed?

"Potassium chloride is used by Dr. Kevorkian with his terminal patients," he said. "It causes the heart to freeze; it stops muscles from performing. An animal dies in 5 to 8 seconds: a few heart beats, then nervous system collapse. In pigs the injection can be made easily through the plexus of the eye."

"And in bovines?" I asked.

"You'd probably use the jugular vein. In cows you cannot use intra-ocular injections."

Bob argued those were theatrics for our benefit. He kindly drove me back to my motel, told me about changes planned around the Institute and asked how we should contact government. Again, I recommended a sober, quiet, non-flashy approach to the Congressional Research Service as a reliable, low-key, respected gateway to senior legislators.

Hummingbird. Sunday 24 January 1999.

Peter Sturrock tells me his book makes good progress. Indeed, it is sensible, well argued. Unfortunately, his agent uses his own accounting formulas: he gets the first royalty money and reimburses various expenses while CUFOS demands to be compensated for citing any old obscure article so that almost nothing is left for the author. Dr. Hynek would never have authorized anything so crass.

Today a milestone was reached with my team's move into new offices in San Mateo. It was a gorgeous, crisp winter day. Janine and I had coffee at Pete's Harbor, admired the sailboats and made the kind of plan one makes when everything seems easy and bright.

18

Mabillon. Sunday 31 January 1999.

Paris again: Reading Boris Vian, *L'Herbe Rouge*. I left the venture company running smoothly in California, communication systems in place, messages flowing, several deals in the pipeline. France is cold but sunny; not a cloud over the belltower of *Saint-Germain-des-Prés*.

We walked all over Montmartre, shopping for fabrics, but preoccupied by a nasty quarrel with our son. We visited my mother, strong in spirit, her mood occasionally vacillating but her handwriting surprisingly clear, unwavering at 99 years of age.

We spoke about literature, her memory of Proust writings still clear.

A café, Boulevard Saint-Michel. Wednesday 3 February 1999.

Today we celebrate 40 years of life together. My love for Janine is deeper and more soul-searing than ever. The weather is cold and dry, the sky has turned gray. Parisian students walk wearing heavy scarves, their breath a whitish puff. Meetings, interviews: *Le Monde, L'Expansion*, various startups. I love the expectation in the air, the progress it conveys but businessmen get carried away by the new technologies, the famed "convergence" we had forecast. Economists write dissertations about "asset inflation," as if they understood it.

One sudden dark spot in our lives: the injustice of sudden rejection by our son's wife. We don't even understand the reasons for what seems like an eruption of sheer hatred. Annick cheered us up.

Mabillon. Thursday 4 February 1999.

The Board room of Vivendi stretches in high-tech elegance across their headquarters building with a superb ninth-floor view of Paris. It sports a terrace garden that is level with the top of the *Arc-de-Triomphe*, in keeping with the status of its management, considered the top layer of French business today. They act accordingly, with insolent contempt for their associates.

Jean-Marie Messier, Eric Licoys, and the team of Vivendi led our investment committee today in a prestigious atmosphere that left me uncomfortable: this is not the way venture capital works.

Mabillon. Sunday 7 February 1999.

This morning Janine and I took the train to Pontoise, an hour outside Paris on the road to Normandy, to investigate an important series of sightings near the village of Haravilliers. The observations at *La Guibarderie* present one of the best examples of the UFO phenomenon yet to come from the picturesque French countryside.

My friend Gérard Deforge and the main witness, Mr. Delangle, met us at the station with Gérard's wife. When Deforge asked me to step into the case I had requested that we drive directly to the site rather than going to Delangle's house, as he proposed to do, "to hear his theories." So, we took the same road he'd followed that morning when he was going to meet fellow hunters at a country lodge (fig. 16).

The day was Saturday, 20 January 1998 and the time was 7 am, before sunrise. There was no fog, but the temperature was freezing.

Delangle, a 61-year-old retired construction manager specialized in airport control towers and concrete facilities, was driving north through the hamlet of Haravilliers, followed by another car with two friends, when they saw a mass of lights rising above the trees ahead of them. They first assumed someone had built a new communication tower with lights on top, except that the thing kept moving. It passed above them as a very large disk with banks of colored lights.

Ahead of them another witness was waiting, parked in his Mercedes with a moonroof through which he saw the object as well.

I had reviewed Delangle's drawing of the scene, showing light beams converging towards the car. The Mercedes driver was a former calibration engineer for Dassault Aviation, also retired, looking forward to a pleasant day of hunting with his buddies.

Once at the lodge I was introduced to the owner while the caretaker came by, a rough country worker with rubber boots who kept the grounds in shape. I walked over to shake his hand and we spoke about our visit and the strange object. "I saw it too!" he volunteered.

Naturally, nobody had bothered to interrogate that lowly worker. He had been riding his motorcycle a few miles north of the lodge when *he saw what he thought was an airliner flying much too low.*

In summary we have six simultaneous observations over some 15 minutes: the four men in two cars, the man in the parked Mercedes, the caretaker on his motorcycle, all within a 3-mile stretch of road. They hadn't met again as a group until I convinced Delangle to assemble them, using my "special visit" from faraway California as an inducement. Velasco, who only knew the case from Delangle, had treated it as a single-witness episode so he never followed up.

Delangle and his wife had arranged for lunch at their home in Marines, where we met two more witnesses: the owner of a woodworking company and the man in the Mercedes, a construction manager specialized in tunnels. When I showed him the painting he reacted at once: "*That's not what I saw!*" he said. "The light from it fell *vertically* through the moonroof. And it wasn't beams, but globs of light, of bright colors, on my legs and the floor of the car..."

So, I asked him if he remembered his friends driving up to the parking lot, and he had no recollection of it, just as the others didn't remember how they drove through the village. By then the object was long gone, whatever it was. But Delangle developed an eye inflammation that required consultation of a specialist, and treatment with a collyre (eye drops) for which we saw the prescription.

Janine took Delangle's wife aside: she worried about her husband, she said, usually so quiet and disciplined, now swept along by urges to tell the world about stupendous happenings in space, on the moon... But how to alert the authorities, when there is nothing specific, and no proof that the object was ever there?

And why did the caretaker see an impossible airliner?

Sedona. Friday 19 March 1999.

Sky Ranch Inn. Back in the States, traveling again. A sunset full of red shadows slides between the vertical cliffs. Here the desert turns into a Wagnerian scene, a power spot. From the wooden deck a curtain of short trees frames the distant hills, a proper landscape to reminisce with our friends, former Hynek associates Tina Choate and Brian Myers, about our experiences at Norton Air Force Base, our visits to

DAVA in March 1985, and the strange statements we'd heard from General Scott and General Miller (**8**). It's hard to forget the larger world, however, because Vivendi keeps intruding. Janine is patient with me when Paris erupts with phone calls, my partners upset at recommendations I made, going against their wishes: I keep arguing we should invest cautiously, and only in classic qualified deals, but they are drunk with the frothy landscape of the Web as imagined from the distorted perspective of Paris. Office politics are already brewing, their rigidity unable to accommodate the style of an American partnership or the open spirit of Silicon Valley.

Back in France Ira Einhorn has finally been ordered by a judge to return to the United States for a new trial.

Later the same day

General Scott retired in Peyson, said Tina. During her visit at Norton AFB he'd taken Brian and Tina to a room where they saw a massive index on a rotating belt, with page after page of UFO incidents involving military witnesses, illustrated with gun camera photos and radar records. Scott and Miller told Allen, in their presence, that they had something to show him at Edwards, but he declined to go, on Colonel Friend's advice. Colonel Friend said, "they didn't have high enough clearances," but couldn't Miller and Scott have worked within the system if they had wanted to? Was that another missed opportunity?

The discussion had turned to the documentary they were supposedly doing. Scott and Miller had taken them into a vault to produce a list of contacts, including the Coast Guard. The two officers were eager to let information out in stages. The approach changed a few weeks later when I visited them. Then Caspar Weinberger reassigned Miller and Scott and the film project was dead.

Sedona. Saturday 20 March 1999.

Tina and Brian purchase museum-quality crystals they hope to resell at a profit, thus earning enough money to pursue research. I told them that Jeffery Kaye hadn't escaped the keen scrutiny of Simonne Servais when Allen came to Paris: she had reconstructed his Israeli contacts.

As a coyote quietly walked up the road we reviewed the files in their garage, in particular the Lorenzens' original investigation of the Michalak case (**9**). The documents fill a dozen four-drawer cabinets. Their value is uneven. Many simply hold clippings or membership records but there are valuable nuggets. Jim and Coral never felt the need to build an index, or a simple chronological list. Some of the files have been dispersed. And researcher Willy Smith never returned Allen's records.

The Lorenzens were unique in the field for their grasp of the phenomenon and a more scientific approach than NICAP or MUFON. Mention of the latter organization brought a bitter smile: "We saw (MUFON director) Walt Andrus after Allen died," recalls Brian. "He told us we must work for him now as the new leader of the field, and just turn over the files!" Vanity always trumps the desire for truth.

Sedona. Sunday 21 March 1999.

The Dow Jones index broke above 10,000 this week, a psychological threshold but a fragile, unsustainable record.

Today we drove west to meet Matt Kelley, a man with a background as a smoke jumper, psychologist and warrior, who showed up one day in Scottsdale as a volunteer to assist Hynek. His house lies at the mouth of a sacred Indian canyon. A tall, kindly looking man in his early fifties, Matt offered to guide us to the well-hidden power spot of local shamans. This turned out to be an extraordinary trek but as we started climbing the gentle slope I felt dizzy, fell behind the others and actually wondered if I would be able to go on, while my head swam unsteadily. I forced myself to concentrate on the path and managed to resume walking. We stopped at a hidden rock house, hewn out of the mountain by a 70-year old recluse who camouflaged it so well that it couldn't be seen from ten feet away.

We sat by the spring at the base of a huge slanted cliff that showed ritual drawings of circles and serpents (some hundreds of years old).

Matt described himself as a turnaround expert specialized in brain studies, with an office in town where he uses a sophisticated EEG device to research dowsing and other special talents. He told me he'd suggested to Allen to follow contactees with special cameras to capture the phenomena on film and calibrate "the Aliens."

Afterwards we drove to the Bradshaw Ranch where a woman has seen many strange lights. She photographed them and published a series of puzzling pictures. The site is reminiscent of Bigelow's Utah ranch, with stories of entities emerging out of nowhere and objects diving on impossible trajectories.

Spring Hill. Friday 26 March 1999.

Going over my Arizona notes: We spent much time reflecting upon the Norton AFB episode. Tina and Brian recall the file system as a machine, about 12 feet from one end to the other, with index pages attached to belts, turned by a crank, filled with numerous reports.

We tried to visit General Scott but his phone in Peyson was never answered. I am struck by the parallel Miller-Scott-Corso, three military men with distinguished records, reporting contact with Aliens. While Corso's book is a mess hyped up by his promoter it is the colonel's desert encounter that is most significant, and the unique experiences he described to me in private, that aren't in the book.

The latest JSE contains a remarkable paper by Colm Kelleher (**10**). He points to the mechanism of retro-transposons (sequences of the human genome with the ability to alter the functions of genes) as a way of transforming some of the body's properties. Colm relates it cleverly to mystical states, some religious "miracles" and the process of illumination. Also in that issue is Kenneth Kress' assessment of parapsychology experiments at SRI from his point of view at the CIA. In his postface he mentions the disturbing suspicion that Pat Price may have leaked classified SRI data to scientologists.

New York. Monday 29 March 1999.

Central Park Hotel. The TV news shows the tragic exodus of ethnic Albanians from Kosovo; families chased away by the Serbs are fleeing; decent people traumatized, children in their arms, walking in dignity, soberly relating abominable atrocities and the ineffective bombs dropped by American high-tech planes.

In happy San Francisco the only crisis comes from a project by the Sisters of Perpetual Indulgence, a gay men's organization, to hold their 20-year anniversary on Easter Sunday. The Catholic Church is howling that such a celebration would be sacrilegious, a scandal to rival the darkest times in history, as if Christians had not "borrowed" the Easter myth from the Saviors celebrated by older cultures, martyred and reborn, like Mithra and Osiris, always on the Solstice.

New York, too, is ready for spring. Driving into Manhattan over the Queensboro Bridge gives the impression of docking into an enormous space station. In the Village, gentrified by recent waves of stock market opulence, Ingo still lives at Bowery and Fourth. I found him in his basement studio, a bit slower than I had known him, his gait dance-like. He was calm, kind and studious.

"I hate the Art world even more than the Psi world," he told me when I asked if he had a future place in mind for his giant canvasses (Note). On his desk was his current work, a manuscript about sexual energy. Ingo told me an intriguing tale about Gene Rodenberry, who used to come and see him. The idea for *Star Trek* came from a manuscript Gene received anonymously, in the mail.

We also spoke of the mysterious "Mr. Axelrod" who had contacted Ingo for a secret expedition where he saw a hovering UFO. Ingo is reverting to scientology doctrine these days, imagining spaceside entities that have controlled us by telepathy since the dawn of man. Over an Italian dinner he told me that he'd worked with Persinger in Canada. He claims that 43Hz is a psi carrier wave: "What you just witnessed is what the CIA fears most," Persinger told his staff when Ingo completed an especially brilliant series of tests.

On our way back, Ingo spoke to me in confidence of the work "going on in the Southwest."

New York. Tuesday 31 March 1999.

Delightful weather, as nice as I've ever seen in Manhattan. Wall Street basks in the sunshine and the glow of the Dow Jones. Shel Gordon tells me he got out, "having no interest in a market at this altitude." Shel expects the stock market to be healthy "only as long as liquidity supports the heady valuations," and not a minute longer.

(Note): Many of Ingo's works went to the remarkable Museum of Visionary Art in Baltimore.

Naturally we discussed the Einhorn case. Shel was recently called by someone from Philadelphia who gathered signatures against Ira, claiming he had nothing to do with Earth Day. Shel refused to sign: "For all his faults, Ira did help John McConnell organize Earth Day!"

Montréal. Friday 2 April 1999.

Intercontinental Hotel. Italian dinner with Videotron executives who may invest in our Vivendi fund. Cold, clear weather, indifferent city with a tiny old town, disfigured by new construction. The TV keeps showing the disaster in Kosovo.

Valuations of web companies—even those with no profit, no revenue, and even no product—are so high that the latest joke is about the man who catches sight of his neighbor's 8-year-old daughter selling her cat in the front yard:

"Nice cat, $500,000" reads her sign.

He laughs at her, but the next day the cat is gone.

"What happened to Kitty?" he asks. "Oh, I traded him for two rabbits, $250,000 each," the girl answers.

Spring Hill. Saturday 10 April 1999.

To my surprise I now feel indifferent to issues that used to fascinate me. In ufology, I have turned down media contacts, declined opportunities to work with Firmage and I am quite happy to let the French military keep its little secrets, as Hal and Kit are now keeping theirs. So I will keep my thoughts to myself.

Our next trip to France, delayed one week by Jean-Marie Messier, will force me to miss the next (15th) meeting of NIDS. But I do pursue the case at Haravilliers because it has novel physical and psychological features. Staying in the background, I try to help Gérard Deforge who will publish whatever we find together.

As for the abduction conundrum, which is begging for a truly scientific study, it remains badly enunciated, a ship of fools laden with sadistic fables and fraudulent hypnosis.

The lure of French-style corporate venture capital is already wearing thin as well. My new French colleagues are not entrepreneurial innovators. I don't feel at home in their world and they haven't inspired my respect. I am a witness at a discontinuity, but the pompous manifestations of French industrial arrogance bore me. (Note)

Winter lingers: wispy fog hangs on to the damp forest. I relish the closeness, our warm silent bedroom. I spent the morning reading to Janine. Magazines ponder the deepening impasse in the Balkans. Every action by the rational West uncovers more political twists, pointless slaughter and tortuous hatreds than most computer games. It is *Dungeons and Dragons* on a global scale, but with real blood.

We are helpless before the plight of refugees. Once again, we have bungled our own attempts to save their lives, and our dignity.

Mabillon. Monday 19 April 1999.

Suddenly, a rushed flight, two nights in Paris and another dark mindstorm. The team at Vivendi objects to my reluctance to rush into web investments and to the analytical way I look at deals. Like many corporate funds before, they place image and brand management above the hard, humble need to build networks of trust.

I have taken time to construct good relationships and I see no need to sign Internet deals as fast as they wish: I should throw money at dot-com startups, they said, as other VC funds are doing. They aspire to be the little girl of the talc, wealthy and proud with her two rabbits. So, this trip means a collapse of mutual trust that will be difficult to recapture. After using my track record to build up their office in California and raise their fund, their management moves in directions I despise with a style I detest.

I now understand why captive corporate Funds from Europe and Japan, with all their money and power, fail when confronted with the intense creativity and easy style of the SiliconValley culture.

(Note) My decision to resign from the Vivendi venture group was prescient: shortly thereafter a number of previously-hidden financial problems came to light within the firm. CEO Jean-Marie Messier and part of the team were forced out by his board and the company had to be reorganized after a loss of 23 billion euros, the largest in French economic history.

Paris pulsates, a bit crazy, the weather drafty and wet with odd patches of blue. The world is waiting for something, a premonition of horror and collapse. U.S. media hide the truth to avoid spoiling commercial enthusiasm but French reporting about the war in Kosovo is clear: Tears, blood, orphans: the usual stuff of history.

Hummingbird. Tuesday 20 April 1999.

I have deciphered the ugly writing on the wall and decided to leave the Fund I was helping to build. I shall be a lonely warrior again. Others may reap profits from my work, but I have my life and soul. Janine reminds me we could survive frugally if we needed to, cutting down expenses and trips. I have no desire to retire in France. I want to spend the rest of my days in California, with her.

The plane that brought me back broke out of the clouds over the Golden Gate Bridge. Then an aesthetic realization jumped at me: so much hope and spirit in the glow of this city! I felt ashamed at my fears and amazed that I ever doubted that my place was here.

Spring Hill. Saturday 24 April 1999.

On Thursday we had a long, expensive dinner with top executives of Mannesmann and Mercedes-Benz at the Ritz-Carlton, and came home with stomach aches...

For the first time in my life I am threatened with this void, yet here at Spring Hill the books and the woods tell me I am stupid to fly off so often to old Europe, stupid to equate life with a mere job, no matter how prestigious. This fear is not original. Many workers have felt what I feel, in worse circumstances. It doesn't make it any less gripping, this weight over my shoulders, the frozen brain. I should have seen the relationship wouldn't work: twice I left France because of this revulsion at the perverse way they try to control their world.

There are good friends with soothing words: Graham Burnette, currently running Holontech, tells me he would work for me "in a minute, anywhere, anytime." I certainly would love having him as a partner. Fred Adler would be delighted if we were in business again, he says with unusual warmth. Better listen to Janine who insists I should dump the French Fund without pausing to ruminate, without suing for abusive breach, without asking, "Who moved my cheese?"

Hummingbird. Monday 26 April 1999.

Sometimes, in the middle of this uncertainty, I feel a brief sense of imminent freedom verging on enthusiasm. Janine took me to see *The King of Masks*, a stunning Chinese film about change and inner beauty that helped me recover some balance.

If I'm not careful I will surely burn out, however. I parked my car in Palo Alto and couldn't find it after lunch. When Adler's office called about my new business address I couldn't even remember it.

San Mateo. Friday 30 April 1999.

The fear stays with me. I am ashamed of it. I believed I had enough spiritual fortitude to center myself psychically against vile emotions that paralyze the mind and poison the body. Evidently, I am as helpless as the next fellow. Watching the constellations or sleeping among the redwoods I thought I had learned that over the expanse of time things found their own level, that there was nothing ever to fear. But the greed of humans can threaten even the mighty forest.

Spring Hill. Saturday 1 May 1999.

Gabriel called. Our frail mother is in the hospital again with the prospects of a third operation to correct "inflammation" around the scars left by the last one. I go back to Paris with burdened heart, to try to cheer her up while working with people I no longer trust, and who don't like me. Janine doesn't deserve these tensions, the short nights and the rushed trips. As a first step we are going to bring back the most valuable books to the City. Next, sell the ranch.

Now I read the *Journal* of Abbé Mugnier (1879-1939,) friend of every writer of the *Belle Epoque*: Daudet, Proust, Huysmans... He knew Gide and Cocteau, preached in *Les Halles*, dined on Boulevard Saint-Germain, a "humble and sincere" figure, a simple priest with patience and integrity, a keen observer as I would like to be, of the world and its silliness and grandeur. "Such is my life," he wrote in 1921, "to gather words, to note some meetings, to be a parasite of the living and the dead, and then to cultivate all sorts of regrets."

In his Journal it is fascinating to find Sâr Peladan with echoes of Guaita, Boullan, Vintras, a *cortège* of mystics and would-be satanists, with commentaries on the dramatic reality and somber silliness of spiritism. In 1892 the smart young Abbé decided that ecclesiastical honors were not worth attaining: "I shall read, take care of myself, love my mother; I will cultivate beautiful souls, and I will let the dead bury the dead. That's the only way to cut short any regret, any ambition, any sadness." Good advice.

Now Joe Firmage speaks of creating a research think tank with long working sessions, to "get to the bottom of the problem." But Firmage is a convert, and this problem has no bottom.

Mabillon. Tuesday 4 May 1999.

Bad traffic: Suburban train conductors are on strike, an unforeseen consequence of a new law that dictates a 35-hour limit on the work week "to provide employment continuity (!)" In the middle of the night, when I dwelled on the absurd situation, thoughts of suicide even drifted through my tired brain. What saved me was the tender image of Janine that took over my heart, and the warmth of this apartment, my safe harbor in the storm, my refuge.

The fact that I can crawl into this abode of peace with its memories high above Paris streets saved my sanity.

Mabillon. Wednesday 5 May 1999.

Thankfully, New York called with encouraging news: Fred would put me on the payroll in a heartbeat, long enough for us to raise a new Fund, he said warmly. So the air seemed a lot freer and the *Champs-Elysées* let me breathe again.

I did have to attend a dinner with my former partners at a basement bar, the kind of trendy place they love. Slender waitresses dressed in black hovered around us, eerily.

This afternoon I will present two final deals before the top echelon of Vivendi and they will fund them if they want.

I walked over to the Seine for breakfast.

Mabillon. Thursday 6 May 1999.

Unable to sleep, 5:30 am. Among my mother's books is a life of Montherland by Pierre Sipriot that reaches into my own fascination with an era when people still found time to ponder why they were on Earth and what it meant to love. He mentions this observation about corridas, that it's really the tragedy of man that is represented, not of the bull: Man--betrayed all his life, mocked and persecuted, and finally slaughtered by forces he can't understand.

It also reveals a time when people remembered the thoughts of antiquity, like Cato speaking of civil war: "Tomorrow both parties will be mixed together in death, and the day after tomorrow in oblivion."

Later the same day, at "La Défense."

The Vivendi investment committee has approved my two deals, so I am able to leave with my head held high. If their life is a game, they might as well play to win. But I have Janine's love, I've already won.

If I never see the sterile towers rising around the *Grande Arche* like the symbols of a tasteless future I will not regret it. The new world of web services is replete with the fakery of advertising. Let's find a place where we can breathe free, undetectable by their "cookies."

This afternoon I will meet my brother at the clinic, to visit our mother who is recovering from her third operation. On the phone she sounded strong, clear-headed. The surgeon has told my brother that the new operation had gone fine, but he made it obvious he would not operate again if something else went wrong.

New York. Thursday 20 May 1999.

Park Central Hotel. Fred Adler says again he's is eager to get me back, resume our partnership and make new plans. I brought him a short memorandum with clear charts. There is new meaning in the dust of this disaster — an odd sense of beginning.

Spring Hill. Saturday 22 May 1999.

Yesterday I had lunch with Randy Fitzgerald who just published a thoughtful article in May's *Reader's Digest*. He is from Tyler, Texas, and went to school with Ira's victim, Holly Maddux. Randy was surprised I wasn't working on a new UFO book. I told him I detested what the field had become. "When humans don't understand something," I told him, "they turn it into a damned religion."

Even after my encouraging trip to New York I still feel bitter and wounded. Janine, who doesn't cut me any slack when I am in that mood, waits for me to pick myself up and get involved in new projects.

Tomorrow I will print out a new plan and mail it to potential investors, but not today. Today we play badminton and read, we joke with Catherine, we watch the blue jays in their nests.

Spring Hill. Sunday 23 May 1999.

Abbé Mugnier, on the unfair public when one tells the truth: "What people write about the Memoirs of celebrities should discourage us from any confession. Poor Rousseau strips naked before us, so we cover him with blows: 'Ah! You admit such a weakness, you miserable fellow...' We hit him again; an encouragement to live in mystery."

At Spring Hill our tenants receive death threats and we all worry about the illegal "gardens." I've written to local authorities in Ukiah with no result: the illegal pot trade supports the economy, second only to welfare, so officials get co-opted into a lucrative system. It is a dangerous game, because methamphetamine labs and crack houses are now spreading in the area. The innocent hippie pot growers of yore have been brutally replaced by heavily-armed gangs.

Reluctantly, after I'd written to Federal authorities, the Sheriff was forced to send a team to destroy the "plants" on our land. They would have been worth hundreds of thousands of dollars on the street (**11**).

Hummingbird. Tuesday 25 May 1999.

Fred Beckman raves about Joe Firmage's proposed institute. I am too tired to become involved again. What I need is time away from Silicon Valley. I am not the only one: soon a lot of people will be on vacation, including my former partners at Vivendi, because Internet stocks have started to tumble down from their absurd heights.

19

Charleston, South Carolina. Saturday 29 May 1999.

Behind Alain's house runs a river, or rather a slough filled with tidal waters from the Atlantic. Reeds grow in deep muck; when I drag out the canoe clouds of tiny insects rise, mist-like, from their shelter.

The home where Janine's brother lives is a comfortable three-bedroom brick structure with a large, modern pool and a sloping lawn, in an exclusive suburb a couple of miles from the shore. In the morning squirrels, blue jays, and cardinals saunter around the deck where Alain spreads grain for them before leaving for his restaurant. The seagulls look down on this with disdain: they feed on tiny fish and shrimp. There are oysters in the mud, and tasty crabs.

We've left ufology behind. Even NIDS leaves me cold in spite of the great staff work. Hal says the latest session was disappointing: John Mack makes no progress with abduction cases. What did they expect?

Later the same day.

Dear Abbé Mugnier! He confessed Sâr Peladan, knew Anatole France when he was writing *The Revolt of the Angels*, and met St. Yves d'Alveydre and Jules Bois. He even attended spiritualist séances with Eusapia Paladino. What he writes about Hell is wonderful: as a priest he must believe in the reality of Hell but he says there's nobody in it, because life itself is full enough with pain and horror.

Now Annick and Michel have joined us. They brought me the latest book by Houellebeck, *Les Particules Elémentaires*: finally, a Frenchman with something to say, a lucid indictment of the mess of Europe with the tapestry of its metaphysical mutations: Antiquity with its gods, Judeo-Christianity with its Absolutes, and the "sad story" of the materialistic era. It is also an indictment of May 68, the hippies and the New Age with the implausible germ of a spiritual impulse: irrelevant, in view of the biogenetic revolution that is coming fast.

The book has been bitterly criticized by French intellectuals for obvious reasons. Houellebeck shows that the delusions of the late sixties did not lead to the harmonious socialization they were supposed to introduce, but to further isolation of the individual, with violence as its only logical next step, a brilliant insight.

I have just seen what the leading forces of France had become: Greedy sharks mad with an uncontrolled, hyperbolic appetite for flashy display, power, and money. Strikes used to appear irrational to me. Now I see them as predictable components of a larger system that is itself irrational. And that silly anguish of the French, depressed about senility and death when they turn 40!

Brian Pinkerton (**12**) told me over breakfast that he was amazed, as I am, by the speed with which personal privacy was being plowed under by the Web. It has all happened over the last two years. The safeguards about data bases, user profiles and individual information that many professionals like us had fought to preserve, have been blown away by the seduction of online advertising: "People demand privacy, but if you tell them they can have a free burger at McDonald's if they waive all their rights, it's all over!" he observed.

Charleston. Sunday 30 May 1999.

Today we paid a leisurely visit to Alain's superb restaurant and had lunch at a friend's house, a rambling structure with decks and a small boat, a private marina. He served us an excellent tuna salad and rice with gambas, white wine and *Père Patriarche*.

We slept away the afternoon heat, then I took Janine on a canoe trip down the river, supreme luxury as the sun set behind the affluent houses of Mount Pleasant.

Charleston. Monday 31 May 1999.

Abbé Mugnier writes that this is a world of waste, "*tout est raté*." At least he had some fun contemplating the tiresome fiasco and confessing the guilty parties, which is beyond my ability. The break-up with Vivendi is final. I sleep like a dumb animal.

Charleston. Thursday 3 June 1999.

Every evening at high tide I push the canoe out and row along the wide turns of the river all the way to Shem Creek. We've explored the quieter zone upriver where white pelicans flew in circles, silver fish jumped in the air, mallards chased through the cloudless sky. I work editing the Journal from 12 years ago, the earlier crises on Wall Street. It was also the time for abduction tales retrieved under shoddy hypnotism. Is that when paranormal investigation took a wrong turn and began catering to the media rather than sticking to research?

Janine and I visited the town today like tourists, driving from the Yorktown aircraft carrier at Patriot Point to the old city. We went through the Citadel but didn't stop: I've seen enough barracks.

My great pleasure is the river. I love the canals lined with reeds, full of wildlife at sunset when the breeze puts silver ripples on the water. Magnificent white cranes hide in the swamp.

Spring Hill. Saturday 5 June 1999.

We made a fast trip to the ranch before my next trip to France, to reconnect with the open sky and look up references for my book project on *The Four Elements* of finance (**13**). It was a taste of what life could be if I dropped out, not to "retire" but to restructure my activities around new interests, neatly focused.

There was a time when these interests would have centered on the UFO mystery but I'm afraid I have reached the same stage as Aimé Michel did ten years ago. The mystery is still there but its dimensions are misunderstood, the problem ill-posed. A critic could tell me, "Well, what are you waiting for? Restate the problem, Vallee, if you're so smart!" I certainly have the data.

Mabillon. Sunday 13 June 1999.

There's nothing wrong with Paris, the sweet Paris of young lovers and tourists who rush around, maps in hand, a little dazed. Yet darkness lingers inside me: sadness, distress at an uncertain future. I shouldn't complain: French bioscience and the Genopole are paying for this visit and I have many doors open to me, but this is a low point. This apartment is my only refuge, my fortress.

As soon as I go down the first steps of the Métro station, that old smell of iron and ozone, burnt plastic and poster glue drifts up from the corridors, from my past, from our student days. It makes me more aware of the folks around me; it puts me in their world again. They could be characters in a Simenon novel, workers and drifters, pert secretaries and old men, bureaucrats on a routine.

There's something else about the smell of the subway, a whiff of normalcy; a certain magic too, that deceptive imminence of tomorrow. I knew it when I was a young man learning about life. Well, I'm still learning about life. There will be new magic.

Mabillon. Monday 14 June 1999.

Five am. The Left has won the European elections in France but less than half the people voted. On the Right, Chirac's party just disintergrated. European structures are slow in putting themselves into place. NATO has entered Kosovo at last, in a belated, back-handed effort to put an end to the genocide.

Janine's sweet voice on the phone speaks of the future. I keep waking up, stirring reproachful regrets: what could I have done with my work, what could I have managed more efficiently? More importantly: how could I have loved her better?

Dominique Weinstein arrived at the *Suffren* on time, his gray hair cut short. He brought a briefcase full of reports for me, including the IHEDN document we had discussed last time. This "Cometa Report" is a semi-official construct, not a government document at all. Supposedly confidential (but already in the hands of the tabloids) the text is an outgrowth of the *89 Committee* of the rightist RPR, Chirac's party. It was inspired by Gilbert Payan and signed by former associates of the Institute, no longer in function. Its publication was stimulated by our Rockefeller meeting at Pocantico.

Velasco bravely maintains the myth of CNES-Sepra but actually has no budget. He's obsessed with two lawsuits. Recently Weinstein traveled with him to a seminar on UFO history in Chicago where people speculated about what I was doing, reported Dominique: where would my archives go after my death? Richard Haines and I are suspected of "working for the government" simply because Dick has told somebody we'd attended John Alexander's briefings.

The historical work has brought up interesting speculation about pilot sightings, including recordings made from aircraft equipped for UFO detection.

Dominique speculated that the stealth technology might have been derived from UFO studies. I countered with the observation that non-lethal weapons for muscle paralysis were a much more probable parallel. I pointed out that the French worked on this kind of reverse engineering just as much as the Americans.

Paris. Wednesday 16 June 1999.

Sitting in a bistrot near the Pasteur Institute I savor the second cup of coffee of the day. The weather is already warm, with velvet in the air and the eyes of women. It is ironic that I keep being drawn to medical innovation while nothing in my background had prepared me for it. At the Genopole meetings yesterday I found I was able to play a useful role in the orientation of the portfolio and in every decision. Afterwards Gabriel Mergui introduced me to Françoise Moisans at Inserm, who suggested I should manage their seed fund for French biotech. But I would have to move back to France to do it.

Françoise was direct in her assessment of French venture developments in the health sciences.

Several funds are in creation but they risk being captured by academic chapels protecting narrow interests: the same names are on every committee.

There is a sense of imminence and chaos in the European elections and their surprises, the multiple crises in the Balkans opening up and closing like a blood-red kaleidoscopic flower. Both Janine and Steve Millard tell me I should take a couple of months off to assess new opportunities before moving forward again but they know that isn't in my nature. I could work twice as hard, make twice as much money. But I am still at heart a poet too easily distracted by the curious density of passing parades.

I feel inebriated by this city to the point of disorientation. The streets are warm, crowds flow through them like pulsing blood.

Mabillon. Saturday 19 June 1999.

Once again, I watch the morning sun behind Notre-Dame; this evening I will see the sunset over the Golden Gate, an eloquent demonstration of the magical achievements of technology that never cease to astound me. Even more amazing, everyone seems to take such marvels for granted. This trip has achieved something for me, a measure of peace, a release so great it borders on exhaustion.

Above all, I am thankful to have this apartment as a silent retreat, a place where I can crawl back and lick my wounds after a day of confrontations and negotiations. Last evening, I was barely able to get up and get the TV news to shut up, before I fell into slumber.

Hummingbird. Saturday 26 June 1999.

On the beach at Tomales Bay near Inverness, I reclined all afternoon in the warm sand next to Janine, recovering from the blows and turmoil of French business, healing my scars, watching passing kayaks. A perfect trip on the winding road from Fairfax to Bolinas: vertiginous, overhanging cliffs with the blue-green lake below.

Spring Hill. Saturday 3 July 1999.

My friend Peter Beren lives in a typical Berkeley house a mile or so from the University, a structure full of books. In the backyard a well-weathered deck overlooks a lawn and a flowerbed. Beyond the back fence runs Benevene Street where Arthur Young lived and where the psychic intelligentsia of the Bay Area used to get together in the seventies to munch on crackers, discuss Uri Geller, and bend spoons.

A couple of days ago I went to see Peter to tell him about *The Four Elements*. He caught the idea, having worked with Laurence Boldt on his book *The Tao of Abundance*. So as we were sipping coffee on Peter's wobbly wooden table I read what Boldt had written about wealth, citing Yang-Chu (from Lieh-Tzu):

"Society has set up a system of rewards beyond material goods. These include titles, social recognition, status, and political power, all wrapped up in a package called self-fulfillment. Attracted by these prizes and goaded on by social pressure, people spend their short lives tiring mind and body to chase after these goals."

"Perhaps it gives them the feeling that they have achieved something in their lives but in reality, they have sacrificed a lot. They can no longer see, hear, act or feel or think from their hearts. Everything they do is dictated by whether it can get them social gains. In the end, they've spent their lives following other people's demands and never lived a life of their own."

The book I write is a practical guide to everyday money management, but it primarily relates to personal integration and control. Yet I am still smarting from my clash with the forces of greed.

Spring Hill. Sunday 4 July 1999.

Over a recent lunch with Peter Sturrock at the Duck Club he acknowledged that the Pocantico report had had no impact among scientists: "I expected to get a few invitations from other campuses, but the only call came from Irvine, and when they heard about my work on neutrinos they thought it was more interesting, so I flew down and spoke about solar physics, instead of UFOs!"

There were some great lessons in the chaos of the last six months. I saw first-hand, the hard way, that I would never be able to dedicate my life to the business of just making money. As for my ufology work, it is complete: I know nothing, yet I know too much. Conversation with ufologists has become a pointless dance.

Ironically, many of today's sincere UFO researchers were inspired as teen-agers by George Adamski's hoaxes. Let them believe in Jacobs' abduction horrors, Hopkins' floating babes in nightgowns drifting over Manhattan, and CUFOS stories of erotic romps with buxom space Aliens. Hal Puthoff just sent me 15 pages of revelations from yet another confused businessman who claims that Bell Labs reverse-engineered crashed spacecraft to invent transistors.

Now a young buck with a three-foot rack peers at me through the bushes, resentful of my presence on "his" land, near the roses he covets. He slowly turns away to nibble on green shoots near the observatory, waiting for me to leave.

Fig.19: With Stanford mathematicians, Palo Alto, Easter 1999.

Fig.20: Meeting with startup entrepreneurs, Istanbul, Turkey, Sept. 1999.

Hummingbird. Sunday 11 July 1999.

We drove back from the ranch at midnight and spent the day setting up new file cabinets for *The Four Elements.* There was a concert at Old First Church down the street, so we went and listened to Dimitri Cogan in Beethoven's *Sonata no.10.* Afterwards they played the Concerto of Aranjuez, in memory of Rodrigo who died last week. Janine burst into tears as she hugged Dimitri. The concert put a memorable, poignant stamp on our time of such uncertainty.

Hummingbird. Saturday 17 July 1999.

Kit called. He was in San Francisco, where Kristin is giving a paper at a conference of the American Society for Mechanical Engineering. They will come over tomorrow and spend the evening with us. I am using the day to complete the first three chapters of *The Four Elements*, diving with pleasure into this new book.

Hummingbird. Monday 2 August 1999.

During Kit's visit we spoke of Bob Lazar (where is the report about his wife?) and Joe Firmage, whom he has so far declined to meet, as I did. He wonders if all the crash rumors and reverse-engineering stories had to do with protecting a technology source by disinforming the Russians during the Cold War. (Would the Russians fall for that?)

Sadly, I learned that Ingo had recently been operated of mouth cancer. To my surprise Kit didn't know about his book *Penetration.* Ingo worked for the Agency for three years, outside of his SRI contract: reportedly, his remote viewing work was so accurate nobody cared about how he did it, or any science implications.

Local media resonate with Bob Bigelow's space tourism plans and Joe Firmage's launching of ISSO, his "International Space Science Organization." Dick Haines senses Joe Firmage going the way of Steven Greer, towards a form of cultism.

Hummingbird. Friday 6 August 1999.

Last night, a visit by GianCarlo d'Alessandro and Matteo Leone from Italy. Dick Haines and his wife Carol, and Ed Stewart joined us. We spoke of Trans-en-Provence and several other significant cases.

Our apartment is still in shambles, with unfinished work on the kitchen. It seems we have lived in dust and noise all year.

Hummingbird. Wednesday 11 August 1999.

A fine drizzle was falling this morning when I took the bus to the financial center and walked around the area of my old office on Market. In search of private advice, I met with Dick Kramlich, dean of California venture capitalists, whom I used to see at Com21 Board meetings. He maintains a discreet office in an old building on Montgomery, a fine drawing of a bird of prey framed on his wall. He encouraged me to speak to various groups about a partner's position, told me who was respectable or trustworthy and who wasn't. He said he would be happy to serve as a personal reference.

The sun came up in the afternoon. The total eclipse was not visible from the U.S., but Catherine watched it in Paris. Yesterday I went back to visit Ren, under follow-up treatment for a secondary infection. Again, we reminisced about the fact that many people are alive today because of his work—and my software. The space station project, too, was planned in part over InfoMedia's Notepad.

Bayeaux. Saturday 21 August 1999.

Again, the total eclipse has coincided with an earthquake, in Turkey this time, and a smaller one in San Francisco. Two days ago there was another small one north of the City. I wonder what we will find in Istanbul, where I have agreed to give the keynote speech at a conference on technology innovation.

Peter Sturrock has found out that his agent had dissipated the money from his UFO book. I had warned him that a similar problem had befallen Philip Corso, but Peter, as a distinguished English academic, hardly listens to business advice.

When phone calls finally got through to Turkey the organizers of the Istanbul conference told me it was maintained in spite of the earthquake and numerous cancellations. Images from the region are horrible. Yet it would be cowardly not to go: our hosts are eager to find reasons to look forward, and resume normalcy.

Yesterday, as I fell asleep in the train from Paris, Max gave me a kiss and his teddy bear. At age two he is tireless, strong and always cheerful. Catherine is with us here in Bayeux, my son and his wife arrived by the night train; this cool summer gives us a rare chance to pause in the chaotic closing of the twentieth century.

I find no escape in ufology: I have lost my sense of humor about fraudulent claims, as I have about the unethical schemes of the investment sharks that now prowl the depths of the Internet.

Bayeux. Wednesday 25 August 1999.

The weather remains clear and cool. Catherine and I briskly walked the seven miles to Port-en-Bessin. Annick and Michel now own a comfortable four-bedroom house in a modern development where most of the owners are retirees. It's an easy walk to central Bayeux, its magnificent cathedral and fine pastry shops. Next door is a botanical garden hosting century-old weeping willows.

I am puzzled by Velasco's lack of interest for the Haravilliers affair. When he visited the witness he told him not to talk about his sighting and made no effort to learn any details: strange behavior for someone who was officially charged with researching the phenomenon. He could easily have done what I did, summoning together the other witnesses. This also means that the local Gendarmes had not bothered to report the case to CNES in Toulouse.

Bayeux. Thursday 26 August 1999.

Trip to Bécherel with Annick and Michel. Bécherel is a small town on a steep cliff, with a dozen bookstores of some interest. *Mont Saint Michel* looms in the distance, swimming in sunlight. We stopped in Combourg to visit Chateaubriand's massive, ugly fortress. It feels good to be here with Janine, in such quiet places…

I found my voice again to write a dozen pages of the *Four Elements*. And today I finally saw Brittany without any rain. This country is looking for its millennial destiny among technologies it doesn't master and social movements it can only manipulate. Yet the economy is improving; fiscal surplusses feed the unquenchable appetite of the bloated bureaucratic class. This would be a good time to restructure it and cut its extravagant privileges instead of fattening it even more.

Yet there is no evidence of wealth in Brittany. The stone houses of Bécherel are loaded with geraniums and blooming hortensias but a general sense of poverty lurks in every alley. Behind the church with its lurid banners, bright blue and white ("With Mary let us walk towards the Father," says the kitchy teaser) the houses look empty, their windows broken, roof shingles scattered. From the little square at the top of the village we see an abandoned cemetery and a gorgeous landscape of fields and prairies. The greedy countryside supports its economy with armies of pigs, their stench wafting over, polluting the sea where bad algae now proliferate.

Mabillon. Monday 30 August 1999.

John Alexander called from Las Vegas last night. There was something new but he couldn't discuss it over the phone, "especially under the current circumstances," meaning while I was in France. I promised to contact him when I returned.

The only French person connected with our paranormal subject whom I felt like calling was Simonne Servais. She immediately agreed to have lunch with me. We met at *Café de la Paix*. She walked up, dressed in bright red and proud as ever, a colorful shawl on her shoulders and a tiny chain around her neck, with a discreet *Croix de Lorraine* gold pendant. She has lost none of her valiant spirit. She has doubts about Velasco. She reminded me of her sighting of November Fifth (1990) when she saw "a horizontal Eiffel Tower" flying slowly over Paris, certainly not some rocket reentry.

We spoke again of her quiet role in history: In 1968 an emergency meeting held in De Gaulle's absence considered sending troops for a *coup de force* against the refineries around Paris, then in the hands of striking workers. At a break she took aside Giraud, the *Préfet de Police*, forcefully arguing against the idea: it would start an insurrection, she said, and surely lead to shots being fired. Yet De Gaulle could only reassert his power if his return was peaceful. She fortunately prevailed and the 1968 riots ended without blood being spilled, a remarkable achievement, a unique turn in French history.

Simonne uses amusing expressions. Speaking of a renovation project she found too expensive she said *cela coûterait le lard du chat...* ("That would cost the fat of the cat.")

Istanbul. Wednesday 1 September 1999.

The air conditioning system fails to dispell the heaviness that rises from the Bosphorus. Last night, over cocktails and dinner aboard the *Semiramis*, Janine and I met the delegates to this conference centered on Science Parks. Mosques and palaces sparkled in the dusky hills, occasional minarets suddenly emerging from the mist.

Janine is happy here, fulfilling an old dream. There are 2,600 years of history around us, visible from our balcony: a grandiose backdrop to help us put things into perspective. Our hosts are the technologists from Tubitak, an institute linked to the Marmara Research Center, established in 1993.

The Turks are trying to establish a technology corridor with Israel and Taiwan. I was invited to bring the experience of a practitioner. We walked across the Galata Bridge to Old Istanbul, delighting in the colors and smells of the spice market.

Istanbul. Thursday 2 September 1999.

At night the Bosphorus, wide and hot, seems to seep into our rooms like an intruding giant. Yesterday evening we took the shuttle boat across to the Asian shore.

We walked through the Arab markets and the harbor to another little mosque, a modest affair with a sidewalk that was washed over by the waves in the wake of noisy ferryboats.

Istanbul. Saturday 4 September 1999.

Last night's conference banquet was held at the Ciragan Palace, formerly the home of sultans, with marble steps to the Bosphorus. The monumental iron gates used to open up for arriving gondolas.

Business concluded with visits to the Yildiz technical university and its incubator, where a clever student displayed his novel implementation of Linux and spoke of adapting it for Turkey.

Istanbul. Sunday 5 September 1999.

With Janine as my guide this time, I saw the sublime Ayasophia (the Church of Divine Wisdom) and the palace cisterns. We walked all over the old city to the Orient Express train station, and then took a taxi up the Golden Horn to Pierre Loti's house.

In conversations with Turks from all walks of life, from professors and students to cab drivers and street vendors, a clear picture of the corruption of politicians emerges: the earthquake has thrown new light on internal scandals. As a local journalist writes, "The ruins of Turkey's political system lie under the rubble." The military have proven especially callous and incompetent. The régime has even sent back foreign relief teams, afraid that they would give the world a first-hand view of power abuses, nepotism and greed that have led to the enormous toll in human lives over the last few weeks.

Our cab driver spoke French. He told us his family still spent the night outside, afraid to be trapped indoors by aftershocks. His wife hasn't slept for days and many people "are going a little crazy."

At the height of the crisis the government even denied authorization to land to relief ships loaded with drinking water. An American hospital vessel was left idle in the Sea of Marmara while thousands of quake victims with untreated injuries suffered in devastated areas close by. Now the sun shines after a splendid storm. We watched it from our high terrace, thunder rumbling on both sides of the Bosphorus, the minarets detached from the night by eerie ultra-violet flashes, like rockets aimed at the heavens.

Hummingbird. Sunday 12 September 1999.

Tonight, I called Bob Bigelow to apologize for missing the Vegas meeting again. He told me it had gone well but there had been no breakthrough. Since the formation of Bigelow Aerospace, he has been in touch with executives of big companies with whom he is creating a consortium. When he carefully weaves references to UFOs into conversation he finds no negative reaction.

Now I learn what John Alexander wanted to tell me: through new contacts with Dana Rohrabacher, on the Aerospace committee of the House, Bigelow has spoken to Congressional staffers and a Senator who brought up the issue with Clinton. The President was very affable, very casual. He said, "I'd love to know about that stuff." In a recent book (*Friends in High Places*), Webb Hubbell reports that Clinton asked him to find out about two things: who really killed Kennedy, and what the UFO problem was all about.

Hummingbird. Friday 17 September 1999.

An elderly aunt of Janine has made what I thought was an innocent request, to be buried in the same vault where Janine's father is resting in Normandy. This opened up floods of emotions for both of us, when Janine said she had planned to reserve it for herself.

So, as I drove up and down Silicon Valley today I was not thinking of Internet software but of a tiny country cemetery in Yvetot-Bocage. I cried at the prospect of us being apart some day. At the end of the journey, I asked, why can't we be together, united to face eternity, whatever that is? Physics cannot define time, and life has not succeeded in separating us. Why should death? I had imagined our ashes would be mixed together, as our hearts and souls already are; or that they would be sent drifting over redwoods, to feed new life.

We are selling Spring Hill: our lives must change. But my heart will always be with your heart, my beloved, wherever you go.

Hummingbird. Sunday 19 September 1999.

Our friends Gary and Lori got married today at the Lion's Path Kung-Fu studio with much wielding of swords, clanging of cymbals, beating of drums and feeding of dancing dragons. Gary authored his own Chinese fortune cookies: "Your capture of an albino Yeti will be questioned when a can of white paint is found in your garage." Also, "A deceptive shadow in a tropical paradise will conceal a period in a long Faulkner sentence, making it seem even longer."

Hummingbird. Friday 24 September 1999.

Today I turned 60. A few close friends wrote or called: cards from Diana Hall, Dr. Hans Rasmussen and Yuri Lozetsev, the latter a gorgeous musical card with compliments from Voronezh. We will have a celebratory dinner with Catherine.

In all, a happy day, subdued with fine damp fog over the hills of Marin where we started looking for a place where we could preserve the research collections.

Spring Hill. Saturday 25 September 1999.

I went up to the top of the tower in the moonlight to admire this gorgeous landscape one last time. Numerous visitors have left a mark on our hearts here, from our families far and wide to passing souls in search of peace or a pure sight of constellations. Memories linger, of friends and kids, visitors eager for research, or passing poets. The graceful smiles of Diane Darling and Diana Hall, the bright paintings of Eve Berni and Penny Yrigoyen, the jokes and good advice of Keith Harary and Roger Brenner, the serious research with Oberon and Daniel Stewart, the poetry of Robin Rule and Dan Roberts, literary feasts listening to Luisa Teish and Darlene, and the delicately whimsical movies of George Kuchar…

Today we called up an agent to put the ranch on the market. Janine has sold the kitchen table and chairs. Tomorrow we give away the Subaru. We've started to streamline our lives, ahead of the Millennium. Simplification, distillation, calcination, the basic steps in the Great Work.

20

Mabillon. Tuesday 5 October 1999.

As soon as we landed in Paris we felt the coolness of occasional rain, we enjoyed family visits with Olivier and the irrepressible Max.

On Sunday I went and saw my mother again. I thought it might be a good idea to read to her rather than letting her drift into silence. I'd brought *Sky & Telescope*, with an amusing amateur astronomer's story of watching a planetary occultation as a boy. She was delighted at this. When I finished she took the magazine from my hands, to my amazement, and translated aloud the whole story into French, only stumbling once in a while on technical words.

My brother and I hadn't seen her open a book since she moved into the rest home. We had assumed her eyes didn't allow her to read clearly any more. What a lesson that was! Love and spirit can accomplish miracles at any age: how could we have forgotten that?

In a happy mood, she went on to recount memories of her own childhood, her father's great command of multiple languages, and her own travels. At 99 years her fighting spirit is intact: when nurses asked her if she wanted to attend the religious service she sent them away: "I'm not a baby any more!"

It has rained on and off. Bad sleep. Tired, we snuggled up in bed, watching the drizzle over the Sacré-Coeur, far to the north.

The Hague. Thursday 7 October 1999.

The somber ceiling over Holland does little to help us adjust to the time. Janine has gone out to see the town with a group of financial guests of Mees Pierson & Co. I stayed in the room to go over my financial presentation and to call the U.S. One of our companies, Regeneration Technologies, is closing a mezzanine round in Florida.

French researcher Claude Maugé, an astute critic, writes to me that the field of ufology took its plunge towards absurdity when Budd Hopkins published *Missing Time* and evangelized Jacobs, Strieber, and John Mack, whom he calls "pathetic:"

"It's almost impossible for me to accept some of the stories that have grown over the last 20 years. I regard *Missing Time* as the beginning of that new ufology that I see as sheer delirium, often in the psychiatric sense. Yet quite a few ufologists who had a relatively sane view of the problem have now embraced these delusions: Jacobs, Maccabee, Walt Andrus. (Ah, Gulf Breeze! And the Ladonia extraterrestrial skeleton!) With a few exceptions (notably yourself with regard to abductionists, but not strongly enough for my taste) how many ufologists have risen against the mistakes of their peers and their mercantile drift?"

Mabillon. Saturday 9 October 1999.

We came back from The Hague on the night train and slept soundly, lost in a haze of projects and plans about the creation of a new fund with Graham Burnette, full of wise advice. Regrets simmer about the lost opportunities of the past year but the air is fresh; Paris has the vibrancy of a half-forgotten flame.

A blonde girl sits across from me in this café, smiles, asks if she can borrow some paper to write. Later she undoes her long hair and smiles again. I am not in the mood for adventures: at dawn a Lufthansa jet will take me back to the West coast.

Our Paris neighbor, a rotund professor of classics, says that after 40 years in the French education system he is burnt-out from the stress of classroom violence and the hypocrisy of the bureaucracy. Yet an elegant socialist minister, Ségolène Royal, has proclaimed that "social differences have been erased!" because schools provide an extra hour of reading for those from poor families. "In the meantime, the kids threaten to beat us up," says our neighbor, "classes turn into riots, several teachers get killed every year. The students expect to get their degree without working; our role is simply to pass them. If they have a serious assignment they say their heads hurt too much!"

Hummingbird. Tuesday 12 October 1999.

Janine and I had lunch at *L'Olivier* with John Alexander and Victoria today. We spoke of NIDS and of Firmage, who meets with investors this afternoon, unrealistically hoping to raise $250M. John reminisced about his briefing to General Abrahamson; it went nowhere.

We also discussed the complex case of multiple sightings on the joint British-American airfield of Bentwaters, in England. John still believes it was a true close encounter, based on his conversations with Colonel Halt. He told us that Halt had been subjected to harassment by ufologists who went as far as abducting his son to force him to reveal a "truth" he didn't have.

Janine's candid reaction to our lunch: disbelief, an impression of unreality.

Kit is based in Singapore for three years, as the number two man for General Motors Research in Asia.

Corso's family still hasn't seen a cent from *The Day After Roswell*: his son's lawsuit against his agent reportedly drags on. The man says all the money is spent.

Hummingbird. Monday 18 October 1999.

Peter Sturrock's book arrived today, a sober work that will satisfy no one. Many witnesses exposed to the phenomenon will put the book down, impatient with its academic restraint.

The rationalists will find nothing in it to convince them the observations are credible, not even the five chapters I have contributed to the volume.

If Allen Hynek were here he would chuckle, refill his pipe, and turn back to the Sunday cartoons.

Hummingbird. Wednesday 20 October 1999.

Last night Carlo Bartalini sang mightily at our 39th wedding anniversary for an assembly of our friends that included Diana Hall, Tia Helena, Gary Shockley and Lori, Mark and Steve, Peter Beren, Keith and Darlene, and of course our daughter. They were a congenial group of writers, artists and well-travelled folk, so we joked and told stories all evening.

Gary had carved an amazing pumpkin for me, with figures in the shape of Springheel Jack, an Alien apparition that scared the public a century ago.

Hummingbird. Wednesday 27 October 1999.

Moody, nervous hours waiting for decisions, memos, draft agreements that always hang in the air between attorneys, partners and forces-that-be, bumping around in that refined space of finance where nothing is ever quite certain, or straight, "till the deal is done."

Halloween is in the air, a time of tantalizing amusement, but I am tired and so is Janine with only five hours' sleep and all those unsolved riddles hanging over the next few weeks. My fingers, my brain, my whole body tingle with anticipation of a breakthrough that hovers beyond my reach, like those invisible flying saucers of modern legend, or the embers of a faraway flame.

The first rain came, a fine drizzle that made Polk Street seem more wretched, the homeless huddling under green blankets. Many of the bars in the city pulsate with industrial music and display cascades of ferns and flowers. They are proud and loud; those on lower Polk, however, cater to a peculiar fauna that crawls around in search of quick drugs, a sickly bedraggled crowd I see every day on the way to route 101: begging, leery of cops and decoys, or just sleeping away the stoned-out hours with no hope at all.

Hummingbird. Sunday 31 October 1999.

Halloween. We walked through the Castro last night after a light Chinese dinner, Janine in her black cape. I accompanied her as a monk among a jolly crowd of space aliens, beauties dressed and undressed, nuns and playing cards, elves and slaves, ghouls and Pharaohs on parade. The weather was dry, balmy and softly breezy. We went home before midnight for our own, more quiet celebration of the last Halloween of the Millennium.

There was another mutilation on the Utah ranch at the end of September. A calf that had disappeared was found again, its internal organs scattered around in an area that had been thoroughly inspected over the previous two days. The liver showed a marked absence of copper.

This is the sixth case that George Onet has documented in the area with hypocuprosis in animals that suffered neither from malnutrition nor disease. The mystery keeps getting deeper.

Spring Hill. Sunday 7 November 1999.

When she called me two days ago to invite me to a radio panel about computer networking in France, Simonne Servais said she had been re-reading *The Network Revolution* with interest. It was a 1979 book that French publishers had turned down. "They said the Internet would never amount to anything," she recalled with a tired giggle, "do you remember? It was re-issued in England and Germany, never in France..."

Of course, they had the Minitel, so France Telecom spent the next 20 years and lots of taxpayers' money blocking the Internet. I don't have time to go to that panel, organized by publisher Odile Jacob who has just discovered networking. I do miss the French language as a tool. I am a more complete writer in French; the language suits my temperament, allowing me to hint at levels of emotion I don't express well in English. But what's the point, in such a desert?

Simonne has ferreted out the truth about the Cometa report. She says the IHEDN is furious to see its name attached to the document, and even more furious to find it has been manipulated by a vile tabloid like VSD. Payan's operation has backfired on French believers while ufologists continue to rave about the document.

At Spring Hill yesterday, we were greeted by a sky of momentous grandeur, dominated by Jupiter and Saturn in majesty, attended by sumptuous garlands of constellations. In the morning, when the dampness lifted, gold spread from one end of the horizon to the other with the leaves of velvety autumn. The air trembled, the earth sighed as if in expectation of the millennium's end. I loaded the truck with the remaining books.

Hummingbird. Wednesday 10 November 1999.

Annick's husband Michel has abruptly died in Bayeux while under doctors'care. Utterly distraught, she called Janine in panic. It was midnight in France: he'd entered the hospital for benign intestinal surgery, but his heart gave up while he was recovering. We are stunned. Janine flies off to Normandy tomorrow.

Downtown San Francisco. Friday 12 November 1999.

My French colleagues have finally sent us our new Fund's papers. In the financial center where I picked up my Air France ticket I had a quiet lunch at Silks and carefully read the founding memo again. It leaves many important items unresolved, but it is enough to put some structure around our discussions in Lyon next week. It turns the page after the stresses and crises of the last few months.

Montpellier. Wednesday 24 November 1999.

In Lyon yesterday, the city froze in the silence of a winter storm. Dawn: Nothing moved. In the TGV as the landscape of snowy fields and dark woods flew by, Graham and I made firm plans for Euro-America-III. Now many companies are gathered here for a financial meeting. Entrepreneurs talk about big plans with venture capitalists who carry fat checkbooks. The sun rises, turning the city orange and pink, Janine's favorite colors.

Paris. Cercle Interallié. Friday 26 November 1999.

Janine is on the way back to California, where I'll join her on Sunday. Peter Beren tells me a Berkeley publisher has made an offer for *The Four Elements of Financial Alchemy*. My life is there, not in fancy French salons, even if the city is clear and sunny this morning, and at night a sparkling center of old culture, an elegant monster with a soft underbelly of naughtiness, cigar smoke, and the hedonistic caress of the Seine flowing under the bridges, already illuminated for the Year 2000 celebrations.

We had our meeting in the plush armchairs of the *Cercle Interallié*, an environment initially designed for elderly English generals. Everything moves forward, too slowly for my taste.

Mabillon. Saturday 27 November 1999.

The French are good at combining new behaviors with old habits. They can be seen with a cell phone while the other hand holds a cigarette or, in the fancy salons for gentlemen, a large cigar. It takes me hours to recover from such encounters, with raspy throat and stinking clothes, but I continue to wonder, what could these people possibly be talking about on their *portables*? Are they finally revealing to each other that legendary *non-dit*, the unspoken words at the heart of secret human psychology?

Lunch with my brother on place Saint Michel. He told me somberly that he had spoken with our mother's surgeon again. Evidently her liver keeps deteriorating. "I asked the same question you did," said Gabriel sadly. "He's a liar, like all surgeons. But I believed him when he spoke of her extraordinary will to live. It could be weeks, or months." I walked back with him to the Luxembourg Gardens, discussing medical progress, cancer treatments, genetics and his skepticism about possible cures for most tumors: "I've come to believe there is another system involved, an undiscovered system. Why do some people recover from cancer, while others defy every attempt at treatment, under the same conditions?"

When I visited Maman she was sitting in her armchair by the window, smartly dressed all in white, alert. We spoke of our family, then I tried to get her interested in a short story, but she had trouble following it and got tired, so I quietly kissed her goodbye.

Spring Hill. Saturday 4 December 1999.

Farewell to Paradise: even as I go away from this place its poetry and magic tug at my soul and whisper that I am nothing but a fool. (Note) Soon the last books will go into storage again. A glorious sun bathes the dull gold of dying leaves, but the pine trees are already verdant with the sheen of new shoots. Sounds are muffled in the icy air, with a thick carpet of rotting plants underfoot and the gurgle of water rushing to the pond.

Yesterday I visited Accuray Systems for the shareholders meeting: I was on their Board for four years, during their toughest period, and

---

(Note): A month later, as she was alone at the ranch doing some final packing, Janine was surprised to see a large, brightly-lit white shape rushing down the path between the main house and the cottage. It was her second observation of an unexplained light on the property.

I always managed to raise the cash they needed to fight another day. Their new robot can track respiration and treat tumors anywhere.

The newest Mars probe is impacting the South polar cap of the planet but no communication has been established with it yet.

Hummingbird. Thursday 9 December 1999.

Memorable evening, a throwback to the 1970s, combined with the sense of chaos that characterizes the turn of the Millennium: An open house at the new California Institute for Physics and Astrophysics, downtown Palo Alto. Marsha Sims was the hostess as Bernie Haisch held a meeting upstairs. Russell Targ and Jack Sarfatti were there with Dean Brown, debating parapsychology. Russell, Dick Shoup, and Dean Radin have been laid off from Interval Research. Joe Firmage and his crew dream of new spacecraft.

Sunnyvale. Friday 10 December 1999.

At the *Lion and Compass* restaurant, long a favorite hangout of Silicon Valley venture capitalists and high-tech entrepreneurs, I just had lunch with Federico Faggin, a man with an ebullient spirit and great humor. We spoke of the absurd heights of the Nasdaq bubble: Yahoo's value is triple that of Boeing. He laughed at economists:

"They write complicated mathematical equations that fit the well-behaved phases of the economy, leaving aside the peaks and crises: Those are passing catastrophes, non-linear aberrations, of course. But it is during those crises that all money is made or lost!"

We agreed a collapse was coming. The same criticism applies to academics. Federico said the reason they were so arrogant (like Sagan's pronouncements about the impossibility of UFOs) was that they treated everybody as they did their students. There's an example of such arrogance in a recent *New Scientist* in which a reader reported "a bright orange-red glowing object passing overhead" in Bavaria. The magazine printed four answers to that person's inquiry, "Can anybody identify what I saw?" All four answers disregarded the reader's careful note that the object was silent and bright enough to be seen behind some trees. Only one "expert" was honest enough to imply he had no idea what the thing actually was. The others summarily brushed off the report with crude, embarrassing jokes.

Hummingbird. Sunday 12 December 1999.

When I called my mother today she said she was eager to see us. She clings to life and speaks bravely to reassure us, even as she feels she is reaching the end. I am sure she will fight until she sees the opening days of the Year 2000 and knows that she has truly mastered the full century mark. After that, it may be time to continue her voyage beyond our coarse and bitter world. If ever a soul had the power to transcend this plane of fragile reality, it is her's.

Federico told me that as a young professor in Padua he used to be a rationalist. Then he had an out-of-body experience that convinced him that consciousness and brain activity were not synonymous.

"It's a strange experience, when you're over here, and you see your body lying a few meters away... When I came closer to it I felt it pulsing with a series of waves or vibrations, and I stood outside watching, looking for a key, a way of reentering. Suddenly I must have found it, because I felt my arms and legs again, and was fascinated with my ability to command them to move: I couldn't detach myself from the machine of my body: I was part of it."

The conversation with Federico reminded me of Aimé Michel: the same humor, the same wonder and helplessness at the mystery.

Hummingbird. Monday 13 December 1999.

Some days are endowed with sudden intensity, the sense of imminence. There is lightness over Silicon Valley today. I spent the day writing the prospectus for our next Fund and visiting companies.

Tonight, my daughter called, suggesting coffee. We had a delightful conversation over chocolate cake at Quetzal, and then I walked home in the darkness. I felt sad about friends I had neglected or lost this year. But the sadness evaporated, giving place to dizzying happiness, an early sign of the Solstice, like a flame suddenly rekindled at a turn of a road, a comet from space hitting the sidewalk, a fresh idea of the romance of life? During my lunch with Federico the thought came back that all of physical reality was only the crust, the superficial aspect of a much larger, multidimensional information universe.

Hummingbird. Tuesday 14 December 1999.

The contract for *The Four Elements* is signed. I plan to finish the book in Normandy. San Francisco is distorted by the influx of new "Dot Com" companies fueled by venture capital. "Silicon Valley is zapping SF's cultural revolution," writes the *Chronicle* (**14**).

In the old days, legendary columnist Herb Caen described "Soma," the region South of Market now invaded by arrogant wealth:

"At lunchtime, the dice cups rattle and bang in dozens of old-time eating and drinking establishments; shaking for the check is a lusty San Francisco tradition that no amount of (earthquake) shaking can halt. South of Market, South o'the Slot, the ancient paint-starved wooden buildings lean against each other for support along the alleys named for such long-gone but no doubt admirable ladies as Clara and Clementina, Jessie and Minna. Let's hear it for these rickety old wrecks. They still stand, defying gravity, the odds and the inspectors. Truly they are the spirit of old San Francisco, bent but not broken, tipsy but on their feet, stubborn as sin and almost as definitely ugly."

That spirit of a brave city, honest enough to name its downtown streets after memorable prostitutes, has vanished under the overblown arrogance of software startups temporarily flush with money.

Spring Hill. Saturday 18 December 1999.

Dinner with Keith and Darlene at the California Culinary Academy in Napa Valley on Thursday. The wineries along the way are splendidly illuminated for the Christmas season. Keith has difficulty finding the right tone for his book, so we recounted the history of parapsychology since the War. He has been in more labs than anyone else in the field, from Eileen Garrett and Rhine to Honorton at Maimonides, Puthoff and Ed May at SRI and SAIC. Keith is too intense in his complaints, but he is right that many projects miss the point: true abilities lie beyond the statistics. Gifted subjects should not be summarily labeled "psychics" and herded like lab animals.

Larissa Vilenskaya, another figure of that era, was depressed after SRI. Keith remembers long discussions when she was suicidal, distraught at the problems in a project that promised so much.

This may be one of my last opportunities to write from Spring Hill: we now have a solid offer from a buyer for the ranch. We drove up to pick up the last boxes of blue files, under a bright half-moon diffused by clouds, the weather turning crisp.

Mabillon. Thursday 23 December 1999.

California approached the Christmas season with obscene sunshine and blue sky, but Paris stands more properly in her red and green livery and a brilliant display of flocked foliage, sparkling garlands and spinning wheels all along the Champs-Elysées.

I carry with me an undying sense of mystery, many unresolved scientific puzzles, and the memory of my mentors: Kourganoff and De Vaucouleurs, Aimé Michel and Hynek, and my father whose shadow still seems to haunt the halls of the *Palais de Justice* whenever I walk across the Seine. As for my mother, she transcends the chasm of the Millennium with resilient grace: frail but determined, her eyes bright as ever, still hungry for sights of the world.

Bayeux. Saturday 25 December 1999.

A storm has been howling around Annick's house. The rain is steady, with bursts of anger, the sky heavy: no hint of the sun. The only sounds are the clickety-clack of icy drops on the slanted windows and the vague rumble of big trucks on the road to Cherbourg. Olivier came over in time for a warm evening of stories, playful games and jokes. We ate oysters, shrimps and the unavoidable turkey, while a Yule log was the center of attention, the target of Max's eyes. Michel's memory is all around us: his death so sudden and absurd.

In the middle of the night there came a sudden burst of pressure, a great wind that made the stone house vibrate as if caught in the waves of an earthquake; then hail hammered the roof, and claps of furious thunder exploded all around us.

A few minutes later it had passed, all became quiet. Then, the steady rain again.

Bayeux. Sunday 26 December 1999.

Here I can work in luxury before the others get up, the pages of *The Four Elements* spread around. I feel blessed with my children and Max so close to me, Annick who smiles bravely through her tears, and Janine who comes into my arms to soothe my soul whenever the sky threatens to pound us into the heavy mud of Normandy.

The storm we experienced last night was the blasting edge of a tornado that destroyed two farmhouses in Isigny, killing two people. Record winds and rains have battered the northern half of France over Christmas, with 27 deaths already counted.

All train traffic is halted.

Janine and I walked over to the center of town along avenues strewn with broken branches. Large trees have been uprooted in the parks. Near the road to Arromanches a dozen pine trees in a row have been felled; they rest on a fence they have crushed. Everywhere, bits of slate have been blown away from the roofs.

Bayeux. Wednesday 29 December 1999.

Annick has made a fire. I write in the living room while Catherine and Olivier read books and Max cheers us with his babble. A second hurricane, of equal intensity to the first one, has ravaged the central and southern part of France, unprecedented in the history of French weather records. Electrical supply is precarious; diesel locomotives have been summoned to pull a few trains. The death toll rises to 50.

It is "Y2K" minus three days. Thanks to the software of one of our companies, thousands of computer programs have been hurriedly fixed to avoid processing a catastrophic "00" date.

Along the coast of Brittany thousands of volunteers are trying to clean up the insults of an oil leak from the sunken ship *Erika* that drapes black goo all over the beaches, the rocks, the fisheries of a vital tourism region. But the real disaster came with the two Christmas storms. France is reeling, not from the expected computer breakdown but from the hurricanes that ravaged the country.

The phenomenon cut a swath of devastation that is remarkable in its apocalyptic grandeur. It tore down high-power lines, bent huge pylons like cheap coat hangers, twisted telephone poles and uprooted trees in forests and parks. In Bayeux the damage is spectacular. Other regions record deaths of people and animals, farmhouses exploded, houses destroyed. Now the floods have come, cutting off Army support and rescue efforts. Telephone central offices and hospital services running on batteries are disrupted for lack of recharging.

Bayeux. Thursday 30 December 1999.

The book is finished, the bundle of economic notes I brought over from California has been reviewed and used and has gone up in smoke in Annick's fireplace. Under the steady spittle from the Norman sky I drove over to the homeless shelter on the road to Ouistreham with Annick and Janine. We donated packages of clothes and boxes of children's books. We lumber along from brown field to gray hill in poor Michel's Mercedes. Annick intends to sell it too, its memories in tow. Normandy is heavy with mud. Birds enjoy this ponderous weather that brings out earthworms and cleans the air but makes humans feel closed up, locked behind the tall hedges.

Mabillon. Friday 31 December 1999.

A radio station interrupts a classical concert to announce that Boris Yeltsin has just resigned. Russian tanks are pounding Chechnya. TV programs show politicians uttering hopeful platitudes; people around the world rush to celebrations but half a million homes in France are without electricity; nearly 100 people have died.

Later this evening Janine and I will go over to Olivier's apartment and wait for midnight with Maxime. We will walk through the square before Notre-Dame and watch the illuminations. My mother is resting, watching, eager to enter into her 100th year. We will see her tomorrow, bringing our grandson for a kiss and his smile.

The Millennium ends with a mixture of blissful thoughts and stomach-churning images forecasting an ominous future, like the stone face of Vladimir Putin as he paces over a bloody Chechen battlefield with his generals.

REFLECTIONS

As we close this book the curtain falls on a decade marked by a heady sense of discovery. The 1990s were a time of daring innovation in the United States. Technological exploration, from cyberspace to the genome, defied all prior boundaries.

Humanity's grasp briefly seemed to extend to the infinite, challenging reality itself, a dangerous and arrogant undertaking. Indeed, the inebriation of the Internet bubble was destined to crash within months, as Federico Faggin and I had anticipated, taking down the fragile fortunes of the marketing geniuses who had hyped it out of existence. But the structures that survived formed the basis of new industries and new forms of commerce and the architecture of planetary communications on an unprecedented scale.

My main passion during those years was in the support of technological innovation, particularly in medicine and in computer networks. My partners and I were able to spearhead significant companies like Mercury Interactive, Synaptic Pharmaceuticals and Accuray, supporting visionary biologists and entrepreneurs.

Privately, I continued to be fascinated by the changing complexities of unexplained phenomena. In that field, too, evidence was accumulating for the physical reality of UFOs: undiscovered breakthroughs seemed within reach; we learned a lot in Utah from the work on the ranch of Bob Bigelow.

Thanks to enlightened support from him and from Laurance Rockefeller, a small cadre of American scientists had begun to study the phenomena first-hand, at close range, over extended periods, and to openly discuss their findings. In Las Vegas, the National Institute for Discovery Science (NIDS) was able to gather, test, analyze, and document hundreds of unexplained observations. Yet it seems we failed to fully seize the opportunity Mr. Bigelow had offered us.

Looking back on the records of these projects one is forced to recognize the sheer complexity of the observations and the tenacity of the research teams, inventing methodology and new instruments on the fly while covering hundreds of miles day and night, in pursuit of elusive objects or reluctant witnesses. Yet the pioneers of this research were only rewarded with a more precise, better documented rationale for their puzzlement.

From our quiet retreat at Spring Hill, where a different series of experiments with information structures were attempted, I was also gathering my own records of unexplained events, saving them for longer-term study. Our modest observatory served as a focus, a discontinuity, a point of disrupted entropy to study a mystery that eluded us. As for the few scientists who studied the phenomenon behind the fences of Pentagon secrecy, they probably fooled themselves and their sponsors about supposed classified insights.

Thus, the most interesting challenge to man's understanding of the world and of his own consciousness remained a mystery of research within a forbidden science. Those who would have tackled the UFO mystery with the tools of physics—men like Hynek and McDonald in the 60s and 70s, and their followers like Poher, Sturrock and Haines in the 80s and 90s—had been forced to retreat into obscurity. The human spirit of discovery that was so alive and vibrant in biotechnology, electronics, and software, had been blunted here, in part because the challenge was too vast and seemingly so irrational, but also because it touched on truths we would rather not scrutinize: they interrogated us at the level of our beings, our beliefs, our faiths, our fears about what may lie in other galaxies—or under the bed.

I have continued compiling *Forbidden Science* as an archival collection of diary records instead of writing for a wider public. I have no ideology to present and no theory to hype, no politician to lobby and no axe to grind. Future researchers will do with these volumes as they wish. For me, the work is its own reward because, as the flawed mystic Otto Rahn wrote in *The Court of Lucifer*,

Le souvenir est le seul Paradis dont on ne peut être chassé.
(Memory is the only Heaven from which we cannot be evicted)

NOTES AND REFERENCES

Part Thirteen: Alien Rumors.

1. About the Russian UFO incidents at the end of 1989, see the *New York Times* for October 9 and October 12 ("Tass' Thrill: Joking over UFO Report,") San Francisco *Examiner* for October 10 ("Tass says UFO landed in USSR"), *SF Chronicle* ("Soviets now allowing space creatures to land") and *Washington Post* for October 10. The first notice of the case appeared in the local Voronezh paper, *Kommuna*, for October 3, 1989, p.4, written by A. Mosolov and entitled "A Football Game with Aliens."

2. Martine Castello's article about the New Age in America, co-authored with Annick Lacroix, was published in *Madame Figaro* for 27 January 1990. *Jours de France Madame* had previously published an interview of me in (January 1st, 1990.) entitled *Faut-il Croire aux Extra-terrestres?*

3. Michael Murphy: *An End to Ordinary History*. L.A.: Tarcher 1982.

4. The book came out under the title: *UFO Chronicles of the Soviet Union—a Cosmic Samizdat* (NY: Ballantine, 1992.) The Russian word *Samizdat* designates a category of literary works that were banned or very hard to find in the Soviet Union, and which circulated privately as typescripts.

5. I learned in 2016 that Zolotov had been murdered in front of his house.

6. According to researcher Stephan Schwartz "Scott was not Senator Pell's chief of Staff. He was hired as a special assistant (…) Scott's brief was to follow Pell's interest in parapsychology." (Private email, 22 July 2013.)

7. Charonne is the name of a Paris Métro station where a dozen unarmed people demonstrating against rightist policies were clubbed to death or injured by rioting policemen who were never punished by DeGaulle. This event, which took place on 8 February 1962, contributed to my decision to leave France.

8. The Cergy-Pontoise events of 26 November 1979 involved three young men who described a peculiar light and fog surrounding their car. One of them, Franck Fontaine, disappeared for an entire week while police searched for him all over France. It was later claimed that he had been abducted, while the CNES team of GEPAN concluded it was a hoax. See an interpretation of the case as psychological warfare in my book *Revelations*.

9. Gilbert Payan is an important man, a French industrialist and advisor to the military who specialized in high-energy lasers, optics, metallurgy and non-lethal weapons. He was the anonymous author of several quasi-official statements about UFOs, including the notorious "Cometa Report."

10. Dr. Edwin May, a physicist, had a long tenure as a parapsychology research leader at SRI and SAIC, running the remote viewing project in Menlo Park from 1985 to 1995 under several government agencies after the departure of Dr. Harold Puthoff to Texas.

11. Like Adamski, "Billy" Eduard Albert Meier, a citizen of Switzerland, claimed to be a UFO contactee and prophet. He produced many controversial UFO photographs as evidence of his encounters with aliens from the Pleiades. Meier's pictures and films are widely regarded as fakes.

12. Jose Maria de Heredia, poem for his daughter Marie (Maricotte). Quoted in *Les Yeux Noirs* by Dominique Bona. Paris: J.C. Lattes 1989.

13. Simonne Servais (editor): *Regards sur DeGaulle*. Paris: Plon 1990.

14. The GEPA (*Groupe d'Etude des Phénomènes Aériens*) was formed in January 1963 by a distinguished group of French scientists and military officers, including Dr. René Hardy and Général Chassin, at the initiative of philosopher Rene Fouéré.

15. During the 1980s Colonel John Alexander and a small cadre of scientists with high clearances attempted to get funding for a large-scale research project on UFOs, to be sponsored by the Space Command, the Air Force and the Intelligence community. I nicknamed the project *The Secret Onion* because it was supposed to involve several layers of researchers with decreasing levels of access.

16. *Grill Flame* was the code name of a classified parapsychology research program at SRI in early 1979, which carried out hundreds of remote viewing experiments through 1986.

17. In April 1990 Craig Fields (then 43 years old) was terminated from his position at DARPA following a series of political issues when he sought to finance research into high-definition television. "Mr. Fields approached the problem as a technologist, not a politician, and stumbled badly. He proposed to leapfrog the first generation of HDTV sets... This meant funding a host of exotic technologies... but he couldn't find the money to pull it off," said the *Wall Street Journal* for June 6, 1990, in an article by Bob Davis. In late April an emissary from Deputy Defense Secretary Donald Atwood's office reportedly showed up at DARPA and handed Craig Fields a piece of paper with a new assignment. He was told to sign the paper or be fired for insubordination. "He signed and now spends his days in a dead-end job studying the Pentagon's laboratories and looking for work outside the government."

18. Pierre Guérin's book was published as: *OVNI, les mécanismes d'une désinformation*. Paris: Albin Michel 2000.

19. *Daisy* was a leader in computer-based design of electronic circuits.

Founded by an Israeli group headed up by Aryeh Finegold, it was financed in part by Fred Adler and it went public in the United States. It fell on hard times in 1989 and 1990. Bankruptcy was imminent when this was written.

20. Hermann Julius Oberth (1894-1989) was an Austro-Hungarian-born German physicist and engineer. He is considered as Von Braun's mentor and one of the founding fathers of astronautics. He stated: "It is my thesis that flying saucers are real and that they are space ships from another solar system. There is no doubt in my mind that these objects are interplanetary craft of some sort. I and my colleagues are confident that they do not originate in our solar system."

21. See for example: "U.S. soldiers leave their earthly posts to look for UFOs." *The Seattle Times*, 19 July 1990.

22. Fred Beckman was in touch with a sizeable network of private researchers I didn't know, and he loved to keep those contacts mysterious.

23. *Alintel* is the name of a novel I published in 1986 (Paris: Le Mercure de France). An American adaptation was published by Frog, Ltd. of Berkeley under the title *FastWalker* in 1996.

24. My mother's "Passavant" family first appears in historical records in 925 AD with William I de la Haye and his brother Aimery, who descended from a Count of Anjou. It is in 1025 that Sebran de la Haye was given the fortress of Passavant on the shores of the Layon River (now in Maine-et-Loire and still standing). About 1125, as a reward for services during the Crusades, one of his descendants named Geoffroy, a humble knight who lived in Champagne, was granted the right of founding La Haye in the Vosges region and another town of Passavant-sur-Coney on the border between Champagne and Lorraine. He had two sons: Simon and Barthélémy de Passavant. The latter married Elisabeth de Lusignan, who came from a family with a legendary connection to the Fée Mélusine. The couple had three children: a daughter named Elisabeth (who would marry Philippe II d'Armagnac, sire de Nemours), Richard I sire de Passavant who eventually built a church in Martinvelle, and Jehan, sire de Saule. My mother's family is issued from Richard.

25. "Welcome to Annwfn," by Diane Darling. *Green Egg* vol.XXI No.81, Beltane 1988.

26. SangStat Medical Corporation, a company launched in Palo Alto by Dr. Philippe Pouletty and financed in part by our Euro-America fund in 1990, went public in December 1993. I served on the Board of both the US Company and the French subsidiary. Sangstat was acquired by Genzyme Corp. in 2003, thus moving Genzyme into the organ transplant market.

SangStat's lead product, Thymoglobulin (antithymocyte globulin) is indicated for the treatment of acute rejection in kidney transplant patients.

27. After much work and delay, Universal Studios were unimpressed by the script and decided not to make the movie. However they kept the rights, and the ending of the novel inspired the final sequence in Spielberg's movie *Indiana Jones and the Kingdom of the Crystal Skull* (2008).

28. The 1968 Cuban case: this episode was described in detail in *UFO Chronicles of the Soviet Union* (NY: Ballantine 1992) pp.82-85.

29. "Volatile Vacuums," OMNI February 1991 p. 50.

30. *Operators and Things,* by Barbara O'Brien had a hardcover edition by Arlington Books (1958) and paperbacks by Ace (1958) and Signet (1976.)

31. Hubert Curien served as French minister of research and technology from 1984 to 1986 and again from 1988 to 1993.

32. Synaptic Pharmaceutical Corporation, in which I invested on behalf of Euro-America in 1991, went public five years later. It was subsequently acquired by Lundbeck. Synaptic had a number of central nervous system projects focused on depression, anxiety, and psychosis.

33. Marcel Vogel had worked for IBM for 27 years, pioneering the technique of magnetic disk "thin films" that proved to be a major source of revenue for the company. His studies on parapsychology included research on man-plant communication. They were published in 1974 in the anthology *Psychic Exploration* by Edgar Mitchell and in Peter Tompkins and Christopher Bird's *Secret Life of Plants* in 1973. I had met him in 1976 (see Part Seven.)

34. The citations about Jean-Charles Passavant are from *Biographie Universelle Michaud* (Paris: Desplaces and Leipzik: Brockhaus.) There was also a Charles-Guillaume Passavant, theologian and pedagogue, born in Minden (Westphalia) on 27 July 1779, who died on 16 July 1846 in Halle. He was the Preacher at the Detmold Collégiale, later the first Pastor at Our Lady of Bremen. He published a critique of Pestalozzi's method, based on observations made in Berthoud (Detmold, 1804), also sermons (1815) and a treatise: *The Principal Protestant Dogmas and Their Respective Importance from a Moral and Pedagogical Viewpoint* (Bremen, 1830.)

Another writer in the family was German artist Jules-David Passavant, born in Frankfurt in 1787, first destined to be a businessman. He changed his mind, studied art under David and Gros, and went to school in Paris from 1810 to 1813. He is the author of an *Artistic Journey in England and Belgium* (Frankfurt 1833,) of *Christian Art in Spain* (Leipzik 1853) and especially of the classic *History of Raphael of Urbin and his father Giovanni Santi* (Leipeik 1839, in two volumes.) He served as director of the gallery of the Schoedel Institute in Frankfurt. See by Heimo and Leonore Korner: *Les*

Seigneurs de Passavant de la Maison de La Haye, in Archives of Georges Claude Passavant, 1981, in German.

35. Julia Phillips, *You'll never eat lunch in this town again*. NY: Random House 1991.

36. Isocor, a software company specialized in corporate directory servers for internal communications, was founded in Los Angeles. We invested in the company through the Euro-America funds in 1991. It went public on Nasdaq in 2000 under the name "Critical Path."

37. Gulf Breeze: On 11 November 1987 a Florida contractor named Ed Walters allegedly saw a bluish-gray craft over his yard and photographed it with a Polaroid camera. He saw the same craft repeatedly and claimed he was abducted by it, a fact that was enthusiastically endorsed by Budd Hopkins. Walters induced MUFON and Bruce Maccabee to conduct elaborate "analyses" of his experiences, described in a controversial book entitled *The Gulf Breeze Sightings* (NY: Morrow 1990.) Numerous experts questioned the authenticity of the photographs. The book neglected to disclose that Walters had once been condemned to three concurrent sentences of five years for forgery, had served two and a half years in State prison, and had been observed to fake "paranormal" photographs.

38. *October Surprise* and BCCI: In 1989 a parapsychologist named Barbara Honegger who had served briefly on Ronald Reagan's White House staff published a book entitled *October Surprise* (NY: Tudor 1989) in which she argued that Reagan and Bush had made a secret deal with the Ayatollah Khomeini to delay the release of 52 American hostages held in Iran, in order to sabotage Carter's re-election. BCCI, the Bank of Commerce and Industry, was a powerful multinational banking empire that was used by drug dealers, governments, and secret organizations all over the world to launder money.

39. *Scitex*, a leading Israeli company that pioneered digital image processing, was founded by a brilliant scientist named Efi Arazi. Coming to California, he launched another company called *Electronics for Imaging*, in the financing of which my partners and I participated.

40. That book by David Jacobs was entitled *Secret Life: Firsthand, Documented Accounts of UFO Abductions* (NY: Simon & Schuster – Fireside, 1993.)

41. Adam Rostoker's article, entitled *Whence Came the Stranger: Tracking the Metapattern of "Stranger in a Strange Land,"* was published in three parts in the *Green Egg*, respectively in XXV (1992) no.97 page 6, no.98 page 6 and no.99 page 10.

42. Bishop Pike's psychic experiences: A celebrated American theologian,

Bishop James A. Pike wrote a book entitled *The Other Side* (Doubleday, 1968) in which he pondered the poltergeist phenomena that followed the suicide of his son in February 1966. The book was co-authored with his mistress Diane Kennedy. When she committed suicide herself he was propelled into a bizarre quest for the identity of Christ that sent him to the deserts of Israel, where he walked off alone into the wilderness and died. For a general perspective on these events one should read the novel *The Transmigration of Timothy Archer* by Philip K. Dick (Random House Vintage, 1991) and *Divine Invasions* by Lawrence Sutin (Citadel Twilight 1991,) a superb biography of Philip Dick.

43. Clark, David and Roberts, Andy, *Phantoms of the Sky: UFOs, a Modern Myth?* London: Robert Hale publishers, 1990.

44. *SF Chronicle* Tuesday May 12, report by Thomas H. Maugh of *LA Times*: "Magnetic particles found throughout the human brain."

45. IRT Corp., in San Diego, specialized in X-ray inspection systems for industry, radiation hardening for electronic circuits and sterilization of medical equipment using linear accelerators. I served on the board after investing in the company through the Euro-America funds in 1990. The company was eventually acquired by Thermo Instrument Systems, Inc.

46. The book was *Teachings of an Initiate* by Max Heindel, which Allen Hynek had bought in 1929.

47. Howard C. Cross was a senior metallurgist at Battelle Memorial Institute in Columbus, Ohio. In the late 1940s he specialized in exotic metallurgy and titanium alloy research. He served as the head of an early assessment of UFOs, which became known as *Report Fourteen* (1954.)

48. About De Grossouvre see *Le Figaro*, Thursday 13 August 1992, p. 5, article by Nicole Kern.

49. As already mentioned in note (8) above, the abduction of Franck Fontaine, variously interpreted as a hoax, as an exercise in psychological warfare, or as a true UFO event, began on November 26, 1979 in the parking lot of an apartment building in Cergy-Pontoise, France. I have analyzed this "Purple Justice" case in *Revelations* (Chapter 5) published in 1991. My conclusion was that Franck may have been abducted and drugged by a French commando as part of a mind control exercise.

50. *November Fifth*: On that date in 1990, about 7 p.m., sightings of a very large, dark triangle with many lights were made all over France, near the time of the reentry of a Russian satellite. This led to many angry comments from witnesses who disagreed with the official explanation given by Jean-Jacques Velasco of CNES/SEPRA. See my blue file F247 and the book by Franck Marie, *OVNI Contact* (Bagneux: SRES 1993.)

51. On Randolph's organization see *Dr. Paschal Beverly Randolph and the*

Supreme Grand Dome of the Rosicrucians in France by R. Swinburne Clymer (Quakertown, Pa.: Philosophical Publishing Co. 1929). Randolph, who died in 1875, led a branch of the Rosicrucian movement in the mid-nineteenth century, visited France several times. He was a mixed-blood man of remarkable intelligence, and a friend of Abraham Lincoln. He advocated a form of Christian Tantra. (See Serge Hutin, *Histoire des Rose-Croix*, Paris: Courrier du Livre 1962.)

52. The CEPH, or *Centre d'Etude du Polymorphisme Humain*, is an organization started by two leading French doctors, Nobel laureate Jean Dausset and Daniel Cohen. Nadine Cohen was the latter's sister.

53. InferOne was a software company specialized in artificial intelligence. It moved to California under the name Datamind, was acquired by Epiphany, went public on Nasdaq and became generally known as Rightpoint.

54. In vain, I suggested a more quiet way of contacting decision-makers in Washington through the Office of Technology Assessment, where my friend Robert Chartrand had a long-term interest in, and knowledge of, the UFO subject. He had worked closely with Al Gore in connection with our Hearings on Emergency Management a decade before.

Part Fourteen: Hummingbird

1. The "Philadelphia Experiment" hoax: an alleged wartime Navy experiment supposed to have been carried out at the Philadelphia Naval Shipyard, about October 28, 1943. The destroyer escort *USS Eldridge* (DE-173) was claimed to have been rendered invisible (or "cloaked") to enemy devices. The story first appeared in 1955, in letters of unknown origin sent by a "Carlos Allende"to a writer and astronomer, Morris K. Jessup.

2. Labimap, a medical instrumentation company specializing in the analysis and decoding of DNA molecules, was a spinoff of the Bertin Company under the incentive of Dr. Daniel Cohen. Their first product was the "multiblotter" robot that enabled Cohen, a medical pioneer, to produce early maps of the human genome at Genethon.

3. SCIF stands for a "Sensitive Compartmented Information Facility" designed to prevent eavesdropping.

4. Dr. Simon was the Boston psychiatrist who hypnotized witnesses Betty and Barney Hill in one of the most celebrated abduction cases, following their observation of a disk with occupants in 1961.

5. *Anatomy of a Hoax* was published in *JSE* Vol.8, No.1, spring 1994, and became one of their most popular articles.

6. Mr. Steve Yantis wrote to me in December 1992, describing a remarkable observation of a dark green triangular or wedge-shaped object 25 to 30 feet long, 5 to 6 feet high, of which he sent me a model. The object was seen in February or March of 1984 near Fort Lewis Army Base and McChord AFB in Washington State, at about 3:30 a.m. It hovered silently during the observation. Blue File F194.

7. The Pentacle Memo was reprinted in full in *UFO Magazine*, Vol.8, No.2, 1993 and in *Just Cause* No.35, March 1993. See also Blue File F258.

8. The Ummo letters were a hoax, a series of documents allegedly coming from aliens living on a planet orbiting Wolf 424. The letters circulated in the 1960s. Psychologist Jose Luis Jordan Pena admitted to starting the hoax.

9. Gordon Novel also made claims about the Kennedy assassination: "The affidavit was essentially a confession by me admitting to criminally covering up the assassination in 1967 through 1969 for White House and C.I.A. In it I named the assassin on the hill (Slew Montgomery of Dallas); backup assassin (Larry Blancset); weapon 303 Savage automatic with Werbell partial directional silencer; bullet: frangible projectile of powered depleted uranium bake fused in keibeinbill caking; conspirators: Richard Helms, Howard Osborn, and K.G.B. double agent Valery Vladimirovich Kosakov; dead control agents - William Harvey and George de Morenschmidt. I named all the C.I.A. and White House people I worked with to create Garrison's phony investigation and then destroy it to muddy the waters..."

10. See "Inertia as a Zero-Point Field Lorentz force" by Bernhard Haisch, Alfonso Rueda & H.E. Puthoff. *Physical Review A*, Vol.49 No.2 Feb. 1994.

11. This claim of terminal condition on the part of Dr. Targ was fortunately a false alarm.

12. The hoax was exposed in *The Willamette Pass Oregon UFO Photo Revisited: An Explanation,* by Irwin Wieder in JSE vol.7, no.2 pp.173-198.

13. Jim Pelkey was a senior partner at Montgomery Securities who was shot four times by his wife over an episode of infidelity, severing his spine.

14. See the "Winery Frog" case analysis in *Confrontations*, NY: Ballantine 1990, chapter 4, pp.71-78.

15. See *ESP Wars: East and West: An Account of the Military Use of Psychic Espionage as Narrated by the Key Russian and American Players* by Edwin C. May, Victor Rubel, and Lloyd Auerbach. Paperback, 336 pp. Published August 9th 2014 by Createspace.

16. The film was based on the book *In Advance of the Landing: Folk Concepts of Outer Space,* by Douglas Curran (NY: Abbeville Press 1985.)

17. Unarius is a San Diego area UFO group composed of contactees who believe they have come from various planets in previous lives.

18. Linda Falorio is a poetess, writer and artist who authored a remarkable "Shadow Tarot" (Pittsburgh: Headless Press 1988.) She inspired several magicians, such as Mishlen Linden, the author of *Typhonian Teratomas: The Shadow of the Abyss* (Cincinnati: Black Moon, 1991.) According to magical tradition, the Qliphoth are the opposite of the Cabalistic Sephiroth, a sort of mirror image of the Tree of Life. As the Sephiroth express Light, the Qliphoth are said to express Darkness, ruled by hermaphroditic goddesses.

19. The Dr. X story, first revealed by Aimé Michel, centers on the observation of two merging disks in the sky over Sisteron on November 2, 1968, with subsequent observation of skin discoloration on the witness'abdomen and claims of paranormal healing.

20. It is likely that the joke had to do with the fact that the lab was testing invisibility devices of the "low observable" and cloaking type.

21. *Skeptics UFO Newsletter* (SUN) #24, Nov. 1993, by Philip Klass.

22. The paper was entitled "The Role and Limitations of High Technology in Emergency Management: Some Insights from Silicon Valley." Annual Meeting of the American Association for the Advancement of Science (AAAS), San Francisco, 20 February 1994.

George Brown is mentioned in Ann Druffel's biography of Dr. James McDonald as one of his Washington contacts.

23. Dr. John Mack's book was *Passport to the Cosmos.*

24. *La Dernière Heure*. 16 Mars 1994. "Les OVNIs Contre-attaquent."

25. *Newsweek* Magazine, ca.10 April 1994.

26. *Time Magazine* circa 18 April 1994. See also the front-page article "A Harvard Doctor Offers Relief for Those 'Abducted' by UFOs," *Wall Street Journal*, Thursday May 14, 1992.

27. *The Economist*, issue of 16 April 1994.

28. Characteristically, I never received any results from the investigation of these granules. Similarly, Velasco and the CNES never gave me any news of developments after I turned over my OVNIBASE program to them. In contrast, in February 1996 George Knapp gave me the results of an analysis performed by Dr. Lefty Levengood. He found that the granules were consistently spherical; their diameter varied from 0.5 to 0.8 mm. They seemed to be made of a high sulfur-containing glass, and could be part of an electro-optic device.

29. Roussel: *OVNI: Secrets cachés de l'enquête officielle*. Paris: Albin Michel 1994.

30. Rennes-le-Château is the site of the Magdalen tower built by Abbé Saunière, where the secret of the Holy Grail is said to be resting, according to Gérard de Sède and to Michael Baigent, Richard Leigh, and Henry Lincoln, authors of *Holy Blood, Holy Grail* (NY: Delacorte 1982.)

31. *The Unpleasant Profession of Jonathan Hoag*, also his *Puppet Masters*, both of which reminded Ron Westrum of abduction stories, a long time before they began circulating.

32. Accuray Systems succeeded in developing a robotic (stereotactic) surgical instrument for the treatment of inoperable brain and upper spine tumors, later extended to sites throughout the body.

33. About Crussard's psychokinetic experiments see C. Crussard and J. Bouvaist: "Etude de Quelques Déformations et Transformations Apparemment Anormales de Métaux" in *Mémoires Scientifiques de la Revue de Métallurgie*, February 1978.

34. Articles about Ubique appeared in many papers, notably the *New York Times* for Tuesday, September 13, 1994 ("A 'virtual' Trade Show: You Don't Have to Go" by Peter H. Lewis) and the *Wall Street Journal* of the same date ("New Products aimed at Users of the Internet," by Jared Sandberg.)

35. *Second-Order Consequences,* by Raymond Bauer. MIT Press, Technology, Space and Society Series, 1969.

36. See the letter to the editor by David Jacobs attacking me *ad hominem* for my position on abductions in JSE Vol.8, No.3 Autumn 1994, p.407.

37. I had met Al Bielek in 1967 in Evanston (see Volume One, entry for 14 March 1967.) At the time he claimed to be a close friend of naturalist Ivan T. Sanderson.

38. The BSW Foundation's address was 766 Madison Avenue, NYC.

39. Research has been done to interfere with cardiac rhythm through means including electromagnetic radiation and even parapsychology. A 1972 declassified DIA report entitled *Controlled Offensive Behavior–USSR* alludes to psychic Kulagina stopping the beating of a frog's heart in solution and re-activating it. The report adds: "This is perhaps the most significant PK test done and its military implications in controlled offensive behavior, if true, are extremely important." (Source: M. Ullman)

40. Letter by Glenn Krawczyk, of Australia. *New Scientist*, 17 Dec. 1994.

41. In 1995 a videotape projected at the *Dialog with the Universe* conference in Dusseldorf allegedly showed Gordon Cooper stating that a UFO had once landed at an airbase where he was stationed, and that it was filmed as it landed. He had sent the film and documents to Washington. This was mentioned on the Internet on October 28, 1995, according to John Schuessler's newsletter *UFO Potpourri* No.397, December 1995.

42. About the Solar Temple and its simulations of alien contact see the interview of Renaud Marhic in *Phénomèna* No.29, Sept-Oct. 1995, page 28: "As in most secret societies, the ultimate goal of the OTS was transformation in depth of our world. This transformation was accomplished on mystical bases but also on political ones. Therefore it exploited the extraterrestrial theme, evoking alleged beings from Sirius, Venus or Proxima..."

43. In 1988 a Federal Court dismissed a lawsuit by Adler & Shaykin against Linda Wachner, a former managing director, for return of fees they paid to her in their failed attempt to buy a division of Revlon. (*Wall Street Journal Index*, 12/15.)

44. The paintings and sculptures by Hopkins, prior to his public interest in abduction cases, involved flat altars ("altars are sacred platforms") in enclosed spaces and "Guardians" defined as "sentinels, participating in a frozen ritual, fixed—absolutely—within a privileged space," close parallels to the themes he later "discovered" when he hypnotized UFO witnesses.

45. *New Scientist* 18 Feb.1995, 'Nearby Space Could not Support Life' by Benjamin Zuckerman.

46. My classification scheme for anomalies was first published as "Bringing Order Out of Chaos: Definitions and Classifications," an appendix to *Confrontations* (NY: Ballantine 1991, pp.231-244. It was later reprinted in the April 1995 edition of *Omni Magazine,* page 54.

47. Active Measures are a set of intelligence techniques for the dissemination of misleading narratives based on true facts. The planting of stories and memes by the CIA and the KGB became a veritable cottage industry after the spreading of the Internet.

48. Jim Schnabel, "Tinker, Tailor, Soldier, Psi" in the *Independent* on Sunday, 27 August 1995.

49. The obituary of my mentor Gérard de Vaucouleurs was published in the *New York Times* of 12 October 1995. His death came shortly after that of another great astrophysicist, Chandrasekhar, who died in August at age 84.

50. See in particular I. A. Crowford (University College, London), "Some Thoughts on the Implications of Faster-than-Light Interstellar Space Travel." published in the *Quarterly Journal of the Royal Astronomical Society* (1995) No.36, 205-218.

51. *Enquête sur les Extrémistes de l'Occulte*, by Renaud Marhic. Bordeaux: L'Horizon Chimérique 1995.

52. "Consciousness, Culture, and UFOs" in *Noetic Review*, Winter 1995, p.6. This article was widely quoted and reprinted.

53. Bob Gates' claim that the CIA pursued remote viewing "only because Congress made them do it" is hard to take seriously.

54. Blogger and investigator Gary S. Bekkum of STARpod.org reported on the web that "Pandolfi first hit mainstream news pages in the late 1990s, following an investigation of unauthorized technology transfers from American defense contractors to the People's Republic of China."

Bekkum cited Ken Timmerman, writing for *The American Spectator*, who claimed that "Ronald Pandolfi was the CIA's highest ranking scientist when he visited the headquarters of Hughes Space and Communications in El Segundo, California in 1996."

The *Congressional Research Service Reports* state that: "A CIA analyst, Ronald Pandolfi, briefed the Senate Intelligence Committee on what he had found in 1995 about Hughes' review of the explosion of a Long March rocket in January 1995. The CIA then allegedly alerted Hughes about Pandolfi's briefing, reportedly according to an internal CIA cable dated September 23, 1998. The Committee then asked Attorney General Janet Reno for a criminal investigation into whether the CIA improperly obstructed a Senate investigation."

According to Timmerman, "After Pandolfi testified in closed session before Senate Intelligence Committee Chairman Richard Shelby (R-Ala.), he was removed from the China division and put to work on developing alternative energy sources."

Bekkum adds: "Some believe the "alternative energy sources" include exotic spacecraft propulsion systems with capabilities associated with intelligently controlled extraterrestrial flying objects."

55. *Le 54ème*, by Thierry Huguenin. Paris: Fixot 1995. About the second massacre of the Order of the Solar Temple, see *The European* for 4-10 January 1996 ("Solar Cult Lives on in New Guise," by Roger Faligot, and "The Fatal Attraction of Shadowy Cults and Armageddon Theorists," by Peter Ustinov) and *Journal du Dimanche* for 24 December 1995 ("Les Sacrifiés de la Secte").

56. *SF Examiner* 24 Dec.1995: "Tapping the Psychic Powers in Each of us"

Part Fifteen: Wild Cards

1. The tasks envisioned by Petersen ranged from "Create effective networks and liaisons with domestic and foreign people in political, military and scientific environments" (two to five years, one million dollars) to "Establish a campus for NIDS, to include research and teaching" (five to ten years, up to one hundred million dollars).

2. Bob Pratt's book on Brazil was entitled *UFO Danger Zone: Terror and Death in Brazil--Where Next?* (Foreword by J. Vallée) Paperback, 363 pages Published July 1st 1996 by Horus House Press, Inc.

3. Ingo Swann mentioned our conversation in his Report on Project SCANATE (published 29 Dec. 1995) as follows: "I consulted a number of scientists outside of the SRI orbit, but not far away, in Silicon Valley. No one could recommend anything. But Dr. Jacques Vallee recognized the problem as one of "addresses." If I remember correctly, he said that you need an address that gets the perceptual channel to the right place, exactly as one needs a street address to find a house, or an address menu code in a computer to find and call up the desired information." This notion led him to using coordinates in remote viewing and became the basis of the CIA/SRI program methodology.

4. Brig. General Arthur E. Exon was the highest ranking military officer to say directly that Roswell was the crash of a spacecraft and that alien bodies were recovered. In 1947 Exon was a Lt.-Colonel stationed at Wright Field and heard of the incident. He said he also flew over the area of the crash and observed two distinct crash sites and gouges and tire tracks on the ground leading into the "pivotal areas." From 1964-66 he was the Commanding Officer of Wright-Patterson AFB, where crash material was supposedly taken in 1947.

5. Dr. Paul Moller, whom I met about 1989, is a UC Davis (California) aeronautics engineer who attempted to develop the *Skycar*, a prototype personal vertical take-off aircraft (a "flying car"). As of 2018, it seems no Moller air vehicle had successfully flown in free, non-tethered flight, out of ground effect.

6. See my book *UFO Chronicles of the Soviet Union: a Cosmic Samizdat.* (NY: Ballantine, 1992.)

7. "Les Enjeux du Millénaire—Pour une Europe de l'Innovation" in *Management et Conjoncture Sociale* No.478 (19 Février 1996) pp. 10-22.

8. Robertson-Stephens, one of the most successful investment banks specializing in West Coast technology stocks, made huge profits in underwriting the initial public offerings of numerous high-tech companies that went public in 1994, 95 and 96. It blew up, however, during the crisis of the "dot-com" bubble after 2000. Other San Francisco firms of the same type were Hambrecht & Quist, Montgomery Securities, and Cowen & Co.

9. *Venture Capital Journal,* January 1996. My work was later mentioned in the same journal, August 1996 issue, page 25.

10. The body of Raina Shirley was found in early April 1996 at the dam on the Eel River in Potter Valley. In a case that illustrates the ravages of the drug subculture in Mendocino County, a 14-year-old boy eventually pleaded guilty to charges stemming from the death of the girl, who had been drugged, raped, and left to die in the icy waters. Two other counts were dismissed as part of the plea bargain in return for the boy promising to testify against his cousin, 27-year old Arnoldo Jorge Manzo, who fled to Mexico "where authorities have failed to locate him." Raina and a 13-year old friend had accepted a ride from Manzo and his cousin to "go to a party spot on the Eel River and try methamphetamine." Her mother eventually circulated a petition asking that the boy be confined by the California Youth Authority instead of a release on probation. This was the kind of tragedy that led us to leave Mendocino County.

11. *The Rickover Effect*, by Ted Rockwell. New York: John Wiley 1992.

12. Lotta's Fountain, the oldest surviving monument in San Francisco, was donated by singer/dancer Lotta Crabtree in 1875. Lotta began her career as a young girl performing for miners in gold country and went on to become one of America's most popular stage performers. After the earthquake in 1906, the fountain was one of the few remaining structures on Market Street. It became a popular meeting place, precious to San Franciscans.

13. This X-Files episode was *Jose Chung's From Outer Space.*

14. *Confessions of a Barbarian*, by Edward Abbey. Edited by David Petersen, NY: Little Brown 1994.

15. Two men named John Ford and Joseph Mazzachelli were arrested in 1996 for plotting to kill three Suffolk county politicians - including the local chairman of the Republican Party John Powell - by putting a radioactive substance in their car, food or toothpaste. Ford headed a Long Island UFO network. He believed that a UFO had crashed in a park in Brookhaven and that alien bodies were taken away by men in black jump suits to the National Laboratory nearby. (Long Island *Newsday*, Friday June 14, 1996)

16. *Nightmares and Human Conflict*, by John Mack. Boston: Houghton-Mifflin, 1974. On the abduction topic see also *Psychological Inquiry - An International Journal of Peer Commentary and Review*. Mahwah, New Jersey: Lawrence Erlbaum Associates, Vol.7 No.2, 1996. Edited by Lawrence A. Pervin. Also the important article by Leonard S. Newman and Roy F. Baumeister: "Toward an Explanation of the UFO Abduction Phenomenon: Hypnotic Elaboration, Extraterrestrial Sadomasochism, and Spurious Memories," pp. 99-126.

17. The name of the company was FAS Engineering and it was headed up by Dr. Gracio Fabris in Burbank. It specialized in liquid metal electrodynamic turbines and liquid metal MHD energy conversion. The liquid metals they used were tin or lead rather than aluminum, which they told me had too high a melting point to be useful in such machinery.

18. The 4.1 pound rock in question, known as Allen Hills 84001, contained organic compounds known as polycyclic aromatic hydrocarbons. It appeared to have been ejected from Mars by meteoritic impact about 15 million years ago and to have fallen to earth some 13,000 years ago. It was found in 1984.

19. The Mount Wilson ranch is located at 114°27' West and 38°15' North, near the Williams Landing Strip, in the region known as the Schoolmarm Basin, Nevada. The coordinates of the Utah ranch near Roosevelt, Utah are

109°31' West and 40°27' North.

20. Ingo Swann described this episode in his 1998 book *Penetration*: "A network of purple, red, and yellow lightning bolts shot in all crazy directions through the cloud, and I would have jumped up if not held down. And then, there it was. Somewhat transparent at first, but in the next second, as if dang-up (like the movie term) out of nowhere, there IT WAS!—solidly visible over the lake."

21. *La Ville du Ciel*, by Pierre Versins in *Fictions* no.100, March 1962, pp.137-161.

22. *Wedge*, by Mark Riebling. New York: Knopf 1994.

23. Benjamin ("Eddie") Passavant's children were: Philippe, Annie (Hallakon), Jacques (and Evelyn, Air Liquide), Andrée (Aulong), Liliane (Picard), Paule, and Bernard.

24. Edith Cresson became Prime Minister under Mitterrand on 15 May 1991, replacing Michel Rocard. The Mayor of Chatellerault (Vienne département) and member of the National Assembly, this long-time socialist politician had served several times in the Cabinet and also held a CEO position for a while at Schneider Industries Service International. A former student of HEC, she was never accepted as a leader by the French Nomenklatura and left her Prime Minister position on 2 April 1992. Her book, *Histoires Françaises* (Paris: Le Rocher, 2006) recounts her efforts to modernize French industry and information technology in particular.

25. "Pourquoi est-il si difficile de financer l'innovation en Europe?" *Le Figaro*, Thursday 12 December 1996.

26. *Paschal Beverly Randolph: A Nineteenth-Century Black American Spiritualist, Rosicrucian, and Sex Magician*, by John Patrick Deveney. Albany: State University of New York, 1997.

27. In 14 months the Institute had spent close to $1.5 million, broken down into two major categories: an operations budget of $710,436 and capital expenditures of $766,093.

In the first category were payroll ($249,986, the Science Board ($210,000,) travel ($124,000,) rent ($45,000,) supplies ($23,730,) and advertising ($14,572.) Also under Operations were the Mount Wilson ranch ($350,970) and the Utah ranch ($200,108.) The analysis of samples only cost $3,960.

In the second category were furniture and equipment ($50,255,) library ($13,129,) the purchase of John Carpenter's 140 abduction files ($14,000,) the Utah trailer ($49,858,) Hal's communications devices ($23,000,) night vision equipment ($8,211,) camcorders ($9,486,) various other gadgets ($6,979) and live cattle ($8,800.)

28. *La Rumeur de Roswell*, by P. Lagrange. Paris: La Découverte 1997.

29. French archaeologists went on strike in February 1997 because Prime Minister Alain Juppé had issued an edict allowing real estate promoters to bulldoze through medieval ruins in Rodez to build a parking garage and an apartment building over the remains of feudal and gallo-roman walls, evading a law that is supposed to protect such sites until ancient artifacts have been mapped and retrieved.

30. *Open to Suggestion*, by Robert Temple. London: Aquarian Press 1989.

31. The articles I wrote for *Le Figaro* during this period covered the high-technology scene in California, the emergence of Internet services and medical innovation.

32. Accuray Systems was eventually saved and achieved an IPO on Nasdaq in 2007 at a valuation of approximately $1.5 billion. Its robotic device, the Cyberknife, became a standard in cancer surgery.

33. *L'Horreur Economique,* by Viviane Forrester. Paris: Fayard 1996.

34. "L'Europe, un génie qui perd ses moyens?" *La Voix du Nord*, Thursday 27 March 1997, page 18.

35. The Two: About the Heaven's Gate suicides see *SF Examiner* for Sunday, 6 April 1997.

36. *New Scientist* 1 March 1997, page 92.

37. Kuchar, George & Mike. *Reflections from a Cinematic Cesspool*. Berkeley: Zanja Press, Mar. 1997.

38. *New Scientist*: Letters, 29 March 1997 page 55 and 3 May 1997 page 56. See also *Field-effect Electronics* by William Gosling, W.G. Townsend and J. Watson. Butterworth 1971.

In May 2018 Dr. Puthoff wrote to me: "When it comes to Corso having said that fiber optics and transistors came from a flying saucer (which you and John Alexander rightly refute,) I once confronted Corso that it was in his book. He became really upset, saying that exaggeration came from (his agent) Bill Birnes and he was only given a day to review before the book went to press to meet the 50th Anniversary of Roswell.

"He said that the truth of the matter was that they (the Army) held the material close to the chest, not even wanting CIA to know they had it because "they would have confiscated it." Instead, they carefully monitored developments in U.S. labs and when something came close (such as fiber optics with x dB attenuation/m,) he would measure what his treasure trove had. Then he would then go to the fiber optic group and said they found better material from a Russian missile, so please check it out. Same with transistors. They monitored transistor development at U.S. laboratories, and when it approached what it seemed they had from the crash retrievals, he would provide sample under same cover. He stated he never ran to industry claiming 'look what we found from a UFO – can you duplicate?' I'm told that that same sly approach is still being used today to obfuscate sources."

39. I argued that Peter Sturrock's conclusion was biased because he was unaware that the catalogue of sightings he used listed hundreds of entries for a single event (the giant object that crossed the French sky in November 1990) resulting in distorted statistics.

40. Class Data Systems was acquired by Cisco. It developed and marketed corporate intranet and Internet solutions that enhanced the performance of real-time and multimedia applications. The company offered CLASSifier, a solution for networks, which carried time sensitive applications, and management tools necessary to enforce corporate-wide policies in the network.

41. This claim seemed preposterous at the time, in line with other boasting by the group. Later events of medical interference at the Bigelow Utah ranch, however, cast a different light on the matter.

42. *New Scientist* for 26 July 1997, p.6, "Warp Factor Zero."

43. Presentation to the UN in 1978.

44. Luminosity Estimates were analyzed in my article, *Estimates of Optical Power Output in Six Cases of Unexplained Aerial Objects with Defined Luminosity Characteristics*. JSE Vol.12, no.3 Autumn 1998.

45. Council Bluffs case: the highlights are included in my article, *Physical Analyses in Ten Cases of Unexplained Aerial Objects with Material Samples*. JSE Vol.12, no.3 Autumn 1998.

46. Charonne killings: see Part 13, note 6. A political demonstration against the extreme right turned ugly on 8 February 1962 in Paris. Police charged an unarmed crowd, forcing it to retreat down the stairs of the subway station at Charonne. The iron gates had been drawn shut. Still the policemen, many of whom belonged to neo-fascist groups, charged viciously, beating people with clubs and rifle butts, pressing them against the bars, leading to the death of several unarmed, helpless men and women, crushed under the weight. The culprits were never punished. The episode contributed heavily to my decision to leave France in the fall of 1962.

47. See the book *Conjuring Up Philip, an Adventure in Psychokinesis* by Iris Owen with Margaret Sparrow. NY: Harper & Row 1976.

48. See the July 8, 1997 broadcast of *The 700 Club* which featured news of the Mars Pathfinder Mission.

Part Sixteen: Four Elements

1. Regeneration Technologies, Inc., based in Florida, was financed by us alongside Lehman Brothers and the Adler funds. The company, which made new materials like bone paste and products such as artificial ligaments for reconstructive surgery, went public on Nasdaq in January 2002.

2. The Alexandria Colossus: although this was never mentioned by the organizers of the show, by the French museum or by the media, the remains of the Colossus had been discovered at the bottom of the sea by a remote viewing team organized by Stephen Schwartz and his colleagues in American parapsychology. This was the most interesting part of the story.

Beginning in 1978, the Mobius Laboratory used remote viewers scattered around the world equipped with maps of modern Alexandria, Egypt. Each was asked to locate a range of archaeological sites, including the tomb of Alexander the Great, the location of Cleopatra's palace, Marc Antony's Timonium, and the Lighthouse of Pharos. After making their location the viewers were asked to describe in detail both surface geography and subsurface configurations and to describe what would be found at the site.

This data was analyzed and evaluated using a multi-viewer scheme, the *Mobius Consensus Protocol*, and a series of locations and descriptive material to guide fieldwork were developed. Between 1979 and 1981 actual fieldwork took place. The marine portion of the fieldwork in the Eastern Harbor was carried out after a survey using side-scan sonar to provide a comparison of electronic and remote sensing data. This work was done by Professor Harold Edgerton of MIT, the inventor of side-scan sonar.

The electronic survey failed to provide useful location data. Remote viewing, however *located all the sites*, and showed that the ancient city extended considerably further into the Alexandrian Eastern Harbor than was previously believed. Researchers from the University of Warsaw, Oxford University, the University of Alexandria, provided archaeological and anthropological expertise, and conducted subsequent independent expert analysis. All remote viewing data was recorded, notarized, and turned over to a third party independent repository, in order to establish an unimpeachable chronology going from prediction to fieldwork results. The entire project was filmed and photographed as it happened.

3. *The Aryan Christ* by Richard Noll. NY: Random House 1997.

4. The Gulf Breeze scandal was triggered by a series of sensational photographs of hovering saucers by "Mr. Ed." The case was heavily promoted by several groups of ufologists. See note 37 in Part 13.

5. *Cosmic Suicide: The Tragedy and Transcendence of Heaven's Gate* by Rodney Perkins and Forrest Jackson. Pentaradial Press, July 1997.

6. I had met Frank Pace in Manhattan on 27 Oct.1975. See FS Vol.2 p.315.

7. Other findings were as follows: (1) the cut around the eye was made by a sharp instrument, not a laser, no cauterization. (2) The ear was cut with a knife, not a surgical instrument, not predator teeth. (3) The cow had been pregnant, as established by a progesterone test and a pregnancy-specific protein-B test, yet there was no fetus. The uterus was enlarged. (4) The heart was found in a friable condition, non-recognizable as an organ. It was "shredded," yet the pericardium was intact. All other organs were recognizable; some contained white nodules. (5) The blue gel was collected and analyzed. It was found smeared over the hide and there was blue color in the thoracic cavity. (6) The animal gave evidence of sudden death. (7) The animal was in good health when killed, as established by its liver and blood chemistry. (8) The carcass, again, was in a North-South position.

8. DAVA meeting in March 1985 described in detail in FS Vol.3, p.171.

9. Michalak case: On May 20, 1967, Mr. Stefan Michalak was prospecting for quartz and silver in the Falcon Lake woods area in Manitoba (about 150 kilometres east of Winnipeg) when the 51-year-old industrial mechanic was startled by a group of alarmed geese. Looking up, he and saw two cigar-shaped objects with a reddish glow hovering about 45 metres away.

One descended, landing on a flat section of rock and taking on more of a disc shape. The other remained in the air for a few minutes before flying off. Believing it to be a secret U.S.military craft, Stefan sat back and sketched it over the next half hour. Then he decided to approach, later recalling the warm air and smell of sulphur as he got closer, as well as a whirring sound of motors and a hissing of air. He also noted a door open on the side with bright lights inside, and said he heard muffled voices.

He claims he went closer and noted the smooth metal of the ship, with no seams. Looking into the bright doorway, wearing the welding goggles he used to protect his eyes while chipping at rocks, Stefan said he saw light beams and panels of various-coloured flashing lights, but could not see anyone or any living thing. When he stepped away, three panels slid across the door opening and sealed it.

He reached to touch the craft, which he said melted the fingertips of the glove he was wearing. The craft then began to turn counter-clockwise and Stefan says he noticed a panel that contained a grid of holes. Shortly afterward, he was struck in the chest by a blast of air or gas that pushed him backward and set his shirt and cap ablaze. He ripped away the burning garments as the craft lifted off and flew away.

Disoriented and nauseous, Stefan stumbled through the forest and vomited. He eventually made his way back to his motel room in Falcon Lake, then

caught a bus back to Winnipeg, where he was treated at a hospital for burns to his chest and stomach that later turned into raised sores on a grid-like pattern. For weeks afterwards, he suffered from diarrhea, headaches, blackouts and weight loss.
(summarized from http://www.cbc.ca/news/canada/manitoba/falcon-lake-incident-book-anniversary-1.4121639)

10. Dr. Colm Kelleher's paper was published as "Retrotransposons as Engines of Human Bodily Transformation," *Journal of Scientific Exploration*, 13, no 1, Spring 1999, pp. 9-24. He argued that "the historical literature suggests that there are unusual physical, as well as psychological, consequences in humans to the attainment of the exalted state of mind known as enlightenment, nirvana, or samadhi. These reported changes include, but are not limited to, sudden reversal of aging, emergence of a light body and observed bodily ascension into the sky. This paper proposes a "jumping DNA" or transposon-mediated mechanism to explain rapid and large-scale cellular changes associated with human bodily transformation. Only 3 % of human DNA encodes the physical body. The remaining 97 % of the 3 billion base pair genome contains over a million genetic structures, called transposons, which have the capacity to jump from one chromosomal location to another. Transposons that jump to a new location via an RNA intermediate are known as retrotransposons."

11. The situation with the drug scene in Northern California continued to worsen in following years, with numerous crimes that went unreported or were not investigated by police. In August 2011 a man named Aaron Bassler, 35, killed former Fort Bragg mayor Jere Melo while Melo patrolled forest land owned by a private timber company. Bassler was tending two *opium fields* (not marijuana!) when he shot Melo with a high-caliber rifle. The case only made headlines, briefly, because the victim was so well-known.

12. Brian Pinkerton, a brilliant computer scientist of the Internet generation, developed the first practical search engine (the "webcrawler") and later went on to be the founder of several successful web startups.

13. *The Four Elements of Financial Alchemy* was published by TenSpeed Press, Berkeley in 2000.

14. *San Francisco Chronicle* 9 Dec.1999, front page.

INDEX

www.ingramcontent.com/pod-product-compliance
Lightning Source LLC
Chambersburg PA
CBHW071947270326
41928CB00009B/1376
* 9 7 8 1 9 4 9 5 0 1 0 5 6 *